QUANG TRUONG
Composite Architecture

QUANG TRUONG

COMPOSITE ARCHITECTURE

Building and Design with Carbon Fiber and FRPs

Birkhäuser
Basel

COMPOSITE MATERIALS

Contents

CASE STUDIES

EXTERIORS

INTERIORS

STRUCTURES

SPECIAL CASES

FOREWORD

BY JAN KNIPPERS

The projects in this book vary in terms of their formal approach and technical performance but have one thing in common: they demonstrate the great design potential that fiber-reinforced composites offer architecture. In contrast to metal, glass, wood, and most other building materials, they enable the comparatively simple production of complexly shaped components. Their low thermal conductivity in combination with different levels of light transmittance and a multitude of different colors and coatings enables esthetically as well as functionally innovative concepts for building envelopes. Carbon fiber has a similar stiffness but much higher strength than steel. Load-adapted placement of carbon fibers allows for structures of unequaled efficiency and lightness.

Even though fiber composites may seem to be a relatively new material system in architecture, their introduction dates back to the mid-20th century. The famous Monsanto House of the Future was made of glass fiber sandwich panels and built in 1957. It was followed by a series of similar design concepts for houses, which have all attracted much attention but made very limited impact on the general development of architecture. The main reason for this was that their formal esthetics and building construction were based on the conception of serial production of housing units. This approach met with little acceptance from users, as it did not allow for variation according to individual needs. Only recently have various manufacturing processes for fiber-reinforced composites been developed that enable the economical production of large-format individual building components with geometric and functional differentiation. This has initiated a renaissance of fiber composites in architecture, as is impressively demonstrated by this book.

Fiber composites offer new options but also pose new challenges to architects and engineers. Typically, they design and construct using a limited number of materials with well-defined properties. Composites enable fine tuning of mechanical properties through layering, orientation, and stacking of fibers to an extent not possible with any other building material. In addition, they consist of a large quantity of different types of resin, additives, and fibers that can be combined in endless different ways according to the specific requirements of the project. It is not only the building itself but also the material system that needs to be designed. This adds another dimension to the design process.

Many of the possibilities offered by fiber composites have hardly been explored. The use of photochromic or thermochromic additives, as well as the integration of phase-change materials into composites, makes possible building envelopes with physical properties that adapt autonomously to changing environmental conditions. Fiber-optic strain sensors and pneumatic or piezo-electric actuators can be integrated into compliant laminates, a technology that is being investigated in the aerospace industry for morphing wings. With this technology, passive building components may become active elements that can adapt to changing environmental conditions or user requirements.

At the same time, fiber composites are also associated with some challenges that still need to be addressed. In a comparative ecological evaluation, components made of fiber composites perform differently compared to conventional solutions, depending on the application. Bio-based alternatives have been available for fibers and resins for a long time, but their durability requires further investigation and improvement. The main challenge, especially for carbon components, is the development of ecologically efficient end-of-life options. Although initial research approaches are available, they still have to be transferred to industrial application.

All this shows we are still at an early stage when it comes to the use of fiber composites in architecture. However, the many options they offer for design show that it is worth taking these steps.

Bancroft Borg
1970s–1980s
Maple ash laminate
68 sq. in. head size
14 oz.

Wilson T2000
1967
Tube steel
63 sq. in. head size
12.8 oz.

Wilson BLX Team
2011
Basalt and carbon composite
104 sq. in. head size
10.5 oz.

PREFACE

I was first introduced to composite materials, unwittingly, as a child taking tennis lessons. My first rackets were wooden, and it required me to be of a certain age to even be able to lift one up, much less swing one (I couldn't imagine at the time trying a one-handed backhand with one of those beasts; I was lucky to be coming of age when two-handed backhands were a newly acceptable technique). A certain dedication to the sport early on meant that my parents, even though such a purchase was quite expensive for them at the time, gave me a metal junior tennis racket for my birthday. Definitely a step up from wood, in those days. It wasn't many birthdays later when I was given a tennis racket made from composites—the same material that was used in the rackets of all the professional tennis players at the time. It was a Prince Spectrum Comp. I would gaze at it for so long that I can still lovingly recall the tiny multi-colored flecks of paint scattered throughout the racket's white surface that were only visible from inches away. Though at the time I wouldn't have been able to verbalize why a composite racket was different, it was appreciable even to me at that age that the design, esthetics, and functional performance of a racket made of this kind of material were completely different from those of the wooden and metal ones I had previously used.

As I grew up, a fascination with cars and airplanes was added to my list of interests, furthering my dalliance with composite materials; this stayed with me until graduate architecture school at Yale, where I took a studio with Greg Lynn. Greg accompanied his twelve students that year to yacht factories, naval architects, and on board an all-carbon-fiber America's Cup yacht, as part of an investigation into the potential for technologies outside of architecture to contribute to building science. This studio, taken concurrently with courses taught by Mario Carpo, the architectural historian, began to sketch a path of architectural inquiry for me that stretched both into the past and toward the future.

Not too long after graduate school, I found myself employed by Diller Scofidio + Renfro (DS+R). A client came in, wanting a beach house, and co-founder Liz Diller turned to me; the project fell into my lap. Due to some combination of: a young architect not knowing any better, a structural engineer who was willing to entertain any challenge, clients that saw themselves as patrons of the arts, and a contractor that had experience in boat building, composite materials were proposed as a primary material for that beach house. Some years later, that house was completed; it was made out of structural fiber-reinforced plastic (FRP)—a seamless and jointless monocoque construction that was both the architectural finished surface and primary structure—the first and only of its kind as far as anyone involved with it was aware.

After the house was completed, and my first child was born, my family and I moved from New York City to Portland, Oregon, where I took a position with a fledgling firm just starting to get some publicity for work with mass timber buildings. The change was probably more drastic than I could possibly have anticipated; from one end of the spectrum to the other in terms of budget and professional culture, from working with the most cutting-edge materials to probably the first ever used. There I learned even more about the challenges of non-conventional material choices in architecture as I gained insight into working with mass timber. What became apparent in the experience of operating at these different ends of the spectrum was the role of regulations and building culture in the architectural profession and, by extension, in the built environment.

During this time, I had come to think of materials, technology, and processes as the dominant issues of architecture. A fourth, sustainability, provides the overall context for the other three. Composite materials embody the potentials and challenges of all four. This material, and these issues, demarcate an inflection point for architecture—a change from how architecture was previously studied and practiced.

The previous generation of architects, gestated in a period of relatively slow technological progress, could occupy itself with introverted academic pursuits: a search for autonomy, criticality, and prestige. But in a time of significant technological progress, being active participants in the future of the built environment means extending architecture beyond traditional boundaries of the discipline—engaging material science, technology, and all of the social and political systems that form the basis of production. This book is a reflection and investigation into the past 15 years of practicing and studying architecture with those experiences.

At this point, I would like to acknowledge those who have helped shape this book in its current form, and offer a variation of a maxim I remember hearing once; any positive attribute or credit for anything in this book is due to the grace of others, any deficiency or error is mine alone.

As the number of primarily composite-structured buildings in the world is small, I know that the number of architects with knowledge of the building issues surrounding this material is also small; my experience working on that beach house for Diller Scofidio + Renfro formed much of the practical foundation for my knowledge of these issues. Without the inimitable gifts of Liz, Ric, and Charles at DS+R, none of this would have happened. I was also fortunate to have felt the strong advocacy of Ben Gilmartin and Chris Andreacola on my behalf during that time. The contractor felt like a partner, as did Antonio Rodriguez, David Kendall, Amber Otto, and James Kotronis. Furthermore, Dan Sesil and Holly Chacon's roles on that project cannot be minimized. The many collaborators and coworkers who also contributed are too numerous to mention, and I hope that they may forgive the absence of a name-check here.

When I first sought to undertake the writing of this book, conversations with Joseph Mayo, Brian Libby, Fran Ford, Jonah Gamblin, and Randy Gragg were helpful in shaping the scope and structure; conversations with my childhood friend Melissa Maerz and her husband Chuck Klosterman were helpful for advice about writing in general.

The Architecture Foundation of Oregon awarded me a fellowship allowing me to visit buildings, factories, and conferences throughout Europe and the US for a year, which laid some of the research foundations for this book. Jane Jarrett and Susan Myers were and continue to be very supportive; their generosity took its forms in many ways that I cannot repay.

During the writing of this book, one of the main challenges was striking the appropriate balance between the technical and the general. As there currently exist no other books about composites in architecture, this book needed to broadly introduce this relatively new material to a design- and construction-oriented audience, yet be valuable for professionals who perhaps wanted to seriously pursue building with it. Conversations with Bill Kreysler were both enjoyable and informative during that time—his capabilities as a fabricator and thinker shaped much of the way I view the changing nature of architecture's relationship with technology.

The author's graduate school thesis project with Professor Greg Lynn, a composite manufacturing facility.
Quang Truong. "Fluid Motion." Digital rendering, 2008.

Dr. Bridget Ogwezi at Granta Design was especially helpful in acquiring some of the comparative material data in charts used throughout this book, as well as for reviewing some chapters. I have always had an affinity for working with structural engineers, and Eric McDonnell was my partner on the mass timber projects I was involved in; Antonio Rodriguez and David Kendall on the composite ones. Elena Lake has become a valued sounding board for my ideas and information about sustainability-related issues, which throughout the course of writing this book only continued to grow in weight and importance.

In terms of education, I owe a great debt to my professors at Yale. Peter Eisenman, Kurt Forster, Greg Lynn, Mario Carpo, Mark Gage, and the late Vincent Scully were particularly influential on my architectural thinking and have continued to provide me with points of guidance at various intervals since. From them I learned to "see" architecture, and to this day I don't know how else I could have learned that without the gift of knowing them. My classmates Pierce Reynoldson, Tala Gharagozlou, Stephen Nielson, and Nick McDermott are/were my architectural sparring partners, and against whom I cannot say I have ever won an argument, nor deserved to.

Special thanks go to my children, Katie and Nicholas, though I know that, due to the special relationship between parents and children, these thanks will pass unheeded and unrepaid. Their birth and the experience of knowing them have changed me in way that I will describe simply thus: before them, architecture was, to me, about the contemporary; once they were born, my work became about the future.

Lastly, and most significantly, thanks go to my wife Anna. She is the *sine qua non* of my life.

The author in front of the composite-structured beach house Blue Dream.

COMPOSITE
MATERIALS

1 INTRODUCTION: MORE WITH LESS

Man's stock of tools marks out the stages of civilization, the stone age, the bronze age, the iron age.

Le Corbusier, *Towards a New Architecture*

Advanced composite materials are relatively new, especially in consideration of the long history of architectural building materials. But, like many other new tools and technologies, this comparatively recent class of materials has the potential to be an important part of our future. Composites are already integral to many other industries—they are commonplace in the automotive, aerospace, naval, consumer goods, and energy industries; how and why they may improve our built environment is just starting to be explored.

Broadly defined, a composite is something made up of two or more parts or elements. As it pertains to materials, a composite is simply one that is composed of various component materials. This contrasts with single-phase materials such as stone or metal. The definition of a composite material is broad enough to accurately describe many age-old building materials such as concrete (made of mineral aggregate and cement), brick (straw and mud), and plywood (wood and glue). Newer composite materials include technical ceramics, metal matrix composites, and fibrous polymer composites. The world of composite materials is extremely broad and complex, and becoming more so as material technology advances.

However, in many industries, the term composite has come to refer to a specific kind of material: fiber-based polymer composites. That type of composite material will be the focus of this book; they are more accurately referred to as fiber-reinforced polymers, FRP composite materials, or FRPs. There are many subset classifications of FRP composites, such as fiberglass (also known as gFRP or GRP) and carbon fiber (cFRP). Kevlar™, a well-known proprietary formulation of aramid, is an FRP composite material. For the remainder of this book, this broad class of fiber-reinforced polymer composites will generally be referred to as FRP composite materials, FRPs, or, for brevity, simply composites.

opposite
A pavilion by the ICD/ITKE at the University of Stuttgart, exploring the use of composites for biomimetic and robotic production methods.

previous page
The Smart Slab by the Digital Buildings Group at ETH Zurich uses 3D-printed formwork for casting concrete, allowing geometrically complex shapes, eliminating traditional formwork, and increasing structural and material efficiency.

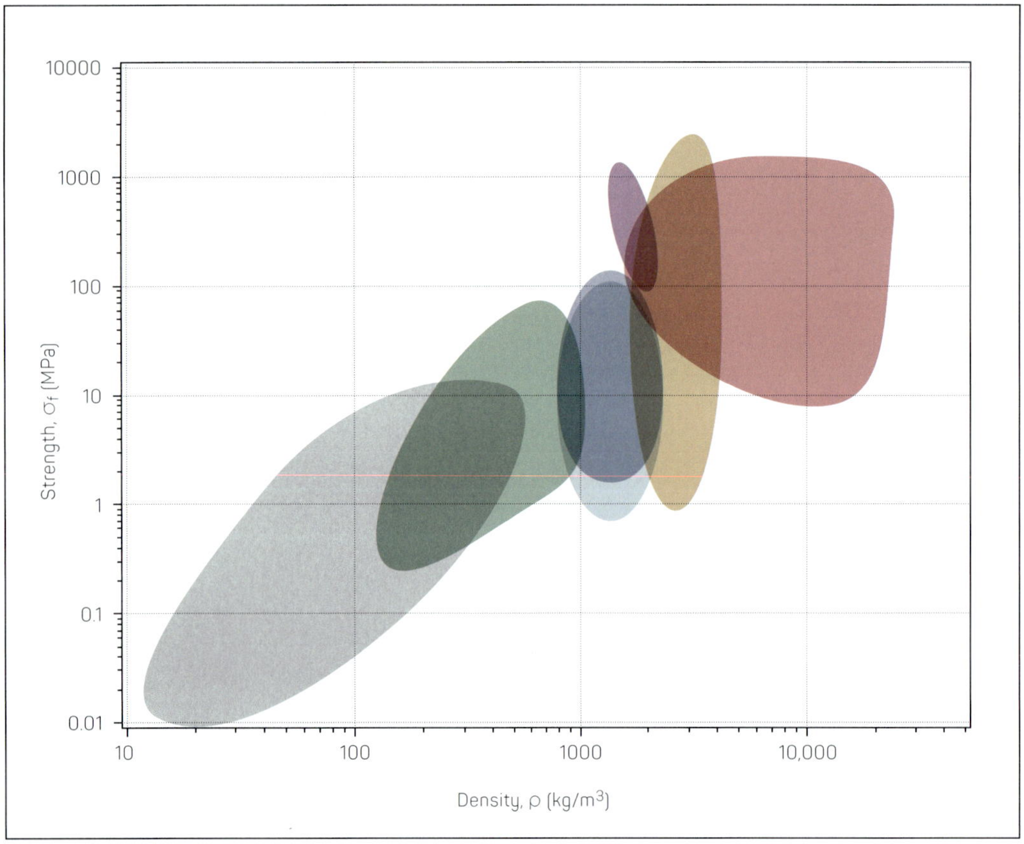

Bubble charts plotting the strength against density values of different classes of materials. From these charts, it is easy to see that composite materials, as a class, offer a unique combination of structurally important properties. It is important to note that the values on the x- and y-axes are logarithmic.

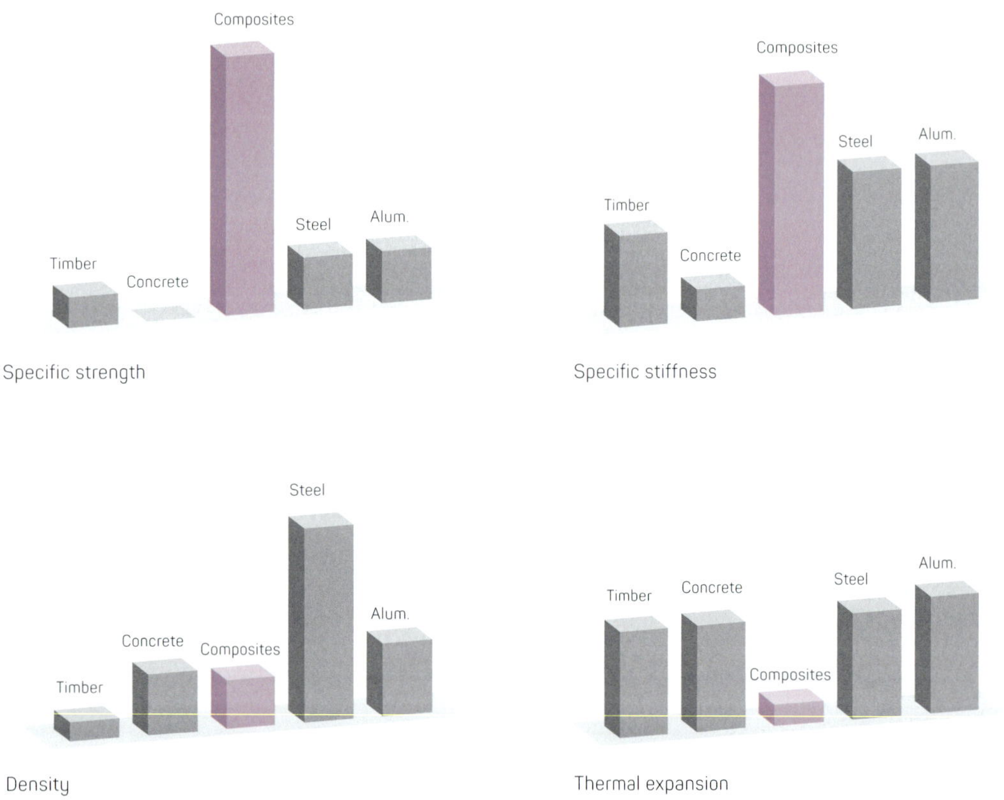

Material property comparisons.

PERFORMANCE AND PROPERTIES

Polymer composite materials possess a combination of properties that would seemingly lend themselves immediately to architecture. Primary among those properties: they are stronger and lighter than most other commonly used construction materials. This combination of stiffness, strength, and reduced weight can bring significant efficiencies to structural design, construction logistics, and sustainability considerations. For building materials, either increased strength or reduced weight as an isolated property would be compelling, but those two properties in combination makes their scope of potential applications even greater. This combination of properties has made composites commonplace in any situation where strength and weight are at a premium.

Charles Eisen's engraving for Laugier's Essai sur l'architecture (1755), depicting the Vitruvian primitive hut.

A student at the University of Stuttgart monitoring the CNC-controlled robotic placement of glass and carbon fiber for the 2016 ICD/ITKE pavilion.

Furthermore, FRPs do not corrode or rust. They can also sustain stress cycles that would irreparably damage other materials. This durability has made composites commonplace where durability and serviceability are paramount, such as in commercial airplanes and marine craft. The same is true in civil engineering and infrastructural applications, where composites are used to supplement, reinforce, or retrofit structures that have suffered damage due to prolonged use or environmental exposure.

Composites also have good thermal properties, which is beneficial in numerous situations. They don't conduct thermal energy well, making them useful as insulators. Pultruded composite parts are substituted for metals in exterior enclosure assemblies to increase the energy efficiency of building envelopes. Composite materials can also be engineered to be dimensionally stable across wide temperature ranges, reducing the need for complicated joints and seams. Not only have they been used to create seamless and jointless façades spanning over 100 meters, but at another extreme, as the material for the rocket cones in spacecraft. These thermal properties, in combination with their corrosion resistance and durability, have meant that composite materials have been successful as the primary architectural enclosures in extreme environments such as Antarctic research stations.

Fiber-based composites are also anisotropic, meaning they have different properties in different directions. This contrasts with isotropic materials, such as stone, metal, and concrete, which have the same properties in every direction. Thus the geometry and orientation of FRP materials have an impact on their structural performance, infusing the design of the material with another layer of import and meaning.

Performance and properties are only part of the reason why materials are selected for architecture; cost is another. But while it is often assumed that composite materials are more expensive than traditional materials, that is too simplistic a generalization. First of all, polymer composites have a vast range of costs, many of which compare favorably with traditional materials, especially since composites can meet similar performance criteria with reduced mass or quantity. Secondly, the process for selecting a construction material should weigh up many other considerations. Upfront costs may be dwarfed by installation, transport, or maintenance costs over the life of a structure. And lastly, prices are influenced to an appreciable extent by the available production infrastructure: certain composites, such as engineered lumber and fiberglass, are relatively cheap due to increased production; others, such as high-modulus, long-strand carbon fiber, still remain relatively expensive (though this is becoming cheaper).

For many kinds of composite materials, production is rising, while costs are falling. This summary of the global composites market was recently published by the market research and consulting company Grand View:

> The global composites market size was estimated at USD 77 billion in 2017. It is projected to expand at a [compound annual growth rate] of 7.7 percent, over the forecast period [2018–2024]. Rapid industrialization in developing economies from Asia Pacific and increasing demand for wind energy are expected to augment market growth. High demand from automotive industry is anticipated to further propel market growth ... Composites are most widely used as a replacement for steel on account of their higher strength to weight ratio ... Carbon fiber is expected to register fastest growth over the study period.[1]

In short, composites can do more with less, in the structural and the material sense. But just as importantly, they can also allow us to do more from the standpoint of design.

opposite right
The patented double-m-hull shape of the U.S. Navy M80 Stiletto boat, using carbon fiber, the largest composite hull at the time of production.

opposite left
The Luca Brenta-designed Chrisco CNB 100 sailing yacht, utilizing carbon-fiber hull and sails. Note the placement of visible carbon-fiber strands on the main sails.

opposite bottom
By May 3, 2009 all structural tests required on the Boeing 787 Dreamliner were complete. The final test occurred April 21, when the wing and trailing edges of the static test airframe were subjected to their limit load – the highest loads expected to be seen in service. The load is about the same as the airplane experiencing 2.5 times the force of gravity.

The BMW i8 and i3 are the first production cars to feature a carbon-fiber chassis, manufactured at their factory in Leipzig, Germany.

opposite top
The Halley VI Antarctic Research Station, clad in FRP exterior panels designed to withstand temperatures below -50 °C and wind gusts over 169 kph (105 mph).

opposite bottom
The Apple store in Zorlu, Turkey (2014), a 10 m² (32.8 ft²) carbon-fiber roof supported entirely by glass.

right
A wind energy farm utilizing composite blade turbines.

First of all, they can be processed into infinitely complex shapes and forms that defy what is feasible in wood, stone, concrete, or steel. They can be 3D printed. Their combination of strength, durability, corrosion resistance, thermal qualities, and process of manufacture means they can effectively replace entire conventional architectural assemblages. And in contrast to those other materials, they function extremely well structurally in tension, opening a vast spectrum of novel tectonics.

This is not to say that composite materials are without challenges. As a synthetically derived material, polymeric composites are composed from non-renewable sources and are not biodegradable. Just like any other product, the strengths and disadvantages of these materials must be weighed against their alternatives—plastic products form an essential part of our world, from safety devices to medical equipment, and their use in certain applications can certainly be justified by cost-benefit analysis in a life-cycle assessment. The extreme durability of synthetic polymers is a big problem in limited-lifespan products such as product packaging, but can present significant advantages in applications intended to last for at least a century, such as our civil infrastructure. New technologies and research in composites recycling and bio-composites aim to address some of the issues that remain for certain applications. These properties of advanced composite materials hint at the possibilities available to architecture through the exploration, understanding, and application of this new class of materials.

MATERIALITY TOWARD A DIFFERENT CONCEPTION OF ARCHITECTURE

Indeed, while the focus of this book is on one specific class of materials (FRP composites), there is much to be gained from a study of materials *in general*. It is this broader goal for which this close study of one material class is relevant. These are possibilities that pertain not only to a building's design, structure, and construction, but also toward broader ideas about the production of architecture within a larger ecology.

It is difficult to overstate the importance of materiality to architecture. The selection of a material delimits structural possibilities, informing the size, scale, and economy of building. Each material then has specifics for its procurement, transport, and fabrication, lending itself to certain localities and technologies, and each with a corresponding impact on the environment. And not least of all, materials have an impact on the sensual experience of architecture, mediating light, acoustics, tactility, and the thermal effect of finished spaces. Materials inform possibility, dictate the means, and produce the effect.

Considering this, it may come as a surprise to many that in recent books, the study of materiality, which may seem so fundamental to the practice of architecture, is described as "a secondary consideration,"[2] or "regaining currency."[3] But the roots of this bias against material study in Western architecture may trace their way back to Alberti, who in his fundamental writing on architecture distinguished between design and material (*lineamenta et materia*); the former issuing from the mind of the architect, and the latter from nature (*natura*) and thus outside the architect's control. This distinction has had far reaching implications, structuring architectural education, scholarship, and practice, and positioning the discipline in relation to science, technology, and labor.

But new material technologies mean that we are essentially designing materials and processes themselves, thus blurring traditional distinction between design and material, or indeed, perhaps between design and nature. As Neri Oxman writes, "design remains constrained by the canon of manufacturing and mass production. Assembly lines still dictate a world made of parts, limiting the imagination of designers and builders who are indoctrinated to think and make in terms of discrete elements with distinct functions. Even the assumption that parts are made from single materials goes unchallenged. [A] Material Ecology considers computational design, digital fabrication, synthetic biology, the environment, and the material itself as inseparable and harmonized dimensions of design."

As information technology and computational power have reshaped the way we interact with our environment, our buildings and architecture will necessarily change with it. Our ability to measure, quantify, and specify the performance of buildings has increased, and with it the expectations and ambitions that we ask our architecture to fulfill. This may best be exemplified by the discourse surrounding sustainability. Relatively recently—within the last generation or so—sustainability has become a prominent, if not primary, point of discourse within architecture. The broad definition of sustainability puts the measurable health of the entire world, now and for future generations, within the scope of consideration for a building. As Manfred Hegger wrote in the preface to the book, *Energy Manual*: "Sustainability affects the totality of the active planning and running of a building, social, economic and ecological concerns. It is a development where today's society considers the needs of future generations."

opposite
The Otaared structure by Neri Oxman, in collaboration with descriptiv (Christoph Bader & Dominik Kolb). Part of the Wanderers project, a series of computationally grown and multi-material, 3D-printed wearables.

While this may seem daunting or overly complex, this points to an idea of building as an integral part of a larger ecology—tied to ideas of economic, social, and environmental production. The building is no longer an inert artifact to be experienced once mystically materialized from the mind of the architect, but organic and alive: built, nurtured, and maintained by the vast systems of life and the environment all around it.

Each generation of architects is tasked with the project of re-establishing the meaning of architecture in society. Architecture, through an understanding of technology and materials, can lead through a proactive control of information and processes, as opposed to reacting to constraints such as construction conventions or code prescriptive methods. This all begins from a study of the basic materials and tools from which we build. It is from materials that we understand place, time, and technology—in short, how we think about architecture.

In this way, we can begin to understand the potentially revolutionary impact of composite materials on architecture. Developed in the middle of the 20th century and quickly adopted for use in the defense, transportation, and civil engineering industries, these materials are only starting to find prominent use in important buildings throughout the world. Much in the same way as these materials have impacted and transformed other industries, so too are they beginning to affect the way we construct and experience buildings.

The general qualities of these composites are probably roughly familiar to the public, in part because of their increasing visibility in those other industries, but composite material specifics as they are professionally applied to the famously conservative building industries are only starting to be understood.

BOOK STRUCTURE

This book introduces the technology underpinning composite materials, assesses their applicability to architecture, and surveys examples of their use in buildings around the globe. Currently, no other book on the market examines this material as applied to architecture and buildings. But the striking architectural results of recently completed buildings by world-renowned architects point toward an increasing desire to understand and apply this technology to the practice of architecture.

This book is organized in two parts. The first part contains chapters introducing composite material issues within architecture, engineering, building, and construction. The second part of the book surveys recently completed buildings that have utilized composite materials to achieve interesting technical or architectural ambitions.

The next chapter gives a brief overview of the history of fiber-reinforced polymer-based composites, as used in architecture as well as in other industries. The third chapter begins to introduce some of the technology around composite material production and fabrication. Sustainability, a complex topic to which composite materials may offer both significant contributions and challenges, is introduced in the fourth chapter. The fifth chapter of the book studies the application of this technology, specifically focusing on practical considerations important to buildings. These are considerations that are necessary given existing building codes and construction realities. Fire safety, weathering, interfaces and joints, thermal considerations, and other construction concerns are reviewed here. The final chapter in the first part of this book theorizes the future of this material in architecture.

The second part of this book examines notable completed buildings that utilize composite materials. Projects by Foster + Partners, Morphosis, Zaha Hadid, Snøhetta, Herzog & de Meuron, Diller Scofidio + Renfro, Kengo Kuma, and SHoP utilizing composite materials have recently been completed around the world, but are shown together for the first time in this book. The new Apple Headquarters in California and newer Apple stores in cities throughout the world, which utilize composite materials to striking architectural effect and have generated much popular fascination, are documented here. This book showcases these projects with photographs, text, drawings, diagrams, and construction photographs, with a goal of explicating the architectural ambitions achieved and the engineering, building, or construction solutions realized.

The case studies are organized by how the composite materials are used in the building—as exterior cladding, as interior finish, or as structure. As an exterior element, composites probably offer the most valuable contribution to contemporary building issues, while also having fewer constraints on their immediate use as an architectural product. For this reason, there are many case studies available that can provide meaningful instruction. While the use of composites in the interior has the longest history, due in part to fewer engineering demands and code constraints, for that same reason the instructive value is the least and this section of case studies is slighter. The most avant-garde role of composite materials in architecture is as the primary structure. Here, the age-old Vitruvian architectural values of durability, use, and beauty find their most striking expression in this new material. The engineering, life-safety, and building code constraints are greatest when dealing with new structural materials, and the case studies in this section are deservedly more In-depth.

As we will see throughout the book, many different architectural ambitions and construction solutions have been realized utilizing composite materials. Whether used as cladding, interior finish, or structural material, these are designs for buildings that spring from the conceptual promise unleashed by this new materiality. However, their realization is directed and shaped in different ways: by the architects' and clients' priorities of program; esthetic or spatial experience; engineering, fabrication, and construction constraints; building codes; or other challenges of construction. We also see that with these new technologies come new challenges—in terms of both architectural theory and construction. The diversity of architectural ambitions and novel solutions to building problems showcased here points to the possibilities for architects and buildings brought by composite materials.

1 "Composites Market Size, Share & Trends Analysis Report By Product (Carbon, Glass), By Resin, By Manufacturing Process, By Application, By End Use, And Segment Forecasts, 2018–2025." Market research report by Grand View Research. Accessed from [https://www.grandviewresearch.com/industry-analysis/composites-market] 8/30/2019.
2 Loschke, in book abstract.
3 Prof. Dr. Ákos Moravánszky, Torsten Lange. *Doctoral Seminar: Materiality in History and Theory of Architecture.* 2013. ETH Zürich. Online PDF. Referenced 29 August, 2019 from https://www.gta.arch.ethz.ch/courses/materiality-in-history-and-theory-of-architecture.

2

A BRIEF HISTORY OF COMPOSITES

Composite materials, at least some of the fiber-reinforced polymer kind, are relatively familiar to the general public, even if most don't really know what they are. Fiberglass, carbon fiber, and Kevlar (aramid) are all well-known thanks to their commonplace usage in many different applications, including surfboards, bicycles, other sporting goods and equipment, automotive components, boats, and many more.

But the acronym FRP and the term fiber-reinforced polymers are likely vague concepts or simply unknown to most people—architects included.

There is some confusion about the exact definition of the word composites, and even more about the term fiber-reinforced polymer composites. Though these materials are currently around us everywhere, there is a general lack of knowledge as to how they came to be such a common part of our world, and the role they may potentially play in our future. Thus, it is worthwhile to spend a little time discussing the definitions of these terms and reviewing the history of these materials.

DEFINITIONS

The definition of the word composite is broad enough to encompass many different things. While the exact wording varies wherever you look, a composite can be most basically defined as something made up of two or more constituent things. The word comes from the Latin *compositus*, meaning "put together."

Both naturally occurring and synthetic materials can be accurately described as composites, such as wood (lignin and cellulose), bone (calcium phosphate and collagen), adobe (straw and mud), and carbon fiber (fibrous carbon and polymer resin); thus, the history of those materials stretches back as far as humanity itself.

The scope of this book concerns itself specifically with fiber-reinforced polymer composites, also known as FRPs. FRPs are themselves a subset of a larger class of materials sometimes called polymer matrix composites (PMCs), polymeric composites, advanced polymer composites (APCs), or advanced composite materials (ACMs).[1, 2] Fiber-reinforced composites may include metal matrix composites (MMCs) or ceramic matrix composites (CMCs); because of their current extremely limited commercial usage within architecture, MMCs and CMCs are not discussed here.[3] And within the class of FRPs there are even more specific subset classes of FRP, typically distinguished by the type of fiber used, such as carbon fiber (cFRP), fiberglass (gFRP, or GRP), boron/basalt (bFRP), or aramid/Kevlar (aFRP).

opposite, from top left to bottom right

A 100 × microscope image showing the fibrous nature of quercus (oak) wood.

A wall made of raw earth, mud and straw in the Andean Puna between Chile and Argentina.

A close-up view of a roll of carbon-fiber weave.

Glass fibers used in fiberglass reinforcing.

It is understandably easy to get confused with the deluge of acronyms and their relationships to one another, especially since the terminology and acronyms seem to vary from text to text and over time. They sometimes seem to be interchangeable or have minute differences that are unrecognized from one text to another. Thus, a graphic chart as provided here may be useful. Currently, within most of the advanced materials industry, there seems to be a general consensus around the term FRP or fiber-reinforced polymer. Thus, for the sake of clarity and brevity, this book will use the terms composite, composite material, or FRPs to specifically refer to fiber-reinforced polymer composites.

The Institution of Structural Engineers, London, adopted a very comprehensive definition of advanced polymer composites, and will be discussed in greater depth later in this book.[4]

It is worth mentioning that the term composite is often used in architecture to discuss the extremely common structural codependency of concrete and steel, such as in metal pan decking with reinforced concrete (sometimes referred to as composite deck construction). The use of the term composite is accurate in these circumstances, as it refers to the combined structural action of those materials. However, the argument could be made that that usage is much more specialized, pertaining most specifically to structural engineering, and is seldom used outside that field. Meanwhile, the word composite has arguably developed a solid purchase in the common public sphere in specific reference to the FRPs common in automotive, marine, aerospace, and sporting goods applications.

The main components/ ingredients in any fiber-reinforced composite.

+

+

=

Fibers
Fibrous reinforcement such as glass, carbon, aramid, biofibers, or others. The length, ratio, and geometry of the fibers contribute to the final properties.

Matrix
Polymer resin, either thermoplastic or thermoset, such as polyester, vinyl-ester, epoxy, or phenolic. The matrix binds the fibers together, distributes the loads, and protects the fibers.

Additives
Fillers, additives, or other ingredients used to add fire resistance, increase durability, aid in the curing process, or contribute other characteristics.

Composite
The resultant material made from the combination of fiber, matrix, and additives. The process or method of combining those ingredients has an impact on the final properties.

REINFORCEMENT IS TO MATRIX AS FIBERS ARE TO POLYMERS

Fibers and polymers are the two key constituent materials that combine to form the composites in question. More specifically, the fibers serve as the reinforcement in a matrix or field of polymers. The two materials work together to provide resultant properties superior to those of each independently.

Because FRP composite materials can be engineered with regard to the fibers, the matrix, and the ratio of each within the final product, this gives them specificity and variability in response to any application. Methods of manufacture and fabrication contribute significantly to their final performance, adding another layer of variability and control. The various elements of FRP production that can be engineered and controlled are both a source of their potential and a challenge, particularly when it comes to architectural uses.

The fibers in a fiber-reinforced polymer composite can be naturally occurring, such as flax, linen, and hemp, or synthetic, such as fiberglass, aramid, and carbon fiber. The polymers commonly used include phenolics, epoxies, polyesters, vinyl esters, and others. A more complete description for each will be discussed in a later chapter.

Since the history of fibers used in FRPs includes both naturally occurring fibers and synthetic fibers, and the history of polymers includes naturally occurring polymers as well, the history of FRPs that is most relevant to our understanding of the material picks up at the beginning of the 20th century, when the first industrially produced synthetic polymers and fibers were derived.

Guide to composite material nomenclature and acronyms.

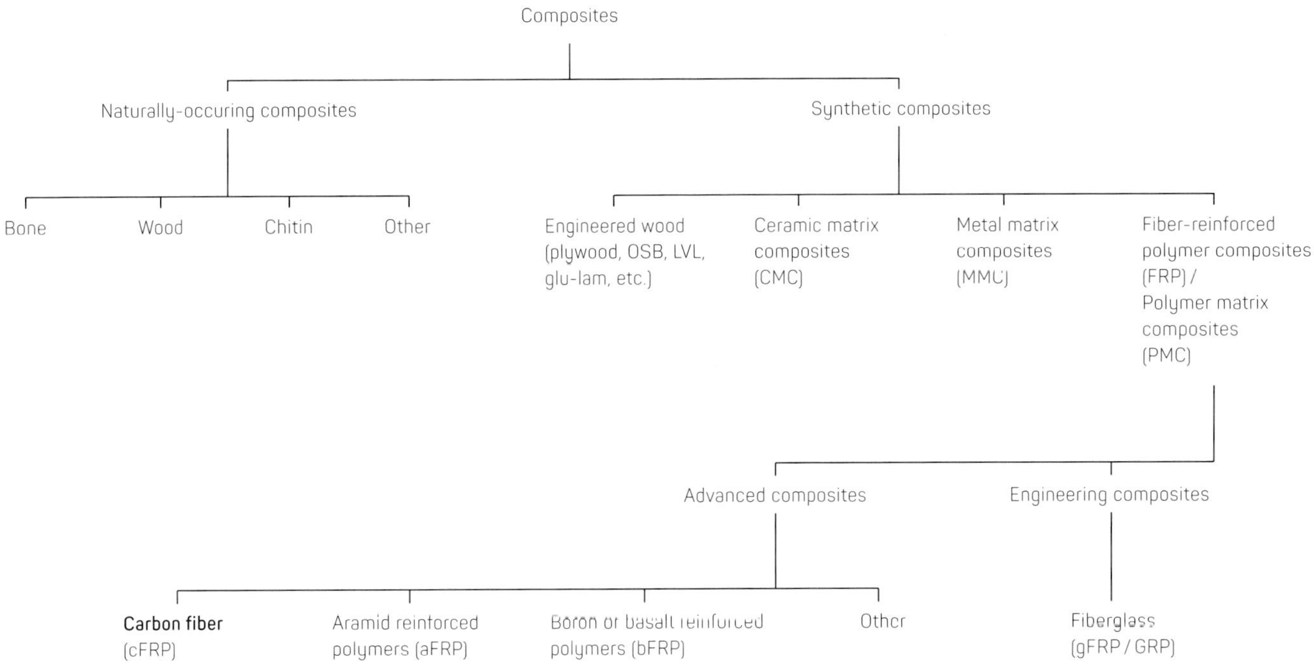

ONE WORD: PLASTICS

Plastics most indelibly imprinted themselves in the minds of a certain generation of the public in the 1967 movie directed by Mike Nichols called *The Graduate*. In the movie, an impressionable young college graduate, uncertain about his life and career prospects, is told there is just one word that represents the future: plastics. Today it may be hard to appreciate how utterly true it has since come to be.

It is worth discussing the word plastic for a moment. The terms plastics and polymers are often used interchangeably, even within the composites industry. [5] But the two terms have slightly different meanings.

To start with, all plastics are polymers, but not all polymers are plastics. Polymers refer to a broad class of materials that are defined at the molecular level by long strings of chemically bonded monomers of organic molecules.[6] Polymers include naturally occurring materials such as cellulose, rubber, amber, and silk. Within this broad group of polymers are plastics, which are defined as "a synthetic material made from a wide range of organic polymers that can be molded into a shape."[7] It derives from the Latin *plasticus* meaning, "to mold."

Within the ability to be both synthetically derived and molded into shapes lie the fundamental advantages and challenges of FRPs. It is also these characteristics that differentiate composites from traditional building materials.

Composites further distinguish themselves from plastics through their incorporation of reinforcement. This is an important distinction, as the material properties of the reinforcing fibers provide qualities far beyond what is possible with the plastic polymers alone. The distinction is significant enough to warrant completely separate industry organizations, journals, trade groups, and branches of engineering and academic study.

FIBER-REINFORCED POLYMERS

Although today functionally quite distinct, the development of plastics and composites has necessarily been intertwined. The developments in composites are fundamentally linked to advances in polymer or plastic technology. The first attempts to synthesize plastics were for use as a substitute for naturally occurring polymers such as shellac.[8]

In 1907, Leo Baekeland derived a phenolic resin that was marketed as Bakelite—this is often pointed to as the first synthetic plastic.[9] Then, around 1931, the Owens Corning company, a joint entity formed by the Owens Illinois Glass Company and Corning Glass Works, began selling molten glass that had been forced through fine orifices as "fiberglass."[10] The Douglas Aircraft company, a precursor company to the aerospace company now known as McDonnell-Douglas (which has since merged with Boeing), began experimenting with the Owens Corning fiberglass and phenolic resin to produce molds for metal aircraft parts.[11] These molds were probably the first synthetic fiber-reinforced polymer parts, and thus the first modern composites as we understand them today.

The Graduate. Directed by Mike Nichols. Screenplay by Calder Willingham and Buck Henry. Hollywood, CA: Lawrence Turman Productions, 1967.
This scene shows the main character being told that one word represents the future: "plastics".

From here, incremental advances in the chemical composition and methods of manufacture of both fibrous reinforcement and polymer matrices have expanded the capabilities and properties of composites. Polyester resin was patented in 1936, epoxy in 1938. Both offered process and structural advantages over phenolic resin. Carbon fiber was first patented in 1961 and offered commercially by Union Carbide in 1959. Aramid fibers were developed by DuPont in 1971 and commercially marketed as Kevlar. And along the way, there were developments in composite coupling agents, fillers, stabilizers, plasticizers, flame retardants, additives, and other process or manufacturing developments too numerous to mention here.[12]

Photograph of Bakelite resin and varnish development laboratory. Image from Bakelite Review: silver anniversary number, 1910–1935 published by the Bakelite Corporation. New York, NY: Bakelite Corporation, 1935, p. 17.

Photograph of Bakelite telephone, originally produced by Ericsson in 1931 (design by Jean Heiberg).

Organization and classification of polymers.

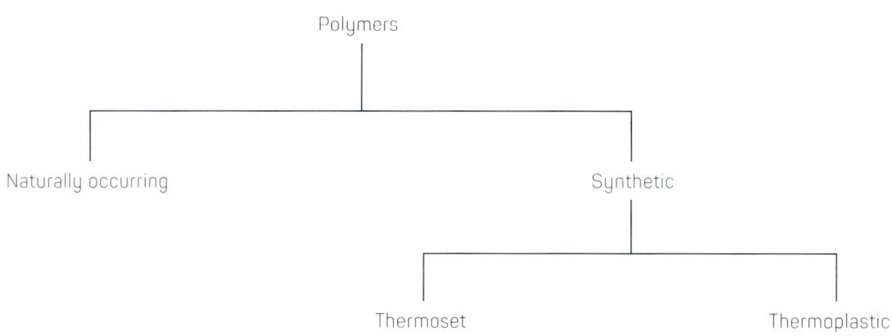

top
Northrop Grumman B-2 Spirit bomber, composed primarily of a carbon-graphite composite.

left
Lockheed F-117A Nighthawk, with composite parts throughout.

bottom
Boeing 787 Dreamliner composite material make-up by weight.

Materials used in Boeing 787 body

- Fiberglass
- Carbon laminate composite
- Carbon sandwich composite
- Aluminum
- Aluminum / steel / titanium

Total materials used by weight

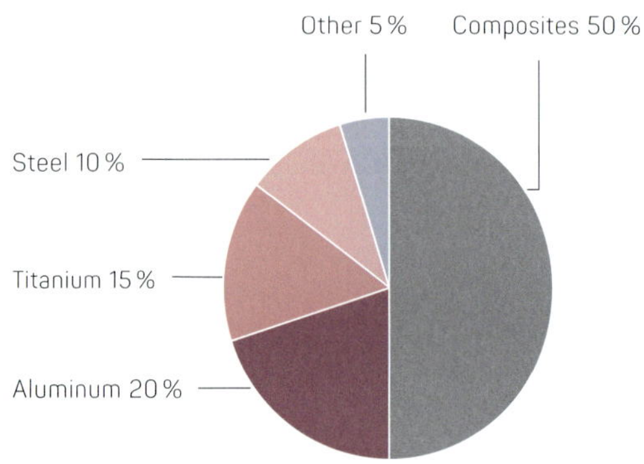

top left
McLaren MP4/1, the first car with an all carbon-fiber monocoque chassis to compete in Formula 1 racing (1981). The material is now ubiquitous in Formula 1 racing.

top right
1953 Corvette, with fiberglass composite body panels.

PLANES, SHIPS, AND AUTOMOBILES

Advances in this branch of material and process science coincided with (or were spurred on by) two great geopolitical events during the middle of the 20th century, World War II and the Cold War. For this reason, composite materials found their first and most rigorously tested applications in the military—for air, marine, and space craft.

As previously mentioned, fiberglass-reinforced resins and polyesters were first put to use for aircraft parts and parts manufacture almost immediately after fiberglass was invented. Early parts for WWII air craft included engine covers, radomes, and structural wing boxes.[13] Composite parts continued to make up a larger and larger share of the total weight of the aircraft, leading up to the development of the F-117A stealth fighter and B-2 stealth bomber, which took advantage of composites not only for their strength and light weight but also their low radar visibility.[14]

Today, the most recent commercial airliners from Boeing and Airbus utilize composites throughout their primary structures and airframes, with the 787 Dreamliner being comprised of 50 percent composites (the next largest material share belongs to aluminum, at 20 percent). The decision to grant such a primary role to the use of composites within their airliners came about in part through extensive research into the lifecycle costs of the aircraft, examining not only traditional factors such as weight, strength, and initial cost, but also build cost, reliability, durability, and maintenance.[15] This lifecycle design perspective holds interesting lessons for the use of composites within the construction industry.

Only slightly later than the aerospace industry, the automotive industry sought out the advantages of composites. The strength-to-weight ratio of composites provided significant gains in the quest for faster and more fuel-efficient cars, as the two goals are mutually related in transport. In 1953, Chevrolet introduced the Corvette, which had 41 fiberglass resin composite body parts, comprising the entirety of the exterior body.[16] In 1981, McLaren debuted the first carbon-fiber monocoque MP4/1 in the Formula 1 circuit, to overwhelming racing success.[17] To this day, nearly all Formula 1 racecars are composed of a monocoque carbon-fiber chassis, utilizing cFRP in pursuit of speed, safety, and fuel-efficiency goals.

In the consumer market, cars such as the BMW i-series represent the first mass-production consumer automobile with a carbon-fiber structure. While previously limited to supercars such as Lamborghini and Ferrari, carbon-fiber chassis have since been embraced by other consumer carmakers, notably Volvo, who have started to mass produce them for their consumer-market vehicles.

As a side note, the issue of crash safety is usually brought up as a concern in the discussion of all-carbon-fiber or FRP chassis vehicles. There are two primary structural goals in the engineering of crash safety: to protect the inhabitants from incursions and to dissipate the energy and force of the collision.[18] Composite materials have properties that lend themselves well to both of the goals if engineered properly.[19] Formula 1 teams using carbon fiber soon discovered the advantages of carbon fiber's behavior in crashes, finding that the energy-absorbing properties of composites "made a great contribution to the safety record of the sport."[20] In consumer vehicles, the all-carbon-fiber chassis BMW i3 has been thoroughly tested by National Highway Traffic Safety Administration (NHTSA) and Insurance Institute for Highway Safety (IIHS), receiving top marks in almost all categories tested.[21] The famously safety-concerned Swedish carmaker Volvo recently announced that initial crash testing of their carbon-fiber-structured flagship Polestar vehicles have been completed, with successful tests which "confirm that carbon fibre supports the highest safety standards."[22]

Boats and submarines and other marine craft have been a natural fit for composites ever since reeds were used to reinforce pitch in the Middle East in 5,000 BC.[23] Besides from strength, stiffness, and light weight, ships benefit from composites' corrosion resistance, durability, and ease of repair. In the modern era, using synthetic polymers, boats have been made of FRP for at least 50 years. A definitive history is hard to pin down, but most sources point to the era around WW II as when the first FRP boats started being made. The US Navy quickly adopted composites to produce small marine craft between 1940 and 1960, driven by the need for enhanced operational performance in stability, range, payload, and stealth, but also for the reduction in ownership costs for maintenance and fuel consumption.[24] The first reported all-FRP boat was produced by Bassons in 1945.[25] The use of composites grew to encompass larger and larger naval ships, with all-composite ships of 80- to 90-meter lengths in production today. In recreational sailing, yachts entered in the America's Cup use high-performance composites for various components, including structural hulls, masts, and mainsails. In today's marine industry, FRP composites have the greatest penetration found in any industry, making up the vast majority of material used, far more than competing materials.[26]

The fiberglass-hulled "Patrol Boat, Riverine," or PBR, used from 1966 to 1972 during the Vietnam War.

left
Detail photo of the Polestar carbon-fiber body in production.

below
Crash test of the Polestar 1 car with carbon-fiber body.

below
America's Cup racing yachts. Currently the boat hulls, masts, sails, and other components are primarily made of carbon fiber.

SPORTING GOODS

Consumer sporting goods products have probably done as much as any other industry to expose the public to the properties of composite materials. As much as the ubiquity of composites has been well publicized in Formula 1 racecars, fighter jets, exotic sports cars, or yachts, those applications are experienced firsthand by relatively few people. However, composite or carbon-fiber tennis rackets, golf clubs, snowboards, skis, and bikes are enjoyed by vast numbers of people—and the association of those relatively affordable goods with their high-performance applications in the transportation industries is probably something the sporting goods manufacturers are all too happy to take advantage of.

The case of tennis rackets is a particularly interesting one. A history of building material science could seemingly be written through the lens of tennis rackets. Tennis rackets, as many remember from the beginning of the Open era, were heavy, wooden frames wielded by stars of the game, including John McEnroe, Bjorn Borg, Arthur Ashe, Chris Evert, and Tracy Austin. Soon after, metal rackets were introduced and became ubiquitous, most notably the Wilson T2000 that was used by Jimmy Connors and Billie Jean King. Not long after that, sometime around the 1980s, composite rackets were introduced, most famously the Wilson Pro Staff 85, which advertised a graphite/Kevlar braided construction and was used by Pete Sampras, Steffi Graf, Stefan Edberg, and Mary Pierce, among others.

Composite rackets gained acceptance with the general public, and then soon became the de facto standard rackets. Because tennis had a willingness to allow experimentation with materials in racket frames and the short timelines of development to market for these consumer products, there is a large segment of adults today who grew up with intimate familiarity and tactile experience with each material (wood, metal, composite) in the form of a tennis racket. Today's young tennis players, of course, know only composite tennis rackets and polyester strings.

Advanced surface profiles and cross-sectional geometries of a contemporary, composite-material-based tennis racket.

Björn Borg playing a double-handed backhand shot with a wooden racket at the 1979 ABN World Tennis Tournament.

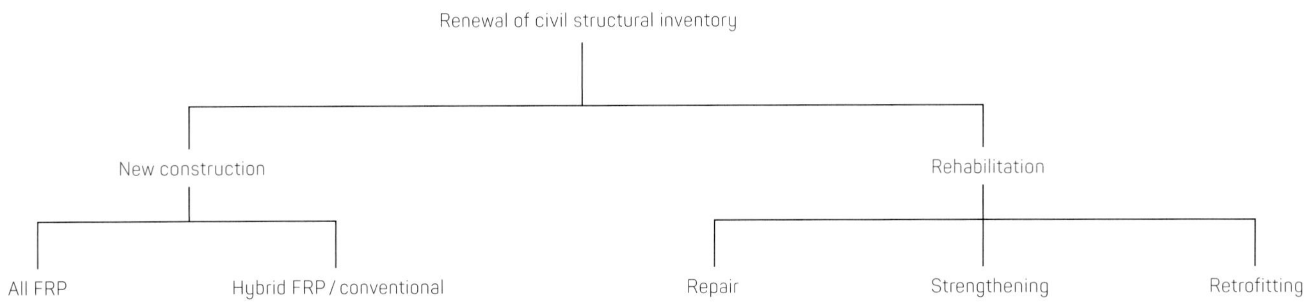

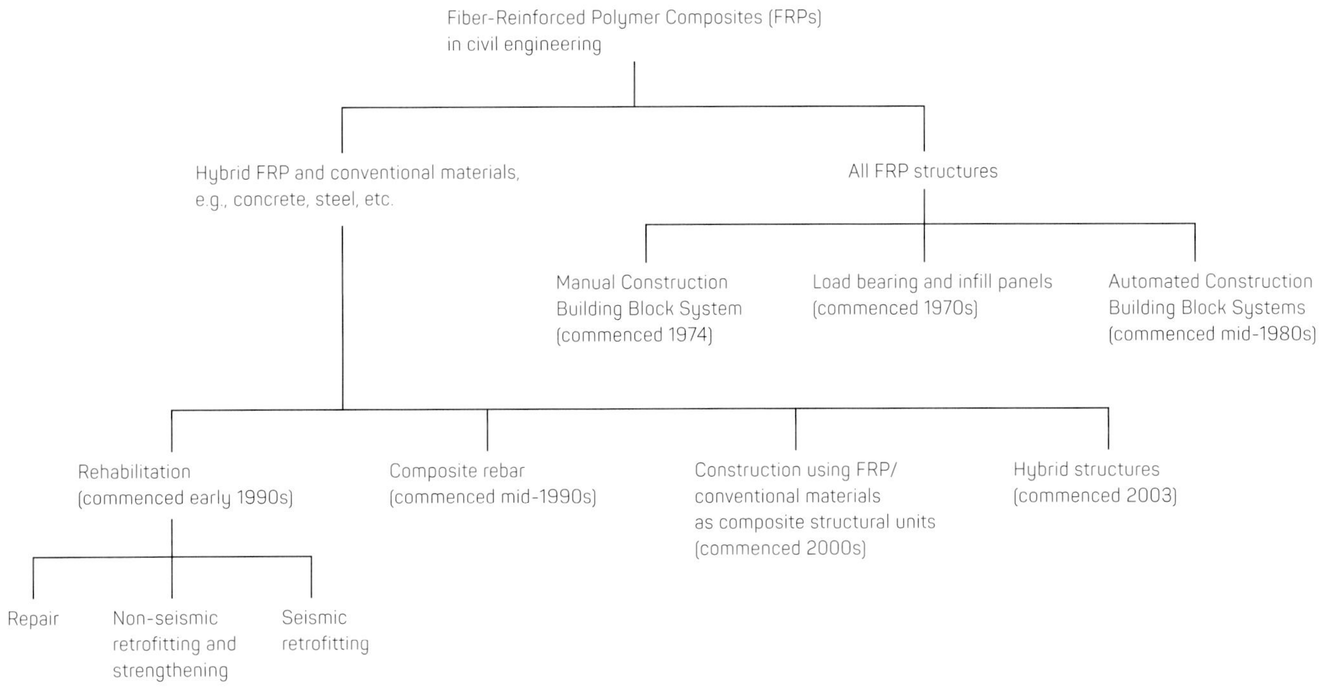

top
Chart categorizing different uses of FRP materials in civil infrastructure. Adapted from Van Den Einde, Lelli, Lei Zhao, and Frieder Seible. "Use of FRP composites in civil structural applications." *Construction and building materials 17*, no. 6–7 (2003): 389–403.

below
Chart categorizing the utilization of FRP composites in civil engineering with approximate dates. Adapted from Hollaway, L. C. "A review of the present and future utilisation of FRP composites in the civil infrastructure with reference to their important in-service properties." *Construction and building materials 24*, no. 12 (2010).

COMPOSITES IN CIVIL INFRASTRUCTURE

Composite usage in civil infrastructure, most notably in bridges, provides some of the most relevant use and engineering lessons for composites in architecture. In civil infrastructure, the issues of structure, safety, and durability are primary. Also, civil construction must contend with analogous issues of scale, fabrication, and erection.

There are two primary ways in which composites have been utilized in civil infrastructure; in combination with other conventional materials to create hybrid structures, and in all-composite structures. This chart from Len Hollaway (previous page, below) summarizes the development of FRP composites in civil infrastructure.

Many of these applications involve the repair, rehabilitation, or retrofitting of existing structures. Changes in use and/or structural degradation have meant that many concrete, metal, and masonry structures are in urgent need of repair.[27] And older structures may have been built to a different set of criteria, particularly in regard to seismic forces, and now may require retrofitting.

The durability, high strength-to-weight ratio, corrosion resistance, and ease of tailoring properties and attributes offered by FRPs has meant that their use has been steadily increasing over the past few decades for retrofitting, strengthening, and rehabilitating civil infrastructure. This has come in the form of composite rebar (for both new and retrofitting applications), chemically and/or mechanically bonded plates for flexural and shear strengthening of slabs, beams, and columns, and all-FRP composite bridge decks, FRP cables and tendons, barriers, and cladding.

Many firsts are claimed in the realm of composite use in civil applications; many of these have to do with specific applications or developments in the integration of FRP components or uses. Because of this, it becomes very difficult to tease out of the journals the significant milestones in the history of composites in civil engineering. The first pedestrian all-FRP bridge was built in Tel Aviv in 1975.[28] The world's first reinforced concrete road bridge to use composite materials as prestressing tendons was completed in Dusseldorf, Germany, in 1986. This two-span bridge spanned a total of 47 meters with a width of 16 meters, using prestressed glass fiber and polyester pultruded rods.[29]

Highly differentiated, locally adapted geometries of a carbon-fiber bicycle frame, this is the Kestrel 4000LTD, back in 2014 the most aerodynamic frame available.

COMPOSITES IN ARCHITECTURE

The documented record of composites usage in architecture is significantly leaner and starts at a much later date than in the air, marine, and space industries. In fact, there exist only a handful of cases of buildings that use reinforced plastics for components outside of furniture, fixtures, and equipment.

The most often cited example for the first reinforced plastic house was the 1957 installation at Disneyland of Monsanto's plastic House of the Future, designed with MIT's architecture department, including Marvin Goody and Ralph Hansen, and structurally engineered by Dr. Albert G. H. Dietz.[30] On display for roughly a decade, it attracted some 20 million visitors during that time. The architects, obviously attempting to differentiate the structural and esthetic capabilities of this new material from traditional materials, sculpted gently curving enclosures and cantilevered the main spaces off a central structural core. However, when it was disassembled in 1967, the future of building it envisaged did not seem any closer to reality.

But just slightly before that, a house by Ionel Schein, Yves Magnant, and R. A. Coulon, called the Snail House, was exhibited at the Paris Exhibition of 1955. Completed entirely of plastic and gFRP, it prominently featured a nautilus inspired plan, structural fiber-glass exterior panels, and an all-plastic bathroom.[31] Though it was built and displayed before the Monsanto House, it is the latter that is more often cited as the first polymer-based architectural house.

The Finnish architect Matti Suuronen created one of the most iconic images of a futuristic house, at least as it was imagined in 1968. His Futuro House was composed of ellipsoid fiberglass-reinforced polyester resin panels, with ellipsoid windows, door handles, and electrical receptacles as well. Initially, Polykem hoped to mass produce the house, but eventually only about 100 were built, of which an estimated 30 exist today.[32]

In 1974, the Mondial House in London was constructed using a reinforced concrete beam and column structure with gFRP cladding. The largest telecommunications center in Europe at the time of completion, it sat right next to London Bridge and was designed by Hubbard Ford & Partners.[33] It was demolished in 2006. In 1977, the American Express Building was completed in Brighton, UK, with semi-structural, load-bearing infill gFRP composite panels.[34]

Perkins Bridge in Belfast, Maine, completed in 2010, a composite arch bridge project completed by Advanced Infrastructure Technologies. The bridge has a 14.6 m (48 ft) span, using 16 FRP composite arch tubes, which act as reinforcement and formwork for cast-in-place concrete.

La Maison Bulle (the Bubble House) by Jean Maneval, 1964–1968.

Matti Suuronen's Futuro House of 1968.

top
The Monsanto House of the Future, on display at Disneyland from 1957–1967. Reportedly visited by roughly 20 million people during that time.

Buckminster "Bucky" Fuller, that inimitable, iconoclastic architect and educator, completed a fiberglass shelter called the Fly's Eye Dome, a structure that "embodied design attention to all that I had learned not only throughout that fifty-year development period but in all my thirty-two earlier years."[35] Composed of fiberglass Y-shaped panels, it was lightweight, rapidly assembled or disassembled, and available in either 24 ft diameter or 50 ft diameter sizes. Initially displayed in 1981, it seems that several restored versions exist throughout the world, including one in the private collection of Sir Norman Foster.[36]

A few other scattered examples of built uses for FRPs were completed in the intervening decades between WW II and the start of the 21st century. Alison and Peter Smithson completed a prototype plastic house for the Ideal Home Exhibition in London, 1956.[37] Rudolph Doernach completed a house composed of four identical gFRP exterior shell elements in 1959.[38] Renzo Piano used fiberglass structural roof panels for a warehouse in Rome and a factory in Genoa, both completed in 1966.[39]

Mondial House by Hubbard, Ford & Partners, completed in 1974 and demolished in 2006.

Buckminster Fuller's Fly's Eye Dome, initially displayed in 1981, installed here in the Miami Design District.

Many applications of FRP have appeared at World's Fair Expositions. At the 1958 Brussel's World Fair, the US Pavilion featured an FRP roof with panels supplied by Kalwall.[40] The 1964 World's Fair showcased a house sheathed in Formica, and the Bell Telephone pavilion had 60-foot-long FRP façades.[41]

Many structures took advantage of the strength-to-weight ratio of composite materials to create long-span, lightweight coverings. In 1978, a 100-foot-diameter prefabricated FRP roof was installed in Argenteuil, France.[42]

Although it is hard to separate the history of composite materials used strictly for interior or exterior ornamentation, it is relatively safe to say that fiberglass composite materials have been used quite extensively and commonly for this purpose for a relatively long time. For non-structural and purely ornamental uses, many constraints on the selection of materials do not exist, opening up the possibilities for the use of novel materials. One early mention of the use of composites for ornament was in 1984; the Bob Evans restaurant chain used FRP components to simulate Victorian-era façades.[43]

It is also worth making a special note about the late architect and structural engineer Frei Otto, whose work at the University of Stuttgart and the Institute for Lightweight Structures continues to inspire many architects currently studying composite materials. His research, which explored minimal surfaces, lightweight structures, naturally inspired forms, and new materials, has found a fresh generation of students who are utilizing new tools and technologies to explore the themes established by his life's work. This can best be seen in the work of the students currently at the University of Stuttgart in the Institute for Computational Design and Construction (ICD) and the Institute for Building Structures and Structural Design (ITKE), whose pavilions are testing many ideas surrounding new material technologies.

Renzo Piano's Mobile Structure for Sulfur Extraction of 1966, with a fiberglass (gFRP) panelized barrel vault.

THE PRESENT AND FUTURE

As we have seen, the history of composites, at least the FRP kind in question, is relatively short, especially in comparison to other building materials. But the history of composites also demonstrates their ability to achieve design and performance goals in many industries, some of which necessarily share overlapping criteria with architecture.

Recently, however, a handful of buildings have been completed that have utilized composite materials in significant ways. The present state-of-the-art of composites in architecture is showcased in Part II of this book, surveying recently built structures that utilize FRP composites. From this we can see how different architects, clients, and builders have made the most of the material to achieve different design goals.

As a concluding point, it is worth considering whether the composites industry would benefit from a branding exercise. The name composite, as we have seen, is and probably will always remain vague, given the broad scope of materials that can accurately be described as such. Fiber-reinforced polymers are too much of a mouthful to be easily remembered, or understood, although that term most accurately describes the materials that may hold potential solutions for many applications. Its corresponding acronym, FRP, is still an acronym, and branding experts will tell you there is a limit to the effectiveness of an acronym to communicate ideas to most people.[44] A succinct name to replace the term fiber-reinforced polymer, or FRP, would potentially go a long way to clarifying the specific class of materials in question, and thus their inherent properties and ability to improve built products.

1 Bank, 1.
2 Strong, 7. Strong differentiates between FRPs, which he calls Engineering Composites, and Advanced Composites, based on the length of fibers and the performance characteristics of the matrices. I find this distinction a bit too fine and counterintuitive and propose a separate classification order here.
3 Hull and Clyne, 3.
4 Hollaway 2001, 3.
5 Strong, 19.
6 Hollaway, 7.
7 Oxford English Dictionary.
8 Rosenberg.
9 Seymour and Deanin, 105.
10 Seymour and Deanin, 57.
11 Strong, 5.
12 Seymour and Strong.
13 Strong, 6.
14 Strong, 8.
15 Hale.
16 Winfield.
17 Savage.
18 Rowe.
19 Volvo press release date 01.11.18; accessed from: https://www.polestar.com/press-release/2018/11/01/polestar-evaluates-strength-of-carbon-fibre-in-successful-first-crash-test.
20 Savage.
21 https://www.iihs.org/ratings/vehicle/bmw/i3-4-door-hatchback/2019.
22 Volvo press release date 01.11.18; accessed from: https://www.polestar.com/press-release/2018/11/01/polestar-evaluates-strength-of-carbon-fibre-in-successful-first-crash-test.
23 Seymour, 58.
24 Mouritz.
25 Winfield.
26 Kazmeirski.
27 Hollaway 2008, xv.
28 Hollaway 2010, 2427.
29 Hollaway 2001, 2.
30 Winfield.
31 Quarmby, 46.
32 Croft, Hodkinson.
33 Hollaway 2008, 2426.
34 Berry, D. B. S. "Tests on full size plastics panel components." *The Use of Plastics for Load Bearing and Infill Panels* (Hollaway L.(ed.)). Manning Rapley Publishing, Croydon (1974): 148–155.
35 Buckminster Fuller Institute (BFI). https://www.bfi.org/about-bfi/mobile-learning/restorations-and-dome-development, accessed 12/11/2018.
36 Rackard.
37 Quarmby, 49.
38 Quarmby, 52.
39 Quarmby, 65–76.
40 Winfield.
41 Winfield.
42 Winfield.
43 Winfield.
44 Keller.

BOEING
CMI Critical Materials
MDF Manufacturing Demonstration Facility
OAK RIDGE National Laboratory
TENNESSEE
THERMWOOD
MDF
MANUFACTURING
DEMONSTRATION
FACILITY

3

TECHNOLOGY: PROPERTIES AND PROCESSES

This chapter gives a brief introduction to the properties, science, and technology behind composite material design and fabrication. As there are already several good full-length textbooks focusing specifically on composite material science, this chapter does not attempt to be a thorough examination of this field. Instead, the target reader is someone who is investigating composite materials for the first time and has an interest in the material as it pertains to use in architecture and construction. Suggestions for further reading can be found at the end of this chapter.

BASIC PROPERTIES

The tables and graphs introduced here give a general overview of how composites, as a class of materials, compare to other common building materials. For structural uses, the key properties are stiffness (how a material resists deformation in response to force: Young's modulus), yield strength (when a material begins to irreparably deform, both under compression and under tension), and density (mass per unit volume). In short: stiffness, strength, and weight. For other architectural uses, sustainability concerns; or more specialized construction issues; properties such as thermal expansion, thermal conductivity, and embodied energy; carbon footprint; and cost are also important to consider, and will be expanded upon in other parts of this chapter or book.

Finding data on material properties can be a cumbersome process and wading through the vast number of sources available to find such data (such as engineering textbooks, fabricator spec sheets, or industry guides) can often be overwhelming. For building professionals, the lack of easy reference to material properties can be an impediment to material-based design thinking.

Furthermore, even within specific classes of materials, for example metal, there is a wide range of properties commercially available. Steel has very different properties from aluminum, and then even within steel many different grades or alloys are available.

It is no different for composites, which offer an even greater range of available properties. For architects and designers seeking to begin an investigation into a material-driven approach or design process, it is thus helpful to begin with a broad comparative understanding of different material classes in key performance metrics.

In architecture, this would allow designers to isolate and compare the criteria most relevant to the function and use required (barring, of course, code, economic, or construction constraints). For instance, it is helpful to know roughly how strong composites are in relation to their alternatives in structures—wood, concrete, and metals.

opposite
3D-printed mold for a composite wind turbine blade measuring 13 m (43 ft) in length. A joint development between Sandia National Laboratories, Oak Ridge National Laboratory, and TPI Composites, 3D-printing the mold cut one year of development time from the blade-making process.

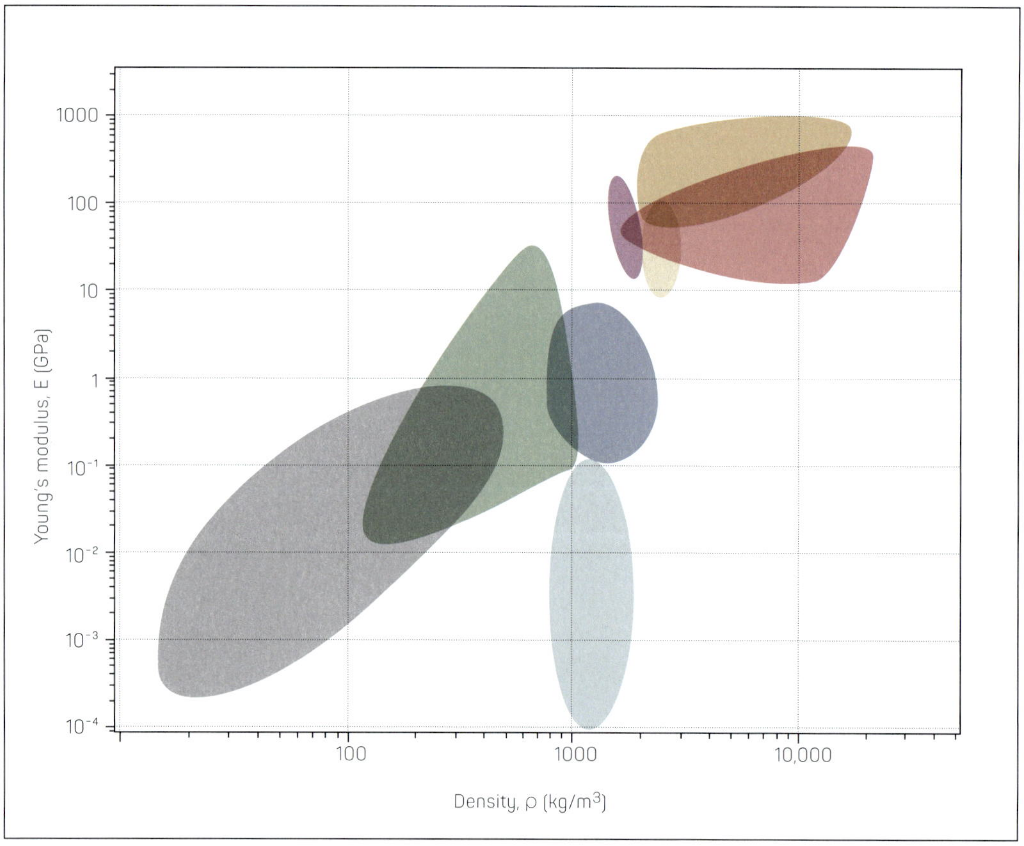

top and bottom
These charts plot the stiffness, or Young's modulus, of different classes of materials against density. The Young's modulus measures a material's deformation, or strain, in reaction to stress. Values to the upper right have greater stiffness and density. The top chart displays only broad material categories (see the legend below). The bottom chart identifies specific materials within those broad categories. It is important to note that the values on the x- and y-axes are logarithmic.

- Metals
- Technical Ceramics
- Non-technical Ceramics
- Composites
- Polymers
- Elastomers
- Natural materials
- Foams

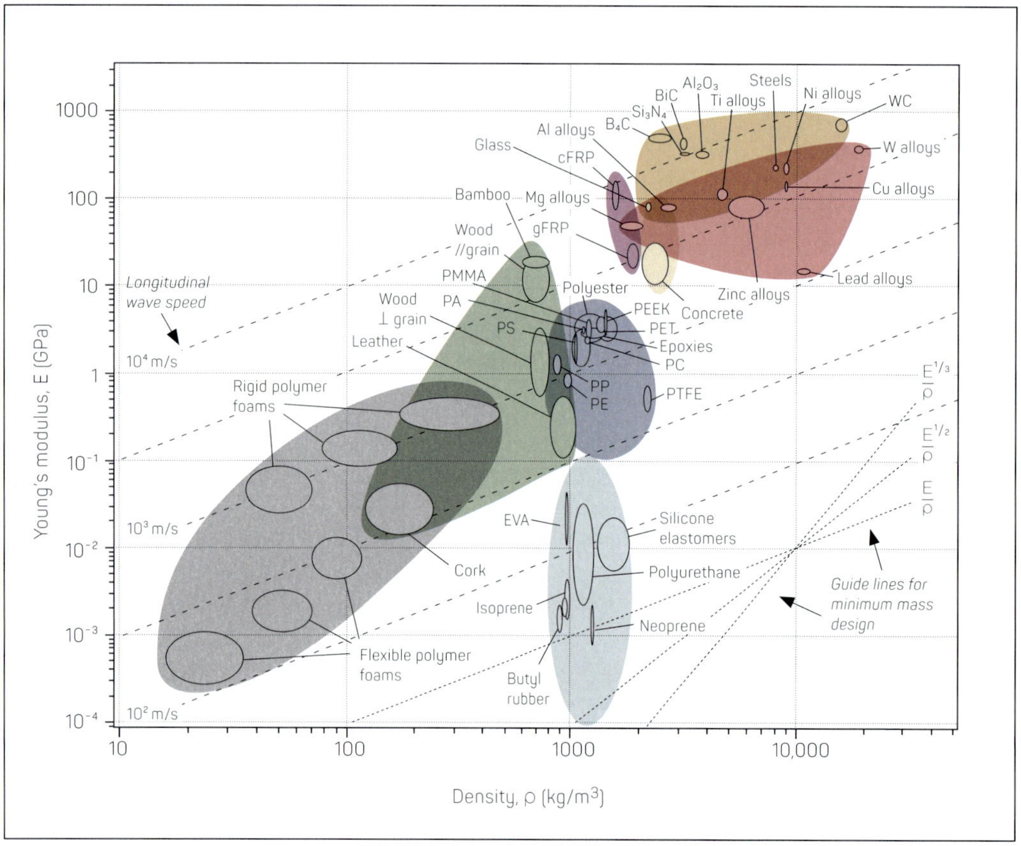

This chart plots the strength of different classes of materials against density. The strength of a material is its ability to withstand an applied load before failure or plastic deformation. Values to the upper right have greater strength and density. It is important to note that the values on the x- and y-axes are logarithmic.

Metals and polymers: yield strength, σ_y

Ceramics, glasses: modulus of rupture, MOR

Elastomers: tensile tear strength, σ_t

Composites: tensile failure, σ_t

- Metals
- Ceramics
- Composites
- Polymers
- Elastomers
- Natural materials
- Foams

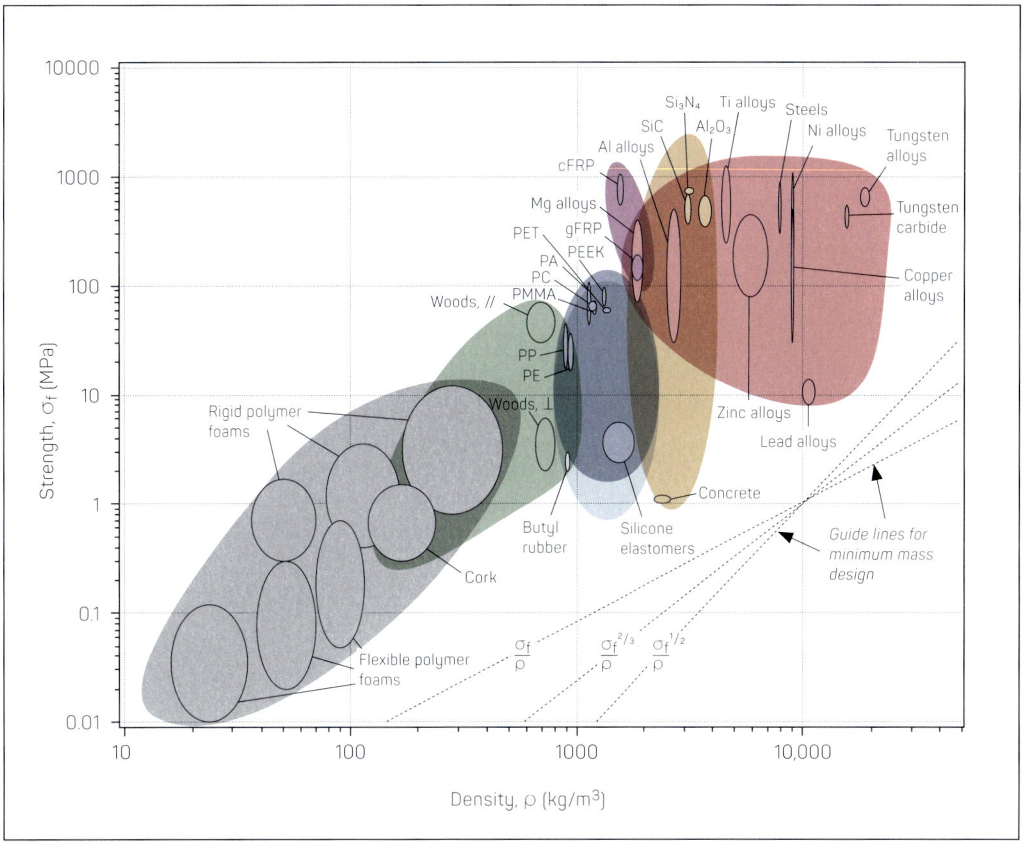

This chart plots the fracture toughness of different classes of materials against Young's modulus, or stiffness. Fracture toughness is the critical stress intensity factor of a sharp crack where propagation of the crack suddenly becomes rapid and unlimited. Values to the upper right have greater fracture toughness and stiffness. It is important to note that the values on the x- and y-axes are logarithmic.

- Metals
- Technical Ceramics
- Non-technical Ceramics
- Composites
- Polymers
- Elastomers
- Natural materials
- Foams

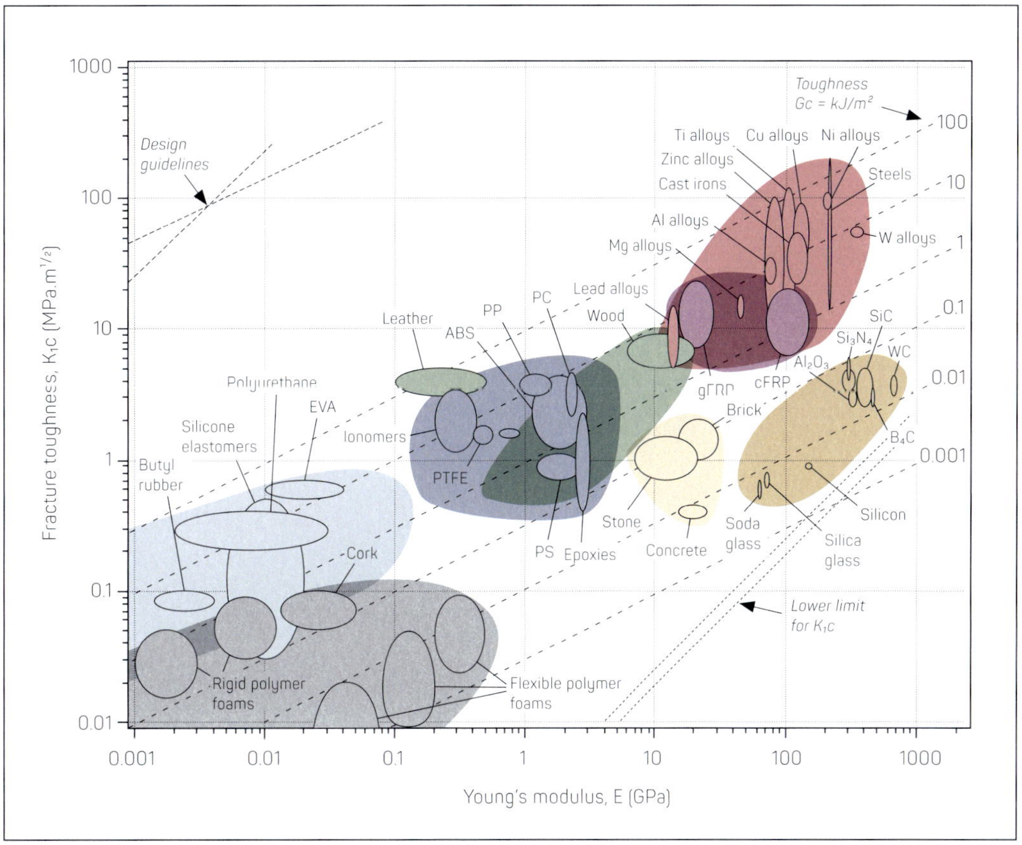

The graphs shown here, from Granta Design, illustrate the key properties of commonly used building materials in relation to each other. They are represented as clouds or bubbles, indicating the range of specific values attainable. The charts are intentionally approximate and are intended for conceptual design purposes—they are not sufficient for detailed design calculations. However, from these charts, the potential for composites as a class of architecturally relevant materials should be clear.

Other properties of composites relevant to architecture, such as their durability, resistance to corrosion, thermal conductivity, and thermal expansion, will be discussed in greater detail as they pertain to those types of composites that possess them.

EXPANDED DEFINITION

At this point, before diving a bit deeper into the technology of composites, it is worth looking at a more detailed definition than the one provided in an earlier chapter. The definition adopted by the Study Group on Advanced Polymer Composites of the Institution of Structural Engineers, London, in 1989 is as follows:

Composite materials consist normally of two discrete phases, a continuous matrix which is often a resin, surrounding a fibrous reinforcing structure. The reinforcement has high strength and stiffness whilst the matrix binds the fibers together, allowing stress to be transferred from one fiber to another producing a consolidated structure. In advanced or high performance composites, high strength and stiffness fibers are used in relatively high volume fractions whilst the orientation of the fibers is controlled to enable high mechanical stresses to be carried safely. In the anisotropic nature of these materials lies their major advantage. The reinforcement can be tailored and oriented to follow the stress patterns in the component leading to much greater design economy than can be achieved with traditional isotropic materials. The reinforcements are typically glass, carbon or aramid fibers in the form of continuous filament, tow or woven fabrics. The resins which confer distinctive properties such as heat, fiber or chemical resistance may be chosen from a wide spectrum of thermosetting or thermoplastic synthetic materials, and those commonly used are polyester, epoxy, and phenolic resins. More advanced heat resisting types such as vinylesters and bismaleimides are gaining usages in high performance applications and advanced carbon fiber/ thermoplastic composites are well into a market development phase.[1]

In the preceding definition, the major components that define composite materials are succinctly explained and related to each other. These are the fiber reinforcing, the polymer matrix, the geometry of the reinforcing, and the resultant anisotropic nature.

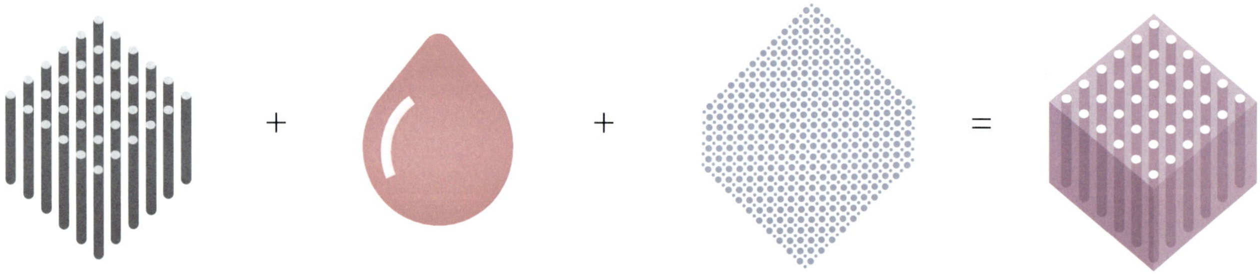

Fibers
Fibrous reinforcement such as glass, carbon, aramid, biofibers, or others. The length, ratio, and geometry of the fibers contribute to the final properties.

Matrix
Polymer resin, either thermoplastic or thermoset, such as polyester, vinylester, epoxy, or phenolic. The matrix binds the fibers together, distributes the loads, and protects the fibers.

Additives
Fillers, additives, or other ingredients used to add fire resistance, increase durability, aid in the curing process, or contribute other characteristics.

Composite
The resultant material made from the combination of fiber, matrix, and additives. The process or method of combining those ingredients has an impact on the final properties.

TECHNOLOGY OVERVIEW: MATERIALS, GEOMETRY, AND PROCESSES

The only thing that needs to be added to the preceding definition is a discussion of process. The process by which the composite is manufactured has an impact not only on the final resultant mechanical properties, but also on the formal shapes possible, the equipment necessary, the volume of production, and the cost of the part.

Thus, as an organizing principle, it may be beneficial to structure the discussion of composite technology around the concepts of materials, geometry, and processes. Each has an impact on the performance and capability of the final material, and each has a history of technological advancements that has further pushed the capabilities of the material as a class. Taken together: composite materials are distinguished by the ability to be manipulated and engineered at three different co-dependent levels: material, geometry, and process. The rest of the chapter goes into each of these technological concepts in greater detail.

Materials

Fiber Reinforcements

Fibers and polymers are the essential components of FRPs. Composites are often known in shorthand by their type of fiber reinforcement: glass fiber-reinforced polymer composites are colloquially referred to as fiberglass, and the same applies to carbon fiber-reinforced epoxy parts. Fiber reinforcement provides strength and stiffness to the final composite material. Fibers are much longer than they are wide or thick—this differentiates them from particles or granules, and this shape and orientation is responsible for their anisotropic properties. Their lengths can range from microscopically short whiskers to long fibers, sometimes meters in length. Generally, as the fibers get longer, tensile strength, modulus of elasticity, and flexural strength increase.[2]
From this fibrous property, which is a result of a combination of the process of fiber manufacture and molecular orientation, comes one of composite materials' most important attributes, that of anisotropy.

Anisotropic materials do not have the same properties along all axes.
This contrasts with isotropic materials, which have the same properties in all directions. Wood is an example of an anisotropic material, with different properties in directions along versus across the grain. Concrete and steel are examples of isotropic materials, which have the same structural properties regardless of axis of orientation.

Isotropic versus anisotropic.
A material which has the same properties in all directions, or regardless of orientation, is considered isotropic.
A material that has differing properties based on orientation or direction is considered anisotropic. Fiber-reinforced composites are almost always anisotropic, though they can be engineered to be quasi-isotropic.

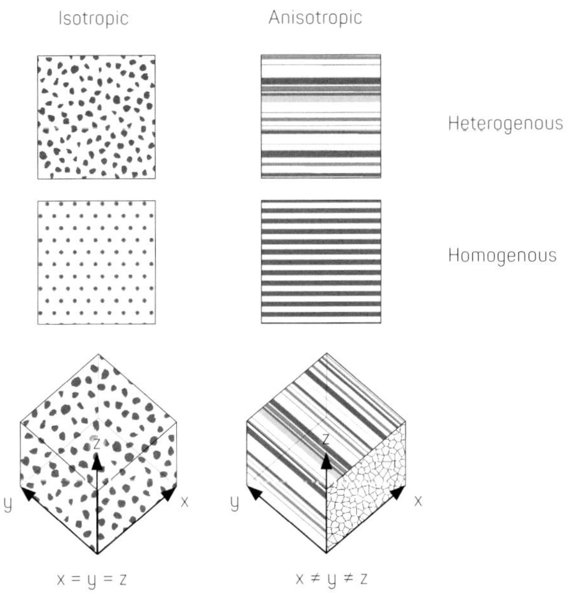

Polymers, without fibrous reinforcing, are isotropic. With fiber reinforcing, particularly with long fibers, they are distinctly anisotropic. This feature of composites plays a big role in final composite component design, which will be discussed as part of the concept of composite geometry.

Glass fiber is the most common form of composite reinforcing, and together with a polyester or epoxy resin is commonly referred to as fiberglass. Fiberglass parts can be found everywhere, and everyone is familiar with boats, automotive parts, furniture, bathtubs, and many other fiberglass products. Its history as one of the first composite materials has meant that the extremely high volume has led to low prices. Fiberglass is formed by forcing molten glass through small metal orifices and is available with different strengths, thermal properties, and electrical behavior.

Carbon or graphite fiber has famously high strength and stiffness. Derived from polyacrylonitrile (PAN) or pitch (a by-product of oil refining), carbon fiber is most commonly paired with an epoxy matrix to form final parts for many high-performance applications. Variations in source material and processing contribute to a wide variety of modulus grades, which are often grouped together as standard, intermediate, or ultra-high modulus. They also have the extremely notable property of having a negative coefficient of thermal expansion—that is, they get smaller as they heat up. When carefully engineered, this property can lead to final parts with excellent thermal stability across a wide range of temperatures. As a group, carbon fiber composites (cFRP) are among the strongest materials commonly available today.

Aramids occupy a sort of middle position between glass and carbon fibers, with distinctive properties that have proven valuable in specific applications. Aramids are roughly as strong as carbon fiber (and thus stronger than glass) but are not as stiff. Contrary to being a limitation, this high strength combined with low stiffness has found many useful applications. High elongation, tensile strength, and fibril failure properties give aramid fibers a toughness renowned in ballistic, armor, and blast protection applications. DuPont markets aramid under the trade name Kevlar, by which aramids are famously known. For a time, the terms bulletproof and Kevlar were essentially interchangeable.

In contrast to synthetically derived glass, carbon, and aramid fibers, there also exist natural, renewably sourced bio-fibers for composite reinforcement. In terms of properties, the typical trade-off is reduced mechanical consistency, strength and stiffness, offset instead by lower costs and the sustainable benefit of a potentially renewable source. Flax, spider silk, hemp, cotton, worm silk and jute have been used to make composites for commercial and industrial applications, and research in the field is growing.

Images of the variety of fiber reinforcing available, from top left, proceeding clockwise: taffetta weave patterned fiberglass; a selection of different biofibers; carbon-fiber weave laminate available in roll form; and aramid fiber yarns.

Thermoplastic
Analogous to butter, a thermoplastic resin is one that is typically heated in order to be shaped into a form, before setting into a solid at room temperature.

Thermoset
Analogous to an egg, a thermoset resin is usually liquid at room temperature, then solidified into its final form (cured) by some process. Thermosets are more commonly used than thermoplastics with fiber reinforcing.

Polymer Matrices

Polymer matrices serve to bind together the fiber reinforcement, transfer structural loads to the reinforcing, and protect it from environmental damage. The terms polymer matrix, plastic, and resin are often used interchangeably.[3] In the finished composite material, the properties most defined by the choice of matrix material are the thermal properties, resistance to solvents, fire resistance, electrical properties, UV resistance/optics, and toughness.

There are two major classes of polymer matrices, thermoset and thermoplastic. Thermoplastics are solid at room temperature, shaped into their desired form by heating, and then set in a mold to cool. Often, thermoplastics can be reheated and reshaped multiple times. In contrast, thermosets are usually liquid at room temperature, and then solidified (or cured) by some process. Thermosets, as their name implies, cannot usually be reshaped once they have been set. Thermosets are the most common form of polymer composite materials.

Unsaturated polyester (UP), thermoset polyester (TP), or simply polyester, is currently the most commonly used polymer resin in the composites industry, including in construction.[4] This can be attributed in no small part to its comparatively low cost. Other advantages include ease of curing, molding, and a wide range of possible properties readily available in the market. Disadvantages include relatively poor durability (compared to other resins), brittleness, and concerns about off-gassing and air quality in the curing process.

Polyester resins are extensively used for automotive parts, boats, recreational vehicles both on land and at sea, household appliances, plumbing fixtures and fittings, including bathtubs and shower units, as well as many other applications.

Epoxies are the second most commonly used thermosetting resin for composites. They are familiar in construction for their non-reinforced use as a coating, paint, setting, or adhesive. Epoxies are thermally stable, have good mechanical properties, low conductivity, and high dielectric strength. They are commonly paired with carbon fibers in the high-performance composites market. In particular, the high shear strength of epoxies makes them favored over other commonly available thermoset resins. In comparison to polyester, they are stronger and stiffer, tougher, and more thermally stable. But they often cost much more than polyesters.[5]

Vinylester, or vinyl ester, or epoxy vinyl ester (EVER), is often described as occupying the middle ground between polyester and epoxy. The cost is halfway between the two; and vinyl ester has better mechanical properties than polyester but cures more easily than epoxy. Vinyl esters have relatively low flammability and smoke production values.[6]

Phenolic, or phenolic resin, was the first synthesized thermoset plastic, and it still plays an important role in reinforced composite materials. While phenolics are generally more expensive than unsaturated polyesters, they are not as expensive as epoxies. The primary advantages are excellent flammability performance, low heat transfer, high thermal stability, and good adhesion. They are currently used frequently in plywood, glulam, and other timber products, as well as in many electrical components, automotive parts, and household wares. Their flammability performance is so remarkable that phenolics have found widespread use in the transportation and aerospace fields, where flame spread and smoke-developed indices requirements are extremely strict. In fact, the flammability performance of phenolics are good enough for them to have found use as parts in the flow path of rocket engines, where temperatures reach in excess of 6,000 °F (3,300 °C). Difficulty in processing phenolics is often cited as a reason for their relatively small market share of polymer resins.

Other thermoset resins less common in the construction industry include polyimides, bismaleimide, cyanate ester, polyurethane, and dicyclopentadiene (DCPD), each with their own advantages and disadvantages.

Thermoplastics are less used in construction for two main reasons; the first is cost and the second is the difficulty of processing thermoplastic resins with reinforcing fibers. The relatively small usage within construction contrasts with the entire synthetic polymer market in general, of which thermoplastics make up about 80 percent.[7] However, thermosets dominate the reinforced polymer market, which equates to 20 percent of the overall market. Over time, process innovations may lead to thermoplastics gaining a larger market share, and thermoplastics have one major advantage over thermosets in that they may be relatively easily re-melted and thus recycled.

Common thermoplastic resins include polyether ether ketone (PEEK), acrylic (polymethyl methacrylate (PMMA)), nylon (polyamide or PA), polyethylene terephthalate (PET), polyvinyl chloride (PVC), and acrylonitrile butadiene styrene (ABS).

A wide range of properties are available within all these matrix resin groups, due to the specific molecular make-up and method of processing of the resin, but also because of the great variety of curing agents, coupling agents, inhibitors, solvents/dilutants, and other additives. Of course, the final properties of the composite also depend on the fiber reinforcing material selection, as well as the manufacturing process.

The descent engine rocket nozzle used on the Apollo lunar missions, made of phenolic composite. The engine could be throttled between 4.44–44.4 kN (1,000–10,000 lbf) of thrust, and measures approximately 2.43 m (8 ft) in length and 1.52 m (5 ft) in diameter.

Careful layering of directional and/or randomly oriented fibers can create specific directional or quasi-isotropic characteristics.

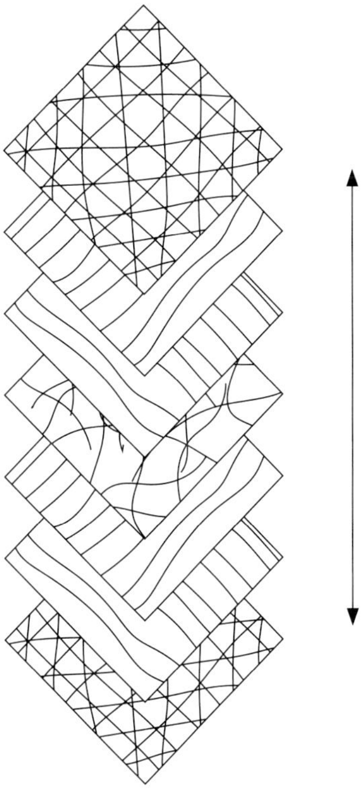

Geometry

Fibers are oriented in different ways in relation to each other and within their matrix, and this has a significant influence on the performance of the final product. The property of their orientation and arrangement is what I am referring to as geometry, though it is also sometimes called reinforcement form. Broadly, the geometry of fibers includes weaves, knits, braids, chop (chop strand), mats, preforms, and whiskers. Certain types of fibers lend themselves better than others to certain geometries, and certain geometries in turn lend themselves better to certain manufacturing processes. Much of this technology is shared with the textile industry, and advancements in textiles suggest applicability to composites as well.

A note about terminology here: a single fiber is often called a filament, or monofilament. Groups of filaments are called strands, rovings (in the case of fiberglass), or tows (in the case of graphite/carbon). Yarns are twisted strands, whiskers refer to extremely short fibers (below 0.20 in (0.5 cm)), and chop or chopped strand is typically anything longer than a whisker up to about 3 in (8 cm).[8]

Woven and knitted reinforcements come in the many different patterns and geometries familiar in textiles: basket, twill, satin, harness, crowfoot, leno, or triaxial, among many others. Each has mechanical properties derived from the type of weave, as well as the thread counts, strand thickness, and other variables. Among the most important properties of a weave or a knit is orientation, wherein a specific type of textile will have predominant directions of fiber placement relative to the x- or y-axis, whether unidirectional, biaxial, 30°, 45°, 60°, for example. Manufacturers often publish technical information about the wide range of reinforcing cloths produced and their properties.

Prepregs are a special type of partially processed reinforcing for composite parts. Fibers come in sheet form, loosely bound together with partially cured resin. These fibers are pre-impregnated with resin and are thus known as prepregs. The pre-impregnation gives a precise and uniform distribution of matrix throughout the fibers, which can otherwise be difficult to achieve. Prepregs have very stringent handling and storage requirements, but can allow unidirectional strand sheets and predictable draping/shaping performance, depending on the desired shape of the final part. They are usually placed in an autoclave under heat and pressure to cure into their final form.

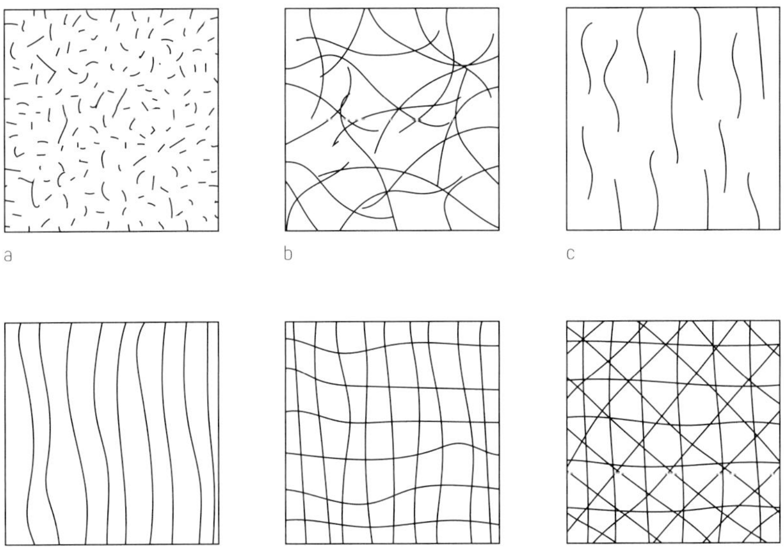

a b c d e f

Fiber reinforcing geometries:

- a short whisker fibers
- b discontinuous randomly oriented fibers, or chop strand
- c discontinuous aligned short fibers, or short fiber uni-directional
- d continuous aligned fibers, or long fiber uni-directional
- e continuous fiber 0° and 90°, or long fiber bi-directional
- f continuous fiber multi-directional, or long fiber multi-directional

Chopped fiber and chopped strand mats are exactly what they sound like, which is a bunch of shorter strands of fiber arranged in a random orientation. Chopped fibers are sometimes sold as loose fibers to be used in spray-up applications, while chopped strand mats come in preformed sheets of chopped fiber. With lower densities of reinforcing, they are typically less strong but also lower cost.

Weaves, knits, and mats have the fibers oriented in the x-y plane. Thus, they are essentially two-dimensional, with weak properties in the z direction. However, certain geometries can approach three-dimensionality. Braided forms, stitched laminates, and computer-numerically-controlled (CNC) weaves allow more fibers to be oriented along the z-axis, giving them enhanced properties in the z direction. The advantages of three-dimensionality can include improved mechanical properties of shear, toughness, progressive failure, ease of handling, and improved formability.

Three-dimensionality can also be approached through the lay-up and stacking of multiple sheets (lamina) of knits or weaves. Alternating or controlling the bias and directionality of the laminae can provide a pseudo-isotropic nature, meaning they will have similar properties along all axes.

Preforms and advanced CNC 3D weaving further advance the concept of specific fiber placement control using CNC technology. The idea is to place fibers exactly where they will be needed in the final shape they will assume. This is opposed to placing fibers in a sheet product that is later shaped into the form of the final part. Recently developed technologies such as 3D weaving, robotic filament placement, and additive manufacturing technologies begin to approach this conceptual ideal of perfect efficiency of fiber placement.

An example of a CNC flat-knit product, with variable weaves and differentiated fiber materials to create a locally differentiated textile.

Contemporary flat-knit machines, with multiple threaded heads and CNC thread placement, capable of producing custom weaves or knits with variable mechanical properties throughout a surface.

Manufacturing processes

So far, we have discussed the general properties of final composite parts, their material make-up, and the geometry of those materials within the final part. The manufacturing process is the method of integrating the fibers and matrix together, setting them into place with their desired orientation, and allowing them to harden and cure into the final part shape. The choice of resin and fiber will to some extent determine which processes are appropriate, and vice versa.

The shape and topology of the final part will also inform which manufacturing method to choose, as certain forms are possible with certain processes but not others. For composite material design, we see here how the material, geometry, and process are intertwined.

The geometry of the reinforcing is often tied directly to and co-dependent on the means of manufacture. In fact, in many cases, it is difficult to separate the two, as one form of reinforcing geometry is specific to certain means of manufacture, or vice versa, such as chopped strand, prepreg, or filament winding. More advanced technologies begin to blur the distinction between the two, as CNC 3D weaving or additive manufacturing technologies are essentially both geometry and process integrated.

The relationship between the final part complexity and the fiber geometry and manufacturing process is worth discussing further, as one or the other may be a driving parameter in the design of a composite part. For architecture and construction, composite parts will most likely fall toward the simpler side of the part complexity spectrum due to their size and scale (most architectural parts do not approach the finer complexity and dimensional tolerance requirements of composite parts made for the medical industry, for example). But architectural parts often demand lower costs and more limited runs of production, especially in comparison to other industries that use composites (such as automotive). Triangulating a position for composite parts in architecture between those parameters is a factor in each project and market application.

Manufacturing processes can be roughly grouped into four main categories: open molding, partial closed molding, closed molding, and non-mold processes. Or more generally, they may be grouped by processes that require molds and those that do not, or by processes that are automated versus manual.

Matrix comparing the various capabilities and costs of composite manufacturing processes. Adapted from Larry Cox, Structurlite Composites Consultants.

Composite Process Capabilities and Costs Matrix

Category	Method	Initial equip. cost	Tooling cost	Labor cost	Production rate	Finished part cost
Open molding	Hand lay-up / spray-up	Low	Low	High	Low	Mid
	Filament winding	Mid	Mid	Low	Mid	Low
Partial open / partial closed molding	Wet lay-up vacuum bag	Low	Low	High	Very low	Mid
	Prepreg oven cure	Mid	Mid-high	High	Very low	High
	Prepreg autoclave cure	Very high	Mid-high	High	Very low	Very high
Closed molding	Vacuum infusion molding	Low	Low	High	Low	Mid
	Resin transfer molding (RTM)	Mid	Mid	High	Mid	Mid
	Light resin transfer molding (RTM)	Low	Low	Mid	Low	Mid
	Compression molding	High	High	Low	High	Low
	Pultrusion	High	High	Low	High	Low
	Continuous lamination	High	Low	Low	High	Low
	Reaction injection molding	High	Low	Low	High	Low
No mold	Additive manufacturing / 3D printing	Low	None	Low	High	Low

Open Mold
Fibers and resin are typically applied by hand into a one-sided mold, with the finish side usually against the mold.

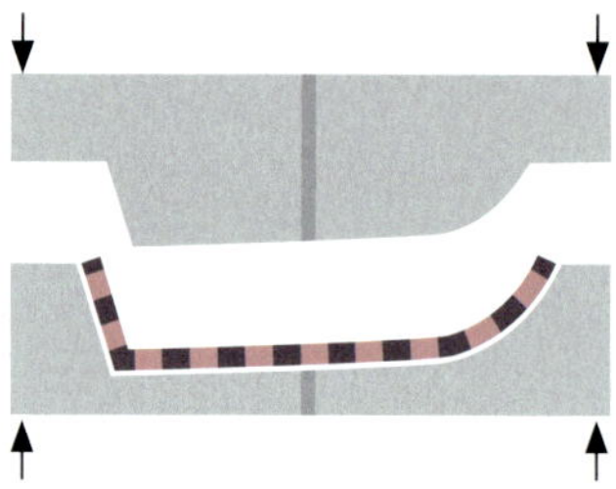

Closed Mold
Fibers and resin are applied by hand or machine into a closed two-sided mold, with the assistance of heat, pressure, vacuums, or resin infusers.

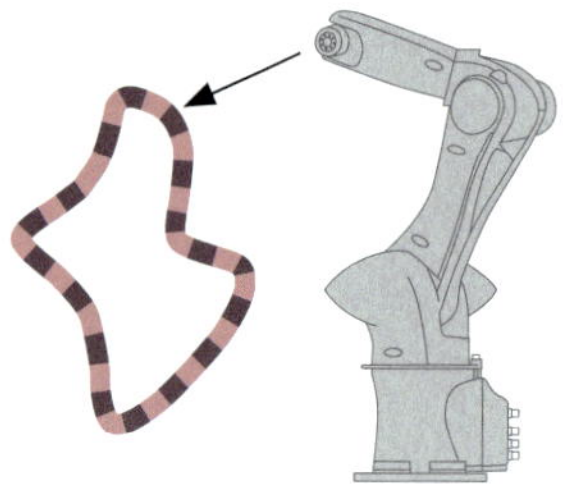

No Mold
Additive manufacturing, 3D-printing, robot assisted, or other fiber and resin placement not requiring a mold.

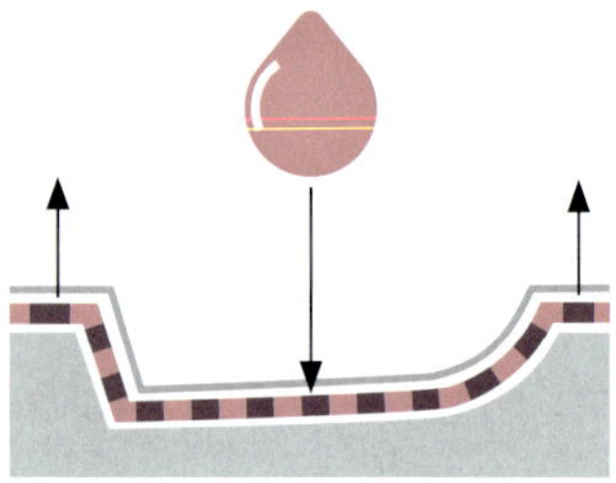

Vacuum Infusion / Light RTM
Fibers are typically applied by hand into a one-sided mold, and vacuum bags and/or pumps are used to distribute the resin throughout the part.

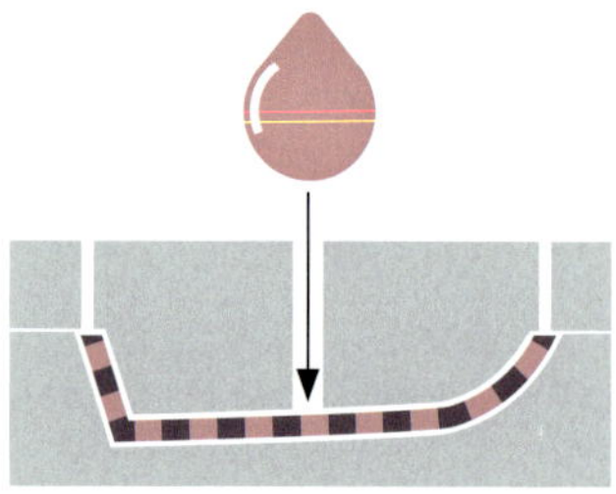

Resin Transfer Molding (RTM)
Fibers are applied by hand or machine into a closed, two-sided mold, with the assistance of pumps, vacuums, heat, pressure, or resin infusers.

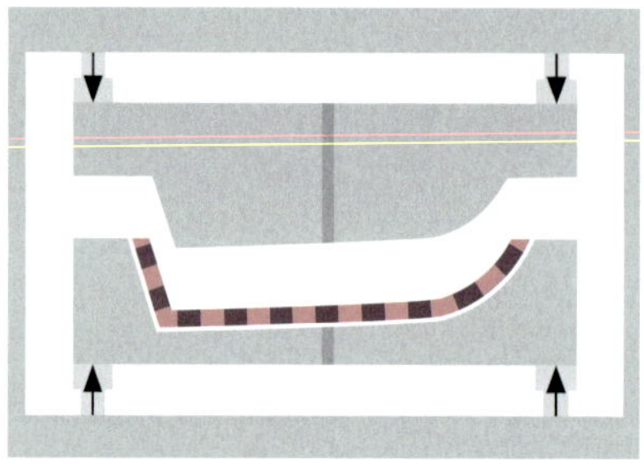

Compression Molding
Molding compound containing fibers and resin in sheet or bulk form is placed in a hydraulic press, which uses heat and high pressure to cure the part into shape.

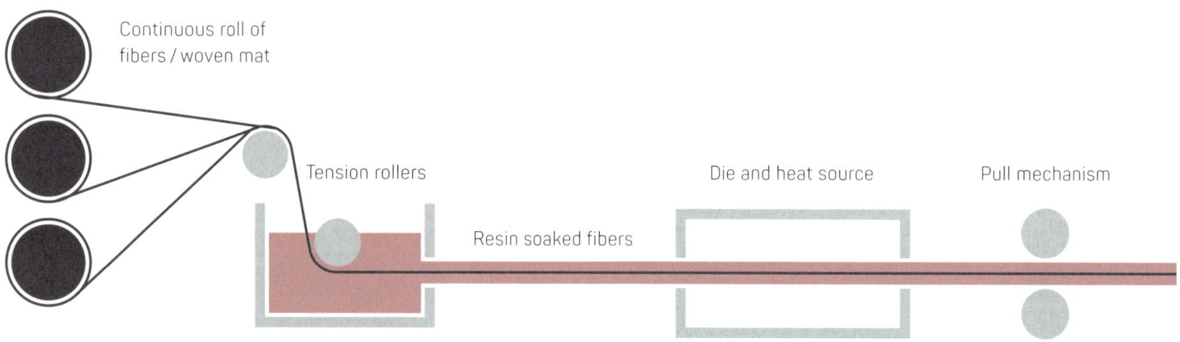

Pultrusion
Fibers and resin are pulled through a die to form parts with a single cross-sectional profile.

In open molding processes, the fibers are usually laid by hand, or sprayed, against an open mold, and then resin is applied (also usually by hand) and allowed to cure before the part is removed from the mold. This process is also called wet lay-up and is still used today for many large parts such as boat ship hulls, wind turbine blades, or bathtubs, for example. It is a very manual process and therefore has both the attendant advantages and disadvantages of a handmade product—a certain amount of part complexity, variability, and detail is achievable, but mechanical consistency, the need for skilled labor, a single finished side, and high-volume production can present challenges.

Filament winding is an open mold process whereby strands of fiber are placed around a spinning mandrel, similar to a wood lathe. New technologies allow many axes of rotation and filament placement.

Partial closed molding processes are similar to open molding techniques in that the fibers are placed manually into or onto molds from which they must be released after curing. The difference comes after the fibers are placed; these processes then utilize vacuum bags, bladders/balloons, ovens, or autoclaves to enhance the resin and fiber integration. These devices apply pressure, which consolidates the plies of laminates, eliminates air pockets, and distributes the resin for a more even and thorough wet-out or saturation.

Prepreg fibers are cured by heating them in a closed oven or an autoclave, which adds pressurization to the heat to assist with laminate consolidation. Prepregs can also be cured and pressurized from within through the use of inflatable bladders or balloons, which define the outer shape by exerting pressure against the mold. This is how tennis rackets and bike frames are often fabricated.

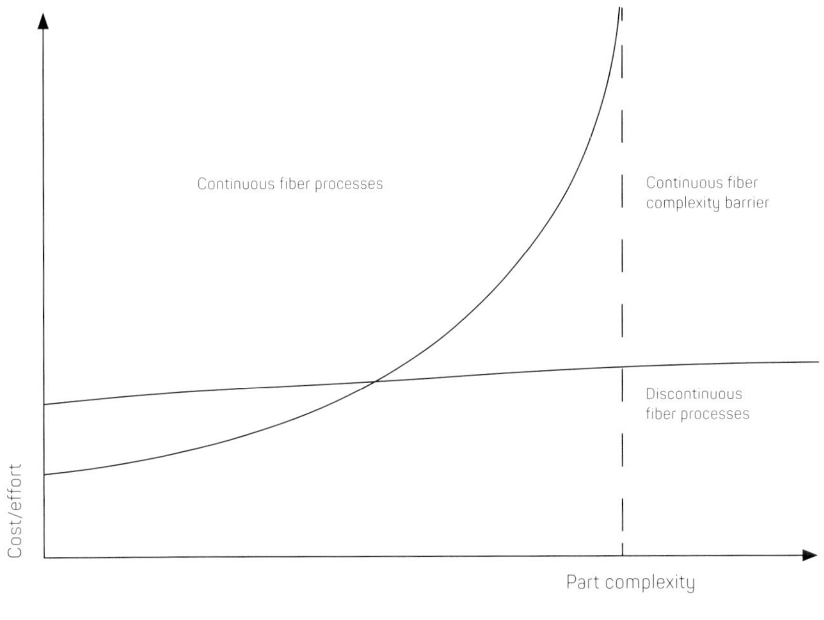

Conceptual chart diagramming the relationship between part complexity and composite manufacturing processes. The dashed line represents a theoretical limit on the part complexity possible for long, continuous fiber-reinforced parts. Discontinuous fiber processes include additive manufacturing, patch-based processes, and other short fiber-based methods.

Siemens B75 wind turbine rotor blade, at the time of production (2012) the largest fiberglass part cast in a single piece, at 75 m (246 ft) in length. It is made from glass-fiber-reinforced epoxy with no seams or joints, manufactured as seen here in a wet-layup process. It weighs about 25 tons; carbon fiber would reduce the weight by an additional 10 to 20 %.

Closed molding processes, as may be inferred from the name, usually involves two or more molds completely encapsulating the finished part. In general, the use of closed molds allows greater control over the finished surface on both sides of a part, better distribution and penetration of resin throughout the reinforcement, and higher volume production. As these processes require two or more molds, they typically offset the higher cost of machinery and tooling with lower manual labor costs over a sufficiently high number of parts.

Of the closed molding processes, compression molding is currently responsible for the greatest share of parts produced in the composite industry. Many applications where multiple small to medium-sized parts need to be produced economically use compression molding technologies. In this process, composite compound material is placed in a press between two matched molds. Bulk molding compound (BMC) and sheet molding compound (SMC) are mixtures of reinforcing fiber and resins prepared for use in compression molding presses. A large hydraulic press then compresses the compound material under high pressure and heat to cure the part into shape. The advantages of this process are a high volume and quality of parts at the expense of greater initial machinery and set-up costs.

Vacuum infusion molding, resin infusion, and resin transfer molding (RTM) are processes by which the reinforcing is laid dry into the molds and vacuum and/or pumps are used to distribute the resin thoroughly throughout the part. These processes allow for more consistent distributions of resin and thus part performance properties. The difficulty of designing the molds, and the locations of the inlets and outlets, adds complexity to the process design.

Pultrusion is a process whereby reinforcing fibers and resin are pulled through a die to form continuous parts with the same cross-section. This process is low cost and achieves excellent consistency, provided the design limitations of the single cross-sectional profile are acceptable.

Non-mold processes

As others have noted, the use of molds for composite part production presents issues for architecture. The cost of creating molds demands economies of scale and high-volume replication of parts, which theoretically may inhibit design freedom (Blonder). While this has long been an architectural problem, it has led some architectural theorists to consider whether current technology allows us to escape those earlier constraints (Carpo).

Thus, some of the emerging composite process technologies aim to free composite production from the use of molds or significantly reduce the cost of mold-making.

This may explain, in part, why additive manufacturing is currently one of the fastest developing technologies in the field of composite processing. In fact, at the most recent North American industry conference at the time of writing (CAMX 2018), around 10 percent of the papers published had additive manufacturing or 3D printing in their titles. The technology is so new that little or no mention is made of additive manufacturing in composite textbooks from just ten years ago. Neither additive manufacturing nor 3D printing relies on molds, and both can produce incredibly complex parts and shapes, while offering impressive material economy with minimal waste factors, and can potentially utilize recycled and reclaimed composite materials.

Not only has additive manufacturing been used to create actual final parts, but also to 3D-print the molds themselves, thereby relying on tested processes while lowering the cost of tooling or mold-making.

The ICD and ITKE at the University of Stuttgart have been pioneering the use of automated filament placement, using robots or even drones to intelligently place structural composite fibers only where needed, thus eliminating the use of molds entirely.

3D-printed biodegradable bamboo technology developed by the Oak Ridge National Laboratory. This additive manufacturing technology was used to create finished architectural parts for a pavilion displayed at Design Miami. Photo courtesy SHoP Architects.

Sandwiches

Sandwich composite structures hold significant promise and utility for the architecture and construction industry. Composed of two skins of laminar composite sandwiching a core of some material, they work the same way structurally as a simple beam, with compressive and tensile forces distributed along the plane of the laminates, analogous to the function of flanges in a wide-flange beam. The core is thus analogous to the web of a beam, connecting the flanges along a distance and providing shear capacity. The difference is that whereas a beam acts linearly, providing structure along the length of the beam in one axis, a sandwich structure provides structure in a plane, that is, along two axes.

Because so much of architecture is currently tectonically composed of thin rectangular volumes joined together (walls, floors, roofs), composite sandwich structures can immediately replace many conventional construction assemblies. These composite sandwich structures then bring many of the benefits that differentiate them from conventional construction materials and assemblies—part consolidation, thermal performance, durability, light weight, high strength, material economy, toughness, corrosion resistance, shop fabrication, reduction of on-site labor, and more. Sandwich structures do not require a mold, eliminating a one-time, cost-consuming step in composite fabrication.

Composite SIPs (structural insulated panels) as installed in a residential structure.

Structurally insulated panels (SIP) provide an interesting case study in the use of composite sandwich structures. With a core of insulating material, typically a polystyrene, sandwiched between two layers of composite, these composite sandwich panels (C-SIP) can function as ready-made wall, floor, and roof structures. They replace conventional assemblies made of dimensional lumber, sheathing, and insulation—consolidating parts while also minimizing weight, trade coordination, and on-site labor. Joint details can be handled any number of ways, from adhesive to mechanical methods, and several companies have developed proprietary systems.

With the technologies that exist, there is good cause to explore the concept of composite sandwich structures that are not purely rectangular panels of constant thickness. Structural forces are hardly ever distributed uniformly, and thus a perfectly efficient structure would never resemble a rectangular volume of uniform thickness (which is currently what most architectural structures are composed of). Composite manufacturing technology allows for the placement, orientation, and variation of fibers along the most efficient load paths in three-dimensional space.

These "smart sandwiches" could address material efficiencies while expressing structural logic, both beloved of architects. In fact, a residence built by Diller Scofidio + Renfro utilized this smart sandwich structural concept[9], as do some on-going research projects at the ETH Zurich and the ICD/ITKE at the University of Stuttgart.

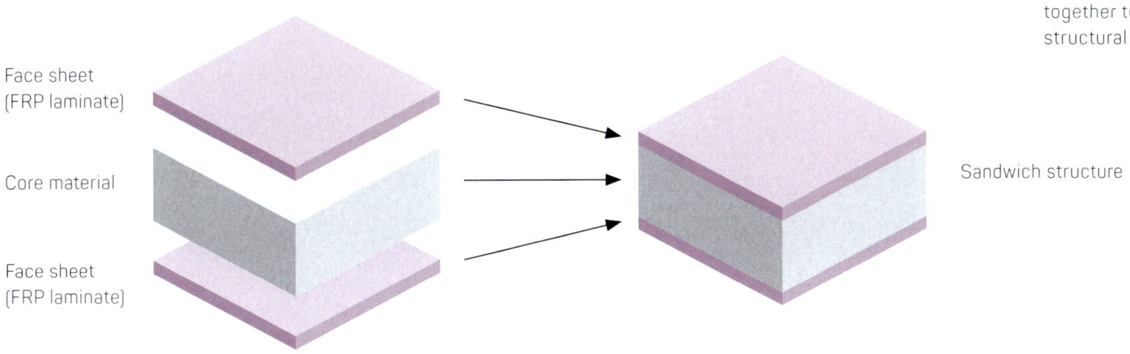

Elements of an FRP sandwich structure. While the face sheets are typically fiber-reinforced composites, the core is generally any lightweight material, such as foam, balsa wood, or honeycomb metal. Adhesive or resin bonds the elements together to form a single structural element.

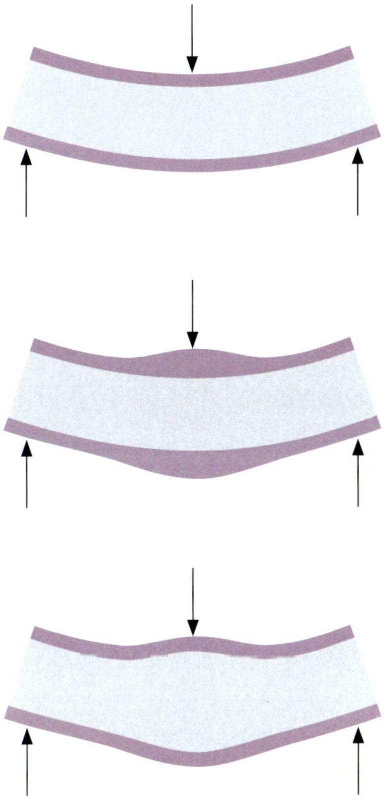

A sandwich structure under simple loading is perfectly analogous to a beam, with the face sheets under tensile or compressive stresses, and the core serving to connect the two face sheets and resist shear stresses. From the fact that any structural member's loading capacity in bending is related to both the depth of the beam and the properties of the material located at the top and bottom ends of that beam, sandwich structures offer a number of different structural responses to loads that are unavailable to simple beams made out of conventional materials (for which the only option is usually to upgrade the entire beam).

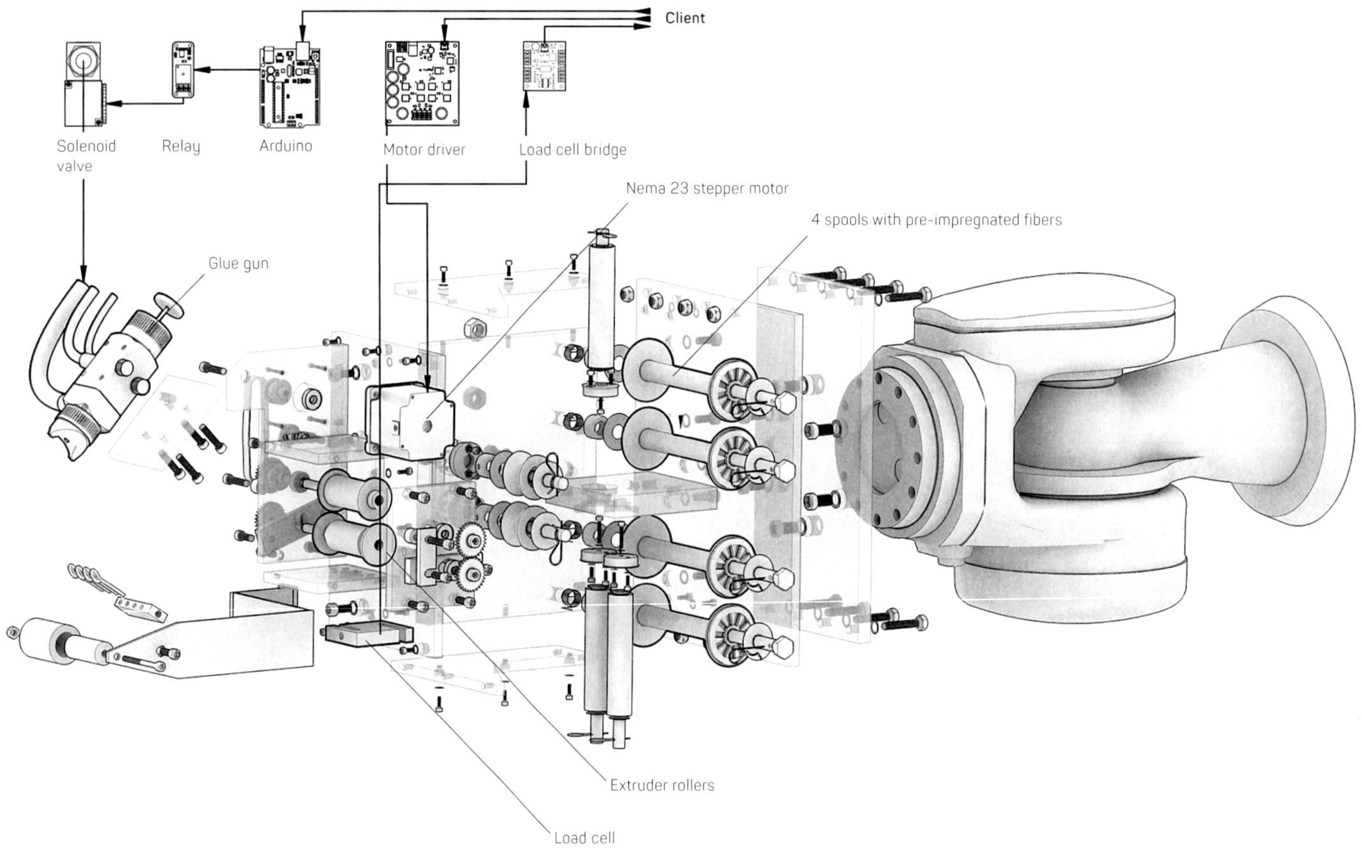

Exploded diagram of fiber-extruding end-effector tool, designed to be attached to the end of a robotic arm and developed by the ICD/ITKE at the University of Stuttgart for their fiber composite pavilions. This tool applies resin and fibers as needed to specific tool paths generated through finite element analysis. More information on this tool can be found in Part II of this book.

COMPOSITE DESIGN

As we have seen, the design of composite materials can be controlled at many different levels. The design of the matrix, fibrous reinforcing, geometry of the laminates, manufacturing process, and/or sandwich structure are all variable, controllable, and interdependent. The material combination of polymer resins and fibrous reinforcing lend each other complementary properties that can be fine-tuned to many different applications, exceeding the capacities of alternative materials. Continuing advancements in the chemical synthesis and processing of polymer resins, fibrous reinforcements, and manufacturing processes mean continually greater performance with fewer drawbacks. Properties can be tailored to applications with a material and design economy impossible with other materials. The design of composites considers knowledge of mechanical properties, intelligent shapes and geometry, and manufacturing and computational power. It is design that incorporates materials, geometry, and processes.

That tailoring, however, is research and design intensive, requiring significant investments at the front-end of the development process for building components. The material, geometry, and process variability are both strengths and weaknesses for composites in architecture. Where composite material technology may lead architectural design in new directions has to do with each of the three components of their design; their inherent material strengths, their geometry and fundamental anisotropy, and our ability to advance and develop their manufacturing processes.

With regard to smart sandwich structures, composite additive manufacturing, and automated filament placement, these technological processes start to point toward freedoms, capabilities, and potentials that diverge from the standardized building assemblies currently responsible for the vast majority of structures today.

below right
The principle of intelligent material distribution, historic geometries, and computationally derived forms are behind some of the work of the Block Research Group at ETH Zurich, including this floor slab made of 3D-printed material. This resulted in a 70 % reduction in raw materials compared to a conventional concrete slab.

below left
A close-up view of the underside of the floor slab developed by the Block Research Group at the ETH Zurich, a slab that reduces material usage through computationally analyzed geometries.

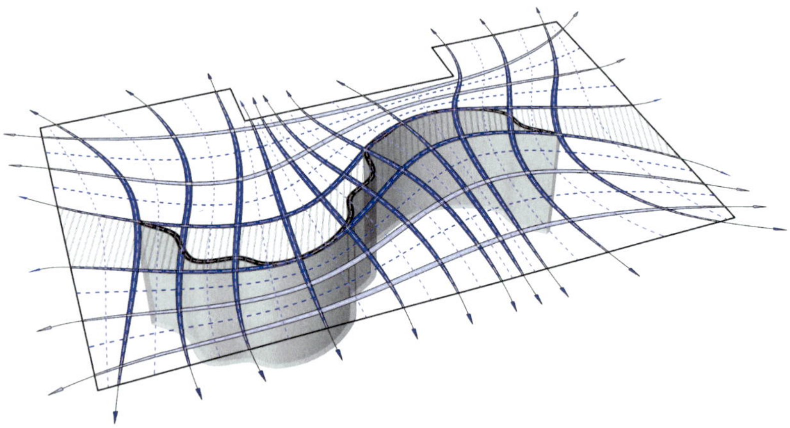

Photos of the Smart Slab, a project of the Digital Building Technologies Chair at the ETH Zurich. The project explores the use of a hierarchical grid of post-tensioned ribs cantilevering from a structural wall. A 3D-printed sand formwork is sprayed with glass fiber-reinforced concrete before being cast into CNC-machined timber to produce the floor slabs. See also photo on page 12 / 13.

For practicing architects, the aim is for this information to allow the ability to engage with clients, engineers, or contractors in a first-principles, fundamental exploration of whether composite materials may be a suitable solution for building issues in a particular situation. Thus, a conscious choice was made here to background much of the discussion using comparisons with other commonly available building materials—steel, aluminum, concrete, and wood. This, along with the information in other chapters of the book, may help interested parties reach a consensus about the suitability of composites for their project. Any decision made to pursue composites further for building solutions would require seeking out adequately qualified professionals. The American Composites Manufacturers Association (ACMA) has produced an excellent guide targeted specifically toward architects in the later stages of a project pursuing composite materials, who may also consult publications by the European composites industry body, the JEC Group (see Bibliography).

For engineers and industry professionals, this information may serve as a brief outline and introduction to the science in advance of further elective study and practice with more in-depth texts.

For students or design enthusiasts, an understanding of the basic material concepts provided here will hopefully spur some investigations and explorations into design or process possibilities.

For a more complete guide to the science behind FRPs, there are excellent books by Ever Barbero, Lawrence Bank, A. Brent Strong, and Len Hollaway (see Bibliography). For up-to-date information on the procedural and technological advances in composites, the industry groups ACMA and JEC publish periodicals on and hold conventions giving the latest news about composite materials.

1 Hollaway 2001, 2.
2 Strong, 199.
3 Strong, 19.
4 Strong, 47.
5 Strong, 108.
6 Barbero, 52.
7 Strong, 161.
8 Strong, 252.
9 Completed 2016. Quang Truong, project architect.

4 MATERIAL SUSTAINABILITY

But how much does your building weigh, Mr. Foster?

Buckminster Fuller

SUSTAINABILITY IN GENERAL

Sustainability is a complicated topic, but a crucial and important one. This is particularly true for the building and construction industry. Buildings are the largest consumers of energy in the US, consuming approximately half of the energy produced and emitting almost half of the total domestic greenhouse gases.[1] Production of concrete alone accounts for between 4 and 8 percent of the total global CO_2 emissions.[2] But the best accepted methodologies for assessing the impact of a building on the environment are still evolving. The continually revised LEED standards (with its classification tiers such as Silver, Gold, Platinum), as well as other competing criteria such as BREEAM, Well, Green Globes, Passive House, Net Zero, and any number of other certifications, point to the constantly evolving thinking regarding this aspect of building and construction.

Thinking about sustainability is broad enough to incorporate not just ecological, but also economic and socio-cultural impacts. This is an arena that involves many constituents, including governments, non-governmental organizations, commercial enterprises, industry, and citizens in general. Indeed, the building industry is inextricably tied to social, political, and economic systems, which all vary from one locality to another. Any meaningful change to the systems that produce buildings and architecture invariably affect all those groups. It is true, when it concerns the ecological environment in general, every living being is affected and interconnected.

As Manfred Hegger put it, "The entirety of the architectural production is up for discussion, i.e. economic, ecological and social aspects must be considered in their mutual dependencies."

It is beyond the scope of this book to fully dive into many of the finer points of this broader discussion, or even whether one metric or term is better suited to representing all the relevant concerns. At the time of writing, there remains a robust discussion as to which term best represents the full suite of building concerns, whether it be sustainability, resilience, green, wellness, health, among many others.

Going forward, the vast set of concerns regarding a building's impact on, and performance with regards to, the larger environment will be summarily referred to as issues of sustainability. The use of the term sustainability here does not intend to give endorsement to the word over other terms and acknowledges the inherent limitations of the word with regard to certain environmental considerations.

opposite
Andreas Gursky. "Les Mees," 2016.

MATERIAL CONSIDERATIONS

For architecture and buildings at the time of construction, it is primarily the materials used that determine a structure's ecological impact. Afterwards, during a structure's use and operation, many other factors besides material composition may play a large role in its sustainable impact (such as heating and cooling equipment, lighting equipment, building placement and orientation). In the case of composite materials, the greatest potential advantages come from the material's high strength-to-weight ratio and its durability. The greatest potential downsides come from its relatively high embodied energy and its durability.

Thus, for composite materials in construction, the fundamental consideration is this: over the intended life of the structure and in comparison to viable alternative materials, can the performance gains, weight savings, and design ambitions achievable with composite materials offset the higher initial energy cost and any end-of-life concerns? Or, more generally: do the properties of the material support the design ambitions of the project?

It is this question that we will be exploring for the rest of this chapter.

A couple of things need to be understood in order to answer the previous question. First, we need to understand the properties of the material. Previous chapters discussed some of the properties of composite materials, mainly addressing their use as building materials, but in this chapter, we will discuss how those properties may have sustainable advantages or disadvantages.

Second, we need to understand the design ambitions of the project. There are many and varied valid ambitions for the construction of a building, of which ecological impacts may be prioritized to greater or lesser degree. Careful control of a project's inputs and expected outputs is part of its design. In short, design is how a building is made and what it does; and that includes its impact on the broader ecological, economic, social, and cultural environment.

opposite
A selection of logos for various sustainability or green programs, codes, certifications, and standards. According to some sources, it is estimated that there are currently around 600 green building or product certifications around the world. Along with the fact that their numbers are growing, it is also true that existing certifications and standards are continuing to change and evolve.

Whole building green or sustainability rating systems / certifications / codes, domestic

Whole building green or sustainability rating systems / certifications / codes, international

Multi-attribute product green or sustainability rating systems / certifications

Single-attribute product green or sustainability rating systems/certifications

ARENA	VALUE	DESIGN AMBITION
Socio-cultural	Community	Provide for social functioning Provide enriching program and utility Enable social connectivity Address spatial equity and inclusiveness Enriching for all ages Promote communal inter-dependency and inter-reliance
	Design	Expression and communication of values and dignity Expression of contemporaneity and locality Convey esthetic inspiration and appreciation Create efficient spatial and programmatic functioning Aid in communal technical and artistic development
	Accessibility	Be barrier-free Multi-generational accommodation Geographic sensibility
	Wellness	Promote safety and security Access to sufficient space and utilities Access to light and clean air Access to physical exercise and cleanliness Thermal comfort Acoustic comfort
Economic	Mutual exchange	Enable economic access and availability Allow access to services and goods Allow for productive use of land and space Provide for mental and intellectual health Accessible and equitable systems of financing Incentivize socially and economically beneficial behaviors
	Labor	Provide for labor and skill development Fair utilization and promotion of local and non-local enterprise Enable dignified labor Promote and support productive economic activity
Ecological	Materiality	Materials aligned with design goals Material properties support the design purposes Functional and esthetic material harmony Life-cycle and end-of-life material consideration
	Energy	Proportional and appropriate initial embodied energy cost Efficient operational energy use Generation of energy for operations and grid contributions
	Emissions / Consumption	Material choices that consider cost of production Operational reduction of unclean emitted air, water, and waste Minimal consumption of materials and energy for operations Recycling and reuse of resources and materials
	Landscape	Site coverage aligned with urban/communal goals Promotion of local micro and macro ecological processes Allow flourishing of flora and fauna Esthetic and functional use of open space
	Infrastructural	Promotion of mobility and access Increase efficiency of infrastructural logistics

Introduction to EE and LC concepts

In order to have a more complete understanding of sustainability with regard to materials in general and composites in particular, it becomes necessary to touch briefly on a couple of sustainability concepts. The first is embodied/embedded energy (EE), and the second is lifecycle analysis/assessment (LCA).

Vaclav Smil has an excellent explanation of the first concept: "Before any materials can start flowing through economies, energies must flow to power their extraction from natural deposits or their production by industrial processes ranging from simple mechanical procedures to complex chemical reactions."[3]

In simple terms: it takes energy to make materials in the first place. But the energy cost of a material does not end once it has been made. The energy cost of a material should include an analysis of how it is used throughout the complete usage life span of the material.

The lifecycle analysis/assessment approach attempts to do just that—"quantifying objective indicators of the environmental impacts of materials during their entire life-span."[4] For buildings, this includes measuring the environmental impact of the building materials used in construction—from raw material extraction, to the fabrication and manufacturing process of building components, including the transportation to the building site, and the energy expended to place and install that building component. Furthermore, it also accounts for the energy required to maintain the building's structural and functional integrity throughout its designed life span and how it is disposed of or recycled at the end of its functional use.

The discussion of sustainability initially focused on the consumption and energy efficiency of a building while occupied and in use. Indeed, advances in the thermal performance of roof assemblies, wall assemblies, penetrations/fenestration, and lighting have gone a long way toward improving the performance of buildings as they relate to the efficiency of heating, cooling, and electrical loads during the times when the building is occupied.

But LCA studies have also shown that a sizable, though highly variable, proportion of the energy cost of a building can come from the initial embedded energy. The percentages can vary significantly, from as low as 13 percent to as high as 50 percent for highly efficient buildings in moderate climates.[5]

This variation is to be expected, given the incredible number of variables in construction. Buildings have varying sizes, construction types, uses, local climates, locally available resources, operating efficiencies, and life spans, not to mention varying study methodologies, all of which have an impact on the calculations.[6]

opposite
An incomplete taxonomy of possible architectural design ambitions and considerations. This list suggests the many different, valid ambitions for a construction project, though it is certainly not complete or exhaustive. Nor does this list intend to imply any hierarchy or weight to one goal over another. The balance, weighting, and hierarchy of goals for any project depend on the unique circumstances and parameters of the building and construction team. It is up to the client, architect, and building team to identify and establish the goals and metrics by which a project's success is to be judged, and then to make material and building choices to support those goals.

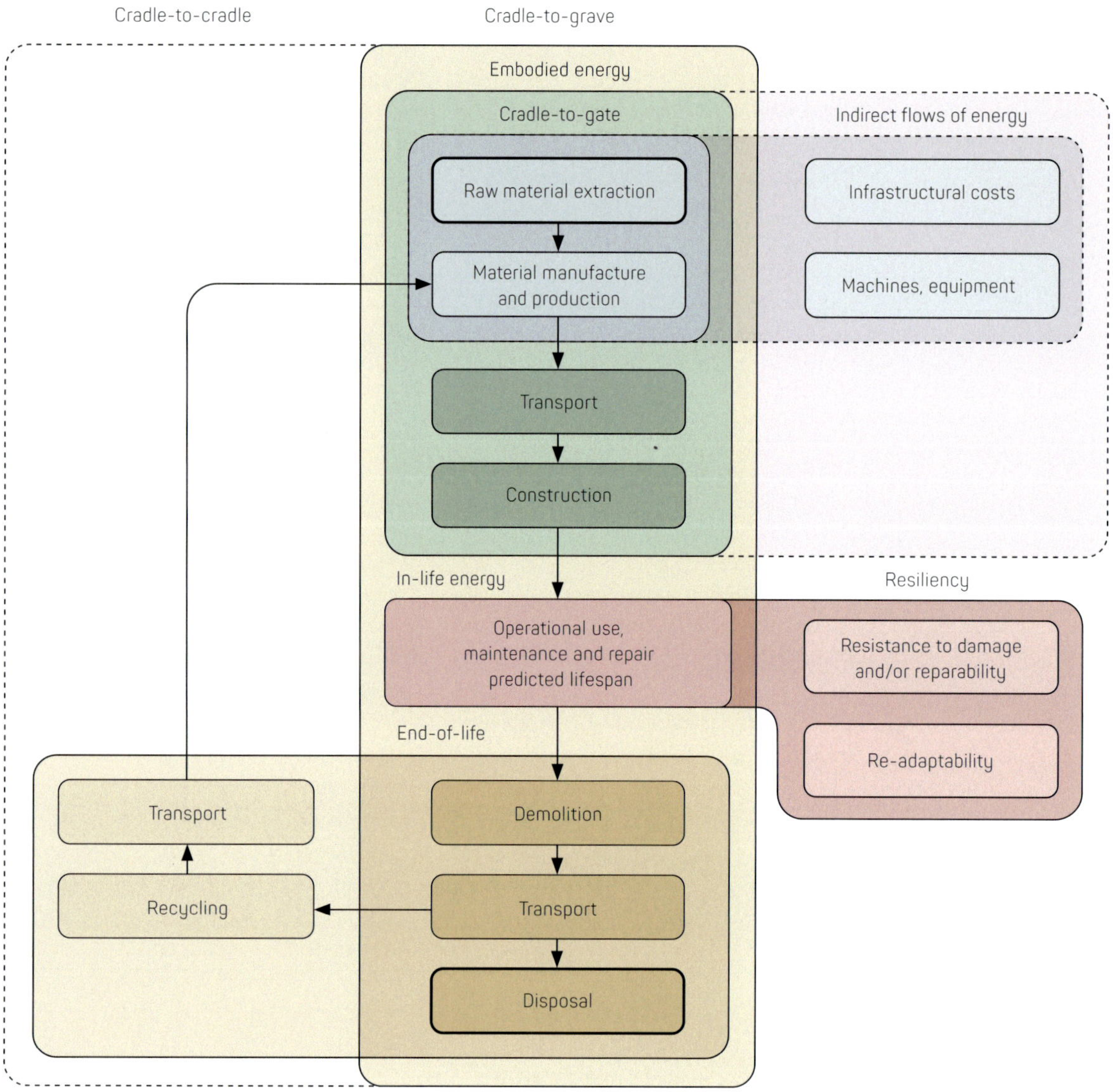

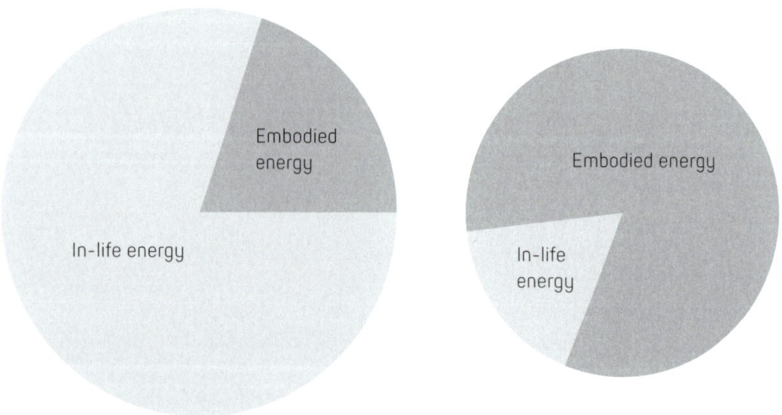

Traditional Building
Lifespan energy cost

High-performance Building
Lifespan energy cost

opposite top
Diagrammatic representation of the factors in a building's lifespan energy cost. While a high-performance building may have a greater percentage of its energy use come from the initial embodied energy of its materials, those materials have the potential to significantly reduce the operational (in-life) and lifespan energy cost of the building. Buildings in certain locations and climates will have differing operational energy demands; another significant variable is the designed lifespan of the building. Certain types of buildings and materials have different functional lifespans to others.

opposite bottom
A diagrammatic overview of life-cycle analysis for materials in construction, incorporating concepts of embodied energy and cradle-to-gate/grave/cradle. Much of the ambiguity and variability in contemporary sustainability studies is due to the complexity of measuring and accounting for all the inputs and outputs at each of these steps. These methodological differences can often make basic quantitative comparisons for material choices difficult. Combined with the particularities of any one given construction project (geographic location, product and material sourcing, construction means and methods), it means that a true understanding of life-cycle costs is a very complicated affair.

A simple thought exercise will help illuminate how variable LCA study methodologies can be: it is conceivable to have two contrasting buildings in the same location, one composed of high-performance materials that render the building extremely efficient to operate, while the other is composed of low-tech materials that then require lots of energy to comfortably condition and maintain. The first would have a high proportion of the lifecycle energy usage up-front while, the second would use much more energy during its use and operation. We would also then have to consider what the lifespan of the building is intended to be; the assumed lifespan of a residential building may be quite different than for a commercial building (or other type). Other architectural choices, such as building size, solar orientation, mechanical equipment, thermal comfort criteria, daylighting, ventilation, and other variables can have enormous impacts on the operational energy consumption of a building.

It is also worth noting that buildings in different climates require different amounts of energy to operate; materials also have differing embedded energies based on locally available resources (timber, for example, is plentiful in certain parts of the US but scarce in others).

It quickly becomes apparent that materials, though significant, are just one aspect within a complex matrix of calculations needed to assess the environmental performance of a building. The complexity of acquiring and accounting for all the architectural variables should be kept in mind as we begin to discuss the sustainable qualities of composite materials.

SUSTAINABLE PROPERTIES OF COMPOSITES

Initial embodied energy

On a spectrum, the materials that require the least amount of energy to produce are naturally occurring materials that can be sourced near the site of construction and require little or no processing. Think of locally available unprocessed clay (which still houses 30 percent of the world's population)[7]. On the other side of that spectrum are industrially produced materials that require remote resource extraction and high-heat industrial processes, such as certain metals or ceramics.

Composite materials are in the middle-to-higher end of that spectrum (the exception would potentially be for composites made of biofibers or biomatrices). While the numbers for composites may seem significantly higher than for other materials, it needs to be understood that most readily available energy figures are per unit of weight. When we consider that alternatives such as concrete, steel, and timber are much heavier and require much more material to achieve potentially similar goals, we can begin to understand that the higher initial energy costs of composite materials are not without benefits.

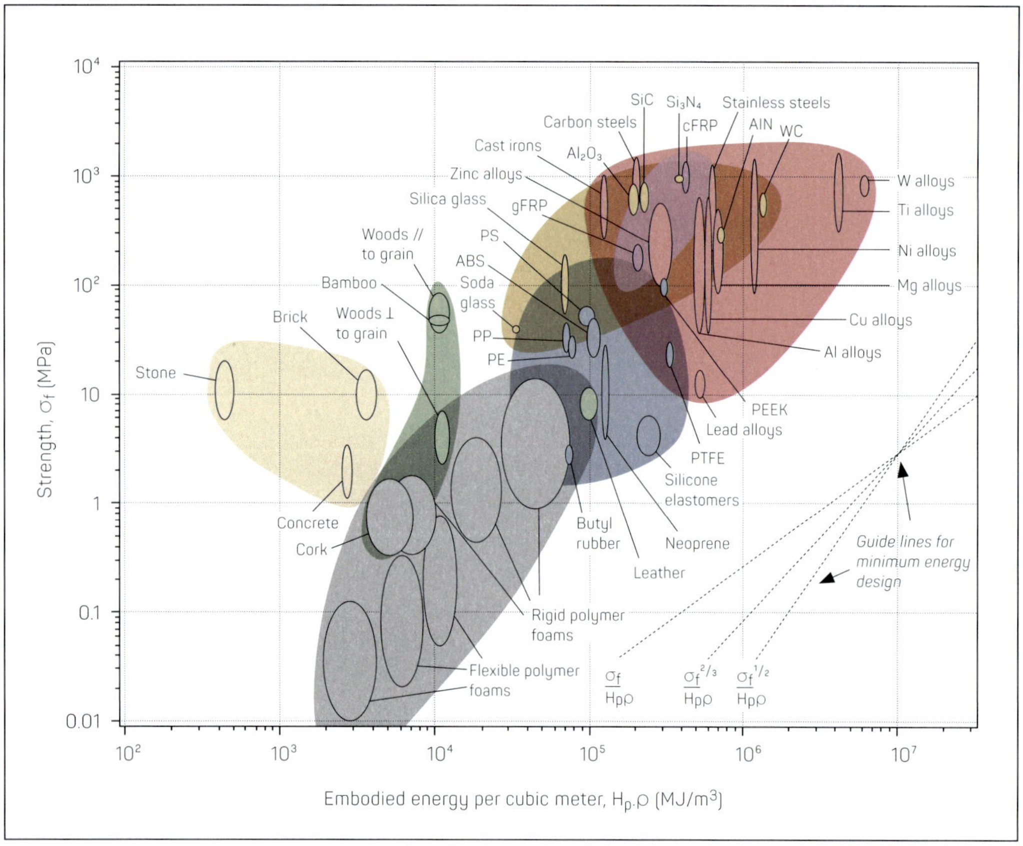

An Ashby chart plotting strength against embodied energy. The chart shows that composite materials can provide the highest levels of material strength available (tensile failure) for a lower level of embodied energy, save for extremely costly technical ceramics. Note that the chart is logarithmic.

Metals and polymers: yield strength, σ_y

Ceramics, glasses: modulus of rupture, MOR

Elastomers: tensile tear strength, σ_t

Composites: tensile failure, σ_t

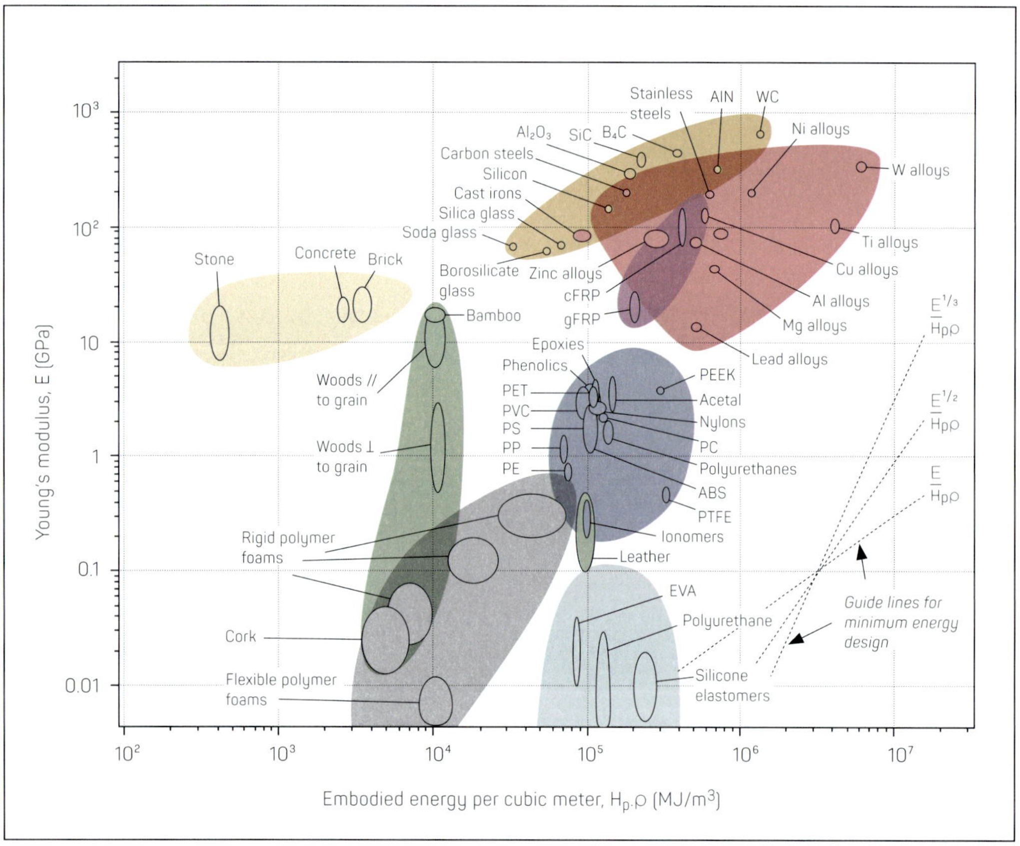

An Ashby chart plotting Young's modulus (stiffness) against embodied energy. As a class, composites are capable of levels of stiffness comparable to many metals with lower levels of embodied energy. Note that the chart is logarithmic.

- Metals
- Technical Ceramics
- Non-technical Ceramics
- Composites
- Polymers
- Elastomers
- Natural materials
- Foams

Efficiency: strength-to-weight and strength-to-energy

The strength-to-weight property of composite materials is a big potential contributor to any sustainability-oriented design goals. Depending on the specific formulation of the fibers and matrix, a composite material can achieve many times the strength of concrete, steel, or timber at only a fraction of the weight. A significantly reduced mass for the same structural performance has significant and cascading effects on the total embodied energy of a building. Less weight on the building also means smaller foundations can be constructed, less excavation is required, smaller machinery for hoisting and erection, and other subsequent energy saving effects.

Similarly, when we look at strength per unit of energy cost, we find that composite materials as a class perform exceedingly well. Per unit of energy, composites provide more strength than alternative building materials.

For architectural or structural purposes, the use of composites means less weight and a potentially more efficient use of material. This a significant factor in the overall energy and environmental impact of a building. This is the insight that resonated so strongly when Buckminster Fuller challenged Norman Foster with the retort: "But how much does your building weigh, Mr. Foster?"

A European Commission report on plastics waste in 2013 looked at the sources and treatment of plastic waste.

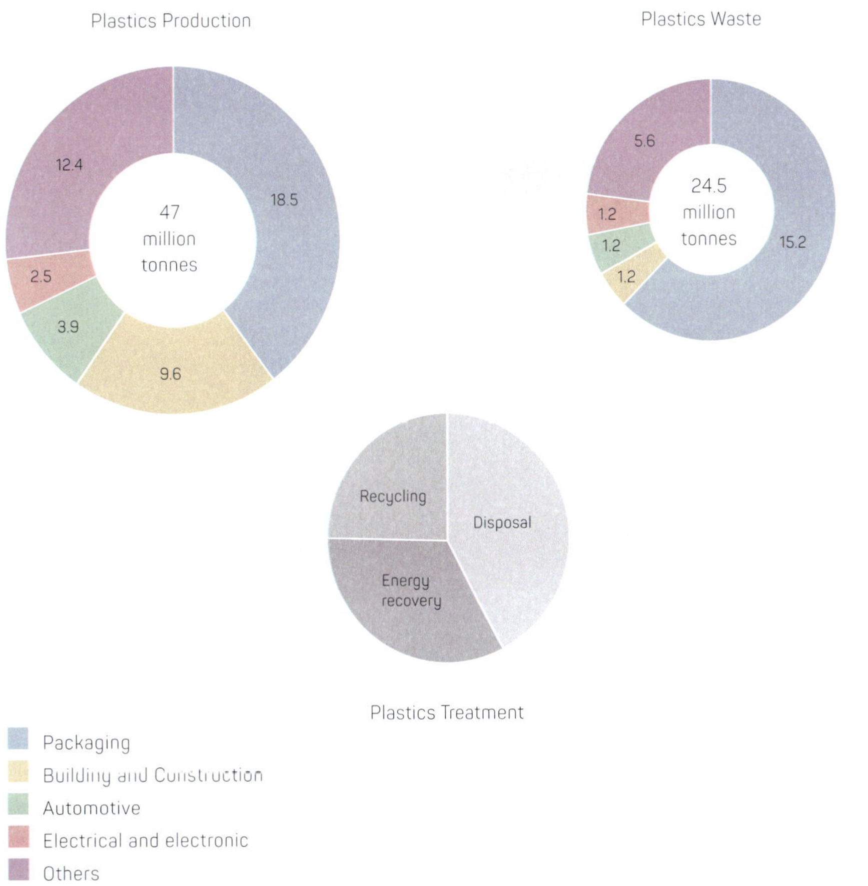

Durability: maintenance and resilience

In addition, lifecycle energy use reductions can be realized through the material's durability, ease of serviceability, and corrosion resistance.

Buildings, like any other product, have an intended life span, during which building parts or components will need maintenance and upkeep in order to remain functional. Maintenance is required due to two factors: natural degradation (wear and tear), or through damage accrued (either naturally or otherwise).

A building's resilience to disaster and damage plays a large role in its functional, economic, and ecological impact. A building that is more resistant to damage, more durable, and easier to repair has significant advantages, both financially and in terms of energy consumption, than a building that needs to be completely replaced when and if damage should occur during its lifespan.

While not always considered an aspect of sustainability, the maintenance and serviceability costs of a building are part of its lifecycle assessment, and when measured appropriately, can significantly influence material decisions in architecture.

Composites also do not corrode. Which is to say, they do not rust and lose their structural integrity due to environmental exposure. They have a durability and relative ease of maintenance that finds favor wherever such demands have special importance. The industries where this has been most acutely significant, and which have thus seen early adoption of composite materials, are aerospace, marine, and infrastructural design.

Thermal conductivity

Composites can also contribute to the in-use energy efficiency of a building through their properties of thermal conductivity. In contrast to metal, masonry, or concrete, composites do not transfer thermal energy as easily. When incorporated with well-designed wall or roof assemblies, composite materials can thus contribute to the efficient heating, cooling, and thermal efficiency of a building.

Composite materials are slowly starting to replace specific parts traditionally made of conventional materials due to these more performative properties; examples can be found throughout curtain wall and rain screen assemblies.

Wellness

Indoor air quality and wellness are two relatively recent concepts of building performance. As such, it is hard to find relevant data on many materials and their off-gassing effects on indoor air quality. This is true of composite materials; more so because FRPs are not commonly used as architectural materials on building interiors (though they are used for ornament, appliances, and countertops). As with many aspects of building performance, this is one that will benefit from continuing and ongoing research.

Durability: end-of-life concerns

There is a flip side to the durability of composite materials, and that is the well-known fact that plastics do not biodegrade easily. The most common matrices and fibers are derived from non-renewable sources, namely petroleum. While it is easy to paint these materials as irredeemably bad, this would be an oversimplification. Plastics and their properties have made possible incredible technological advances on behalf of humanity, from safety features such as helmets and airbags, to advanced medical equipment, to the safe transport of food resources across long distances.

Synthetic polymers are already everywhere in buildings, from insulation, vapor barriers and roofing membranes to piping, wiring, and the glues that bind engineered wood products. Their growing role in every industry is chiefly due to two factors, their performative benefits and low cost. Synthetic polymers are a ubiquitous and inextricable part of our modern lives. Plastics are neither inherently good nor bad; they are a material tool to be used as best suits our design ambitions. Plastics will necessarily be part of our future.

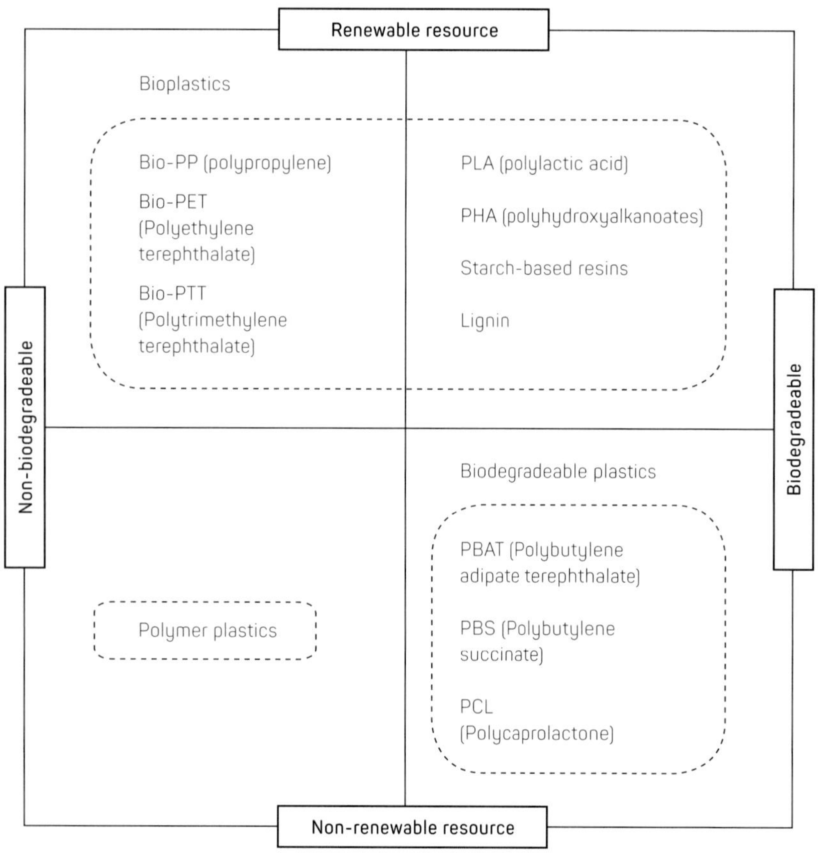

Where LCAs are valuable in many cases is that they offer surprising and insightful results. The most famous early LCA studies looked at the combined environmental impacts of cotton clothing versus polyester or a cotton-polyester hybrid. What they found was that, although producing polyester required a higher initial energy compared to cotton, once the costs of maintenance, agricultural impacts, water usage, fertilizers, pesticides, and lifespan were included, the cotton shirts consumed more energy than those made of cotton blended with synthetics.[8] This is not to say that polyester shirts are therefore better than cotton ones, but we must consider that their impact on the environment is not so simply assessed. We also need to consider that there may be other considerations in our choice of T-shirt purchases; sensual and esthetic concerns must also be considered along with lifecycle energy calculations.

Boeing, the commercial airline manufacturer, has published many studies of the lifecycle assessments they calculated that led them to integrate 50 percent composites and carbon fiber by weight into their newest airliner, the 787 Dreamliner. Using an expanded product lifecycle cost approach allowed them to realize weight savings of 20 percent in comparison to previous generation aluminum structures and significantly reduced maintenance (both scheduled and non-routine).[9]

The civil infrastructure industry has also seen basic lifecycle assessments point toward the adoption of composite materials in lieu of or supplementing conventional materials.[10]

The durability of composite materials is thus a property that needs to be designed for its application—considered within the context of its initial generation, use, maintenance, and lifespan in comparison to alternative materials.

The carbon footprint of a building or material is another way of quantifying or measuring the energy impact of construction choices. Coal, a significant contributor to atmospheric carbon emissions, can potentially be repurposed to create carbon fiber and thus become a carbon sink.

Carbon footprint

There is another property worth mentioning here, specific to the use of carbon fiber composites (cFRPs): the material has potential to repurpose coal plants toward carbon fiber production, reducing the amount of carbon that would have otherwise been released into the atmosphere.

Research into repurposing coal plants toward the production of carbon fiber is ongoing. Instead of burning coal to generate power and releasing hydrocarbons into the atmosphere, these processes could capture the hydrocarbons and turn them into a precursor to carbon fiber (known as pitch). This would allow the coal industry to shift from CO_2-emitting power generation to carbon fiber production, taking advantage of the vast coal reserves in many locations, repurposing existing facilities, and reducing atmospheric carbon emissions.[11]

Emerging sustainable composite technology

In the realm of emerging sustainable composite technologies, there are two main avenues of research and development. The first is in biomaterials—naturally occurring and/or renewable sources of fibers and resins. The second is in recycling.

Both technologies attempt to address some of the potential downsides to composite material use—their non-renewable sources and their end-of-life concerns. Typically, the trade-offs come in the form of reduced strength, stiffness, and consistency over polymer matrices and synthetic fibers.

Soybean oil, cashew nut oil, and cellulose have been used to replace thermoset and thermoplastic resins. Flax, hemp, cotton, silk, and many other fibers have been used in place of synthetic fibers. Hybrid formulations of bio and synthetic materials are also possible, and in combination with CNC or locally controlled fiber placement can further improve the efficiency and performance of composites.

Jute fibers being prepared, potentially for use in bio-composite materials.

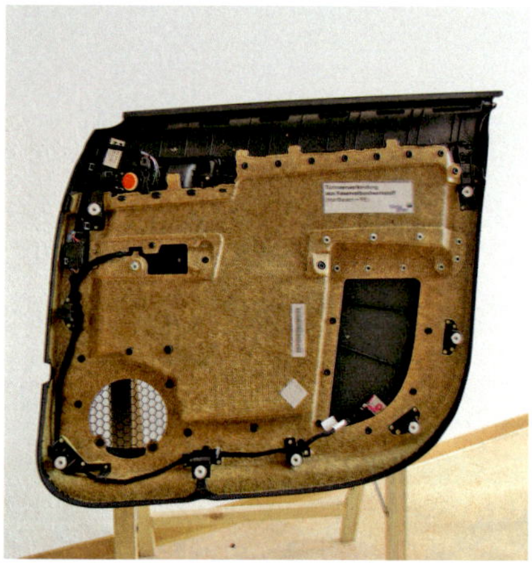

Biocomposites (biofibers and bio-resin) being used to create automotive parts.

The auto maker Porsche has recently studied incorporating biocomposites into the body panels of its 718 Cayman GT4 to complement the high-performance carbon fiber structural chassis. Produced as part of the project Elcomap, which stands for Environmentally Friendly Lightweight Composite Materials for Aerodynamic Body Panels, these parts use cashew nut oil and flax reinforcement.[12]

For the recycling of composites, the difficulty often lies in collecting and separating materials into homogenous categories. Composites are naturally heterogeneous, so the breakdown and reuse of the materials presents additional challenges. Recycling processes can basically be broken down to two categories: mechanical recycling and fiber reclamation.

In mechanical recycling of composites, reclaimed fiber-reinforced polymers are cut up, milled, or ground to short scrap. The ground-up material can be reused in new composites. Both the resin and the fiber are recovered and reused, at the expense of degraded mechanical properties and limited manufacturing process options.

Fiber reclamation processes break down the FRPs through thermal or chemical treatments that dissolve the matrix. Pyrolysis, fluidized bed combustion, chemical, and enzymatic recycling are processes by which the fibers and resins can be reclaimed with little to no mechanical degradation. These components can then be reused for many different composite part applications.[13]

Both technologies, biocomposite and composite recycling, are relatively new and will benefit from continuing research and process development.

top
Waste carbon fiber being prepared for chemical and mechanical fiber reclamation.

bottom
Nonwoven mats made of 100 % recycled carbon fiber, ready for use in composite parts.

Chopped recycled carbon fibers, called tow, in varying fiber lengths from 6–12 mm (0.24–0.47 in).

Nonwoven mats are produced with recycled carbon fibers combined with thermoplastic fibers. Various thermoplastics can be used, such as PP, PA and PPS, with typical carbon fiber content being between 25 and 40 %. This recycled product is ideally suited for press molding.

Part consolidation

Composites also possess a unique ability in architecture due to their multi-varied properties; and one of those is part consolidation. Part consolidation refers to the ability of a single composite structure to take the functional place of an assembly of conventional materials. The clearest example of this is in the case of C-SIPs, or composite structural insulated panels. In this case, a sandwich structure of composite material and insulating foam can replace the traditional multi-trade assembly of structure, insulation, air barrier, sheathing, and water barrier.

As building performance demands increase, particularly with regard to thermal U- and R-values, conventional materials used in exterior assemblies, such as metal and glass, which are highly thermally conductive. Composite materials and assemblies hold many practical advantages for the design of high-performance envelopes.

below
Diagram depicting various building exterior enclosures, showing a range of structural systems, weather (air and water) resistant barriers, thermal protection, and cladding/siding (typically for residential or light commercial structures).

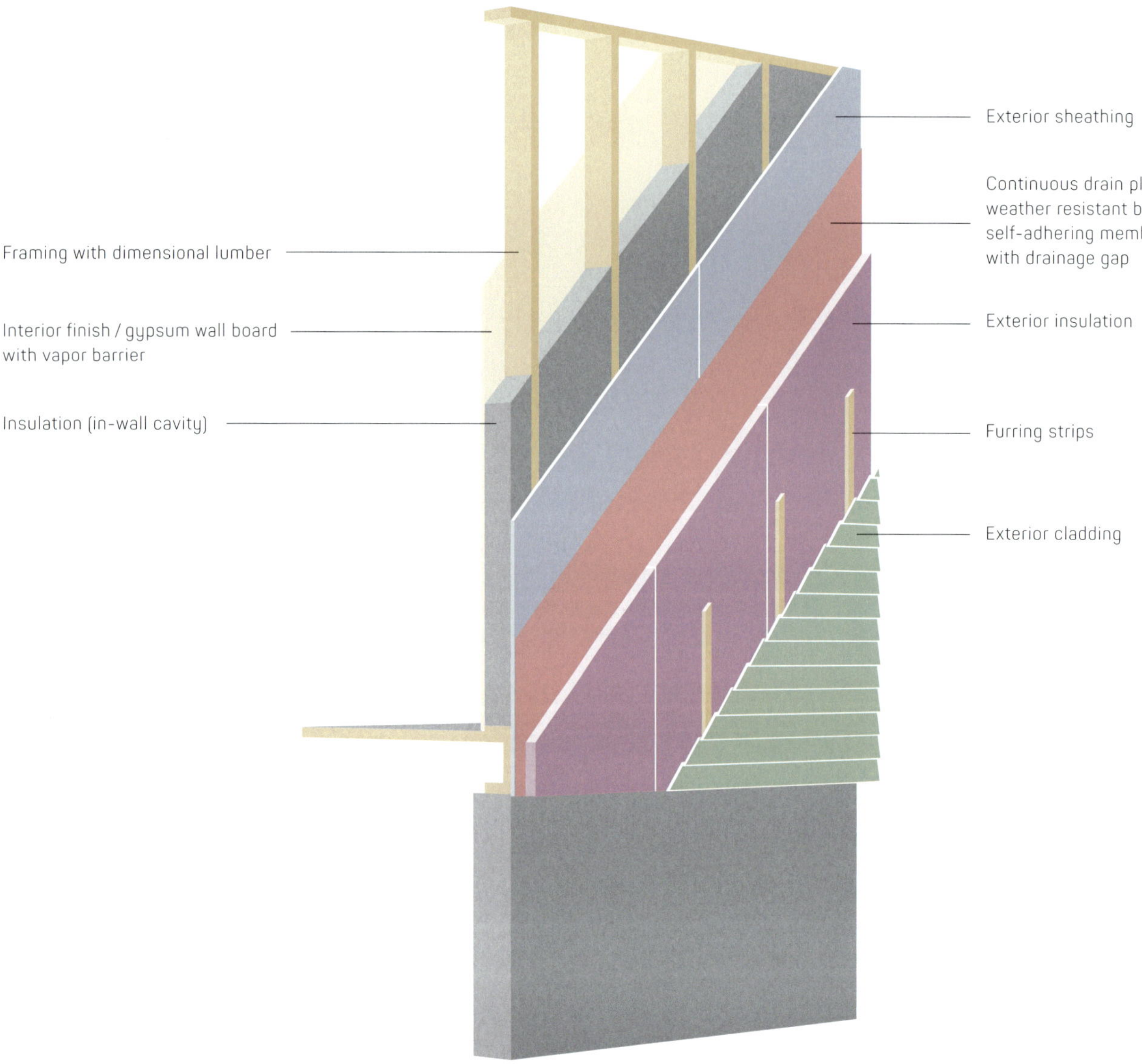

In sandwich structures, the core material between layers of composite laminates also offer intriguing possibilities. In a sandwich structure, the core functions to mechanically connect the inner and outer laminates and resist shear stresses (like the web in a wide-flange steel beam). They are typically made of foam insulation, balsawood, or other light-weight materials, and have the added benefit of serving as thermal insulation. But there exists the possibility of recycling plastic waste to fulfill all these functions. One company in particular, Armacell, is taking plastic water bottle waste and recycling it into usable PET foam for many applications, including architectural composite sandwich structures. Their product has found application in several built projects throughout the globe and has the added sustainability benefit of reclaiming and repurposing a huge amount of plastic waste, which would otherwise find its way to landfills or the oceans.

DESIGN AMBITION AND SUSTAINABILITY

The properties discussed so far rely on our abilities to quantify effects in order to make judgments: initial energy, strength, durability, lifecycle assessments, and carbon footprints are all attempts to numerically value the effects of material choices. But there is a limit to what we can quantify.

Lifecycle assessments, while great tools for expanding our understanding of ecological impacts, are always going to be incomplete. This is not a methodological critique. In a system as vast and complex as the earth's ecology, we cannot fully understand all the repercussions of our continued economic and material production. And beyond what is difficult to quantify are those things that are unquantifiable—the things that are qualitative.

Sustainability impacts for composite material usage in the built environment

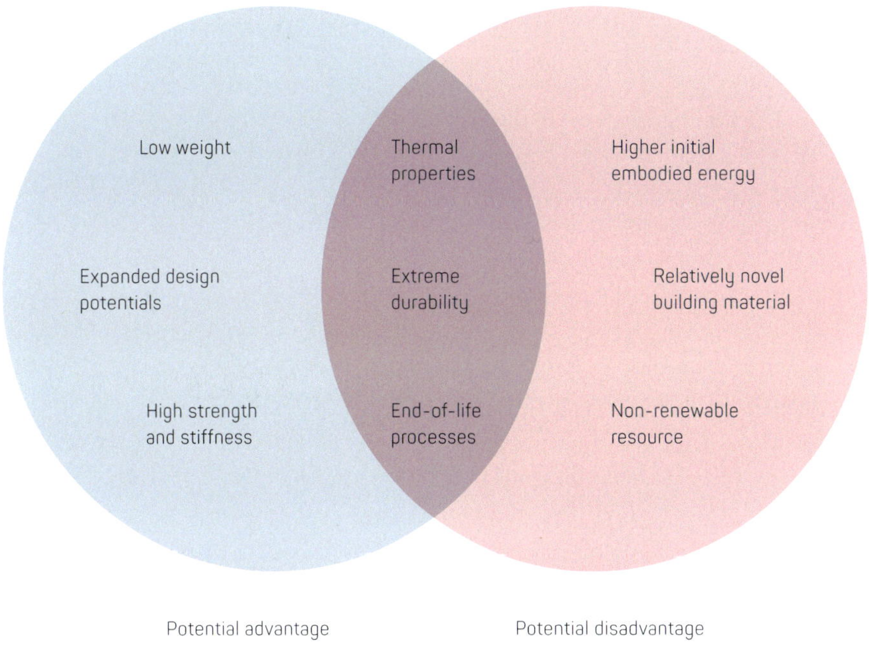

After briefly touching on the many considerations possible regarding the sustainable properties of composites, it is now worth revisiting the question posed at the beginning of this chapter. Do these properties support the design ambition?

As we discussed, the scope of architecture and design has broadened over the last generation. Sustainability concerns are now an important and unavoidable aspect of how building performance is judged. Though the exact definition and parameters for this are still being debated, architecture clearly has a scope of responsibility now that is greater than what it was, even in the recent past.

We can and should endeavor to quantify the performance of buildings in many ways, including our understanding of materials. We should also beware of those who say that the future is homogenous and singular, composed of one material only. There are too many diverse and distinct goals and contexts for architecture for which a broad spectrum of materials would be enriching.

A polyethylene terephthalate (PET) foam made of 100 % recycled plastic water bottles and specifically formulated and qualified for use as a structural composite foam core. This product reclaims plastic waste and repurposes it for structural use, such as in the dome structure used for a church in Paris.

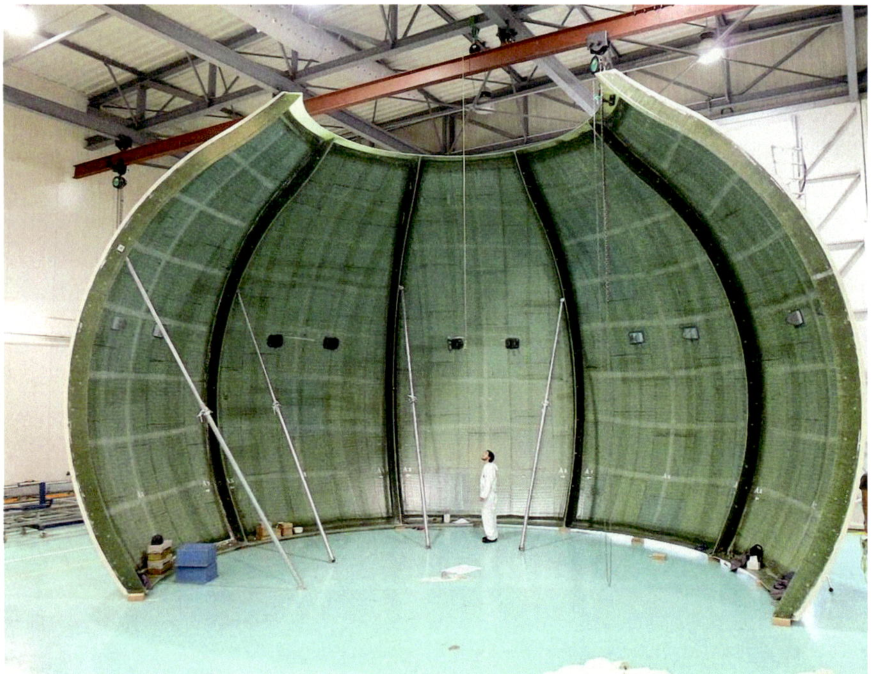

Indeed, it seems that the best-case future is heterogenous, diverse, and hybrid (which is similar in meaning to composite). Composite materials find some of their best applications in support of or in conjunction with other materials; as reinforcing or retrofitting. They may provide the best answer for the rehabilitation and reuse of much of our infrastructure and building stock.

But we should also be aware of things we cannot quantify that may be equally or more important in the design of a building.

If ecological impact was our sole design concern, then there is a case to be made that we should not build at all. Of course, this would ignore all the positive things that a building can do: house families, provide productive workspaces, heal the infirm, educate the young, and enrich the mental and emotional lives of citizens. While a bit reductive, this rhetorical device may help us to clarify and focus on the design ambitions that animate our work.

There is a network of weighted design considerations in the making of buildings, some of which are sustainability goals, and some of which are not; there are social, cultural, sensual, and humanistic ambitions for architecture as well.

This is just to say that we need to understand what the design ambition for the project is, and then test whether certain materials support that ambition. All materials have inherent properties that may or may not lend themselves to certain quantifiable or unquantifiable goals, composites included.

For each of these concerns, in each building context, the weight of one goal may outweigh another. That balance of qualitative and quantitative concerns is what identifies each material, building, context, design, and designer.

1 Russell-Smith, Sarah V., et al. "Sustainable target value design: integrating life cycle assessment and target value design to improve building energy and environmental performance." *Journal of Cleaner Production 88* (2015): 43–51.
2 Lehne. Global Carbon Project: [https://www.globalcarbonproject.org/] Accessed 23 Apr 2019.
3 Smil 2014, 94.
4 Smil 2014, 103.
5 Smil 2014, 100; Berge 2009, 19.
6 Cabeza.
7 Berge 2009. Smil 2014, 52.
8 Smil 2014, 103.
9 Hale/Boeing.
10 Hollaway 2010. Ilg 2015.
11 Milberg, Evan. "Utah Researchers Look to Turn Coal into Carbon Fiber." *Composites Manufacturing*, November 7, 2016. Accessed from [http://compositesmanufacturingmagazine.com/2016/11/utah-researchers-look-turn-coal-carbon-fiber/] Apr 24, 2019.
12 Perkins, Chris. "Porsche's Natural Fiber Is Like Carbon Fiber Made From Plants." *Road & Track* online 7 Jan 2019. Accessed from [https://www.roadandtrack.com/motorsports/a25776025/porsche-natural-fiber-718-cayman-gt4-clubsport/] 24 April 2019.
13 Ali, Zaara and Asmatulu, Eylem. "Sustainable and Green Manufacturing Options of Fiber Reinforced Composites." Department of Mechanical Engineering at Wichita State University. Presented at CAMX 2018, Dallas.

5 BUILDING ISSUES

The architectural design opportunities afforded by composite materials may be gleaned from a study of the materials' properties, technology, and history, as discussed in earlier chapters. But the reality of building involves many additional considerations and constraints. For the vast majority of structures built today, architecture's two most visible and immediate partners on any project are the owner and the contractor. Owners control the financial means of building, which exercises considerable, if not ultimate, power. Contractors are responsible for the physical manifestation of the building, including the implementation of much of the technology used to create buildings (euphemistically dubbed "means and methods of construction"). But there is also a less visible though equally important partner: the authorities-having-jurisdiction (AHJs). These are the building departments, regulatory bodies, local fire departments, reviewing officials, and other persons who have jurisdictional power to approve or deny any building project or specific facet of a building. Building codes, regulations, and standards are as responsible for the form of our built environment as any other single consideration or relationship. This chapter will briefly introduce some of the building issues relevant to the relationships with AHJs and contractors.

Primary among any considerations for a product in our built environment is the protection of life safety, which requires an understanding of composite material performance and integrity under thermal, mechanical, and environmental loads. The material's flammability, structural failure modes, weathering, and durability are briefly introduced in this chapter. As demonstrated by their wide-ranging use in other industries, composites have properties that satisfy far stricter requirements than those typically demanded by architecture. But it is nonetheless worth being explicit about their capacities in these regards.

While a scientific understanding of a material may begin to address any concern we may have about its performance in real-world scenarios, building codes and regulations impose an entirely separate set of criteria. These criteria are different, but related to, our scientific and engineering understanding of materials. When a material's use is not explicitly prescribed in the building code, there are usually alternative means and methods to comply with regulations. These codes are often the first set of requirements that need to be satisfied for any material to find an application in construction.

opposite
Installation of the unitized gFRP wall panels on the SFMOMA.

Understanding current regulations and how composite materials currently fit into the latest building code compliance pathways will help architectural and building professionals understand how best to use composite materials today and recognize where opportunities exist for novel ways of using them. Going forward, this understanding will also engage professionals in how adjustments or revisions to the code may be warranted in the interest of improving our built environment.

If understanding code pathways is generally the first set of constraints toward material selection in architecture, then the second most immediate set of constraints is usually construction or contractor issues.

Certain construction considerations specific to composite materials will be discussed in this chapter. Issues of dimensional tolerance, thermal expansion, connections, transportation, hoisting, and erection particularities will be introduced. And while an entire book could be written about the history and theory of architectural joints and joinery, composite materials offer new architectural possibilities for addressing this age-old professional problem, which will be introduced in this chapter as well.

The issues inherent to these relationships—with codes, regulations, and contractors—are building issues. They bear at least as much, if not more, responsibility for the final form of the built environment as any matter of design or technology. In order to effectively enact any desired change, an understanding of these issues is crucial.

LIFE SAFETY

In considerations of life safety, it can be argued that composite materials have proven themselves beyond reproach in other industries with much more demanding criteria for durable structural integrity and fire performance than architecture. The Boeing 787 Dreamliner and Airbus A380, two commercial airliners made predominantly of structural composites, are prime examples illustrating the point. Antarctic research stations composed primarily of composites, such as Halley VI, are located where any access to external assistance is remote and fail-safe performance is life critical.

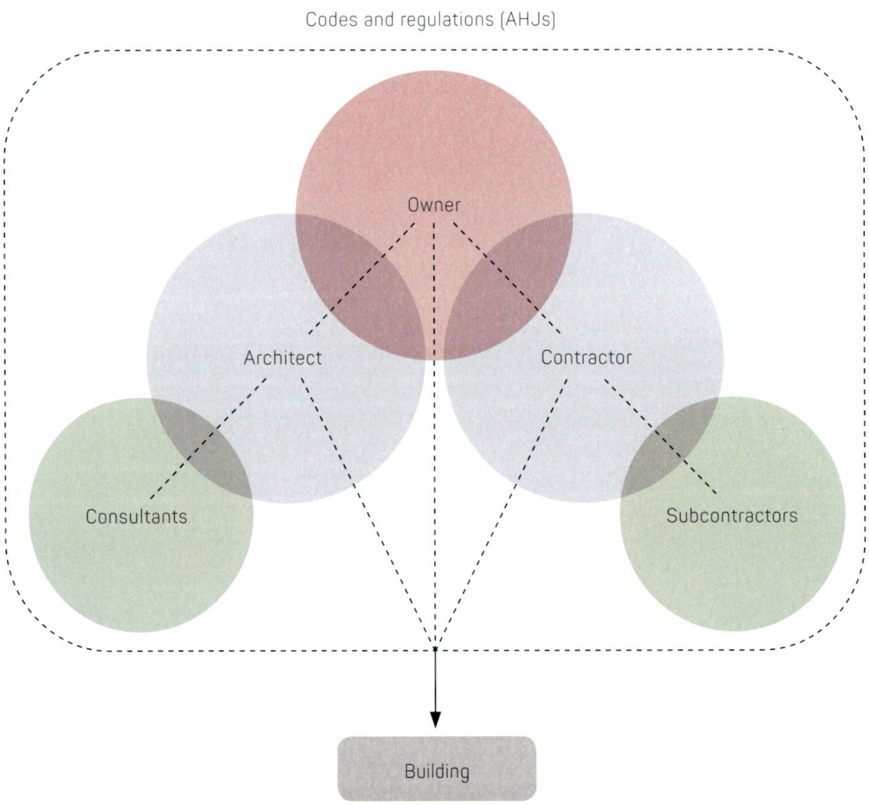

Diagram illustrating a typical owner / architect / contractor (OAC) relationship in a design-bid-build project delivery method (loosely extracted from the AIA's Contract Relationship Diagrams, published April 2017 (https://www.aia.org/resources/64256-contract-relationship-diagrams)). Note that while typically excluded in these types of diagrams, the codes and regulations govern all parties and have a large role in the final building form and design. Also note that while the architect and contractor must work together, there is no contractual relationship between them. This quasi-oppositional relationship was initially established in order to benefit the owners, who theoretically could use the competing independent interests of the architect and contractor to their advantage. As construction technology and the capabilities of architects and contractors have changed, this has led to inefficiencies in this model, as exemplified by the rise of intermediary parties (construction managers, design assists, etc.).

The composite-bodied Boeing 787 Dreamliner has passed stringent standards for structural integrity and maintainability in high-use and high-stress applications.

A detail view of the Boeing 787 composite fuselage interior.

The composite-clad Halley VI Antarctic Research Station proves the durability and logistical advantages of the material in extreme environments.

Composite body panels of the Halley VI Antarctic Research Station being assembled in place.

The composite materials on these airplanes and research stations are subjected to mechanical stresses (structural and wind loads), thermal stresses (heat and temperature fluctuations), and environmental attack (rain, moisture, ice, and heat), not unlike but much more severe than in most architectural applications, and the penalty for unpredictable material behavior in their situation is catastrophically unacceptable. Suffice it to say, composite materials can be engineered and specified to meet stringent demands for resistance to structural and thermal failure, and for durability with regard to wear and tear, and environmental attack.

Flammability

A composite material's flammability and its performance under thermal stress are governed largely by the choice of matrix, and to a lesser extent by the choice of fiber reinforcement. Polymer resins are organic materials composed of carbon, hydrogen, oxygen, and nitrogen atoms and are thus prone to ignition, though not all resins to an equal extent. Careful selection of the resinous matrix, along with consideration for the fiber material and any additives or fillers, can produce a composite material to meet almost any thermal performance criteria. On the one hand, a resin may be viscous at room temperature, or it may have a flammability resistance surpassing most metals. In fact, phenolic resin composites are used for rocket engine cones, where temperatures can exceed 2200 °C / 4000 °F. In summary, composite materials as a group can exhibit a wide range of thermal behaviors.

With regard to a composite material's structural integrity in high temperatures, the critical property that designers need to pay attention to is the *glass transition temperature* (T_g). Similar to but different from the *heat distortion temperature* or *heat deflection temperature*, it refers to the temperature at which the polymer matrix undergoes a change in its physical and mechanical properties from a rigid (known as glassy) state to a viscous (known as rubbery) state. It is related to the *maximum service temperature* (T_{max}) of a material, which is measured using UL, ASTM, or EN testing protocols. This is the point where a polymer-based composite loses its structural integrity, with significant changes to stiffness and modulus.

While the specific *glass transition temperature* (T_g) of different composites can vary significantly due to their particular composition, generally, the thermoset resins most likely to be used in construction (unsaturated polyester, epoxy, or vinyl ester) and pultruded profiles are not suitable for use above temperatures around 180 °C / 350 °F if not protected and insulated in a similar manner to structural steel members. Thermoplastic polymers have been developed that can perform at up to 450 °C / 800 °F. Where extreme resistance to flammability is desired, phenolic resins are usually specified. Phenolic composites are used in temperature-sensitive aircraft, train, bus, and subway parts, as well as in rocket and aerospace components subject to extremely high temperatures, sometimes in excess of 2200 °C / 4000 °F. [1, 2, 3]

Along with careful consideration of the *glass transition temperature* T_g, composite material designers must also pay heed to the smoke-developed and flame-spread properties, as these have clear impacts on user life safety during fire (and for code-compliant usage as interior finish materials). Again, phenolic resins have excellent smoke and flame-spread properties, which makes them an obvious choice where fire performance is critical. Polyester, vinyl ester, and epoxy resins generally perform worse than phenolics for flame-spread and smoke-developed indices, though various additives may improve their performance.

The performance of any given resin selected may be altered by the addition of certain additives and fillers. Additives such as halogen and synergist, alumina trihydrate (ATH), hydrated fillers, or intumescent additives inhibit, reduce, or insulate against thermal decomposition.[4] Alternatively, the presence of voids or impurities in the matrix can alter the thermal (and other) properties of composites, most often for the worse, and must be carefully controlled during processing in order to maintain predictable behavior. Complicating this further is the fact that certain common flame-retardant additives, such as halogen, end up producing toxic smoke, which may be unacceptable in a building application.

Generally, what may be understood from an architectural point of view is that polyester, epoxy, and vinyl ester-based composite parts may be suitable in many architectural applications where flammability performance is not critically important. Adequately designed, detailed, and most importantly, protected from extreme heat, they have the potential to serve as secondary or even primary structural members in assemblies for building types where occupancy, use, egress, and fire suppression technologies are considered in conjunction. In situations where resistance to fire and combustion is crucial, phenolic-based resins provide performance that exceeds most other construction materials, including many metals. Phenolics, however, have trade-offs in manufacturing that need to be considered regarding the fiber selection, final part shape, and processing. All of this, of course, needs to be studied in detail and with due diligence with qualified engineers, fabricators, and regulatory officials before they may be proposed as building materials.

This chart plots the thermal conductivity of different classes of materials against thermal diffusivity. Thermal conductivity measures a materials ability to transfer, or conduct, heat. Thermal diffusivity is the thermal conductivity divided by density and specific heat capacity at constant pressure, pertaining to the rapidity of thermal conductivity. Values to the lower left will have less thermal conductivity and diffusivity, thus potentially serving as better thermal insulators. It is important to note that the values on the x- and y-axes are logarithmic.

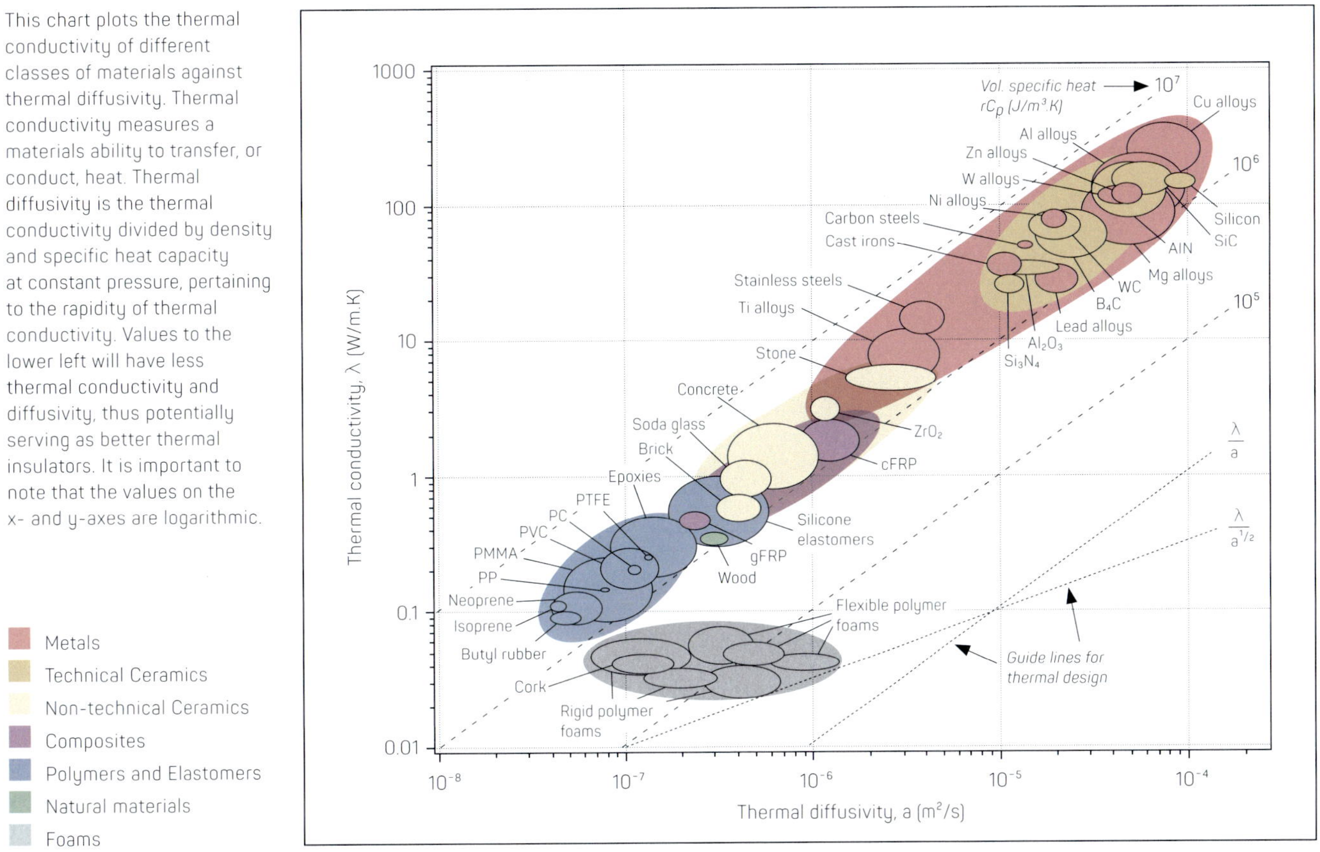

Diagram illustrating the various states of polymer resins in relation to increasing temperature. As temperature increases, the modulus or ability to inelastically resist deformation decreases. The specific point at which each polymer reaches transition states depends on the type and composition of the resin.

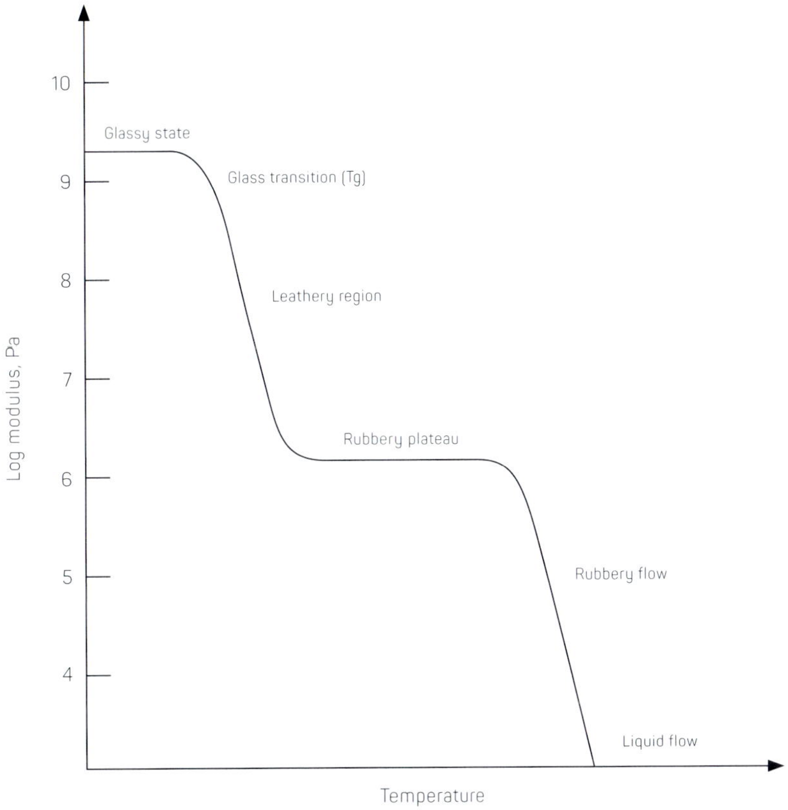

Failure modes

Understanding the way composite materials behave under mechanical or structural loads is complicated by several factors. First of all, composite materials are by definition composed of more than one element and governed by the interaction of those multiple elements, rendering them much more complicated. Secondly, composite materials are fundamentally anisotropic, meaning their properties vary depending on direction and orientation. Thirdly, their compositional make-up is variable among three different interdependent levels, as discussed in Chapter 3: in their material, their geometry, and fabrication. And finally, the varied forms and macro-assemblies in which composites may be applied in architectural settings (pultruded structural sections, sandwich constructions, finish surfaces, etc.) further complicate any attempt to generalize the way that composite materials behave under stress.

In short, the high degree of variability in the design of composite parts means a high degree of variability in their mechanical responses.

Composite laminate parts generally fail in one of three ways: the fibers fracture, the matrix cracks, or the bond between the fibers and matrix fails (interface debonding/interfacial fracture).[5] Sandwich structures will fail much like a beam in the following ways: local crushing of the core, indentation of the skin, transverse shear failure, face material failure, general buckling, shear buckling, or face wrinkling.

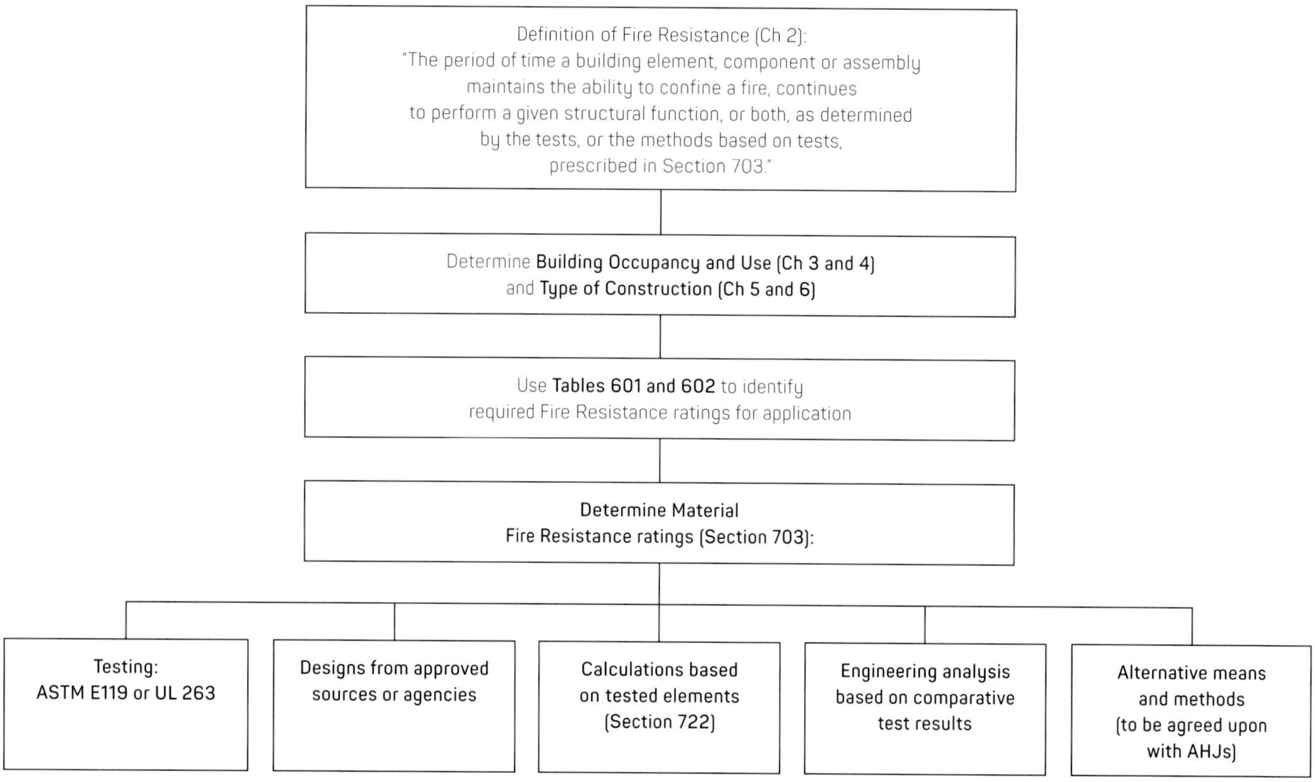

below
Flowchart illustrating the path for determination of the required fire resistance of any building element, component, or assembly, based on the IBC 2018. The fire resistance requirement is a function of the occupancy type, use, construction type, and application. The five methods along the bottom of the chart (based on Section 703) show the many ways that a particular material can satisfy those requirements.

top
Common failure modes for fiber-reinforced polymer composites.

bottom
Common failure modes for composite sandwich structures. They are analogous to simple beam or column failure modes.

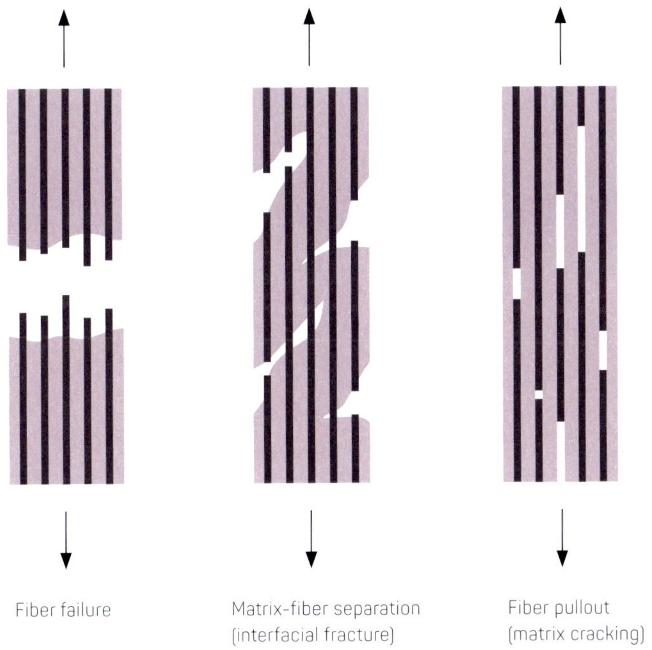

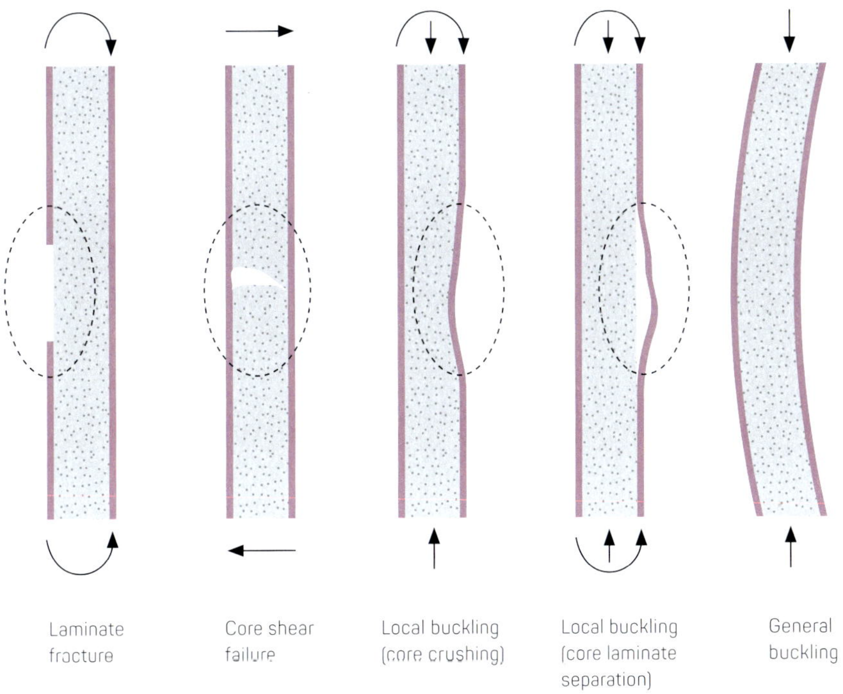

With the design of any structural member, identifiable progressive failure is preferable to sudden catastrophic failure. Designing and engineering to prevent failure, as with any material, means understanding the structural loading criteria, calculating the stresses, designing and engineering the parts to satisfy those criteria, and controlling the process of fabrication to minimize deviations from expected behavior. Any redundancies, safety factors, and other safeguards should be incorporated as deemed appropriate for the application and use situation.

Weathering and durability

The first thing that must be reiterated is that FRP composites do not corrode or rot. This distinguishes them from all conventional building materials except certain types of stone, masonry, and unreinforced concrete. Their structural capacity, and ability to maintain that structural capacity over long periods of time in harsh environments, further distinguishes composites from those other materials. Composite materials' dominant usage in the marine industry is testament to this fact.[6] In terms of their ability to provide structural capacity and maintain integrity in environmentally exposed conditions, their functionality is in a class of its own.

However, distinguished as they are from other building materials in this regard, they are not completely immune to the effects of an extreme environment or extended mechanical fatigue. The choice and design of the resinous matrix is what contributes most to a composite's performance with regard to weathering and durability. Where resistance to fatigue and creep are most critical, a considered choice of resins can provide good initial properties. Additives, fiber-to-resin ratios, and manufacturing processes also have an impact on those properties.

If the initial resin properties, in combination with any additional additives, are not thought adequate for the application, finish coatings and surface applications may further protect the final composite part from the applicable environmental stresses. Paints, gelcoats, cementitious coatings, or other finish materials can work in combination with the composite part to provide resistance to moisture, UV light, abrasion, or any other kind of environmental effect. The durability and weather resistance of composites has the potential to be one of their greatest assets in construction.

BUILDING CODES

Building codes and regulations exist to ensure compliance with standards set for the protection of life safety; "to safeguard the public health, safety, and general welfare of the occupants of new and existing buildings and structures."[7] While they prescribe and codify certain established construction methods for the expediency of regulatory approvals, this expediency can come with trade-offs.

In the United States, the International Building Code (IBC) is the most widely adopted set of standards for building construction. Published by the International Code Council (ICC), the IBC is a complementary set of specialty codes comprising the International Residential Code, International Fire Code, International Energy Conservation Code, International Plumbing Code, and others. Collectively these are known as the I-Codes or the IBC. They are revised and published every three years to incorporate changes that have been reviewed and accepted through their open code development and review process.

Even before building codes come into play, however, local zoning regulations do. Zoning regulations generally contain restrictions on land use—size, height, lot coverage minimums and maximums, floor-area-ratios (FAR), and setbacks are some of the restrictions that are determined at the county and municipal level in the US. They typically do not restrict materiality within construction, though they may often have provisions for exterior or façade materials (usually intended for style or historic preservation reasons). Zoning provisions regarding occupancy types and uses have a cascading impact on the building code pathways possible, and so are usually the first level of regulation that needs to be confirmed with any project.

The issue of compliance with building construction codes is further complicated by the addition, modification, and revision of the base IBC by jurisdictions at the federal, state, county, and municipal levels; the ADA, Fair Housing Act, barrier-free standards, OHSA, local seismic design criteria, energy codes, zoning and other regulatory and legislative codes make design and construction in the US a very complicated affair.

It is thus good architectural practice to review and understand the applicable regulations for a project right at the outset, as these codes are the basis for the relationship between the building team and the authorities-having-jurisdiction.

Performance-based regulations	Prescriptive-based regulations
Performance oriented	Compliance oriented
Sets results-oriented goals	Mandates a design, technology, or equipment
Establishes objectives or tiered standards	Specifies strict methods of compliance
Encourages flexibility and innovation	Prioritizes convention and tradition
Requires mutual consensus and understanding	Requires adherence to written rules
Focuses on outputs and outcomes	Focuses on inputs and products
Naturally progressive; assumes multiple solutions	Naturally conservative; based on proven methods

Prescriptive versus performance codes

In understanding building codes, both in terms of their historical intent as well as for their future development, it becomes necessary to touch upon the concept of prescriptive versus performance codes. A prescriptive code is as it sounds: it prescribes certain design solutions that have previously been deemed to comply with the intent of the codes. A performance code defines the objective and intent but does not prescribe a specific design solution. (See the comparison in the chart above.)

As an example, consider the simple case of handrails. In the IBC version 2018, which is "predominately prescriptive in nature,"[8] to find the code on handrails, you would need to look within Chapter 10: Egress (word count: approximately 36,000). Within that chapter, in Section 1014, approximately 1,200 words are specifically devoted to prescribing code-compliant handrails: when they are necessary, their height, position, relation to stairs versus ramps (which is cross-linked to Section 1012, totaling approximately 1,000 words), maximum and minimum diameters, extensions beyond stairs and landings, clearances from adjacent walls, acceptable amount of continuity or obstructions and support points, resistance to loads both horizontal and vertical (cross-linked to Section 1029, totaling 300 words, unless the handrail is made out of glass, in which case Section 2407 is applicable, approximately 400 words), and many other prescriptions, restrictions, and exceptions.

Of course, if you are designing a residential handrail, then you are looking in the wrong code book, and you need to review the separate and different code for residential handrails (in the ICC Residential Code). If the handrail needs to be incorporated with a guard for fall protection, then check those code sections as well; let's not forget barrier-free and ADA standards. In all, to design a code-compliant, non-residential handrail in a jurisdiction that has adopted the IBC, tens of thousands of words over several books and book sections need to be read, interpreted, and applied to create a construction document, which is then communicated to and confirmed by a building official.

In contrast, the ICC Performance Code of 2015 has only 370 words devoted to egress at all, with not even a mention of handrails, and the stated objectives being: "To protect people during egress and rescue operations," and "Buildings and their facilities shall be constructed to reduce the likelihood of unintentional falls."

This example underlines the difficulty in understanding and evaluating the compliance of new materials in a prescriptive code system, where certain material classifications and assemblies are allowed in specific uses, and other materials or uses must find alternative means of approval. A prescriptive code is reactive in nature, codifying existing solutions that have been previously deemed compliant, and is thus inherently restrictive toward new approaches. This situation is only compounded by the rapid pace of contemporary material, process, and technological development.

Building Element	Type I		Type II		Type III		Type IV	Type V	
	A	B	A	B	A	B	HT	A	B
Primary structural frame[f] (see Section 202)	3[a, b]	2[a, b]	1[b]	0	1[b]	0	HT	1[b]	0
Bearing walls									
Exterior[e, f]	3	2	1	0	2	2	2	1	0
Interior	3[a]	2[a]	1	0	1	0	1/HT	1	0
Nonbearing walls and partitions Exterior	See Table 602								
Nonbearing walls and partitions Interior[d]	0	0	0	0	0	0	See Section 2304.11.2	0	0
Floor construction and associated secondary members (see Section 202)	2	2	1	0	1	0	HT	1	0
Roof construction and associated secondary members (see Section 202)	$1^1/_2$[b]	1[b, c]	1[b, c]	0[c]	1[b, c]	0	HT	1[b, c]	0

Table 601 of the 2018 IBC, showing the required fire resistance of building elements as a function of their construction type. Construction type is determined by building occupancy and use.

a Roof supports: Fire resistance ratings of primary structural frame and bearing walls are permitted to be reduced by 1 hour where supporting a roof only.

b Except in Group F-1, H, M and S-1 occupancies, fire protection of structural members in roof construction shall not be required, including protection of primary structural frame members, roof framing and decking where every part of the roof construction is 20 feet or more above any floor immediately below. Fire-retardant-treated wood members shall be allowed to be used for such unprotected members.

c In all occupancies, heavy timber complying with Section 2304.11 shall be allowed where a 1-hour or less fire resistance rating is required.

d Not less than the fire resistance rating required by other sections of this code.

e Not less than the fire resistance rating based on fire separation distance (see Table 602).

f Not less than the fire resistance rating as referenced in Section 704.10.

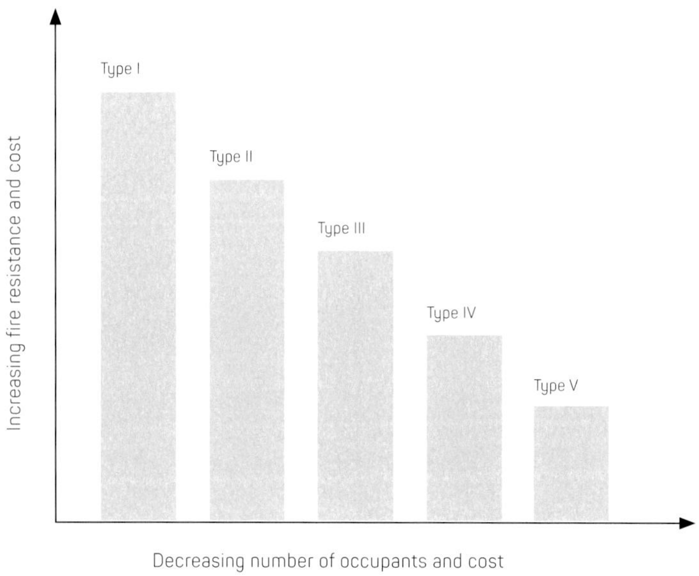

A diagram illustrating the theoretical relationship between construction type and cost, fire resistance requirements, and occupancy. Exceptions, optional fire protection measures, and special uses or cases (such as new types for mass timber buildings set to take effect in 2021) mean that the relationship between building types is not so easily generalized.

Currently, the IBC is understandably cautious in its attitude toward the development and application of new materials and technologies in buildings of certain sizes and uses. This is due not only to a conservative approach to the overall goals ("to safeguard the public health, safety, and general welfare"), but also to the origins of the code in the US as a means to placate insurance underwriters.[9] Performance codes have certain advantages, giving "designers more freedom to comply with the stated goals. They also require the designer to take on more responsibility for knowing the consequences of their design actions." But prescriptive codes also have advantages, "for speed, clarity, and assurance of compliance during design review."[10] As is the case in much of the US, matters of risk, liability, and responsibility are at the heart of the matter.

For composite materials, the material science and engineering industries, and the building industry as a whole, it is worth reflecting on the state of the current regulations and the directions that we would like their development to progress in so as to achieve the overall building and environmental goals we have in mind.

In the US, under the predominantly prescriptive approach of the IBC, there is a system in place for the revision and modification of the codes, as well as the first two versions of the ICC's Performance Codes (issued in 2015 and 2018). Researching, proposing, and then supporting amendments to the codes may be one way to gain increased prescriptive compliance for non-conventional materials in buildings under the IBC; another would be to lobby for acceptance of performance codes in more and more jurisdictions.

Currently, there are multiple paths to the acceptance of materials for use as a building element (Section 703), and those could be explored by industry groups to fast-track the viability of certain composite assemblies for use in building. The composites industry, or advocates of non-conventional materials in buildings, may take lessons from the mass timber industry, which successfully lobbied for changes to the IBC to allow the use of timber structures previously outside of a prescriptive path. With continued research, development, and outreach with regard to our building regulations, composites can significantly contribute to the achievement of our future design goals.

Materials in the IBC

The IBC is structured and arranged to "follow sequential steps that generally occur during a plan review or inspection."[11] For the IBC, this means the first order of business is establishing use and occupancy classifications (Chapter 3). Special use cases, such as high-rise buildings, are covered in Chapter 4. From those classifications, general building height and area limitations can be determined (Chapter 5) in conjunction with "Types of Construction" (Chapter 6).

It is these Types of Construction that determine material use, application, fire-resistance rating requirements, and other requirements. Allowable materials and their uses and locations are specifically laid out in Section 603. Further requirements are detailed in chapters devoted to specific materials. For fiber-reinforced polymers, this means Chapter 26: Plastic.

To summarize briefly here: Type V buildings are permitted to use almost any material in any building element. Type III buildings are buildings that use noncombustible materials in the exterior walls and any material (including FRP) on the interiors, and Type I and II buildings have all building elements made of noncombustible materials, except where otherwise specifically allowed.

The ACMA has published excellent decision-making trees/flow charts for architects looking to utilize FRPs, or manufacturers intending make FRP products for use as exterior wall assemblies. These charts illustrate the complexity of the rules surrounding FRP use in one specific application.

The handrails, guards, and ramps of Le Corbusier's Villa La Roche in Paris, France would be non-compliant for many applications.

In the case of FRP composites, it generally breaks down like this: they may be used anywhere and anyhow in Type V buildings, on the interiors of Type III buildings, and on the interiors and exteriors of Type I, II, and III buildings with many contingencies. In practical reality, though, it is the contingencies that determine everything. Some, but not all, of the contingencies are helpfully diagrammed by the ACMA decision trees represented over the next five pages.

What these diagrams from ACMA do not cover are uses outside of exterior wall assemblies. For any other use, including structurally, a detailed understanding of the IBC is required. There are multiple paths to acceptable uses, generally detailed in IBC Section 703, including laboratory or full-scale mock-up testing, engineered or calculated results, and/or in conjunction with the explicit approval of any authority-having-jurisdiction (AHJ).

For composites, which as a class are generally considered "combustible" (ASTM E-136 is the test specified by the IBC to determine combustibility), there are many different mechanical responses to thermal stress. As we discussed earlier, phenolic-based resins have incredible thermal performance, while other resins quickly lose structural capacity under heat. The first design solution may be to design a composite that meets the thermal loading criteria. Another option, perhaps more readily feasible given the process technology available, is to apply a layer of thermal protection onto thermally sensitive composites (in the form of cementitious or intumescent coatings, for example). This is a solution that has parallels with our treatment of structural steel.

For any project, a mutual understanding of the properties of the material in question between the engineers and architects, building officials, owner, and contractor is essential, particularly for non-conventional building materials. Qualified experts and engineers in composites and code experts should be sought out for retention on any building project considering such materials.

opposite and following pages
IBC Fire Decision Tree.

Abbreviations and Definitions of Common Terms

FP Foam Plastic Insulation*: A plastic that is intentionally expanded by the use of a foaming agent to produce a reduced-density plastic containing voids consisting of open or closed cells distributed throughout the plastic for thermal insulating or acoustical purposes and that has a density of less than 20 pounds per cubic foot (pcf) (320 kg/m^3).

FRP Fiber Reinforced Polymer*: A polymeric composite material consisting of reinforcement fibers, such as glass, impregnated with a fiber-binding polymer which is then molded and hardened. Fiber-reinforced polymers are permitted to contain cores laminated between fiber-reinforced polymer facings.

FSI Flame Spread Index*: A comparative measure, expressed as a dimensionless number, derived from visual measurements of the spread of flame versus time for a material tested in accordance with ASTM E 84 or UL 723.

CRS Corrosion Resistive Steel*: Steel that has the ability to withstand deterioration of its surface or its properties when exposed to its environment.

ASS Automatic Sprinkler System*: An automatic sprinkler system, for fire protection purposes, is an integrated system of underground and overhead piping designed in accordance with fire protection engineering standards.

PVC Polyvinylchloride**: A synthetic thermoplastic material made by polymerizing vinyl chloride.

PP Polypropylene**: a plastic polymer used chiefly for molded parts, electrical insulation, packaging, and fibers for wearing apparel.

SDI Smoke Developing Index

* definitions directly from IBC

** definitions from dictionary.com

Color Key for Decision Trees

Type I-IV Construction

- Plastics
  - FP & FRP
  - Plastic Siding
- Wood
- Combustibles other than Plastics and Wood

Type V Construction

- FP & FRP
- Plastic Siding
- Materials other than Wood, Plastics, and PP Sidings
- PP Siding

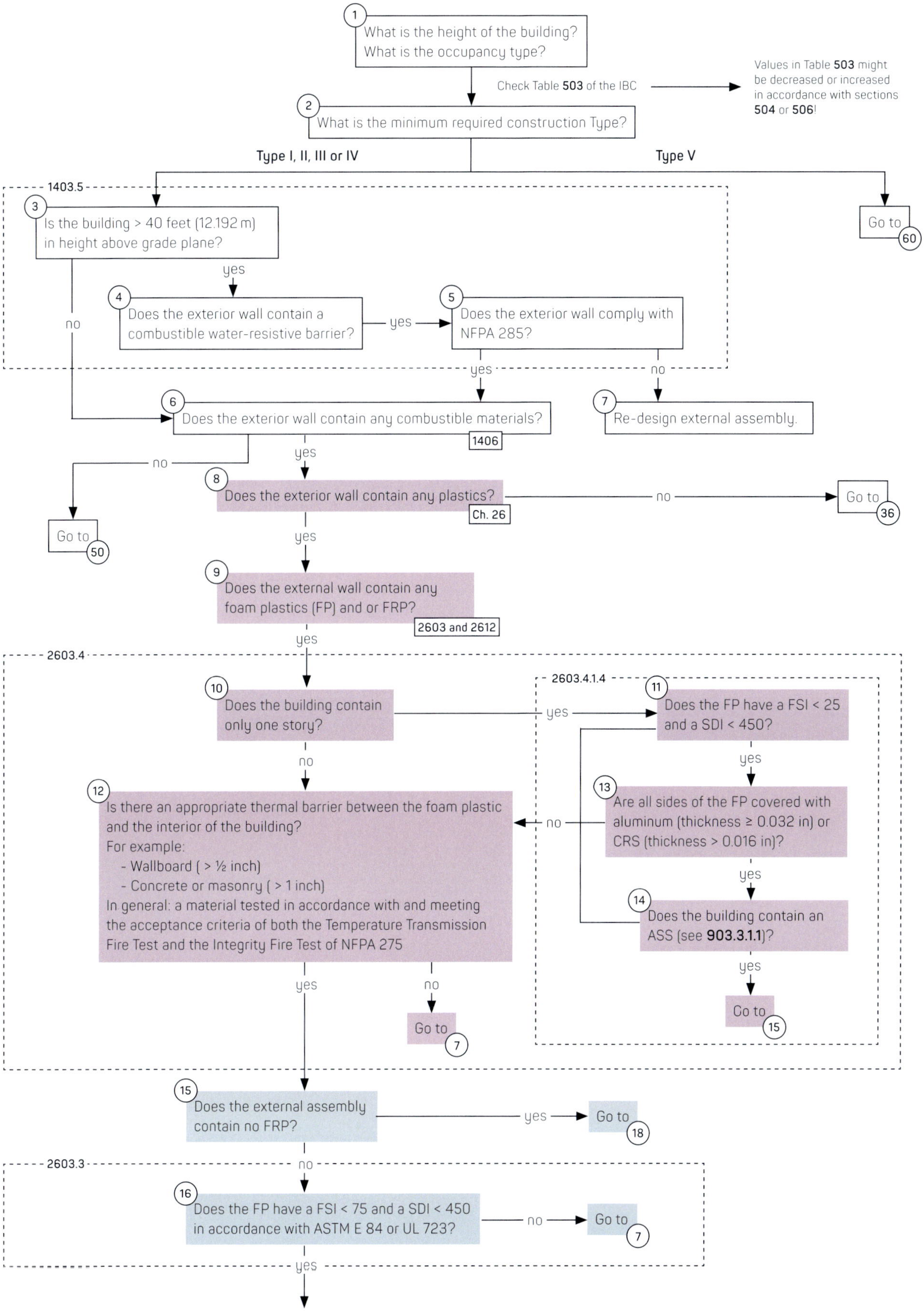

continued next page

continued from previous page

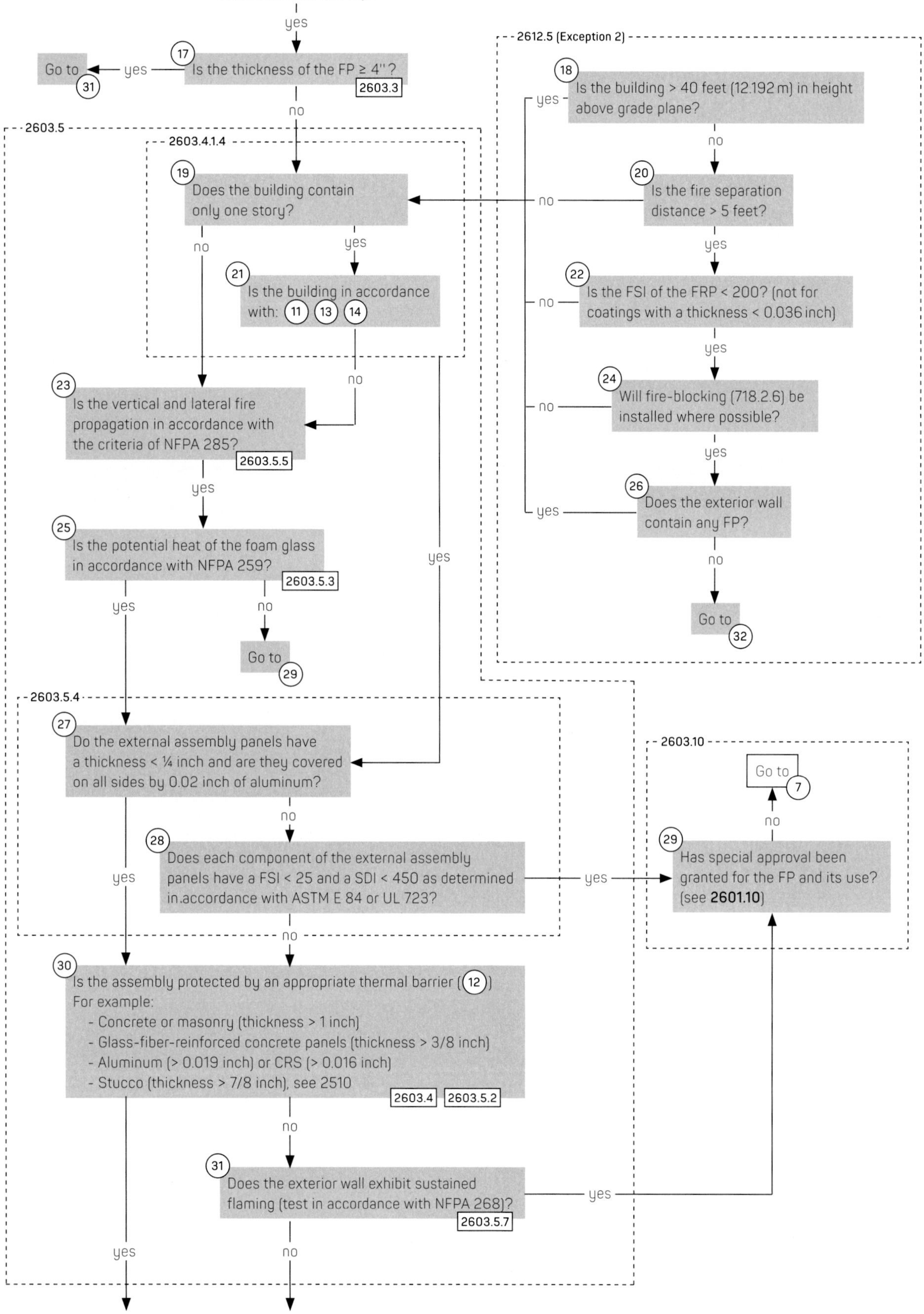

continued next page

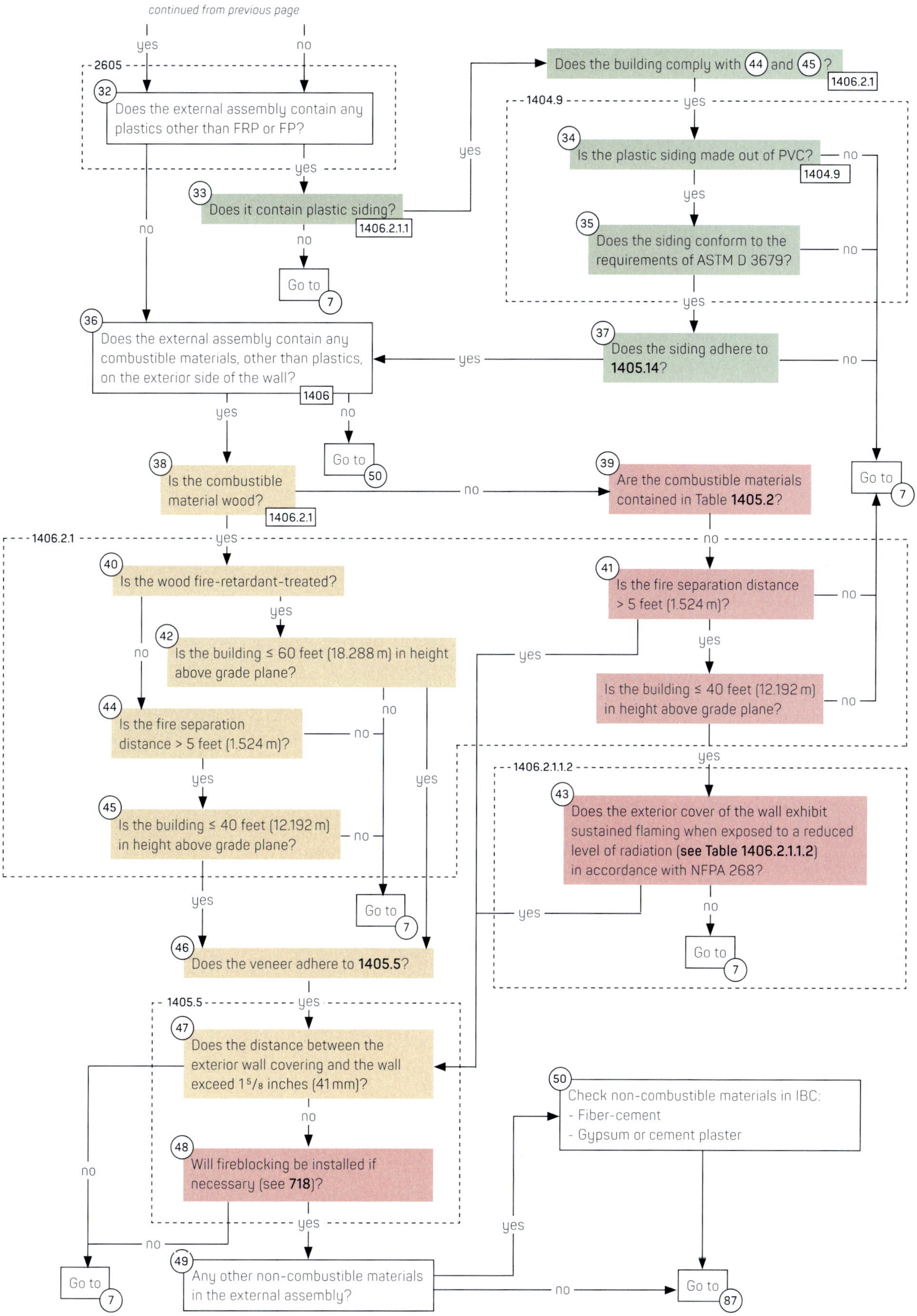
continued from previous page
yes
no
2605
32 Does the external assembly contain any plastics other than FRP or FP?
yes
33 Does it contain plastic siding?
1406.2.1.1
no
Go to 7
yes
Does the building comply with 44 and 45 ?
1406.2.1
1404.9
yes
34 Is the plastic siding made out of PVC?
1404.9
no
yes
35 Does the siding conform to the requirements of ASTM D 3679?
no
yes
37 Does the siding adhere to 1405.14?
no
yes
36 Does the external assembly contain any combustible materials, other than plastics, on the exterior side of the wall?
1406
yes
no
Go to 50
38 Is the combustible material wood?
1406.2.1
no
39 Are the combustible materials contained in Table 1405.2?
Go to 7
1406.2.1
yes
no
40 Is the wood fire-retardant-treated?
yes
no
42 Is the building ≤ 60 feet (18.288 m) in height above grade plane?
41 Is the fire separation distance > 5 feet (1.524 m)?
no
yes
yes
Is the building ≤ 40 feet (12.192 m) in height above grade plane?
no
44 Is the fire separation distance > 5 feet (1.524 m)?
no
no
yes
yes
yes
1406.2.1.1.2
45 Is the building ≤ 40 feet (12.192 m) in height above grade plane?
no
43 Does the exterior cover of the wall exhibit sustained flaming when exposed to a reduced level of radiation (see Table 1406.2.1.1.2) in accordance with NFPA 268?
yes
Go to 7
yes
no
Go to 7
46 Does the veneer adhere to 1405.5?
1405.5
yes
47 Does the distance between the exterior wall covering and the wall exceed 1 5/8 inches (41 mm)?
no
no
48 Will fireblocking be installed if necessary (see 718)?
50 Check non-combustible materials in IBC:
- Fiber-cement
- Gypsum or cement plaster
yes
yes
no
Go to 7
49 Any other non-combustible materials in the external assembly?
no
Go to 87

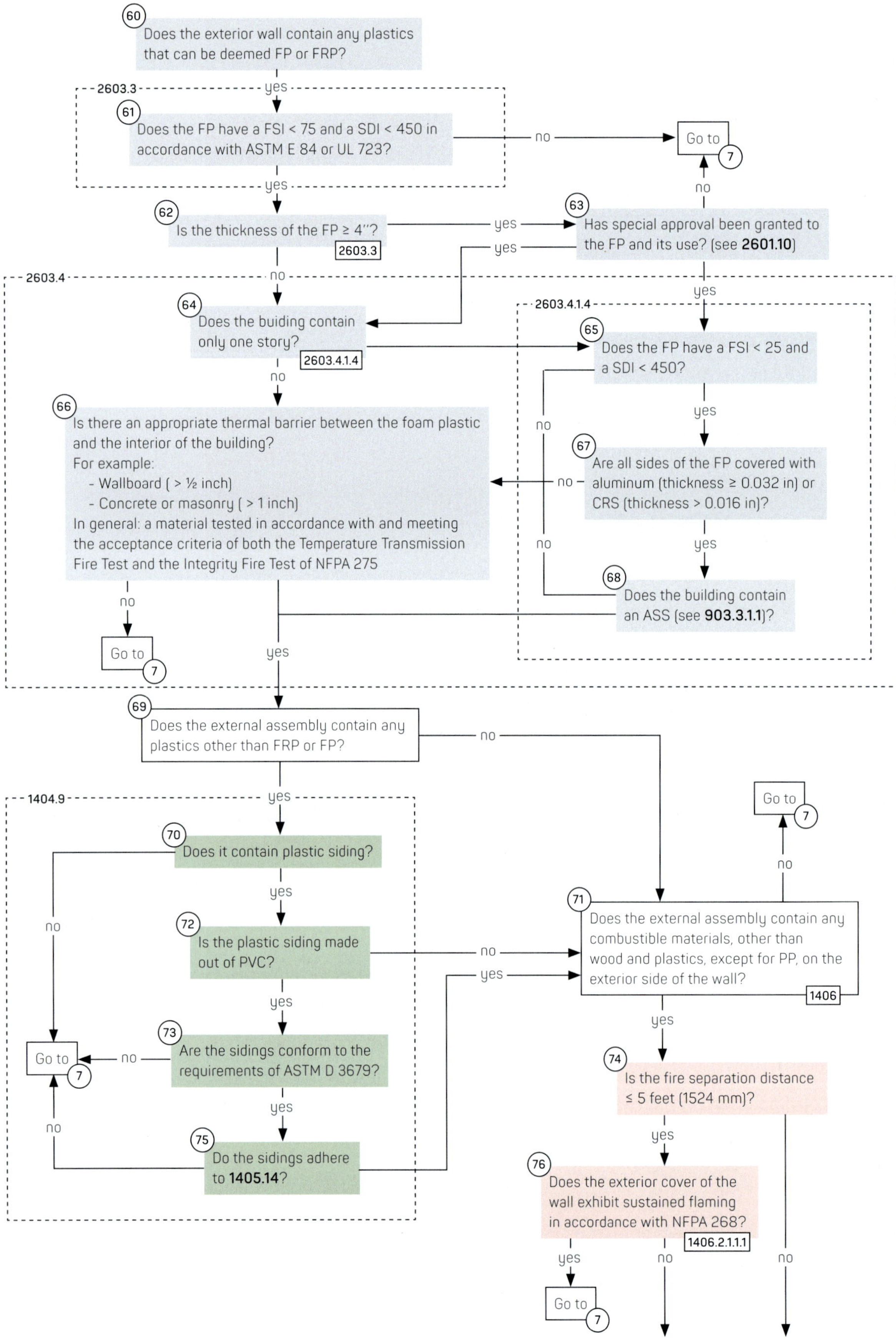

continued next page

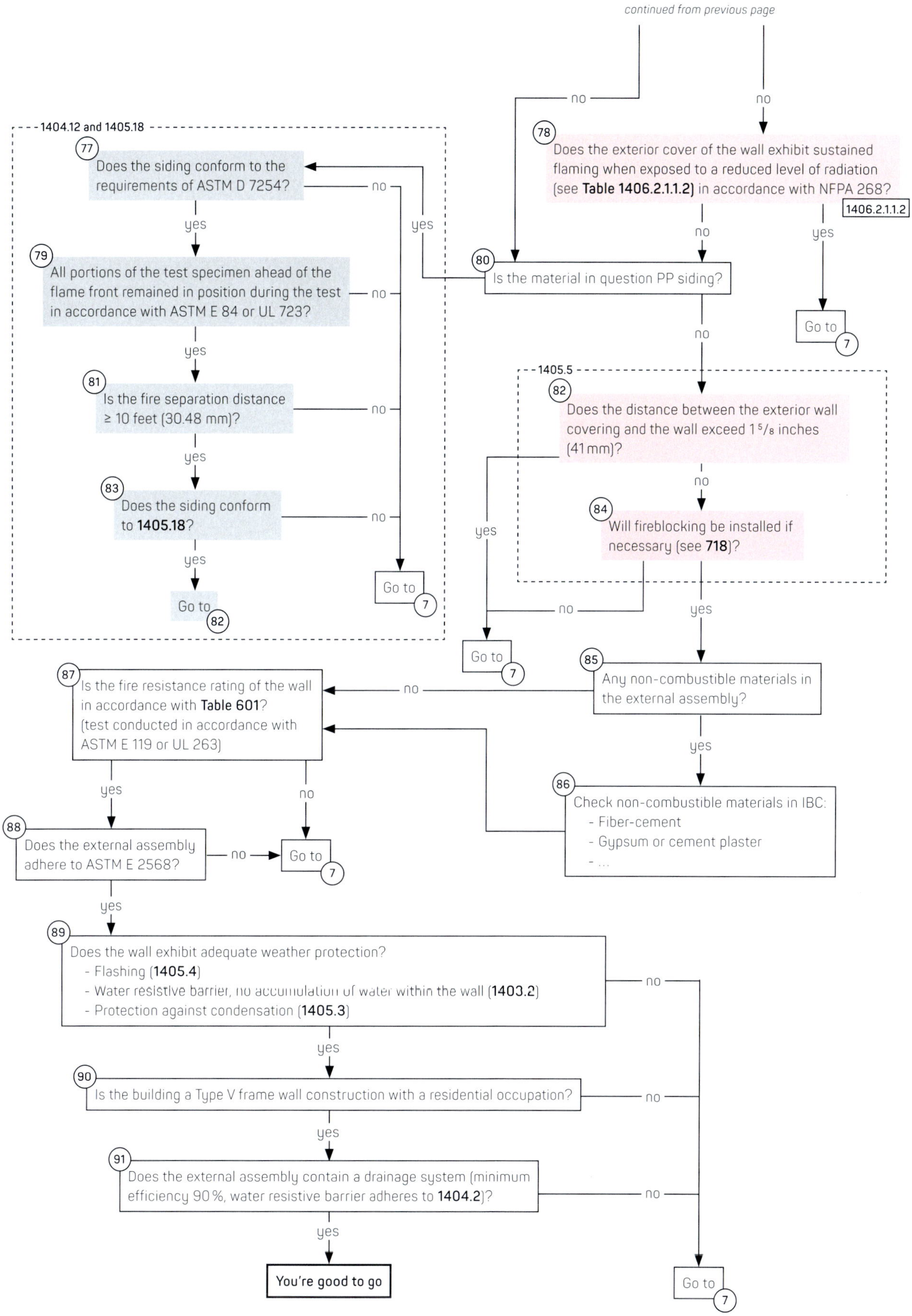
continued from previous page
no
no
1404.12 and 1405.18
77 Does the siding conform to the requirements of ASTM D 7254?
yes
no
yes
79 All portions of the test specimen ahead of the flame front remained in position during the test in accordance with ASTM E 84 or UL 723?
no
yes
81 Is the fire separation distance ≥ 10 feet (30.48 mm)?
no
yes
83 Does the siding conform to 1405.18?
no
yes
Go to 82
Go to 7
78 Does the exterior cover of the wall exhibit sustained flaming when exposed to a reduced level of radiation (see Table 1406.2.1.1.2) in accordance with NFPA 268?
1406.2.1.1.2
no
yes
80 Is the material in question PP siding?
Go to 7
no
1405.5
82 Does the distance between the exterior wall covering and the wall exceed 1 5/8 inches (41 mm)?
no
yes
84 Will fireblocking be installed if necessary (see 718)?
no
yes
Go to 7
85 Any non-combustible materials in the external assembly?
no
yes
86 Check non-combustible materials in IBC:
- Fiber-cement
- Gypsum or cement plaster
- ...
87 Is the fire resistance rating of the wall in accordance with Table 601? (test conducted in accordance with ASTM E 119 or UL 263)
yes
no
88 Does the external assembly adhere to ASTM E 2568?
no
Go to 7
yes
89 Does the wall exhibit adequate weather protection?
- Flashing (1405.4)
- Water resistive barrier, no accumulation of water within the wall (1403.2)
- Protection against condensation (1405.3)
no
yes
90 Is the building a Type V frame wall construction with a residential occupation?
no
yes
91 Does the external assembly contain a drainage system (minimum efficiency 90 %, water resistive barrier adheres to 1404.2)?
no
yes
You're good to go
Go to 7

Compliance for non-prescribed (alternative) means, materials, and methods

In Chapter 1, Section 104.11 of the 2015 and 2018 IBC, it states: "The provisions of this code are not intended to prevent the installation of any material or to prohibit any design or method of construction not specifically prescribed by this code, provided that any such alternative has been approved. An alternative material, design or method of construction shall be approved where the building official finds that the proposed design is satisfactory and complies with the intent of the provisions of this code, and that the material, method or work offered is, for the purpose intended, not less than the equivalent of that prescribed in this code in quality, strength, effectiveness, fire resistance, durability and safety." As Francis Ching and Steven Winkel write, "[the IBC] recognizes that there will be innovations in building types, such as covered malls, mixed-use buildings, and atrium buildings that do not fit neatly into prescribed occupancy classifications. The code also recognizes that there will be innovations in materials and construction technology that may happen faster than code revisions are made."[12]

In short, what this means is that for any building project team proposing non-IBC-prescribed materials, designs, and methods of construction, a mutual understanding between them and the authorities-having-jurisdiction (AHJs) must be established in order to obtain approval for those alternatives for construction.

This section, with the cooperation of the AHJs, starts to push the IBC toward the functioning of a performance code. It is easy to see how this relationship between the building teams and the AHJs becomes crucial for the future of building using progressive materials and technology.

Materials in the Eurocode

The Eurocode is the set of building regulations that govern most of Europe and parts of Asia, the Middle East, and Africa. They function to supplement local building regulations and provide a unified set of guidelines for most of Europe. For building products, the EU Construction Products Directive (CPD) sets the standards for "fit for purpose" products throughout the EU.[13]

Like the IBC, use (purpose group) and size have an allowable set of construction methods and materials. Materials are classified according to their performance in reaction to fire, from A1, A2, B, C, D, E, & F, with A1 offering the highest level of performance and F offering the lowest (this is not to be confused with similar classification ratings from an ASTM E-84 test, which also rate materials based on flame-spread and smoke-developed indices—which also have an A, B, C level rating system). These fire performance classifications are then used to determine the material's suitability for use within certain building components and assemblies.

A 2016 policy report commissioned by the European Commission Joint Research Centre entitled "Prospect for new guidance in the design of FRP" aimed to create a harmonized European set of standards for composite structures.[14]

CONSTRUCTION CONSIDERATIONS

The contractor is arguably the architect's most visible partner in the delivery of completed buildings. Any successful building project necessitates a well-functioning relationship between architect and contractor (or construction manager / builder). Currently, contractor involvement in a traditional architectural delivery process can be divided into two equally important phases: pre-construction services and construction.

During pre-construction, the contractor's skill, comfort, and familiarity with materials and techniques is a large factor in the viability of a design, assuming code compliance has been met (or there is a strategy in place for compliance). With any non-conventional building material or technology, it is a given that the majority of contractors will be uncomfortable. Most often, this lack of comfort (which may be the same as knowledge and confidence) translates to negative impacts on a project's schedule and budget.

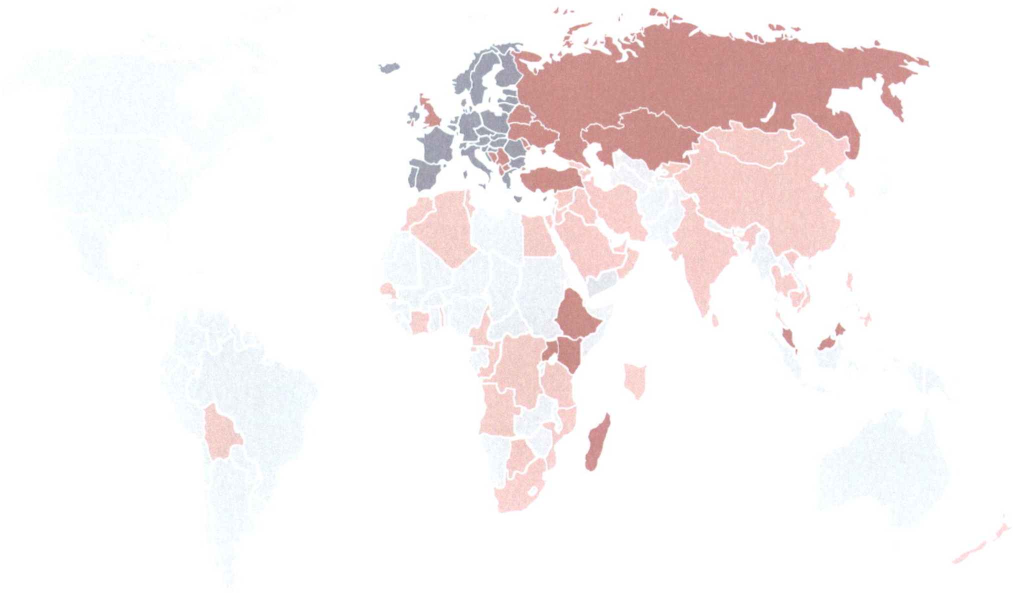

A map showing the adoption of the Eurocodes throughout the world.

- Eurocodes adopted (EU-EFTA countries)
- Eurocodes adopted or in process of adoption (non EU countries)
- Expression of interest in Eurocodes adoption (non EU countries)

Chart plotting material strength against cost. Note that the values along the x- and y-axes are logarithmic. The high strength and potentials of composites currently come at a cost.

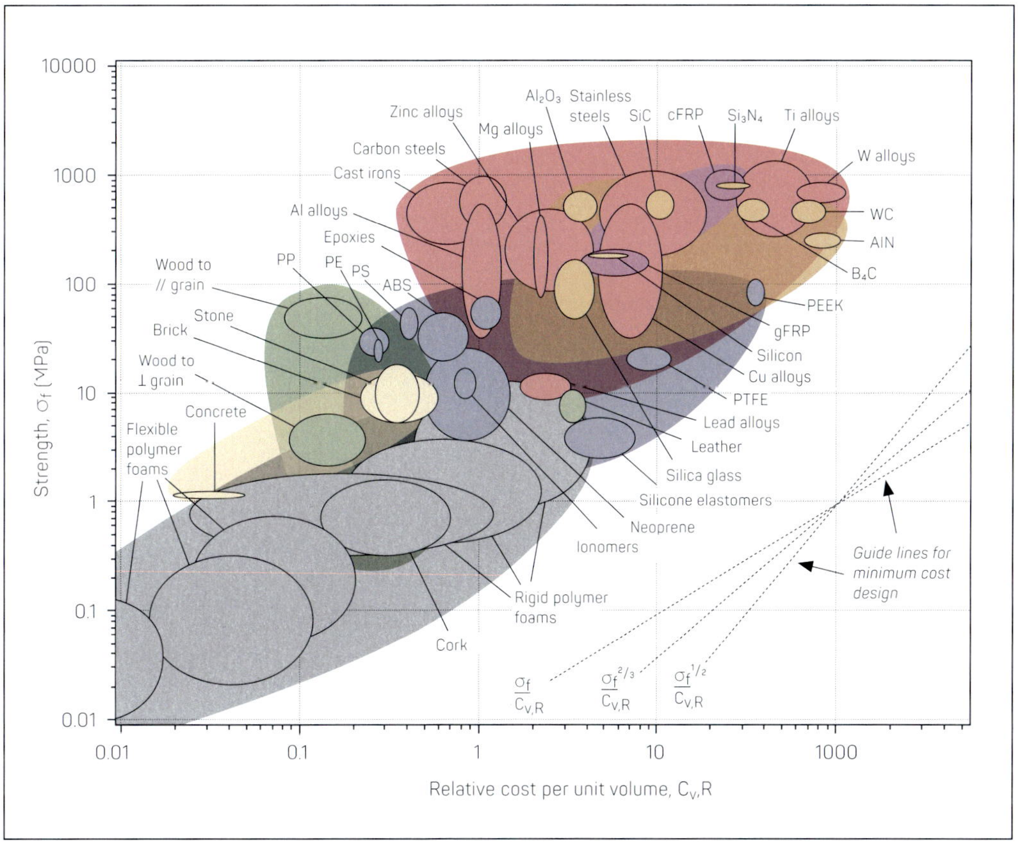

- Metals
- Technical Ceramics
- Non-technical Ceramics
- Composites
- Polymers and Elastomers
- Natural materials
- Foams

Cost is the root of the issue here, and lack of familiarity with composite technology is a challenge in this regard.

There are a couple of ways to approach this on a very general level at the pre-construction phase. The first and most immediate way is to bring in partners who can provide the requisite knowledge and skill to accommodate the proposed design. These may be engineers, fabricators, or outside industry contractors who can complement the incumbent abilities of the general contractor.

In a way, this response is like what has been happening in architecture with design-assist consulting firms such as Gehry Technologies.

The second is a more general and long-term building-industry-structure response—and that is to shift many of the variables, uncertainties, and assurances of new materials in construction to the fabricators of those new architectural products. Essentially, this shifts the burden from the general contractor, liable for typically only a one-off building, to a high-tech manufacturing facility that can research, develop, and scale architectural product solutions across many buildings. In essence, it is a move toward vertical integration. This response attempts to align risk and incentives toward those who can profit from them; it may be the general direction where construction is headed in the future.

During construction, contractors are responsible for the handling, erecting, and installing of any proposed composite parts. Generally, in the case of composites, this represents significantly fewer complications than for other building materials because of the reduced weight of composite parts. For the SFMOMA project in San Francisco by Snøhetta, this meant the ability to install unitized composite exterior wall assemblies by hoisting and without the use of extensive scaffolding.

The linearity, sequential dependency, and potential for misaligned objectives in a traditional building delivery model can be a source of inefficiency or conflict. The rapidly growing complexity of the information and processes to be managed will only increase the potential for these inefficiencies and conflicts; the emergence of specialized professionals such as construction managers, design assists, and others highlights the expanded scope and value that can be claimed in the building industry.

Professional roles and relationships in the contemporary building environment have evolved. In part, this is due to changing technology and the expanded technical scope of any building project.

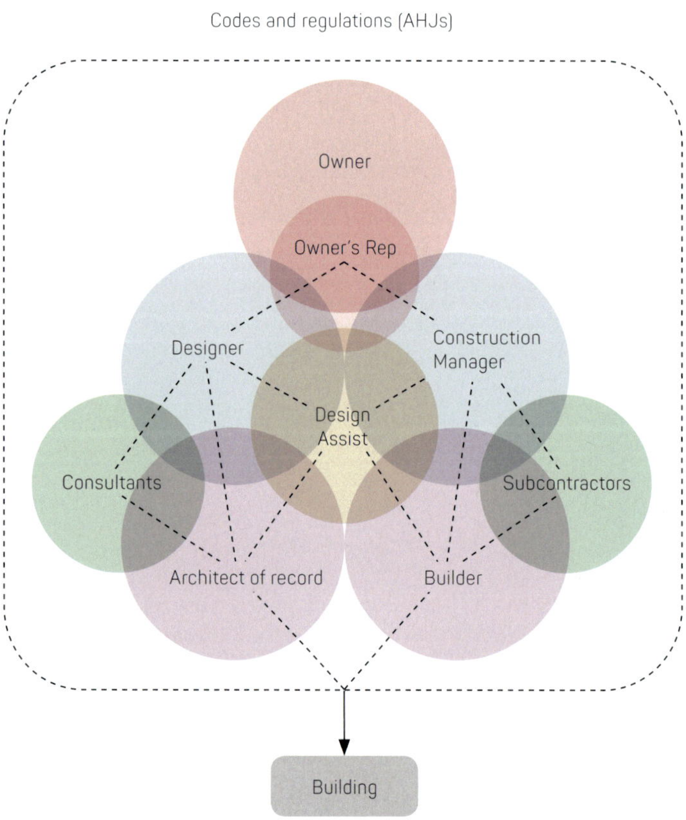

Joints and joinery

There may be one area of composite design with which both contractors and architects may be equally unfamiliar; and that is the design of joints in composites. There is a long history of joints and joinery in architecture. The three main reasons for any joint in architecture are: sizes, stresses, and tolerances.

The first is the constraints and limits placed on the dimensions of architectural component parts in sourcing and then transporting them to the building site. Few materials occurring naturally or produced industrially are available in sizes that can span architectural distances in one piece; even those are limited in their dimensions by what can be transported (a notable exception is architecture made from stone carved in situ, such as the temples in Jordan or the churches of Lalibela). What can be shipped and transported to the building site is usually much smaller than the building itself—sizes are limited by trucking and roadway dimensions; this necessitates the aggregation of smaller parts to make a building. Joints are the expression of the boundaries between those parts (and indirectly about our transportation infrastructure).

Secondly, joints transmit, transfer, and control stresses from one part of the building to another. They may function structurally, transferring lateral loads to shear walls or moment frames, for example. They also allow for movement between differing materials due to differentials in expansion, contraction, and/or bending stresses. These joints control the mechanical movement of materials over distances; hence the term "control joints." Joints address the reality of molecular level responses to thermal and mechanical loads over architectural scales.

The famous geberettes and exterior structural bracing of the Centre Pompidou in Paris, France, a building that celebrated the materials and engineering of the late industrial age.

Thirdly, joints help manage the many imperfections inherent in construction. It should not come as a surprise that building components are not always placed exactly where they were intended to be and may not be precisely the size they need to be; the accumulation and accommodation of those inexactitudes is the construction tolerance. Industry groups such as the AISC publish standards for the acceptable deviation of members and their placement from the ideal. These joints express a forgiveness for material and procedural imperfection.

The mechanical and esthetic management of joints is a history of architecture itself. Modernism invented the reveal as a novel way to express the intersection between two different materials, in contrast to expressed trim or moldings at material intersections. The reveal was a detail that corresponded with the theoretical and meta-architectural aims of the epoch.

Composites joinery (connections between different composite parts or with other materials) generally falls into two categories: mechanical (such as bolts and rivets), chemical (such as adhesive bonding), or some combination the two. The possibility of in-situ chemical bonding is what distinguishes composite joinery from that of other materials. In contrast to mechanical connections, which typically occur at points; chemical connections act over surfaces.

Composite materials can change the way joints function and are expressed in architecture. This is because they can be fabricated on site, with appropriate site conditioning, and be engineered to internally withstand mechanical and thermal stresses without control joints, as in the Stedelijk Museum in Amsterdam (opposite). Seamless and jointless surface expressions are possible with composite materials, unlike any other conventional building material.

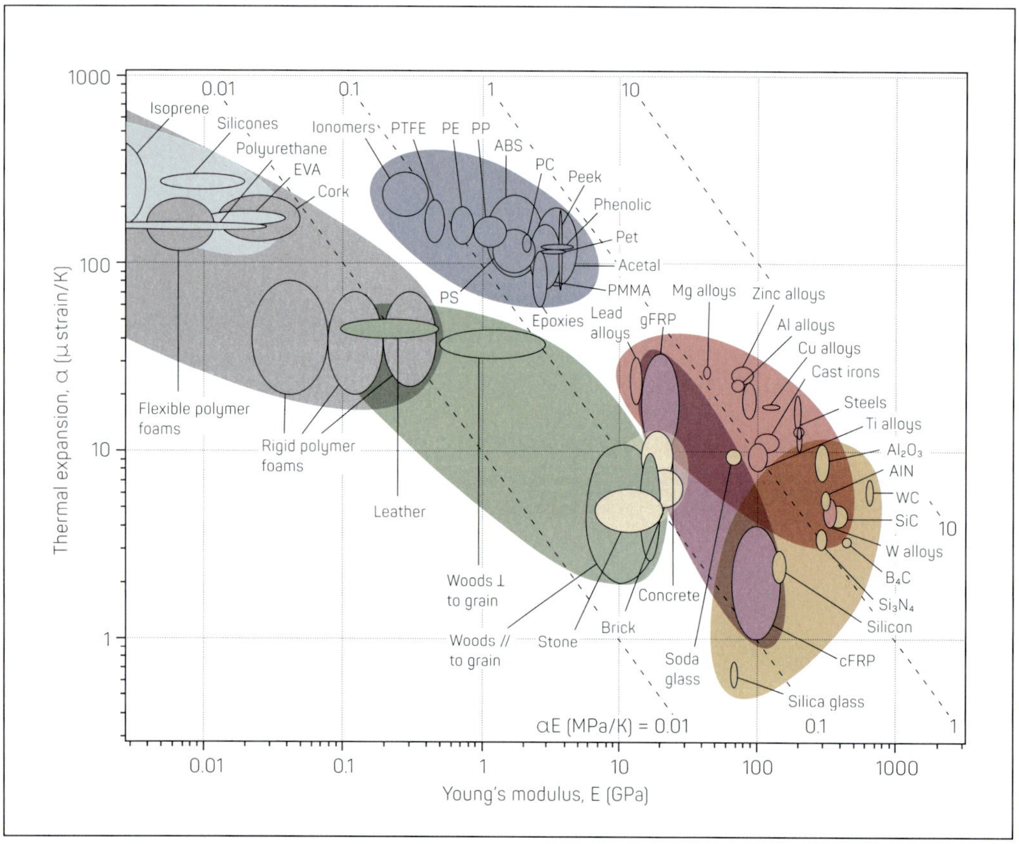

Chart plotting coefficient of thermal expansion against stiffness (Young's modulus). Note that the values along the x- and y-axes are logarithmic. Materials toward the bottom right of the chart offer the greatest strength and dimensional stability over temperatures.

CONCLUSION

The issues discussed in this chapter, those pertaining to architecture's relationship to its two most immediate partners, the AHJs and contractors, are geared toward finding productive ways of working to achieve common building goals using materials in construction. It is assumed that the safeguarding of health, welfare, and life safety is a common starting point, and to the extent that composite materials can fulfill those mandates and any others of the building team, their consideration should also be equally routine.

Technology, development, and expanding and changing scopes of risk and responsibility within all building professions mean that a continuing reevaluation of these issues is necessary. All parties have an interest in a materially rich world that can meet the goals of the present and future.

1 Bank, 46.
2 Kreysler, 14.
3 Strong, 127.
4 Kreysler, 26.
5 Hollaway, 77; Strong, 325.
6 Lucintel.
7 IBC 2018.
8 Ching & Winkel, 34.
9 Ching & Winkel, 21.
10 Ching & Winkel, 36.
11 IBC 2018.
12 Ching & Winkel, 11.
13 Ching & Mulville, 2.05.
14 Ascione, L., J. F. Caron, P. Godonou, K. Van Ijselmuijden, J. Knippers, T. Mottram, M. Oppe, M. Gantriis Sorensen, J. Taby, and L. Tromp. "Prospect for new guidance in the design of FRP." JRC Report EUR 27666 (2016). Published in Italy, Luxembourg: Publications Office of the European Union, 2016.

The Stedelijk Museum in Amsterdam, clad with panels made of carbon fiber and aramid composite, has a façade that was engineered to be one single, jointless, seamless piece across its 100 m (328 ft) length.

6 THE FUTURE OF BUILDING

The story of humanity ... would not have been possible without an expanding and increasingly intricate and complex use of materials. [1]

Vaclav Smil

The raw materials that we use have not changed, but as a result of trial and error, experimentation, refinement, and scientific investigation, the instructions that we follow for combining raw materials have become vastly more sophisticated. [2]

Paul Romer

By many measures, buildings have gotten better over time. Especially since the Industrial Age, buildings have gotten stronger, more comfortable, and safer. But further improvement is still possible. Advances in material science, computation, engineering, and fabrication technology hold significant promise for the building and construction industries. Sustainability has become a crucial consideration for construction, and evolving thinking on sustainability will continue to be an important factor in the ambitions for building projects. Composite materials are well positioned to contribute in applications where their material properties are aligned with the project design goals. In construction, their contributions can best progress through two paths: as a cost-driven substitute for other materials or as a high-performance driver. The performance, properties, and process technology of composites open new potentials for architecture and design, and some designers have started to explore interesting directions that highlight these possibilities. To best prepare for a future of building that is technology driven, architecture needs to address disciplinary inertia in practice and education. Careful consideration of the structure and functioning of building code regulations can help foster construction efficiency and innovation while maintaining safeguards on public health and welfare. Although the future of building may see many aspects of performance measured and quantified, it also bears remembering that many unquantifiable aspects of building performance also contribute to a healthy built environment.

opposite
Young & Ayata. Base Flowers. Multimaterial 3D print, Resin, Full color sandstone, 2015.

By many measures, perceptibly and imperceptibly, buildings have gotten better. Perhaps the most perceptible measure by which buildings have improved is thermally. Insulation in exterior walls and roofs makes interior spaces feel more comfortable and require less energy to heat and air condition. Advanced glazing systems, combined with stronger structures, mean that windows are now larger, allowing access to more natural light and better views to the exterior. And glazing units with multiple panes, sealed gas, and advanced coatings mean these surfaces also insulate better, at least compared to the single-paned glass of only a half century ago.

Imperceptibly, buildings have gotten better, too. The building services systems (mechanical, electrical, and plumbing, or M/E/P) have all steadily improved, leading to noticeable functional improvements in the equipment used to service buildings. Standardized and industrially produced materials, such as dimensional lumber, engineered woods, gypsum board, steel, and rebar have meant that buildings have gotten stronger, more consistent, and cheaper to build. Building codes have been incorporated across multiple jurisdictions to more consistently require structures that are more resistant to damage, fire, and earthquakes. Fire protection measures and egress standards have increased due to those same regulations. Buildings today are safer and more accessible than ever before.

Andreas Gursky, Salerno I, 1990.

And yet there are many ways that buildings can still get better. The technologies that drive many of the improvements mentioned above are actually older than we may realize. Fiberglass, used as thermal insulation—the first material that performed well enough in thin enough dimensions to be both cost-effective and architecturally viable, was invented in 1938. Dimensional lumber as we know it and use it today (two-by-fours, etc.) was first published as a set of standards by industry groups at the very beginning of the 20th century, such as the Pacific Coast Lumber Manufacturers Association in 1906[3]. The first plywood panels manufactured from softwoods in the western United States were showcased at the 1905 World's Fair in Portland, Oregon.[4] Structural steel is a product of the Industrial Age and was used as a building element at its start: the first skyscraper was built in 1885, and the curtain wall was invented around the same time. Gypsum wallboard was trademarked in 1926 as Sheetrock, which is how it is still colloquially known today. Concrete, stone, and masonry are, of course, centuries-old structural materials and are still commonly used today.

The potential for improvement in building technology is perhaps best brought into relief when compared to the changes seen in industries outside of architecture. While many buildings today utilize the same technology that was in use 100 years ago, it is difficult to imagine an automobile, airplane, or many other industrial products doing the same. The potential for improvement in our buildings is limited only by our imaginations.

Today, new materials, tools, and technologies hold significant promise for advances and improvements in our buildings and environment. Digital/computational tools, robotic fabrication, information technology, advanced sensors, internet-of-things, generative design, and artificial intelligence are all recently developed technologies poised to be significant factors in the building industry of the future. "These technologies portend a potential seismic shift in both process and role for architects,"[5] writes Phillip Bernstein.

At the same time, the evolving discourse surrounding the issue of sustainability is becoming more and more important. These issues are fundamentally changing the way we understand and assess architecture. As Manfred Hegger put it, "the entirety of the architectural production is up for discussion, i.e. economic, ecological and social aspects must be considered in their mutual dependencies." This is drastically different from how architecture was conceptualized, practiced, and taught but one generation ago.

The expanded scope of design consideration under sustainability marks a dramatic shift from the past. Historically (and for the most part, through to today), architecture has above all served the desires of a specific client. More ambitious architects worked with an idea of an expanded audience that went beyond any sole client—this ambitious architecture may have addressed a greater perceived context, such as in the case of a civic or cultural building. Modernism expanded that scope even further and brought an idea of an international style to architectural discourse. Postmodernism, deconstructivism, and other branches of academic pursuits in the later 20th century addressed an intellectual audience of architecture concerned with ideas of criticality and autonomy. But sustainability has expanded that scope far beyond any of those prior considerations.

When everything is supposed to be considered, it then becomes crucial to be specific about the goals for each project. For, unlike single-purpose built products such as racecars or airplanes, where the concept of better is easily defined and easily quantifiable, buildings have a diverse and varied set of goals, some of which are unquantifiable. There is a vast range of viable ambitions for any architectural project—socio-cultural, economic, and ecological—and the lessons of sustainability have shown us that many of our architectural decisions have measurable impacts. Primary among those considerations for architectural impact is the expanded thinking around lifecycle analysis/assessment (LCA). This leads to consideration of material choices from the moment of genesis, through design, installation, and maintenance, over a specified lifespan, until the building's end-of-life process. With LCA thinking, the gestation, birth, life, and death of a building are part of its design.

The materials we use must be aligned with those goals. Moreover, the durability of a material and the designed lifespan of a product are intertwined. For a limited use or short lifespan product, an extremely durable material is counter to its goals; for something that is intended to last forever, that property of durability is well-aligned. In almost all cases concerning the ecological footprint, all other things being equal, less material and lighter weight (less mass) usually means a smaller ecological footprint.

This alignment between material properties and end goals can be called material efficiency—the effectiveness of a material's properties in meeting its intended goals with a minimum of trade-offs. For different applications in a building, a material will have differing goals; a structural material must be strong, stiff, durable, and resilient; an exterior-facing material will need to have good weathering, durability, and thermal properties.

When and where they are aligned with the overall goals of a project, composite materials can contribute meaningfully to this future of construction. As a class of materials, they are stronger, lighter, more durable, perform better thermally, and allow more design potential. Thus, they can lend those same properties to an overall building project, contributing to the success of a project designed to succeed by those same measures. Composite materials can lead to lighter, stronger, more durable, and better thermally performing buildings that have new formal possibilities.

As the use of composite materials, specifically fiber-reinforced polymers (FRPs), has become more and more essential in many industries, most notably the transportation, civil engineering, energy, and consumer goods industries, the question of when and how composites will start to make an equally significant impact on the building industry is becoming more persistent. The question for the future of composites in architecture, then, is how best to marshal and direct the development of this new material technology toward the future of building.

opposite
The preface of the treatise De re aedificatoria by Leon Battista Alberti, circa 1485. Image from the Olomouc manuscript. De re aedificatoria was the first printed book on architecture, followed shortly thereafter by Vitruvius's De architectura, which, though written in antiquity and heavily influenced the structure of Alberti's treatise, was printed after the Alberti treatise.

LEONIS BAPTISTE ALBERTI DE RE AEDIFICA
TORIA INCIPIT. LEGE. FOELCITER
MULTAS ET VARIAS AR
tes quæ ad uitam bene & beate
agendam faciant summa indu
stria & diligentia conquisitas no
bis maiores nostri tradidere. Quæ
omnes & si ferant præ se quasi cer
tatim huc tendere. Ut plurimum
generi hominum prosint: tamen
habere innatum atq; insitum
eas intelligimus quippiam quo
singulæ singulos præ cæteris diuersosq; polliceri fructus uidean
tur. Namq; artes quidem alias necessitate sectamur: alias pro
bamus utilitate: aliæ uero quod tantum circa res cognitu grati
simas uersentur in prætio sunt. Quales autem hæ sint artes non
est ut prosequar: in promptu enim sunt. Verum si repetas ex om
ni maximarum artium numero nullam penitus inuenies quæ
non spretis reliquis suos quosdam & proprios fines petat & contem
pletur. Aut si tandem comperias ullam quæ cum huiusmodi sit
ut ea carere nullo pacto possis: tum & de se utilitatem uoluptati
dignitatiq; coniunctam præstet: meo iudicio ab earum numero
excludendam esse non duces architecturam. Namq; ea quidem
siquid rem diligentius pensitaris & publice & priuatim commo
dissima & uehementer gratissima generi hominum est: dignita
teq; inter primas non postrema. Sed antequam ultra progrediar expli
candum mihi censeo quemnam haberi uelim architectum. Non
enim tignarium adducam fabrum, quem tu summis cæterarum
disciplinarum uiris compares. Fabri enim manus architecto pro i
strumento est. Architectum ego hunc fore constituam qui certa
admirabiliq; ratione & uia: tum mente animoq; diffinire: tum &
opere absoluere didicerit quæcumq; ex ponderum motu corporumq;
compactione & coagmentatione dignissimis hominum usibus bel
lissime commodentur: quæ ut possint comprehensione & cogni
tione opus est rerum optimarum & dignissimarum. Itaq; huius

Conceptually, there are two ways to look at the potential future of composite materials in architecture. The first way is to view them as materials that can be substituted for other materials in conventional construction assemblies. Incremental improvements in building assemblies can be achieved through the replacement or re-engineering of specific building parts that benefit from the properties of composite materials. In this first path, cost is the essential driver. The second way to view composite materials can be as high-performance materials, offering completely new possibilities, due to their inherent properties surpassing those of alternative materials. Alongside these high-performance material properties, their systems and processes for fabrication are also high performing. Together, high-performance composite properties and processes offer new potential for the way buildings are designed, engineered, fabricated, and constructed, heralding a truly new way of building for the digital age.

The first path forward for composites, as a substitute for traditional materials, is already well underway. Composites have made significant, though varying, degrees of penetration toward the replacement of traditional building materials in many different conventional construction assemblies. Façades, curtain wall assemblies, window frames and trims, insulation, secondary structures, and interior elements are some of the many building components where the properties of composite materials offer advantages over legacy materials.

In these applications, the parameter that exerts the strongest pressure for adoption is cost. Here, the building industry can learn from civil engineering and transportation (among others) in adopting a lifecycle analysis/assessment (LCA) approach. This means quantifying the costs of a material choice to include material acquisition, installation logistics and scheduling, lifetime maintenance, lifespan, and any other ancillary costs. After the quantification of these considerations over a designed lifespan, composites may emerge as a self-evident material choice that has clear advantages.

Process. Axonometric diagram drawing by Peter Eisenman. Frank House (House VI). Cornwall Connecticut, 1973. Tape, ink, and screentone.

Detail view of composite rebar from Mateenbar, an alternative to steel concrete reinforcing bars. Besides the fact that composite rebar will not corrode, published technical information claims a tensile strength of 1,000 MPa (145 ksi) (roughly double that of steel) and specific weight of 2,100 kg/m^3 (131 lb/ft^3) (roughly a third that of steel).

A good example of this is the rebar used in reinforced concrete. Steel deteriorates rapidly when exposed to moisture, even when it is encased in concrete, leading to a loss of structural capacity over a relatively short time. Conventional countermeasures call for expensive epoxy-coated steel rebar, but new composite reinforcing bars offer a compelling alternative. Not only is the strength of this composite rebar comparable or greater, but durability is significantly improved, and the reduction in weight offers significant logistical and installation improvements (composite rebar can be carried by hand and does not require a crane to maneuver it). Over the lifetime of a structure, these improvements can be significant.

The example of composite usage in the civil infrastructure also addresses two common criticisms of polymer-based composites: the end-of-life issues and the high initial embodied energy. Both can best be assessed carefully with lifecycle (LCA) methods. The end-of-life processes for polymer-based materials can be an issue, due to their durability, for products with short or limited lifespans designed to be discarded (such as in plastic water bottles or packaging), but that durability becomes a positive when designing for buildings or structures that are intended to last forever, or for products that can be reused indefinitely. Here, the designed lifespan of the product aligns with the material property.

The second commonly noted criticism comes from the high initial embodied energy of composite materials. It should be noted that while a composite such as carbon fiber can embody more energy per unit volume than steel, it can also achieve multiple times the strength of steel at a fraction of the weight[6]. These properties may yield further efficiencies, depending on other project variables, such as where weight may have additional ancillary costs in transport or installation. A good example of this is the construction of the SFMOMA, where site constraints meant that erecting scaffolding around the exterior to install a conventional façade would have been prohibitive or extremely costly. By developing lightweight, unitized gFRP wall panels, the project team was able to hoist and install the exterior façade elements without scaffolding, all in one pass (as opposed to multiple passes for a typical sequentially phased assembly), contributing to reductions in cost and schedule. A careful understanding of all the properties of materials, in comparison to alternatives and with LCA methods, will help drive appropriate material choices.

When there is a revolution in materials, there will be a revolution in architecture.

Reinier de Graaf, Partner, Office for Metropolitan Architecture (OMA)

We are now in the middle of another revolution, a transition from the steel age to one dependent on other, more advanced materials.

L. C. Hollaway, University of Surrey

The second way of looking at the potential for composites in architecture is as high-performance materials offering new potentials due to superlative properties. This, coupled with the unique processes of fabrication for composite materials, can herald a completely new way of building that integrates design, digital technology, and fabrication capabilities. In contrast to the first way forward for composites (as a substitute for other materials driven by cost considerations), this way forward is driven by performance.

With composite materials, designers have taken advantage of their extraordinary properties to create structures such as the roof of the Steve Jobs Theater, which is strong and light enough to span 47 meters (155 feet), supported without a single column or wall, resting only on glass, and just 1.5 meters (5 feet) at the thickest point in the roof. Utilizing another notable property of carbon fiber and aramid (their almost perfect dimensional stability across vast thermal ranges), the Stedelijk Museum in Amsterdam features a seamless, jointless exterior façade stretching across 3,000 square meters (32,300 square feet). In the pavilions built by the Institute of Computational Design and Construction (ICD) and the Institute of Building Structures and Structural Design (ITKE) at the University of Stuttgart, students and faculty have collaborated to erect pavilions that, borrowing from biological sources of inspiration, explore ideas of integrated design and construction processes, material efficiency, and robotic construction. In all these projects, the performance and properties of composite materials allowed new architectural effects unachievable with any other material.

Process. Finite element analysis (FEA) used for form generation and structural/material engineering in the ICD/ITKE Pavilion of 2017.

Material properties

Carbon FRP
Young's modulus 80 GPa

Glass FRP
Young's modulus 24 GPa

Mixure
porosity 15 %
Young's modulus 40 GPa
specific weight 11 kN/m^3

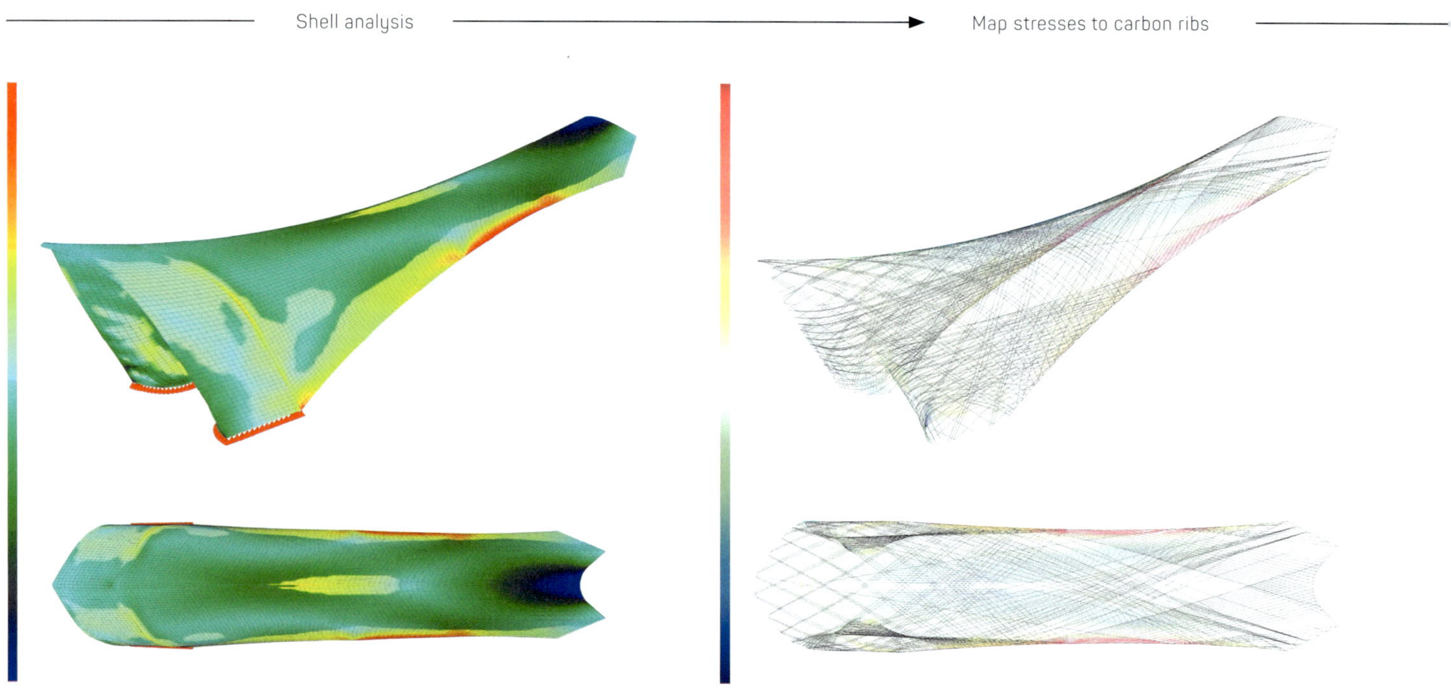

What these projects also demonstrate is a new diversity of formal design language made possible by composite materials. Some of them work from biological sources of inspiration, noting that nature almost exclusively uses fiber-reinforced composites for structures. Cellulose, chitin, collagen, and wood are all fiber-reinforced composites, and, with these, nature has achieved an astoundingly diverse language of design, structure, and functionality. As explicitly stated by the ICD/ITKE, their work "aims to transfer this biological principle of [a] load-adapted and thus highly-differentiated fiber composite system into architecture ... [in] an interdisciplinary exploration of biological principles together with the latest computational technologies."[7] Neri Oxman, who also works with material technology that draws from biological sources of inspiration, calls her area of research Material Ecology: "computational design, digital fabrication, synthetic biology, the environment, and the material itself as inseparable and harmonized dimensions of design."[8] All this work shares in common a pursuit of a materially efficient, computationally-driven architecture that brings with it new formal possibilities.

Beam analysis

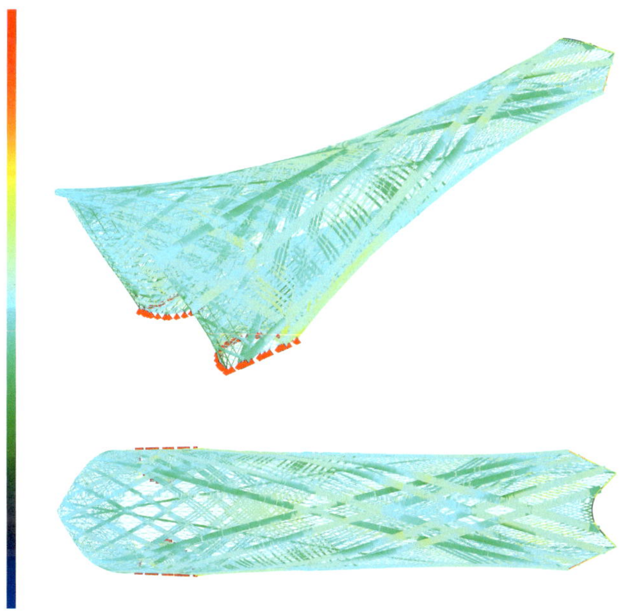

While these two futures for composites in architecture (cost-driven or performance-driven) may seem to be starting from opposite ends of a spectrum, in practice they may tend toward convergence. Developments from a design and performance-focused approach to architecture will symbiotically exchange ideas with the advancements made by a cost-driven world of construction. Substitution of composites for conventional materials will continue to occur more often incrementally, gradually replacing less suitable materials, in situations where proven appropriate. This convergence may well begin with the moment when novel architectural building systems utilizing composite technologies are delivered, in situations that can accommodate them.

We are coming to a time where technology and thinking are perhaps not so separate anymore, and a need to re-examine the methodologies of design is apparent.[9]

Phillip Bernstein, *Architecture Design Data*

To best prepare the field of architecture to be a part of this future means addressing some of the disciplinary inertia in both practice and education. The architect's role in building has always been fluid (nowhere has that been better documented and explicated than in Andrew Saint's book, *Architect and Engineer: A Sibling Rivalry*). This fluidity is due in part to the evolving nature of building technology and the architect's capabilities within that technological milieu.

As Andrew Saint explains, this is perhaps best exemplified in the changing nature of the architect's instrument of service: the architectural drawing. It was not so long ago that large-scale, complex buildings were documented with only a handful of drawings. Today, even very small projects require drawings that number in the triple digits, to say nothing of the specifications book, a complementary text document forming part of any project's complete set of instructions, also voluminous. The percentage of documents serving only architectural purposes are diminishing in proportion to those provided by the systems engineers or consultants—the structural, mechanical, electrical, plumbing, landscape, fire protection, façade, sustainability, specialty equipment, and other professionals involved in the building.

The idea persists that the architect, as master builder, is in control of everything about the building. But this idea is increasingly unrealistic and may impede the development of buildings, which are now so much more advanced than those built decades or centuries ago. "The traditional notion of an architect having a vision of a building and then drawing it either on paper or on a computer and then constructing it isn't really how architecture works and in reality the computer has a lot of influence on design,"[10] says Michael Hansmeyer.

The complex reality of contemporary architectural production necessitates a very high degree of specialization at an increasing number of points, and the productive exchange of vast quantities of data and information is more conducive to this future of construction than any single master builder. A productive and effective architect will not be a master in the traditional sense of the term, but a facilitator—one who can manage complex processes, and harness and deploy resources toward prioritized ends, while remaining sensitive to the diverse and varied goals of any particular building project.

Similarly, architectural education will need to adapt. As recent as certain technologies are in architecture, almost as recent is the idea of an academic institution granting degrees in architecture. The Massachusetts Institute of Technology (MIT) offered the first course of study in architecture situated within a university in 1868 and incorporated the School of Architecture in 1932.[11] The discipline's academic curriculum and pedagogy dances on the boundary between art and science, and venerable institutions granting those degrees have their own set of autonomous goals, quite distinct from the practical world of architecture and construction. Much of this can be exemplified by the ability of a graduate architecture student to converse about the finer points of deconstructivist theory, or generate bogglingly complex projective geometries, but be unfamiliar with the construction of a common wall assembly.

Surprising as it may be to many outside the building professions, there has been a longstanding divide between architecture and engineering (within which one may include material sciences). As Patrik Schumacher writes: "This dividing line emerged over the last 200 years and finally resulted in two distinct, autonomous, even incommensurable discourses … the demarcation between architecture/design versus engineering/science is sharply drawn and ultra-stable. We should not expect any discursive synthesis here. Instead we should expect and work toward the clarification and further sharpening of the demarcation, in terms of the distinct competencies and criteria of success of each side."[12]

The Fountainhead.
Dir. King Vidor. Henry Blanke Productions/Warner Bros. Studio, 1949.
This film popularizes a characterization of architects as independent and uncompromising.

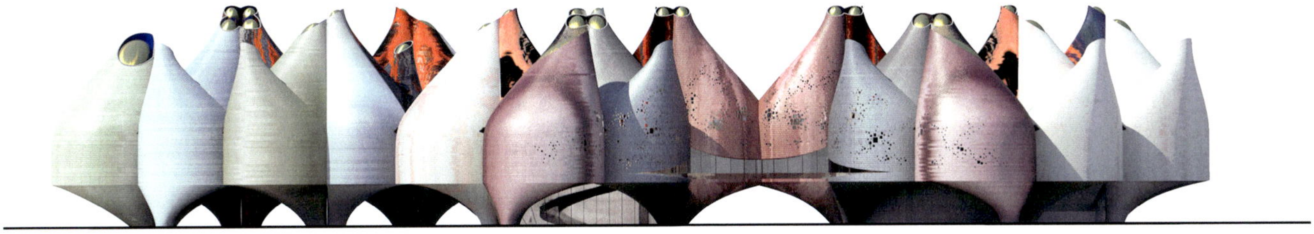

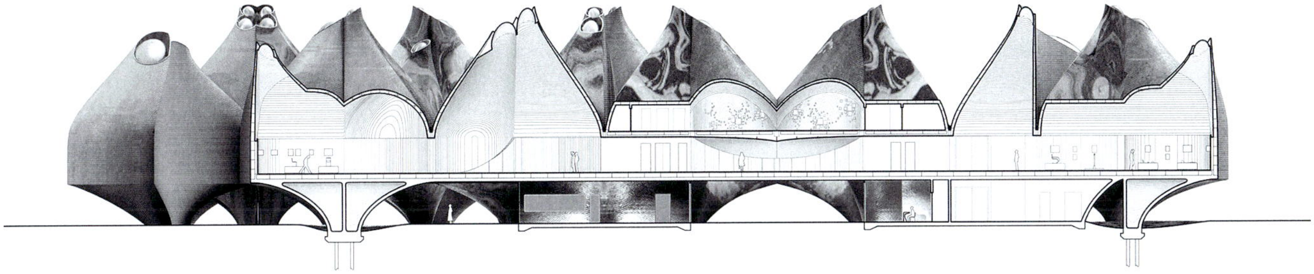

Competition winning entry for the Bauhaus Museum, "Vessel Collective" by Young & Ayata. Each of the vessels was imagined as "clad with small dimension sintered glass tiles made from recycled car windshields".

Joris Laarman. The Bone Chair, 2006. Cast aluminum. Design for the chair began in 1998 in partnership with Adam Opel GmbH, a German subsidiary of General Motors. Using new imaging and simulation software developed with the intent of creating more efficient engine parts that provide optimum strength using a minimum of materials, the Joris Laarman lab repeated generations of the software simulation to develop this form that could be cast in aluminum.

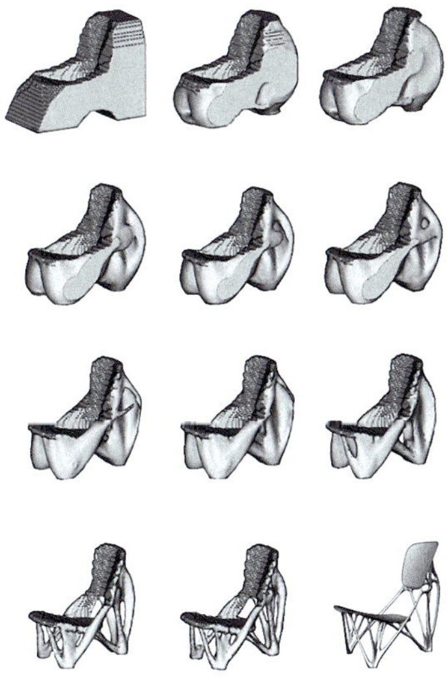

In partnership with Autodesk, the Dutch development and construction company, Van Wijnen explored generative design tools at an urban level. "The project involved the design of a geometric model that could meet the local building code constraints (such as number and location of access streets, setbacks, parking rules, etc.), and satisfy the developer's requirements (such as amount of two-story residential units and apartment buildings). Urban design problems generally present many stakeholders, often representing conflicting requirements and interests, thus intensifying the complexity of the design. Generative design is able to aid the management and structuring of such complexity through the definition of the goals." An evolutionary process quickly generated multiple solutions with measurable outcomes in each of several categories established by the developers.

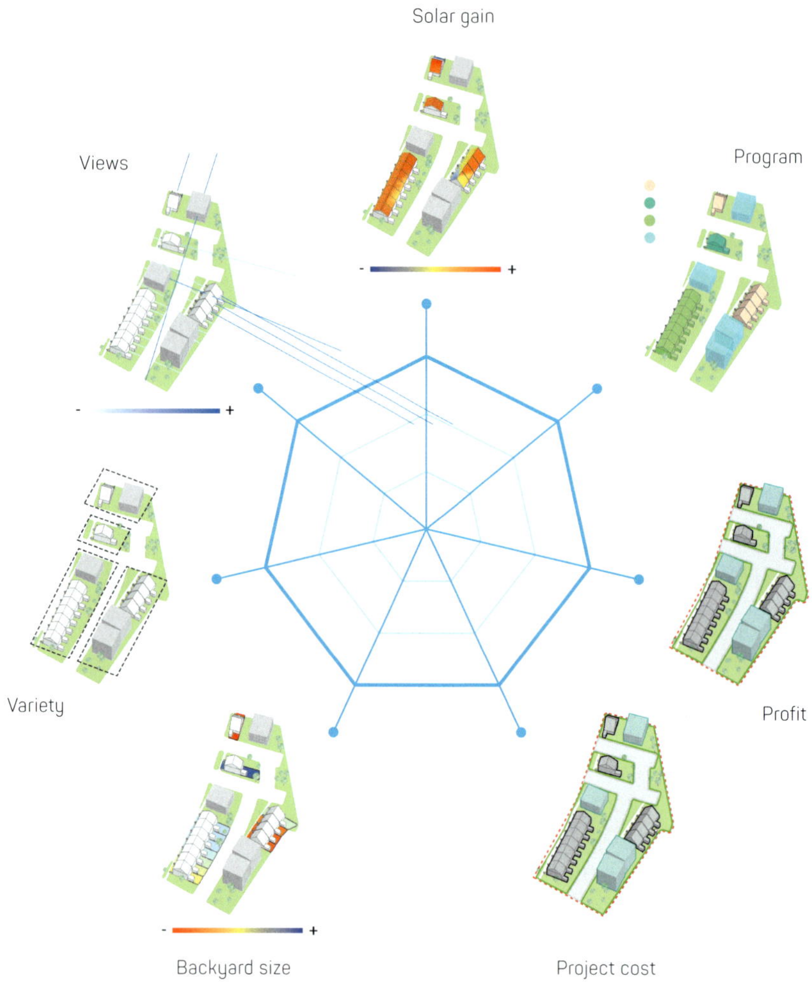

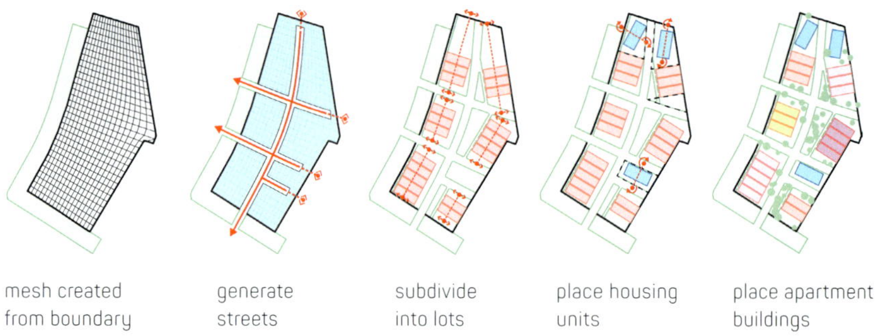

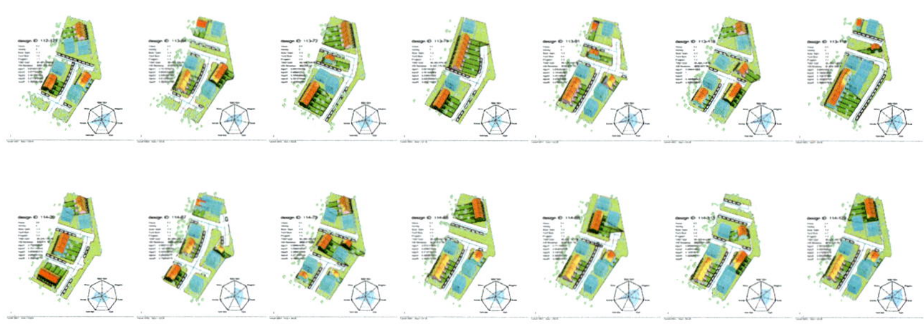

Die Zauberflöte (The Magic Flute), directed by Romeo Castellucci, La Monnaie, Brussels, 2018. The set design by Michael Hansmeyer is entirely 3D printed.

Though this statement may seem extreme and polemical, it may accurately describe the nature of the current working relationship between architecture and technology. In fact, the roots of this conceptual divide may be traceable even further back than what Mr. Schumacher wrote, all the way back to Alberti, who separated design (*lineamenta*) and material (*natura*), or Vasari, who argued for the concept of *disegno*. This disciplinary division still manifests in many ways, from education to professional practice, and has had potentially far-reaching implications.

The "further sharpening of the demarcation [between architecture/design and engineering/science]" may be a counterproductive position when it comes to readying architects for a future spent navigating a professional environment soon to be dominated by new technological tools. Moving forward, the discipline of architecture needs to better incorporate technology into its education, practice, and theory. A moderated and controlled amount of exposure to the realities of professional architectural and building practices, along with encouraged collaborations with technical departments, would be of most benefit, while still keeping intact the sense of curiosity and imagination that is necessary for innovative research and exploration.

Once we enter into what happens when a structure is actually assembled in any age, we find designing and making, architecture and engineering, art and science muddled up together so constantly and utterly that a once-and-for-all process of dissociation in an age of reason or enhanced technology appears implausible.[13]

Andrew Saint, *Architect & Engineer: A Sibling Rivalry*

Within all of this, what is often overlooked is the role of building regulations in shaping the final form of the built environment. Though the idea of building codes is ancient, their shape, specificity, structure, and legislative reach is distinctly new. In the US, the International Code Council (ICC), which publishes the codes adopted by most jurisdictions, was incorporated in 1994. Their history serving insurance underwriters has inculcated an understandably conservative approach to building compliance. Currently, building code regulations govern the compliance of architectural elements as small as the diameter of a handrail, and approved materials are prescribed in specific assemblies. Improvements in the efficiency and efficacy of building codes and regulations will need to be re-examined closely in order to attain the goal of fostering building innovation while maintaining the safeguards on public health and welfare.

Lastly, it bears repeating that the issues brought forth by new technologies and the debate about sustainability have broadened the viable spectrum of ambitions for any architectural project, including goals within socio-cultural, economic, and ecological realms. Throughout the course of human history, we have developed the ability to understand, synthesize, and manipulate materials at increasingly micro and macro levels. Alongside this has been a growing, though certainly not complete, appreciation for the impact those material manipulations have on the larger world. It may be important to remember the humble fact that the impacts and effects of some of these architectural goals may be quantifiable, and some may not (either currently or inherently). As we continue to refine and clarify our goals for any human endeavor, especially within the noble practice of building, it is important to keep in mind the responsibility all of us have toward our larger environment. Those involved with architecture and construction have chosen a profession that is directly responsible for the built world, and that is a role we should cherish. Optimism for the future should be a prerequisite. As Winston Churchill famously said, "We shape our buildings and afterwards our buildings shape us."[14]

1. Smil 2014.
2. Paul M. Romer. "Endogenous Technological Change." *The Journal of Political Economy, Vol. 98, No. 5, Part 2: The Problem of Development: A Conference of the Institute for the Study of Free Enterprise Systems.* (Oct., 1990), pp. S71–S102
3. Wilk, Christopher. *Plywood: a material story*. London: Thames & Hudson Victoria and Albert Museum, 2017.
4. Wilk.
5. Bernstein 2018, 26.
6. Extrapolated from data provided by Ansys Granta, Ltd. Differing methodologies of calculating embodied energy, classes and grades of materials, and other factors can make more precise comparisons difficult.
7. From the ICD Buga Fiber Pavilion press release, 2019.
8. Neri Oxman. "Towards a material ecology." World Economic Forum address, 17 Jan 2016. Accessed from [https://www.weforum.org/agenda/2016/01/towards-a-material-ecology/].
9. Bernstein 2018, 8.
10. "Sci-fi 'gothic' architecture brought to life" by Laura Allsop, www.cnn.com. April 8, 2011.
11. https://libraries.mit.edu/mithistory/research/schools-and-departments/school-of-architecture-and-planning/ [accessed 9/5/2019].
12. Patrik Schumacher, London 2012. "The Profound Social Instrumentality of the Built Environment." Published in: Catalogue/book 'Stefan Polonyi – Bearing Lines – Bearing Surfaces', MAI – Museum für Architektur und Ingenieurkunst NRW e. V., Ed. Ursula Kleefisch-Jobst et al., Edition Axel Menges, Stuttgart/London 2012. Accessed from [https://www.patrikschumacher.com/Texts/] 7 May 2019.
13. Saint, 492.
14. Speech to the House of Commons on October 28, 1943.

Young & Ayata. Base Flowers. Multimaterial 3D print, Resin, Full color sandstone, 2015.

CASE STUDIES

CASE STUDIES
EXTERIORS

previous page
Interior view of the Ding Concert Hall with large interior FRP "sails" designed for acoustic performance.

SF MO MA

SFMOMA

Museum

San Francisco, USA

2015

Architectural ambition

The SFMOMA utilizes an FRP exterior façade to achieve two significant feats: a lightweight, materially distinctive, and geometrically complex exterior form, and the satisfaction of US building code-required fire-testing for the use of FRP as an exterior building material in a high-rise building.

In 2010, architects Snøhetta won an international competition to expand the San Francisco Museum of Modern Art (SFMOMA). At the time, the SFMOMA occupied a stand-alone building designed by Mario Botta in the South of Market neighborhood (SOMA). The Botta building, which was completed in 1995, was part of a city-generated arts district masterplan that was intended to revitalize the neighborhood, which at the time had little pedestrian activity and lots of industrial/commercial buildings and parking lots.

The original Botta building thus took an inward-facing stance with regards to its environs; largely opaque, its brick-clad concrete and stone façades gave an impression of stability, protection, and remove from the streets. Its large internal atrium was a quiet space accessible only to those who could purchase tickets. In the time since its completion, it had come to be an iconic symbol of both the institution and neighborhood, but the city and surrounding area had changed. This presented an opportunity for the institution and its selected architect to re-envision and reshape the buildings' engagement with the public and its surrounding area.

SFMOMA and Snøhetta's goals were to increase public engagement with the institution, taking advantage of the neighborhood's transformation into a lively pedestrian and commercial zone. They wanted to complement the original Botta building, but to counteract some of the building's inward-facing nature, creating public urban spaces and re-energizing pedestrian zones in the immediately adjacent streets. In short, they wanted to create an architecture that expressed permanence, openness, and lightness in equal measure.

opposite
Exterior view showing the gFRP cladding panels.

Design and engineering

The architects, in collaboration with Enclos and Kreysler & Associates, found FRP to be a material well-suited to achieve these goals. As the architects state: "[FRP] is inherently light, but when finished with a cementitious layer, it can take on a monumentality akin to the Botta building, which uses a thin layer of brick mounted on unitized panels to create the perception of a masonry building. We were also drawn to FRP for its fabrication and geometric capabilities. The texture and expressive capabilities of the material, along with how its geometry works at several scales, were key to why we chose it as the material."

FRP is used as the primary façade material on the entirety of the eastern and western façades of the expansion project. The design of those façades is probably best explained by the architects themselves: "It was designed to be evocative of the natural processes of the Bay Area, visually embodying the ephemera of sunlight, fog, wind, and water. Its distinctive rippled geometry is dynamic in all types of light, and its cantilevered and double-curved form maximizes daylight and clear space in the public realm at ground level. This increased daylight access combines with a new public pedestrian circulation pathway and a highly transparent façade to beckon and welcome visitors to the expanded museum.

"The unique rippled surface is naturally animated by the movement of light and shadow throughout the day. The double-curved shape and ripples combine with the strong, clear light of the Bay Area to ensure that the building has a constantly varying profile and brightness. The panels provide a human scale as people approach. Crisp, clean smooth facets at the thinner north and south ends of the building, composed of opaque glass, provide a polished counterpoint to the east and west rippled FRP surfaces, suggesting the merging of natural processes and human made intentional action in one shape. The resulting light sculptural mass quickly signifies the uniqueness of the building, its contents and its purpose."[1]

Early studies for material options looked at glass fiber reinforced concrete (GFRC) as well as high-performance concrete (i. e. Ductal), but the team quickly discovered that FRP allowed for a significant reduction in weight over alternative materials, which in turn translated into cost savings. The FRP was lightweight, about 5 lb/ft^2 (24.4 kg/m^2), which allowed it to be shop-fabricated onto a standard unitized curtain wall system.

This allowed several benefits: the panels could be installed in a single pass by crane, since site constraints precluded scaffolding, and multiple passes were cost prohibitive. But also, it reduced the number of specialized contractors needed to install a typical unitized rainscreen façade. The reduced weight enabled by FRP had cascading impacts, reducing the overall weight of the building, eliminating an estimated 1 million pounds (454 tonnes) of steel, allowing fewer structural columns and braces on the interior, increasing the size and flexibility of the gallery spaces, and ultimately reduced project costs.

1 Interview with Snøhetta architects Samuel Brissette, Chad Carpenter, Aaron Dorf, Lara Kaufman, and Jon McNeal. Feb 22, 2019.

Fabrication and construction

Each of the 710 FRP rainscreen panels is unique, some as large as 1.5 m wide and 9 m long, and together they cover about 55,000 ft² (5110 m²) across the façades and 11 stories in height. The finish layer, a rough grained sandy white cementitious material, is composed of a 1/16 in (1.59 mm) thick polymer coating composed mostly of polyester resin, sand, and additives for UV stability and fire resistance. The color was the result of a custom mixed batch of locally sourced sand and polyester resin.

The fiberglass buildup behind the finish coat is a roughly 3/16 in (4.76 mm) thick layer of roving glass fiber and polyester resin. The rippled geometry was developed in part to provide a degree of self-reinforcement and wind load resistance, but was also supported by a visually concealed lightweight aluminum frame, which also served as the connection point to the unitized aluminum curtain wall.

While the high number of unique panels, each of which required custom tooling, would seem to be cost prohibitive, Kreysler was able to innovate a few methods in order to economically achieve this goal. The tooling was made of expanded polystyrene (EPS) foam, which was lightweight, inexpensive, machinable, and recyclable. In addition, the foam tooling was able to serve as handling cradles for shipping and transport.

The FRP fabrication methods also enabled high-precision geometry. The panels were all prefabricated based on designs generated by Snøhetta using Rhino3d and Grasshopper, which were then given to Kreysler for finite element analysis (FEA) and tool-path generation. Surface fidelity was estimated to be within 1.5 in over the entire 11-story height of the museum.

As this project constituted the largest architectural use of FRP in a US building project, it was subject to and passed NFPA 285 full-scale fire regulation testing. This marks the first time FRPs have been approved for use in such an application.

Maintenance of the FRP panels is accomplished with roof-mounted building maintenance units (BMU) for cleaning. Full-scale mockup testing for a range of impact and ballistic scenarios, including driving a forklift into the panels, left the building team satisfied with the panels' performance, along with the knowledge that repairs would be relatively easy to patch.

Conclusion

The FRP panels offered this project a range of benefits. Flexibility in design, panel size, form, and finish, as well as the cascading benefits of low weight, from ease of erection to reduction in structure and ultimately costs meant that FRP was instrumental in making this project a success.

South elevation.

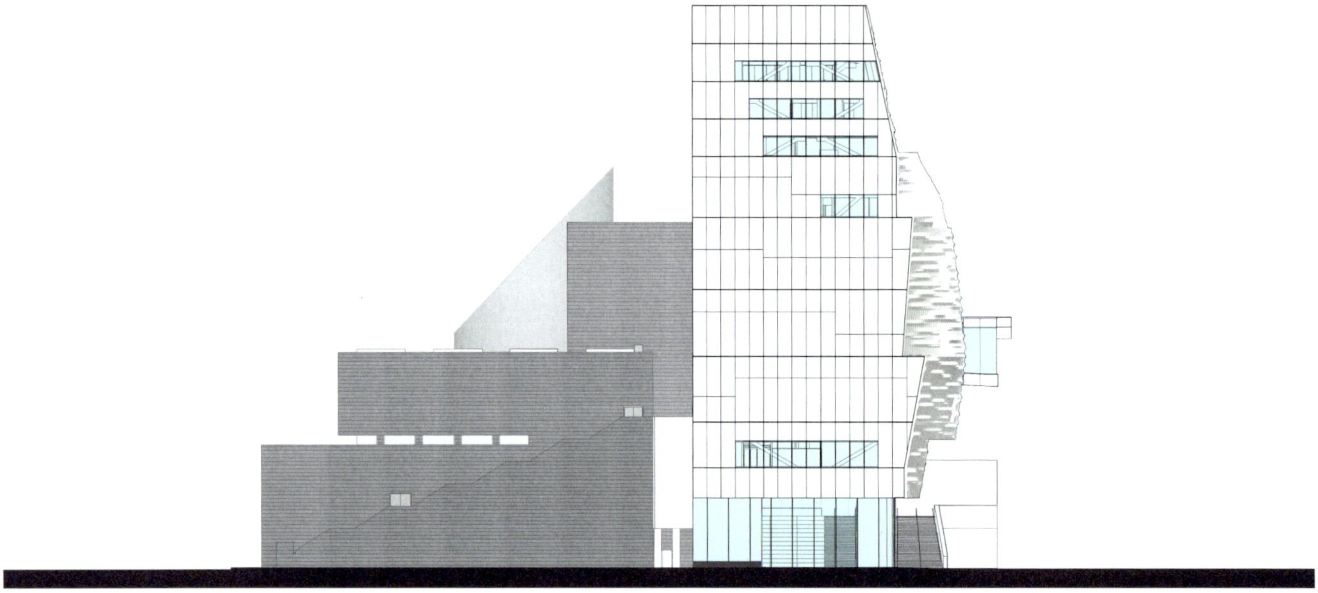

West elevation.

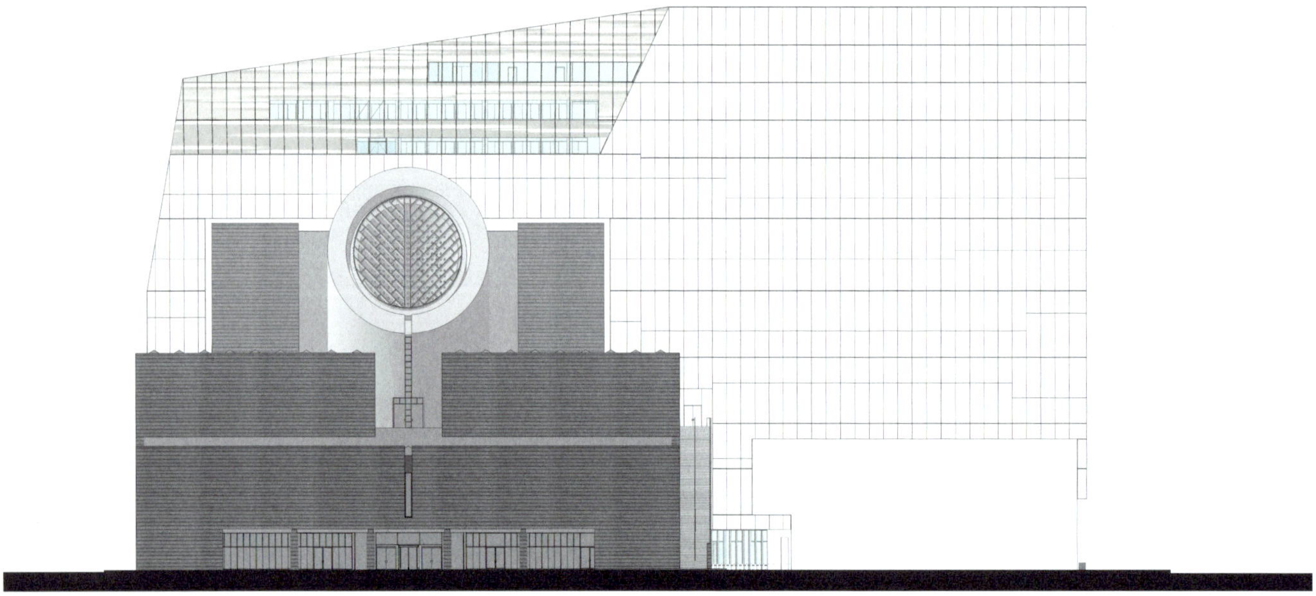

Site plan.

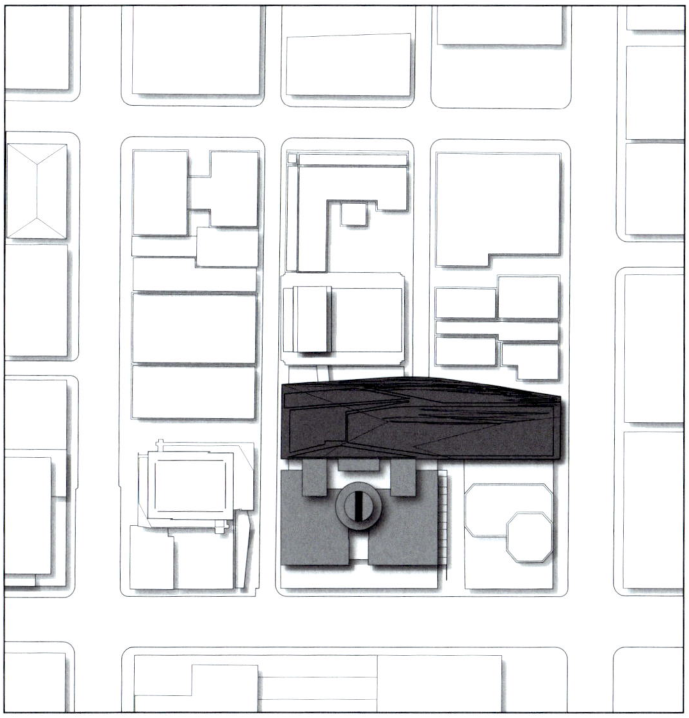

East elevation.

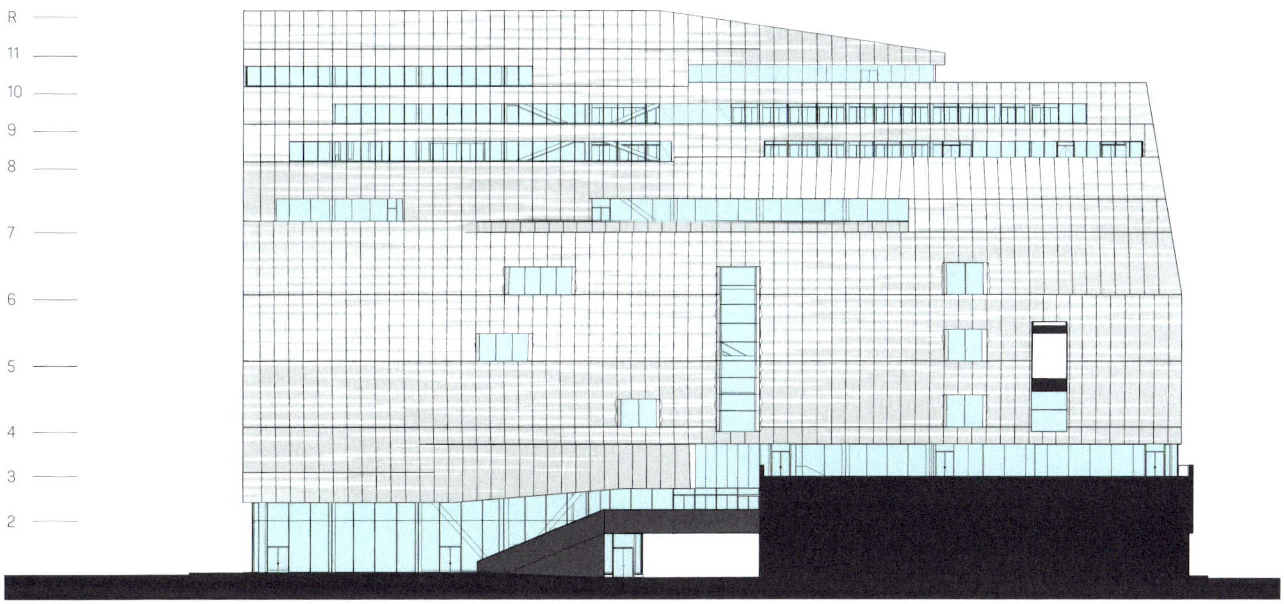

FRP mold preparation; sandblasting of FRP panels at shop facility; packaging and hoisting of FRP panels for trucking to site.

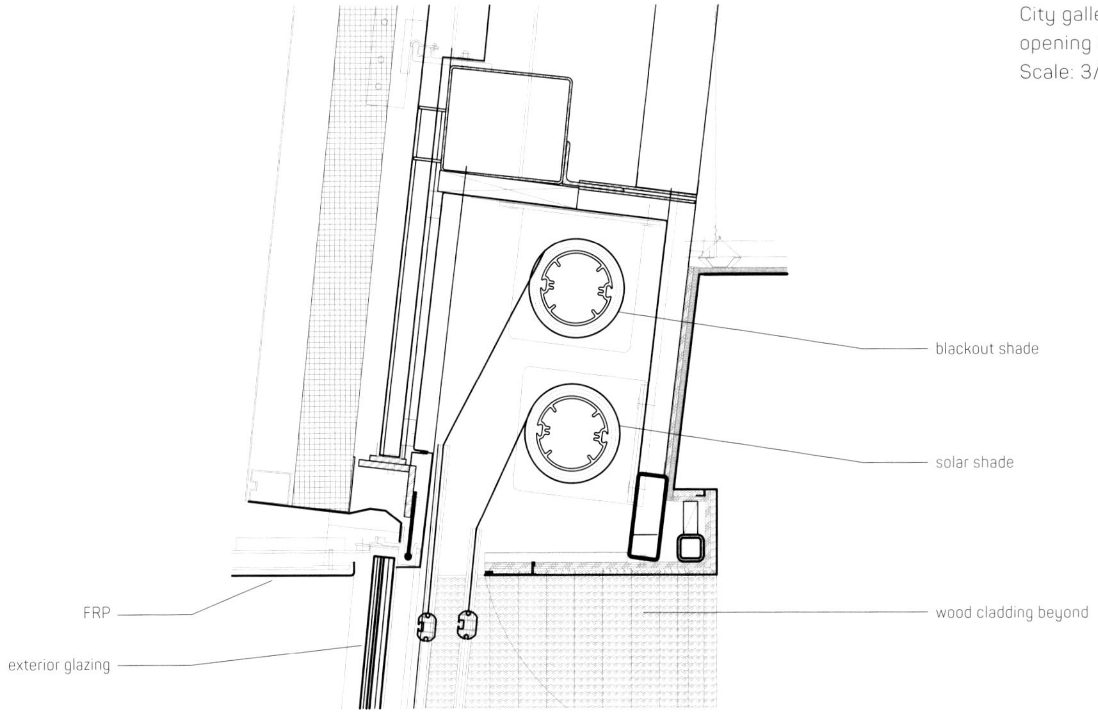

City gallery cased
opening head
Scale: 3/4″ = 1′–0″

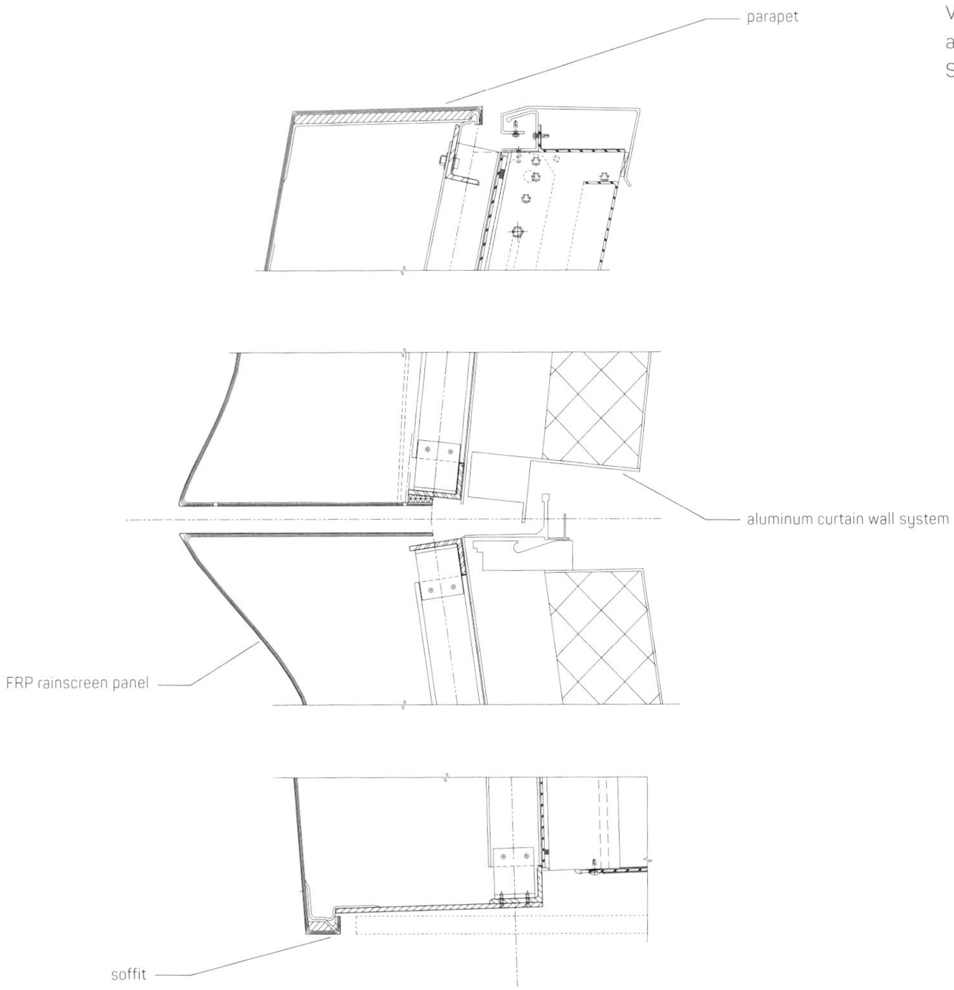

Vertical section detail
at panel joint
Scale: 1.5″ = 1′–0″

left
Detail view of finished exterior FRP wall panels.

bottom
Construction photo: erection of unitized FRP wall panels.

top
Construction photo: erection of unitized FRP wall panels.

bottom
Erection of unitized FRP wall panels above the entrance and sculpture terrace.

Exterior view of the museum showing the east elevation composed of gFRP façade panels.

HEYDAR ALIYEV CENTER

Mixed-use cultural center

Baku, Azerbaijan

2012

Architectural ambition

The Heydar Aliyev Center by Zaha Hadid Architects is perhaps the most fully realized, uncompromised, and ambitious example of the late Iraqi-born architect's design vision. The Center, designed following an international competition run by the post-Soviet Republic of Azerbaijan, aspired to "express the sensibilities of the Azeri culture and the optimism of a nation that looks to the future."[1]

The client, the Republic of Azerbaijan, asked for a national culture center containing galleries, a museum, and a 1,000-seat auditorium on a large parcel of land just outside the main part of the capital city, Baku. Also made clear was the desire for a building capable of serving as an icon and destination for this central Asian republic to the rest of the world.

From the architects: "The design of the Heydar Aliyev Center establishes a continuous, fluid relationship between its surrounding plaza and the building's interior. The plaza, as the ground surface; accessible to all as part of Baku's urban fabric, rises to envelop an equally public interior space and defines a sequence of event spaces dedicated to the collective celebration of contemporary and traditional Azeri culture. Elaborate formations such as undulations, bifurcations, folds, and inflections modify this plaza surface into an architectural landscape that performs a multitude of functions: welcoming, embracing, and directing visitors through different levels of the interior. With this gesture, the building blurs the conventional differentiation between architectural object and urban landscape, building envelope and urban plaza, figure and ground, interior and exterior."[2]

opposite
Main entrance exterior photo.

Design and engineering

The outer skin is the most distinctive and complex engineering feature of the building. A combination of glass fiber-reinforced concrete (GFRC) and glass fiber-reinforced polymer (gFRP) panels form the exterior surface, supported by a steel space frame substructure on top of a concrete superstructure. The space-frame substructure essentially mediates between the flowing, continuous shapes of the exterior skin and the primary load-carrying function of the concrete.

"Our ambition was to achieve a surface so continuous that it appears homogenous,"[3] requiring the coordination of multiple complex functions within that architectural envelope; gFRP was chosen as an ideal cladding (siding) material because it allows "for the powerful plasticity of the building's design while responding to very different functional demands related to a variety of situations: plaza, transitional zones and envelope."[4] Advanced computational modeling was a prerequisite to control and communicate geometric information across all the design team partners, including fabricators and contractors.

Fabrication and construction

Engineering consultancy Werner Sobek, appointed by the contractor DiA as façade consultant, began by recommending a space-frame construction for the exterior cladding. Werner Sobek ended up with scope that included the curtain walls, interior skin, and glass balustrades, among other responsibilities. The demands of the geometry, along with live and dead loads, material expansion, and construction tolerances, led the consultants to a solution that involved "a single-movement joint separating concrete slabs, space frames, and other components into two sections. In addition, expansion and contraction of finishing materials, such as the external and internal skin, are visually suppressed or absorbed into uniform, if not always regular, panel joints and the extent of off-site fabrication is maximized to optimize quality control and precision."[5] The interstitial space frame became a crucial component of the structure, mediating between the outer skin and the secondary support structures, involving "labor-intensive site work" and fine-tuning of the final mounting and fixing points.

Cladding manufacturer Arabian Profile initially set out to manufacture glass fiber-reinforced concrete panels for the plaza and parts of the external envelope rain screen, before proposing gFRP. The gFRP panels, made of hollow fiberglass instead of concrete, halved the production times and reduced the weight by 80 percent. Rigorous testing to match the gFRP to the previously completed GFRC panels was conducted before proceeding.

Microchips attached to the 13,000 gFRP panels and 3,150 GFRC panels (a total of over 16,000 exterior cladding panels) eased fabrication and installation logistics. At the peak of assembly, 70 unique gFRP panels were produced per day.

1 Bekiroglu.
2 Bekiroglu.
3 Bekiroglu.
4 Bekiroglu.
5 Mara.

Conclusion

Zaha Hadid Architects responded to the desires of a republic with an amazing design and technical achievement made possible, in part, by the material expediencies of gFRP.

Site plan.

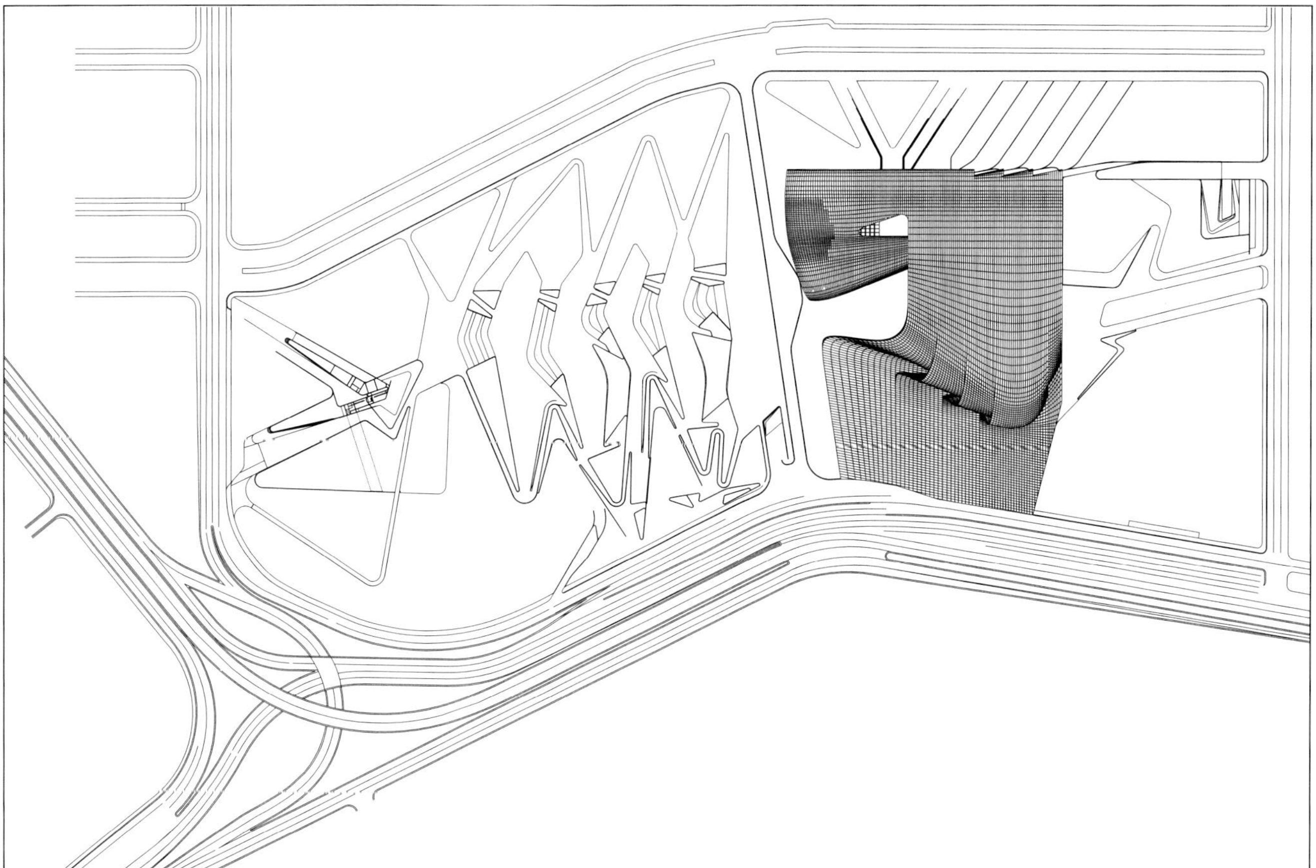

Section, showing concrete, space frame construction and cladding.

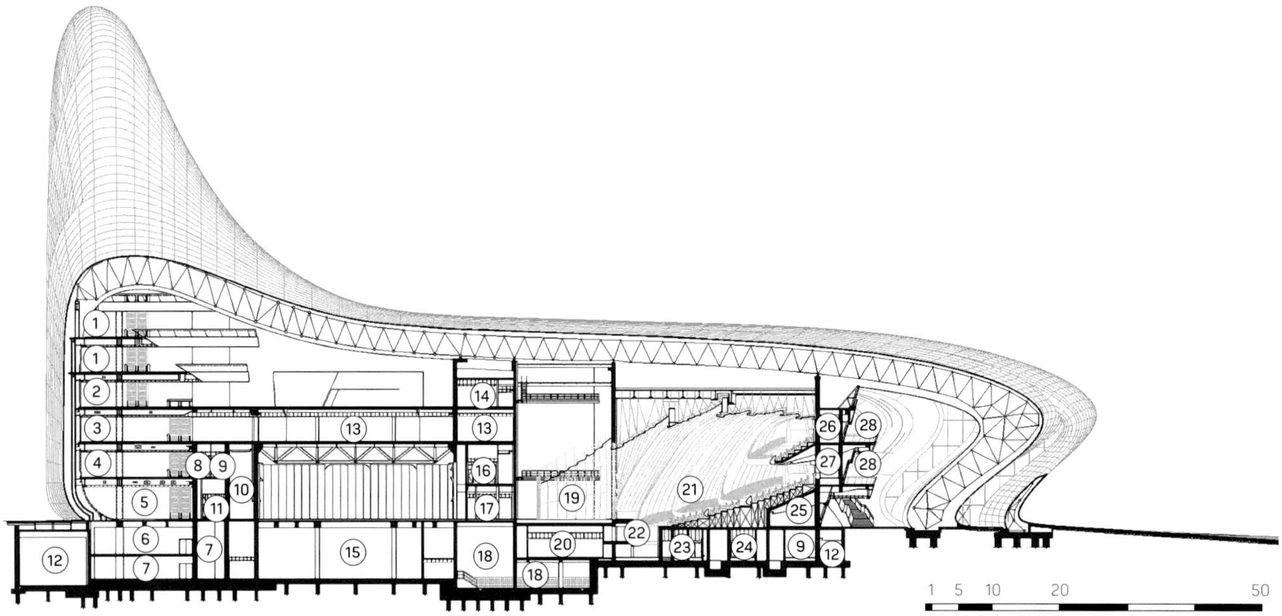

1 Learning and reading zone
2 Multimedia zone
3 Business zone
4 Children's activity zone
5 Welcome zone
6 Library storage
7 Library stack
8 Disabled restroom
9 Janitor's room
10 Conference center lobby
11 Women's restroom
12 Loading bay
13 Meeting room
14 Network room
15 Auditorium / Multipurpose hall storage
16 Men's restroom
17 Service kitchen
18 AHU room
19 Main stage
20 Backstage storage
21 Auditorium
22 Orchestra pit
23 Guest dressing room
24 Women's locker room / WC
25 Cloakroom
26 Translator room
27 Projection room
28 Balcony

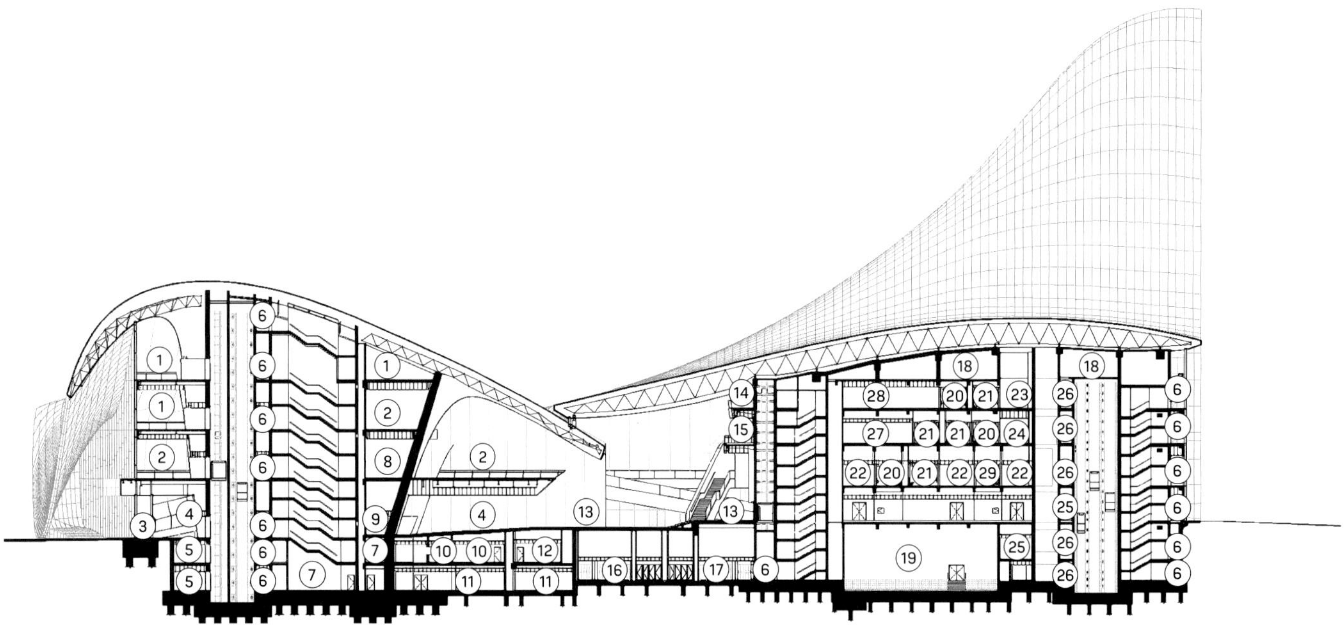

1 Permanent collection gallery
2 Temporary exhibition gallery
3 Security vestibule
4 Museum lobby
5 President / VIP lobby
6 Vestibule
7 Storage
8 Small temporary gallery / darkroom
9 Welcome gallery
10 Cloakroom
11 Registration and art handling
12 Medical room
13 Conference center lobby
14 Organizer's office
15 Meeting room lobby
16 Men's shower / locker room
17 Women's shower / locker room
18 Fan room
19 AHU room
20 Men's restroom
21 Women's restroom
22 Control room
23 Administration offices
24 Mezzanine café
25 Service lobby
26 Janitor's room
27 Meeting room
28 Network room
29 Disabled room

The Heydar Aliyev Center during construction, with the steel space frame and portions of the sheathing visible. The gFRP composite finish panels were then mounted on this space frame.

Exterior view showing the exterior cladding composed of GFRC and gFRP panels.

KOLON ONE & ONLY TOWER

Corporate and research headquarters

Seoul, South Korea

2018

opposite
View looking up at the gFRP sun-shading elements.

Architectural ambition

This building houses the corporate headquarters and research facilities of the Kolon Group, a corporation with business involvements in textiles, chemicals, sustainable technologies, clothing, and fashion based in Seoul, South Korea.

Morphosis was selected to design the building as an expression of Kolon's "commitment to sustainability, technology, and culture."[1] Housing 38 internal divisions across research, manufacturing, and industrial design functions, the building includes office, laboratory, and social spaces designed to maximize interactivity and exchange. The primary visual signature from the exterior is the *brise-soleil* sun-shading elements.

Parametrically shaped to balance daylight, shade, and views, these exterior sun-shading façade elements are "both the performative and symbolic feature of the building." The gFRP façade units incorporate Kolon's proprietary aramid fabric, selected for its structural properties and design capabilities. Fronting a major park in the business hub of Magok, the building architecturally communicates the Kolon Group's commitment to technological innovation, design, and sustainability.

Design and engineering

After initial investigation of metal and GFRC alternatives, gFRP was chosen for the sun-shading elements due to its "ability to be formed into complex shapes, durability, and its high strength-to-weight ratio. The use of gFRP allowed for the iconic and continuous, fabric-like sun-shade assembly which has no visible subframing."[2] Careful repetition of panel types allowed for fabrication consistency and economy of scale across all the parts.

Indeed, it is the unique shape of the sun-shading elements and the way they are deployed across the majority of the west-facing façade that gives the building its distinctiveness. Approximately 3.0 m × 3.2 m in size, they were parametrically designed (with assistance from Gehry Technologies and façade consultants ARUP) to adjust to continuing insights gained from material investigations and mockups. As Stan Su, Director of Enclosure Design at Morphosis, stated, "As it [gFRP] is not a typical material used in façade construction, the design team invested much time in investigations and mockups to understand the material's capabilities and potential for use within an exterior façade."[3]

Another design consideration had to do with codes and fire performance; local regulations in South Korea require all materials above 6 stories to be non-flammable; however, the gFRP sun-shades were considered ornamental and thus outside those restrictions (per drawings the Kolon One & Only Tower is 8 stories tall). Nevertheless, the design team and engineers worked with the gFRP supplier to develop and test a laminate buildup that would exceed local code-required flammability, flame-spread, and fire-retardancy indices.

Fabrication and construction

The sun-shading gFRP elements were fabricated using a hand lay-up vacuum infusion process (VIP) with Kolon's own aramid fiber. Male plugs (positive forms), also made of gFRP for durability, were CNCed and digitally scanned for geometric accuracy. A two-piece gFRP part was then fabricated from those plugs, joined with a minimal joint, and then fitted with mounting hardware and temporary lifting rings. Though the elements were lightweight, hoisting and maneuvering them was complicated by their irregular geometry. This was addressed by using temporary lifting rings at key balance points.

Adhesive and mechanical attachments joined the gFRP part to the stainless-steel mounting plates at each "arm" of the sun-shading elements; this will allow maintenance, removal, or replacement of each sun-shade part when required.

The design emphasized a reading of continuous skin, which meant minimizing the seam between the two gFRP pieces and the connections to the stainless-steel mounting components. The detailing of the monocoque construction had to consider weather intrusion, and vents were introduced to induce airflow and allow any moisture to evacuate.

1 Su, Stan. Interview with the author, May 2019.
2 Su.
3 Su.

Conclusion

A building designed and constructed to visually broadcast a high-tech company's commitment to design, technology, and sustainability chose functional gFRP components to achieve a design esthetic and functional performance impossible with any other material.

Location plan.

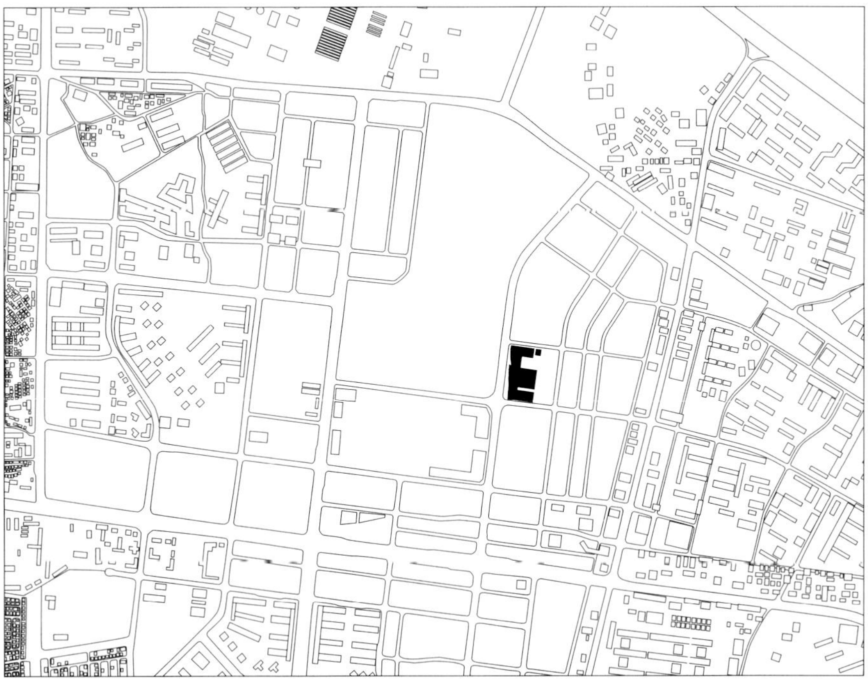

West elevation.

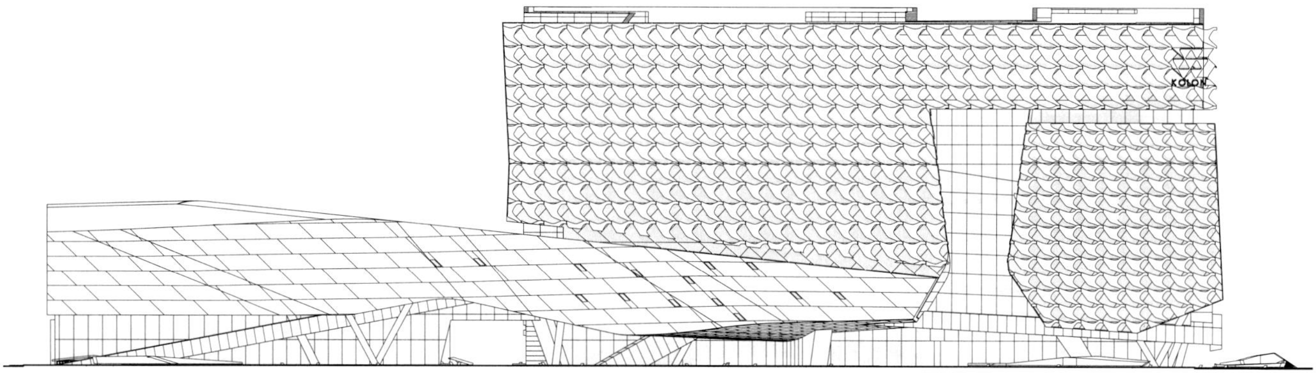

North elevation.

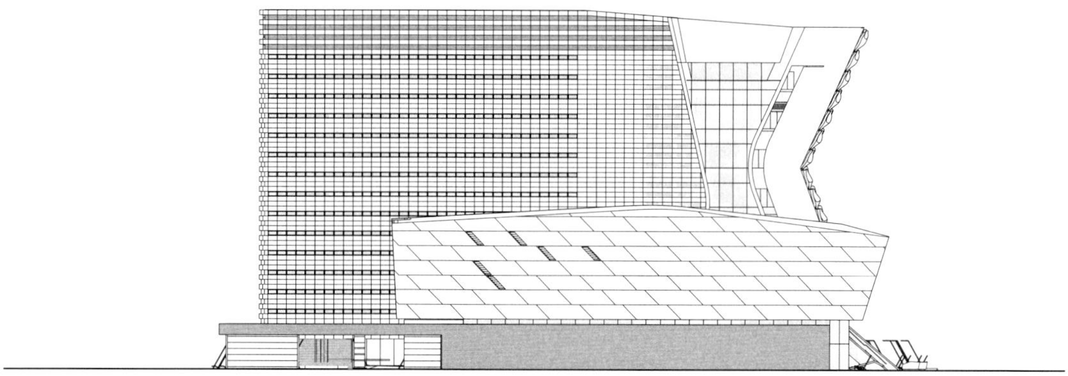

South elevation.

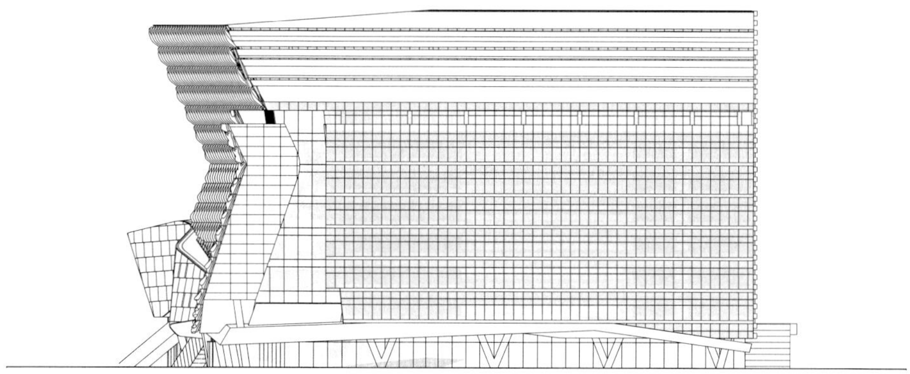

East elevation.

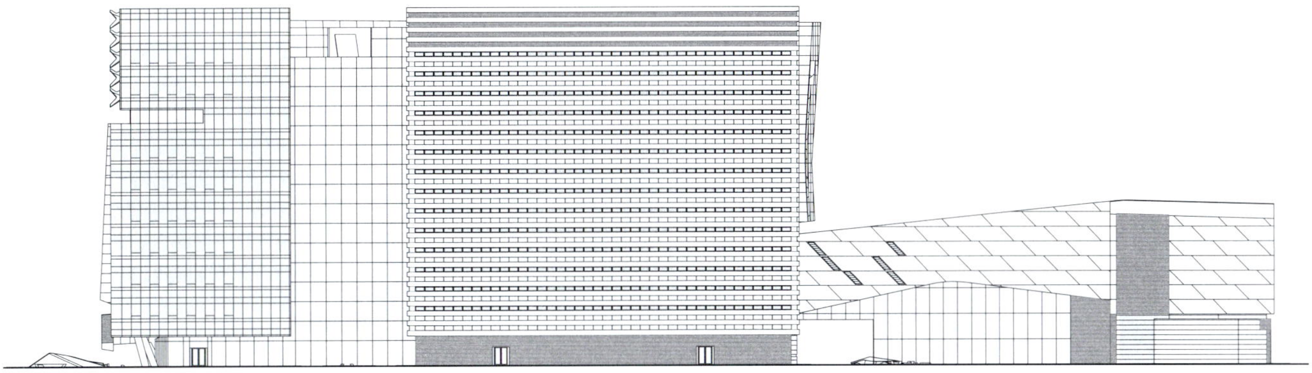

left
Building components, axonometric diagram.

bottom
West façade layers, axonometric diagram.

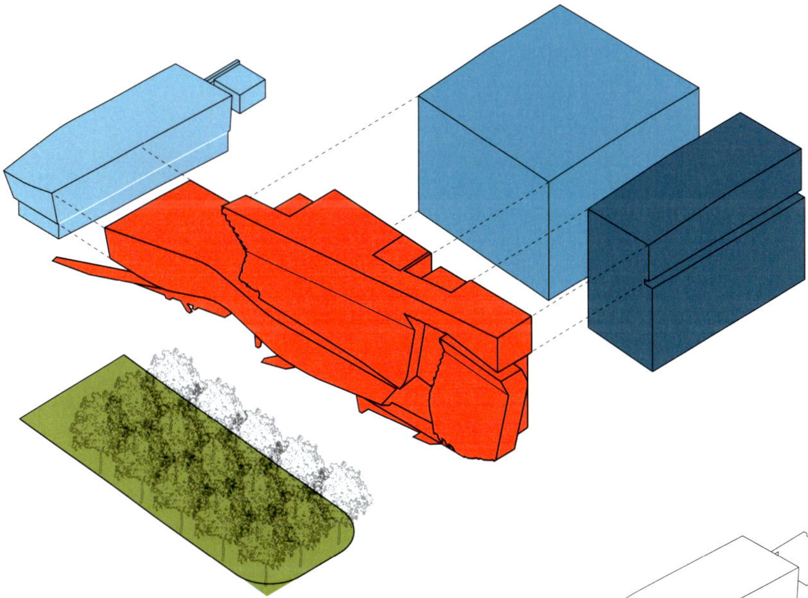

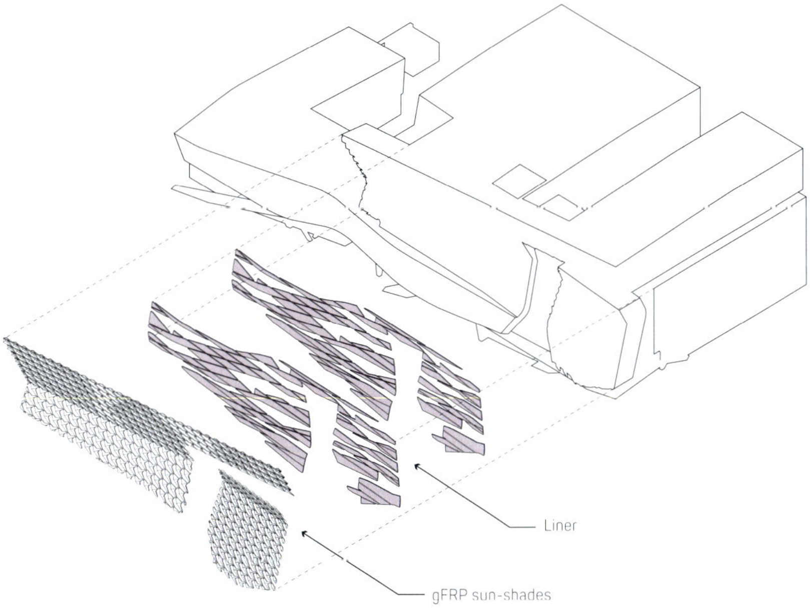

Façade details.

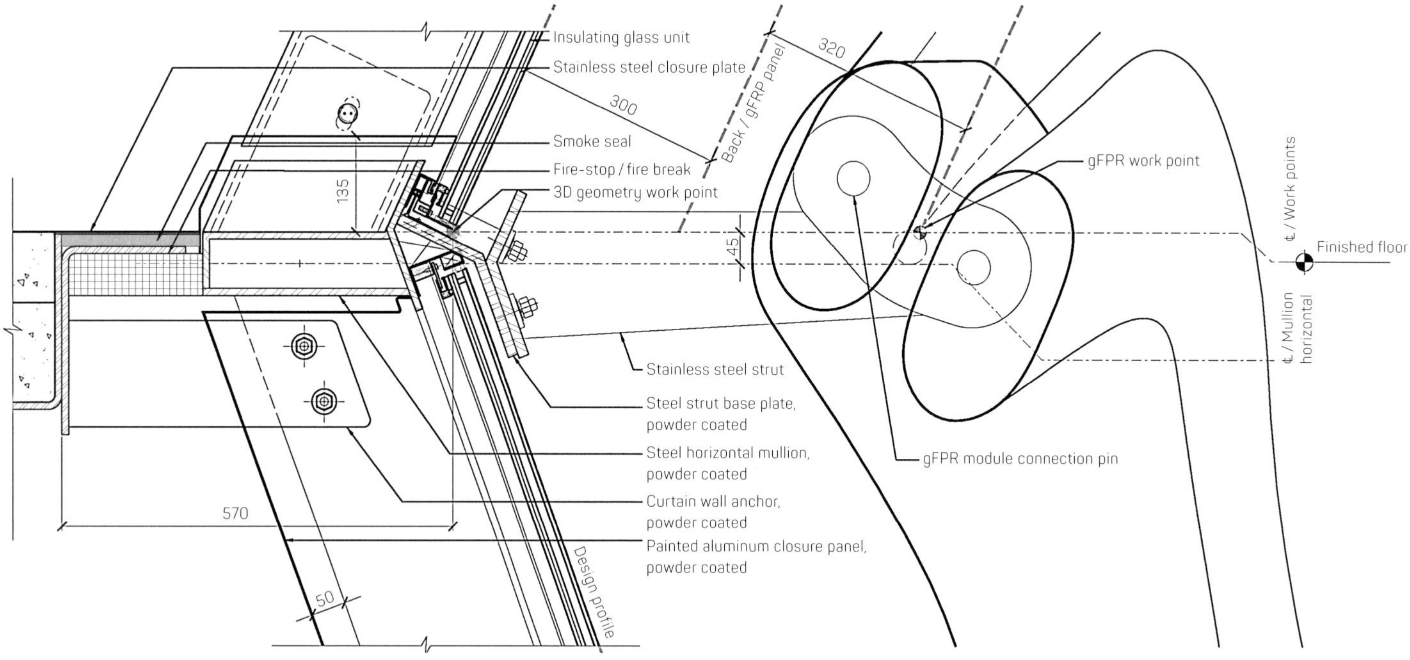

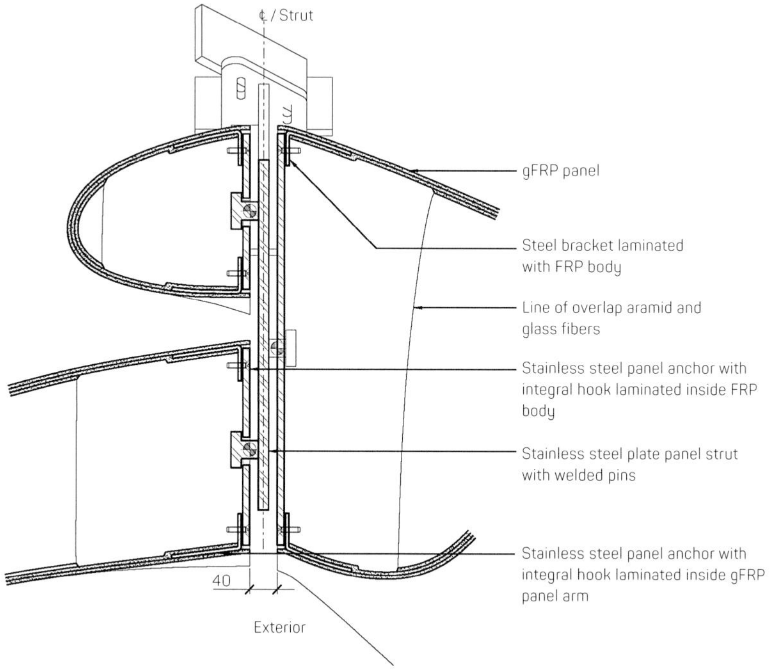

above
Façade model, detail.

right
Façade model.

Detail section through gFRP sun-shade element.

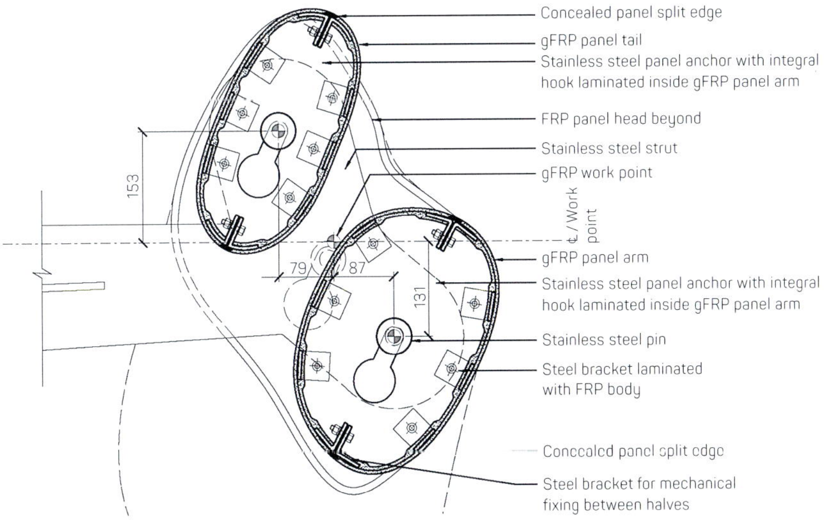

gFRP molds for the façade sun shading elements.

Section.

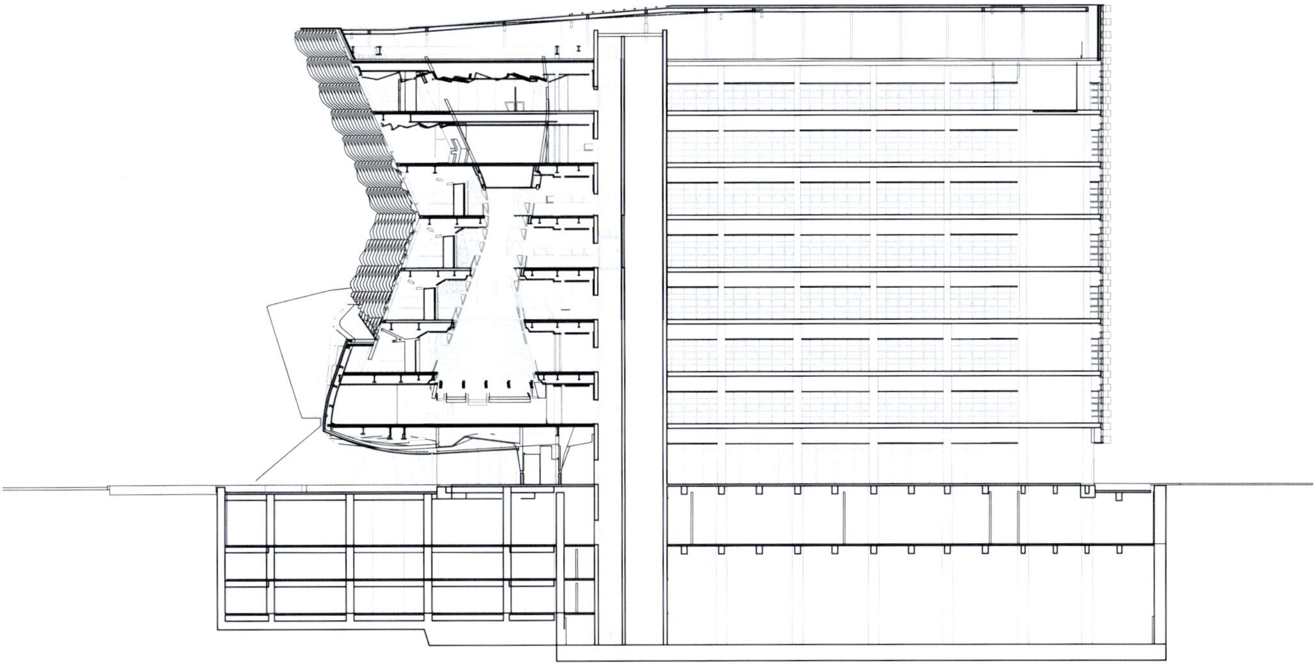

Scale model.

View of the tower from the northwest.

STEDELIJK MUSEUM

Contemporary art museum

Amsterdam, Netherlands

2012

Architectural ambition

The Stedelijk Museum in Amsterdam, Netherlands, achieves an architectural milestone: a 100 m long seamless façade with no visible joints.

Benthem Crouwel was selected to design the extension to the Stedelijk Museum, which previously occupied a 19th-century building designed by Adriaan Willem Weissman. Located adjacent to the Rijksmuseum, Van Gogh Museum, and Concertgebouw in the Museumplein, Amsterdam's museum square, this new addition needed to architecturally convey its modernity and curatorial dedication to contemporary art.

To contrast with the existing ornate and finely detailed 19th-century brick and stone building, the architects began a search for a material that would be smooth and seamless. There appeared to be two paths toward this goal: either to select a material composed of many small parts that in aggregate appeared monolithic, or to search for a material that could truly be monolithic across its entire façade, which stretched 100 m (328 ft) and covered 3,000 m² (32,300 ft²). While a seamless, jointless surface across this length is essentially unprecedented in architecture, the architects found inspiration by studying the aerospace, automotive, and in particular, the rich maritime industry of the Netherlands. A partnership with the composite manufacturing company Teijin, which also sponsored the project, provided the material and impetus for the selection and development of the aramid (Twaron) and carbon fiber composite façade panels.

The final, finished form of the new addition to the Stedelijk Museum, nicknamed "The Bathtub," is a smooth, shiny, seamless white surface that

opposite
View from the southeast.

spans the entire length of the building without any joints or seams, cantilevering dramatically outward at the roof to shelter over 2,000 m^2 (21,000 ft^2) of outdoor plaza space. Housing new galleries, visitor services, a library, and ground floor museum store, the Stedelijk is a striking presence in one of the most culturally dense areas of Europe.

Design and engineering

The first design and engineering challenge was accommodating thermal expansion across such a significant length and surface area. Conventional materials require joints placed at regular intervals to allow for thermal expansion, contraction, and the construction tolerances that are a part of any architectural project, but the ambition for a seamless surface in this building precluded any visible joints.

Engineering firm Solico BV worked with Holland Composites, Teijin Aramid, and Toho Tenax to find a material solution that could satisfy this architectural goal. Not only did the façade need to accommodate the range of temperatures experienced under direct summer sun and in the depths of a harsh winter, but it also needed to be structurally stiff enough to resist wind loads, its own weight, and internal and external temperature differentials. Also, it needed to be exceptionally flat. A smooth, shiny, white surface across such a significant expanse would make any material imperfection or surface irregularity conspicuously visible. The criteria were thus to be dimensionally stable across the entire surface in temperatures ranging from -20 °C (-4 °F) to 50 °C (122 °F), deflect no more than 0.3 percent due to wind or structural loads, thermally expand no more than 0.1 percent, and achieve perfect flatness.

The engineering team finally developed a composite sandwich panel structure that would meet these criteria. The sandwich was composed of two skins of aramid (Teijin Twaron) and carbon fiber (Toho Tenax) in a vinyl ester resin, on either side of a fire-retardant polyisocyanurate (PIR) foam core. Initially, a glass fiber polyester resin make-up was explored, with expansion joints expressed at the corners, but sponsorship by Teijin allowed the relatively more expensive aramid fiber with its more appropriate thermal properties to be chosen. Both aramid and carbon fiber have negative coefficients of thermal expansion, which when composited with the vinyl ester resin resulted in a close-to-zero composite effect.

The second major design and engineering challenge had to do with flatness. Any surface irregularity in a glossy surface would have been perceptible from a distance and therefore unacceptable. Holland Composites constructed huge float glass molds on which to assemble the panels. By floating molten glass on molten metal, the team was able to achieve perfectly flat surfaces measuring over 17 m × 4 m (56 ft × 13 ft) for the composite tooling. Upon these flat tools, the ply layup was set, vacuum bagged, and cured.

Full scale mockup testing was done in cooperation with local authorities to ensure fire-resistance compliance, with the panels ultimately achieving a Class A rating.

Fabrication and construction

The panels, once cured and unmolded, were delivered to the site for installation. The entire building was enclosed in a scaffold tent to control dust and temperature. Custom anchors were developed that bridged between the steel superstructure and the FRP panels, allowing minute millimeter adjustments that could be laser-verified to tolerances within +/- 3 mm (0.19 in).

A custom vacuum clamp attachment for a forklift was also developed to raise and position the panels. The vacuum clamps could handle and accurately place the panels in their desired location without deflecting or placing undue stresses on them at any point.

Once the panels were anchored in place, they were then wet-seamed together to create the final, seamless surface. Carefully detailed edges on each of the panels allowed one panel to be mated to the other to achieve the final joint- and seam-free construction. One panel was overlapped with the adjacent panel at the edge, with small holes allowing vinyl ester to be injected. The injected resin would bond to a backing plate attached to the panel behind. Then, small gaps were filled with PIR foam and covered with prepared strips of aramid and carbon fiber laminate. This was then wetted out and cured, structurally combining all the panels together across the face of the building.

The temperature and humidity within the tented work area had to be carefully controlled to allow for proper resin mixing, spray coating, and curing. This was further complicated by the need to eliminate variation across the entire height and breadth of the work area. Minute differentiations would have resulted in visible variations in the coating.

Finally, the entire surface had to be painted. To avoid any variations in the painting, the complete façade had to be spray painted in one pass for each coating. A UV-resistant paint used in the marine and aerospace industries was chosen and applied by boat painters. The finish has shown little fading and has been remarkably easy to clean.

Conclusion

The architects were drawn to composite materials for the freedom in form and details they allow; in this case, to contrast with an existing 19th-century brick building and to esthetically communicate the mission of the occupying institution. The composite panels were utilized here to achieve a significant architectural feat—over 3,000 m^2 of joint- and seam-free surface.

Site plan.

1 Concertgebouw
2 Van Gogh Museum
3 Diamond Museum
4 Rijksmuseum

South elevation.

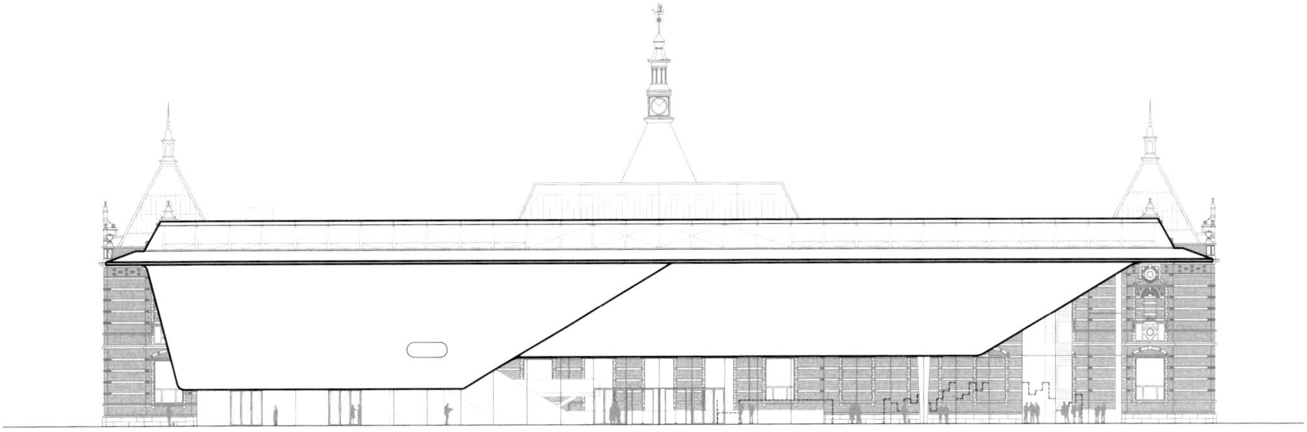

West elevation.

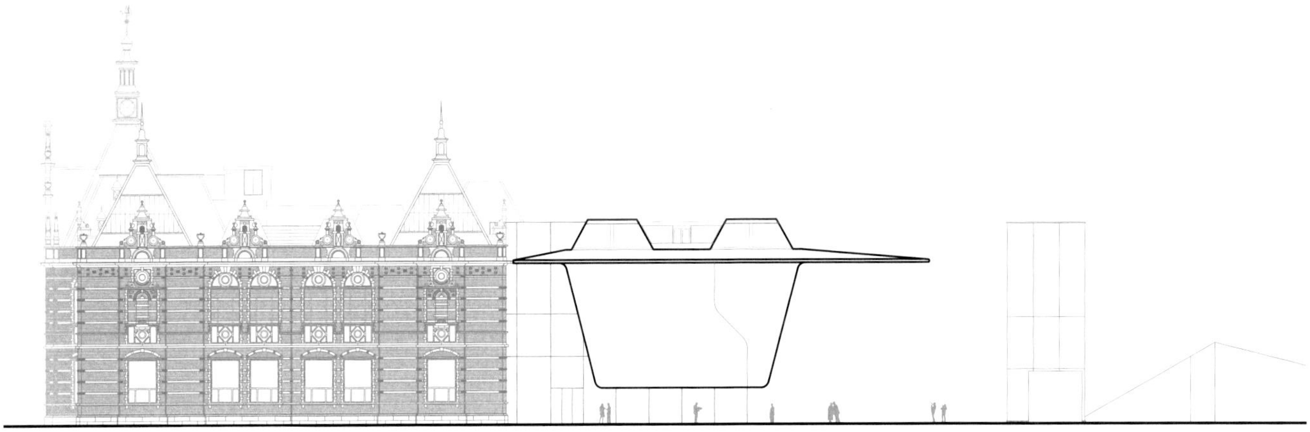

East elevation.

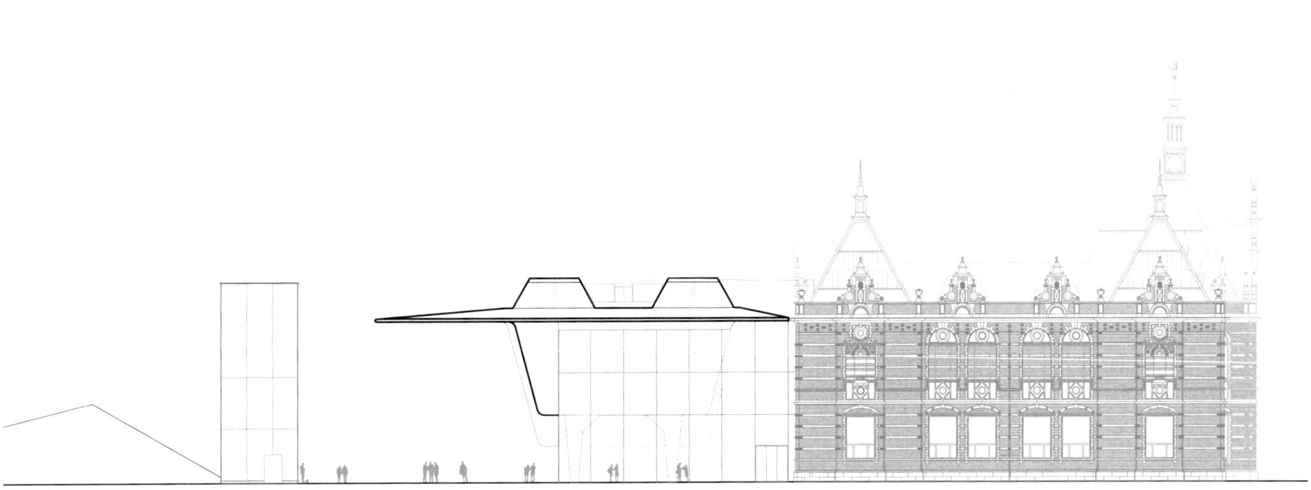

0 2.5 5 15 m

Cross section.

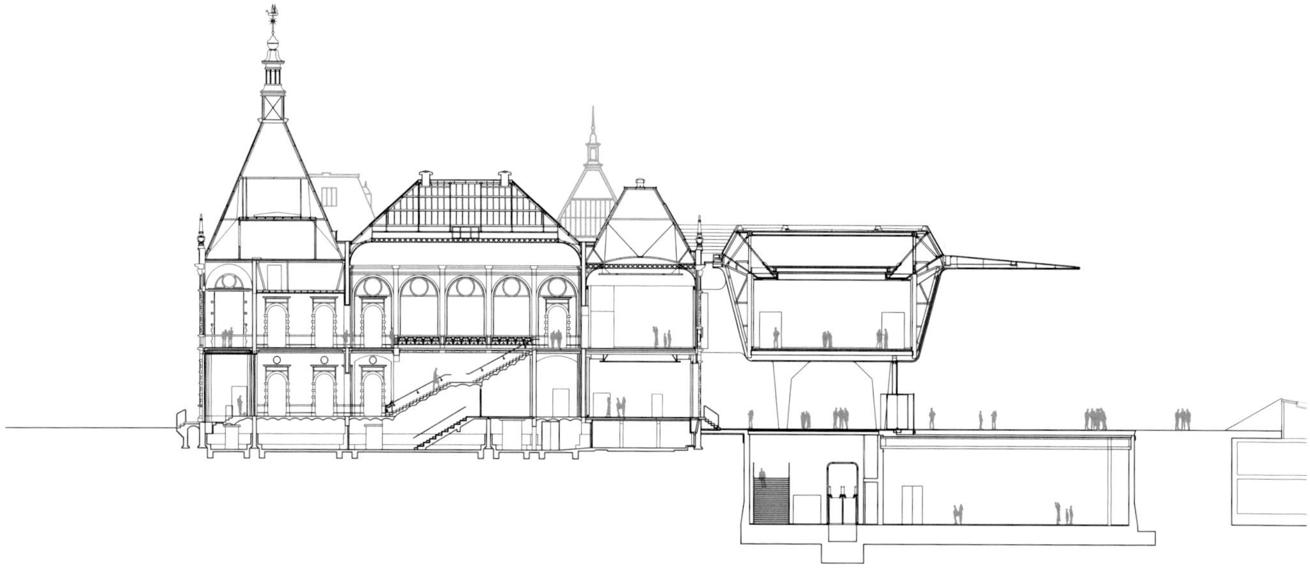

Longitudinal section.

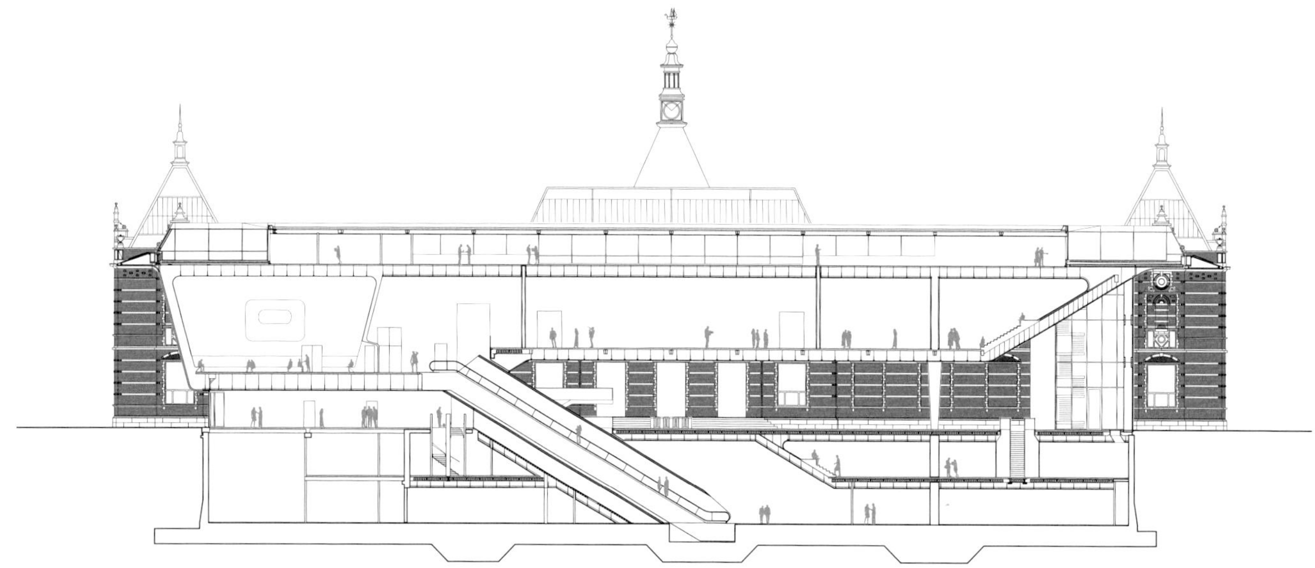

top
Construction photo showing steel structure.

left
Construction photo showing the special lifting brackets that were used to place composite façade panels in place.

Construction photo showing installation of composite façade panels.

Façade section.

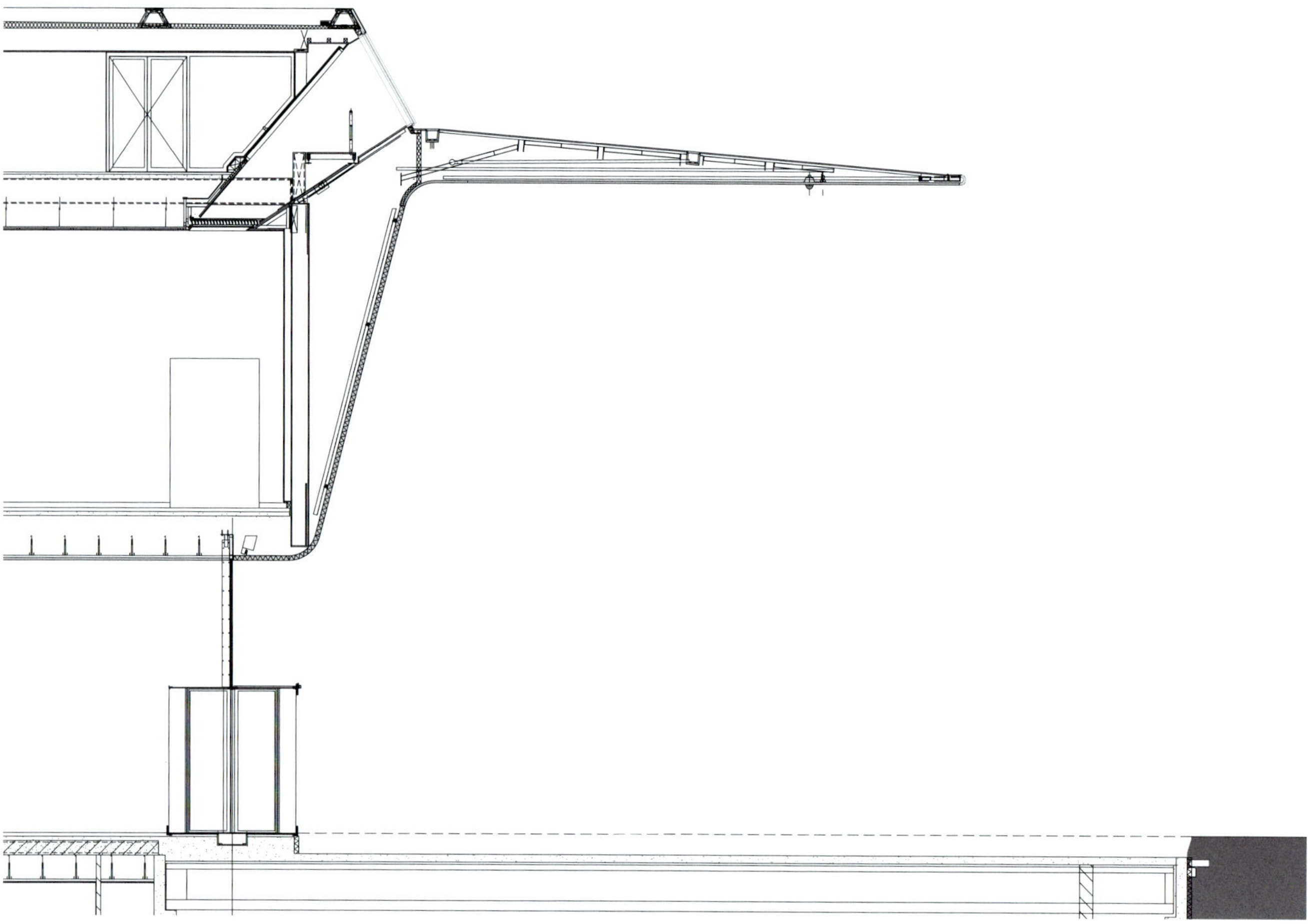

Diagram illustrating the composition of the FRP sandwich cladding panels.

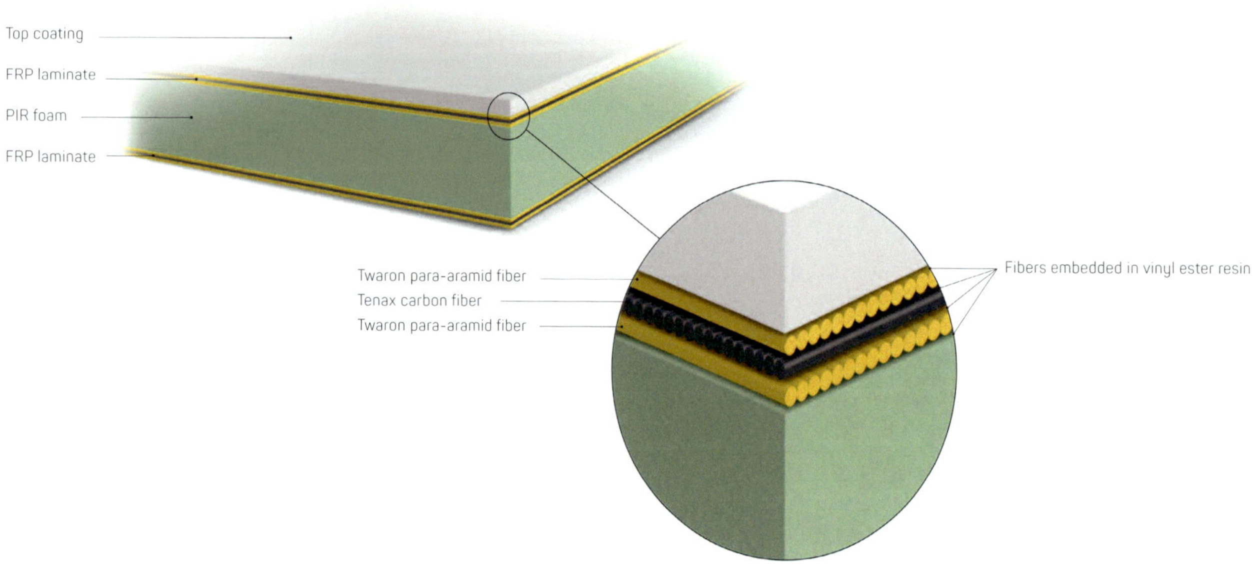

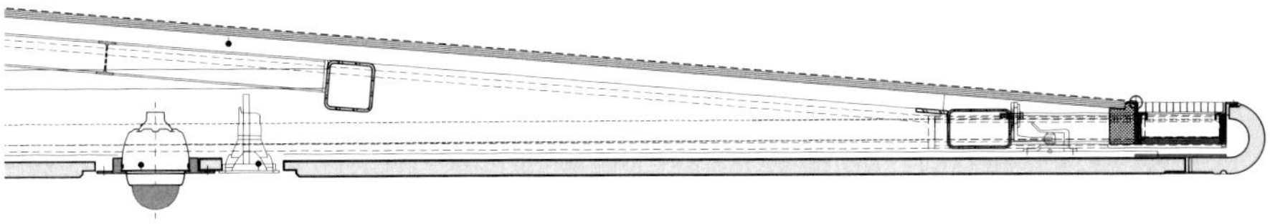

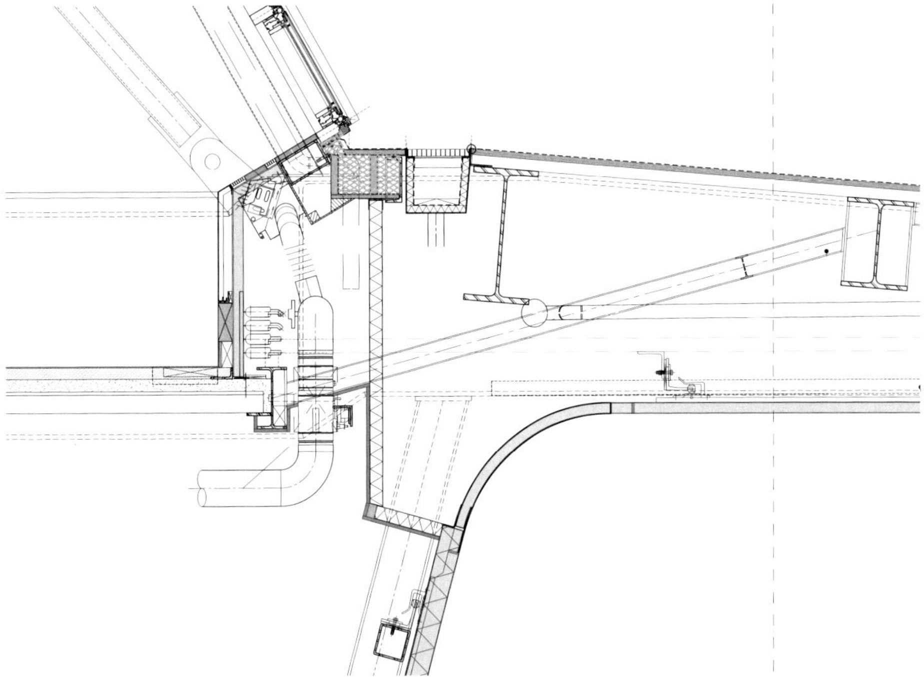

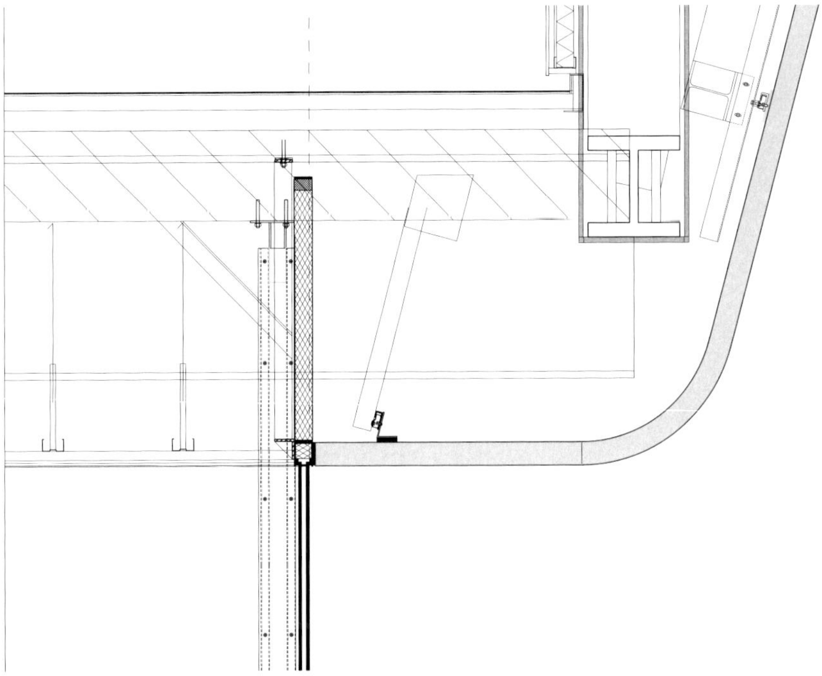

Visit the ALL NEW
Madame Tussauds!

View from the west.

BBVA HEAD-QUARTERS

Bank headquarters

Madrid, Spain

2013–2015

Architectural ambition

A new headquarters in Madrid for the Spanish bank BBVA by Herzog & de Meuron expresses a "raw architecture … informed by the strong influence of the solar conditions."[1] The complex occupies a site of over 636,000 ft^2 (59,000 m^2), over which the architects arranged a "linear structure of three-story buildings"[2] with a large ovoid tower in the middle. Effective solar shading devices were required along the periphery of the buildings and on portions of the tower façade. For this, Herzog & de Meuron developed uniquely formulated and shaped FRP brise-soleil "fins" to modulate the sun, view, daylighting, and thermal loads.

Design and engineering

Over 1600 panels ranging in size from 4.92 ft to 13.12 ft (1.5 m to 4 m) were designed and fabricated with a sandwich panel construction developed in partnership with Innova Composites and Permasteelisa. These extend various distances outward from the face of the façade and have cut-outs on the lower portion to "provide views and daylight where [solar] protection is needed least—resulting in a figurative element that varies in direction and size according to solar angle and program."[3] Designed to meet European EN 13501-1 fire standards and UV weathering resistance, as well as process considerations, the solar fins had to meet all the requisite structural, fire, and mechanical requirements for an exterior building component.

opposite
View of gFRP solar brise-soleil fins.

Fabrication and construction

The brise-soleil fins have a composite sandwich structure. Placed over a PET foam core, a laminate layup of glass fiber filament mats was infused with urethane acrylate resin. Alumina trihydride (ATH) fillers in the resin provided some fire retardancy, which is supplemented by an in-mold spray layer of FR intumescent gelcoat. This was then overpainted with polyurethane for UV resistance.

Closed mold vacuum infused curing and spray gelcoat, along with careful resin engineering, allowed cost-effective production while meeting stringent design tolerance, fire resistance, durability, and performance parameters.

Conclusion

The BBVA Headquarters by Herzog & de Meuron, featuring distinctive solar "fin" brise-soleils throughout the exterior, is an example of how FRP components can serve as an extremely functional, cost-effective, and attractive part of a building that meets the highest standards of design and performance.

1 Herzog & de Meuron. Press release no. 324. "New Headquarters for BBVA Madrid, Spain".
2 Herzog & de Meuron. Press release no. 324.
3 Herzog & de Meuron. Press release no. 324.

Diagram showing orientation of solar fins in plan and section, keyed to building façade orientation.

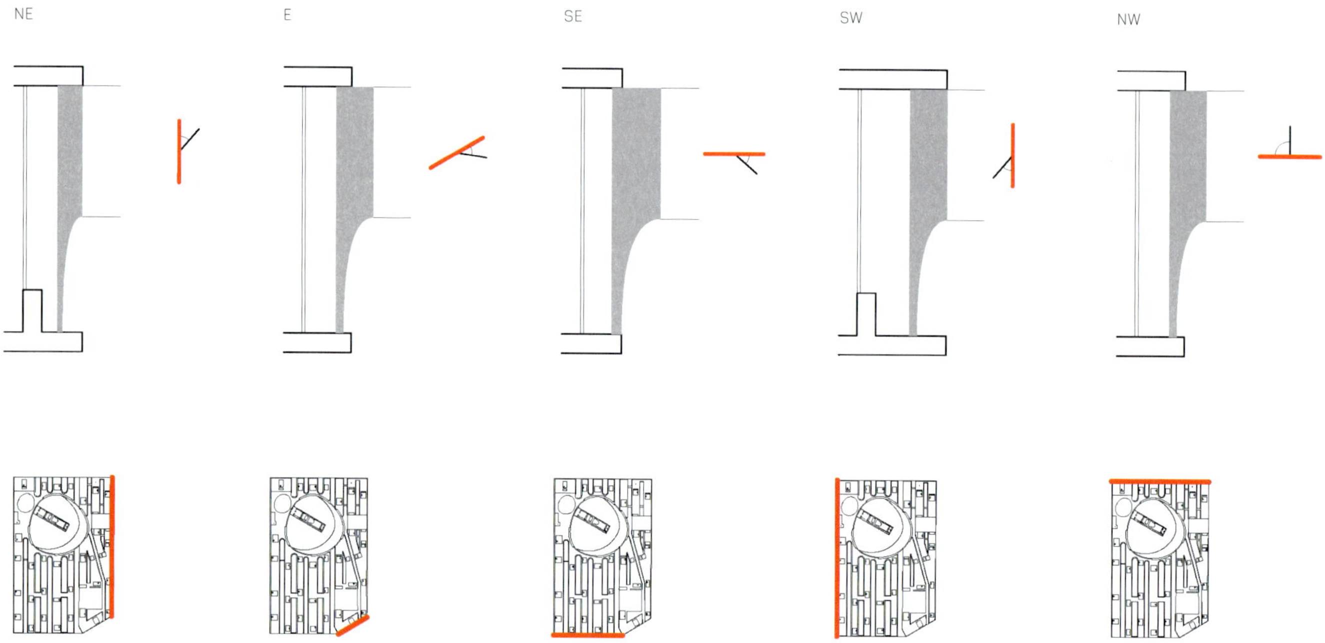

left
Wall section detail showing size, scale, and fixed placement of solar fins along the façade.

bottom
Diagram cataloging various solar brise-soleil fin sizes and dimensions.

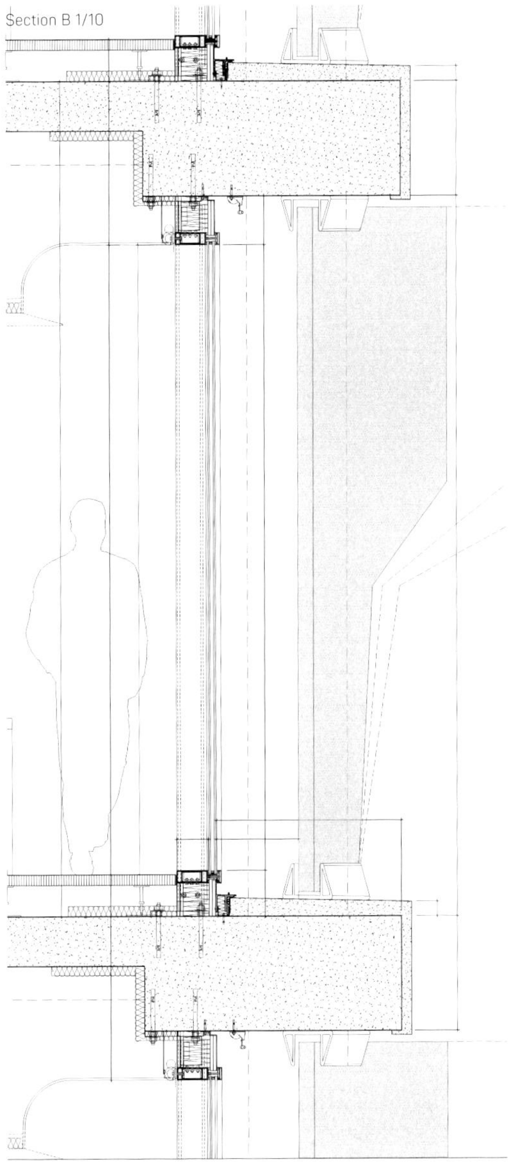

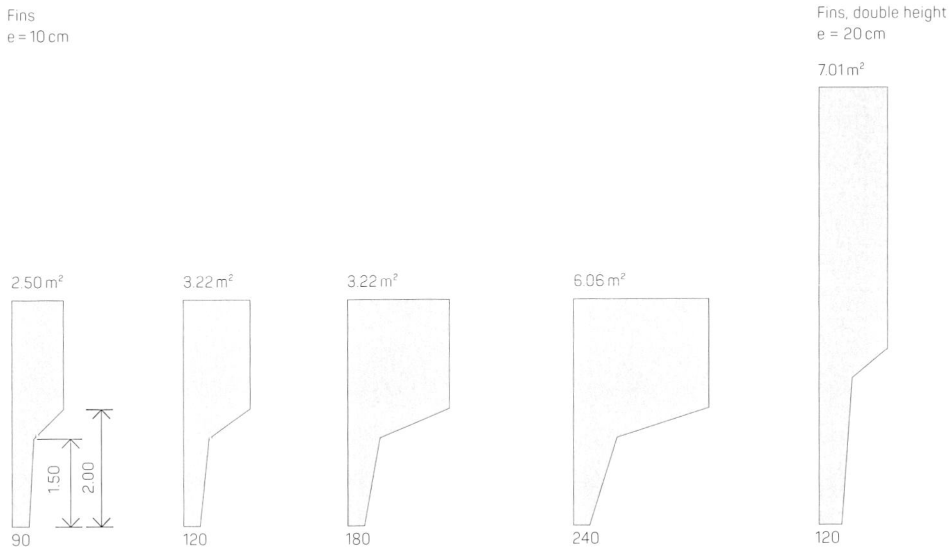

BBVA

Exterior view.

GEBOUW X WINDES-HEIM

University of Applied Sciences, faculties of Journalism and Economics

Zwolle, Netherlands

2010

Architectural ambition

The architects, in partnership with the client, the Christian University of Applied Sciences in Zwolle, Netherlands, wanted to create a building that had the latest and most advanced technology, specifically in relation to sustainability. To do this, special design attention was paid to the curtain wall system, mechanical systems, daylighting considerations, envelope performance, and plan layout.

In fulfilling this goal, a building with a high-insulating, materially efficient envelope allowing an optimal amount of daylighting was crucial. An expressive and distinctive façade would be essential to communicate the project's architectural ambition. A self-supporting composite façade system, developed with the fabricator Holland Composites, was an essential part of meeting the building's performance and esthetic aims.

Design, engineering, fabrication and construction

After an initial study, an exterior glazing ratio of 50 percent was determined as ideal. The architects came up with a design that utilized 3300 triangular insulated glazing units (IGUs), arrayed throughout a unitized curtain wall façade system. Door units are indistinguishable from the rest of the façade, save for a door handle and an additional seam.

The unitized façade system employs a composite FRP sandwich structure. Each of the unitized façade elements is 41 ft × 11.5 ft × 1 ft (12.5 m ×

opposite
Interior view with unitized composite façade in the background.

3.5 m × 0.3 m) and together they make up a total façade surface area of 60,800 ft^2 (5650 m^2). These façade elements are mounted on the concrete or steel structure behind. The exterior IGUs are then structurally glazed within those façade elements.

A single mold was used to prefabricate the façade units off-site, minimizing waste and cost and increasing efficiency and consistency across the façade. The façade units came prefinished and were fully self-supporting off the concrete building structure. No further interior or exterior finishing was required on-site, reducing labor, maintenance, and schedule costs.

Development, production, transport, and assembly of the façade was completed by Holland Composites.

The envelope performs extremely well, with an RC value of 8. In combination with high-efficiency mechanical, rainwater, occupancy, daylighting, and other systems, the building seeks to attain the highest standards of sustainability, resulting in the highest possible sustainability label from GreenCalc.

Conclusion

Increasing performance requirements on curtain wall assemblies are pushing conventional construction materials and techniques toward their limits. The highly integrated composite curtain wall of the Gebouw (Building) X in Windesheim demonstrates many of the high performance, fabrication, and design possibilities available with the use of composite materials.

Elevation.

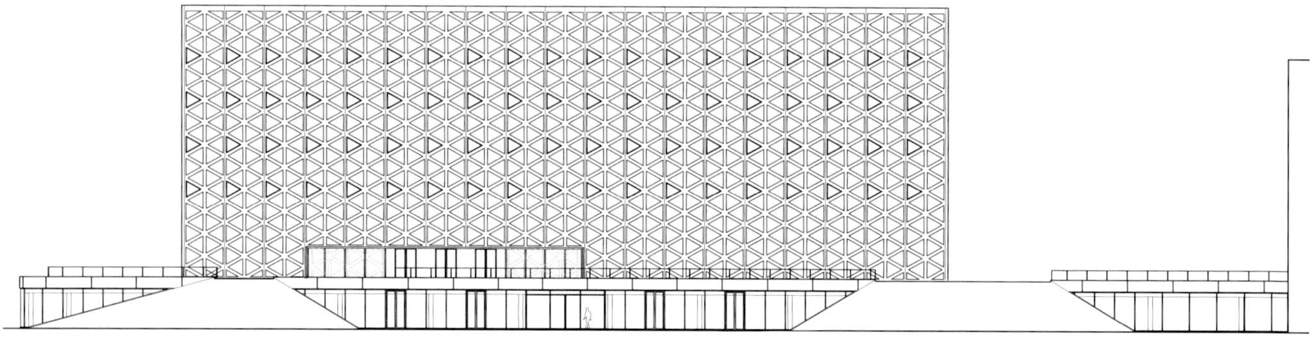

Section.

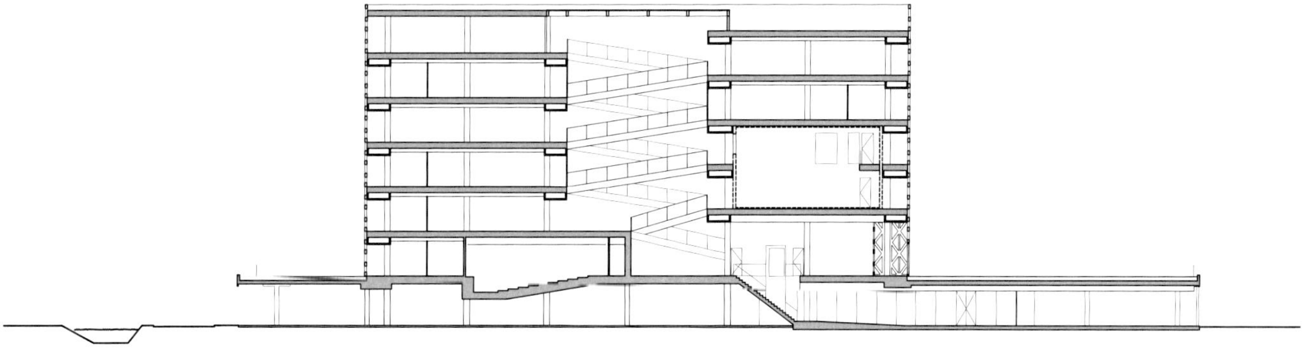

Façade section.

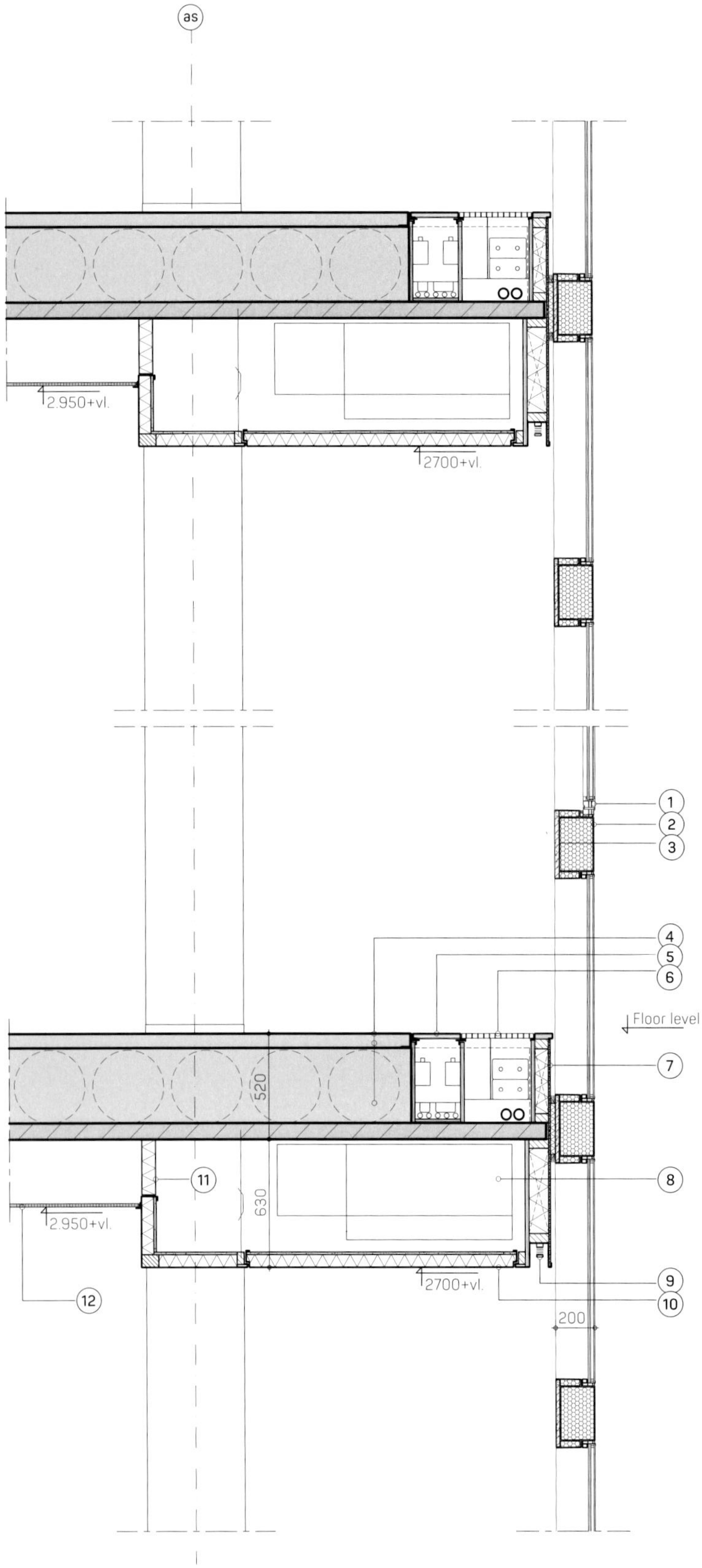

1 thermally interrupted aluminum with insulated glazing
2 FRP and insulation
3 cement-bonded fiberboard
4 floor construction:
  - bubble slab concrete
  - sand cement screed
  - mineral cast floor
5 cover strip as grid
6 convector pit with grate
7 panel
  - gypsum board
  - insulation
  - fiber cement board
8 installation space
9 lighting cove
10 removable perforated metal
11 acoustic isolation
12 dropped ceiling system

Façade details.

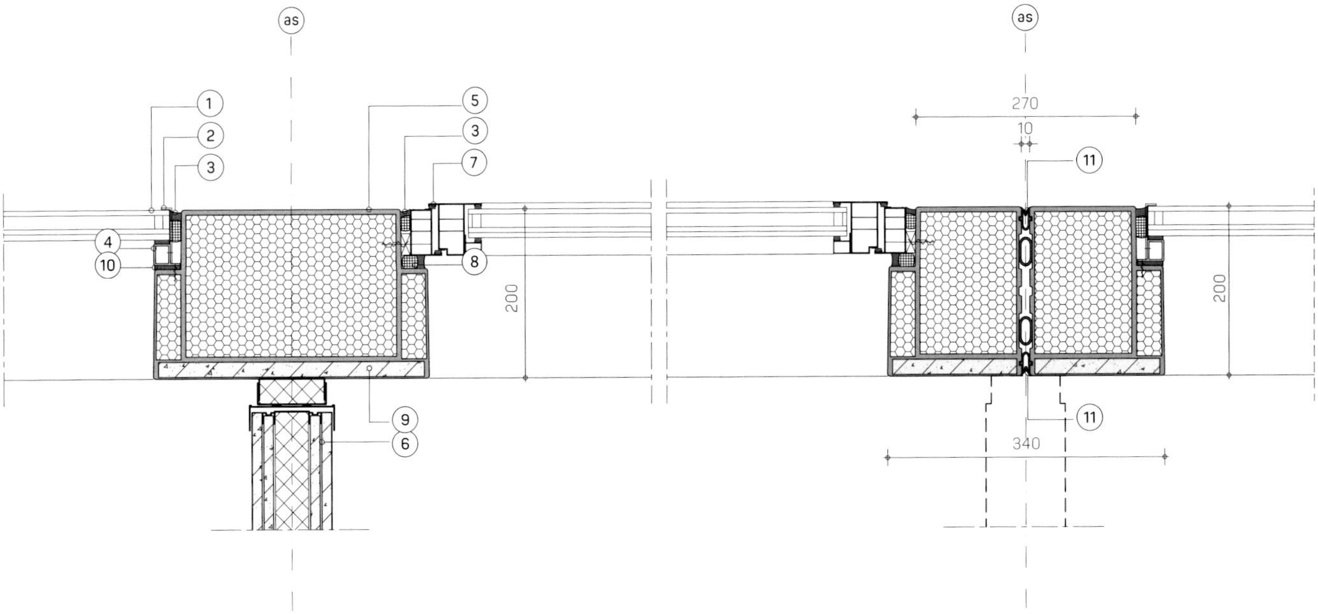

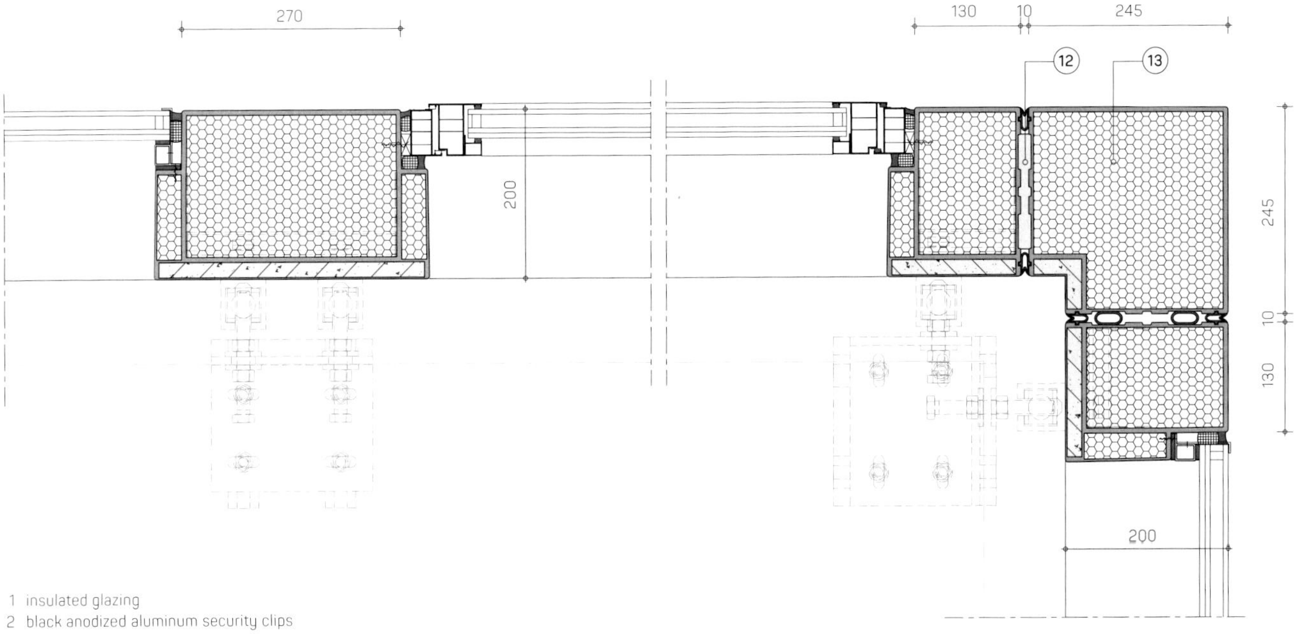

1 insulated glazing
2 black anodized aluminum security clips
3 sealant
4 black anodized aluminum profile and structural sealant joint
5 FRP and insulation
6 partition wall with cement-based fiberboard
7 aluminum window with thermal break
8 closed neoprene cell tape
9 cement-bonded fiberboard
10 closed neoprene cell tape
11 rubber sealing profile color white
12 glued elements
13 corner element

Construction and erection
of the FRP wall panels.

CASE STUDIES
INTERIORS

SAN ROQUE

CARRASCO AIRPORT

International Airport

Montevideo, Uruguay

2009

Architectural ambition

The Carrasco Airport, with its giant curving roof, serves as a thoroughly modern entrance for air travelers to the country of Uruguay.

The gently curving roof of the Carrasco International Airport, officially known as "Aeropuerto Internacional de Carrasco General Cesareo L. Berisso," is located 17.7 km (11 mi) outside Montevideo, the capital city of Uruguay. It measures over 365 m (1,200 ft) in length and shelters all the functions of an airport serving over 1 million passengers per year arriving and departing on international flights.

The design of the roof was inspired by the rolling dunes of the Uruguayan coastline and the surrounding site topography. This shell is designed to appear as a single monolithic form hovering gently above the ground.

Design and engineering

The doubly curved shape of the roof shelters both indoor and outdoor areas, reaches a height of 36.7 m (120 ft) above the ground, and is 39,750 m^2 (427,865 ft^2) in area. The roof is structured with a series of 4 m deep steel trusses in each orthogonal direction and lined with a thermoplastic polyolefin membrane (TPO) on the top surface. The roof's governing structural load comes from an 18,000 kN / 59 kg/m^2 uplift force based on wind tunnel testing.

opposite
Interior view showing the curved composite ceiling.

On the underside, the doubly curved concave surface inhibited the use of a similar system, so sandwich panels made of composite plates with a gelcoat finish over a foam (expanded polystyrene and polyurethane) core were fabricated. These panels were then attached to the steel structure with a secondary aluminum substructure that allowed minute dimensional corrections in placement. The composite panel supplier, MVC-Poloplast Paineis, stated: "Our challenge was to develop a lining system that could meet the requirements of strength and safety, be applied without the need for special equipment and have the greatest resistance at the lowest possible weight." The total dead load of the roof structure and roofing assembly was approximately 122 kg/m^2.

The architects also undertook measures to eliminate any penetrations of the skin for lights, sprinklers, smoke detectors, speakers, diffusers, grilles, access hatches, outlets, conduits, or any other equipment. The result is to reinforce the abstract, continuous, monumental nature of the roof as viewed from below and above.

Conclusion

Composite panels allowed Viñoly Architects to accomplish a complex geometry for the most demanding of programs that reinforced the architects' design goals.

opposite
Exterior views.

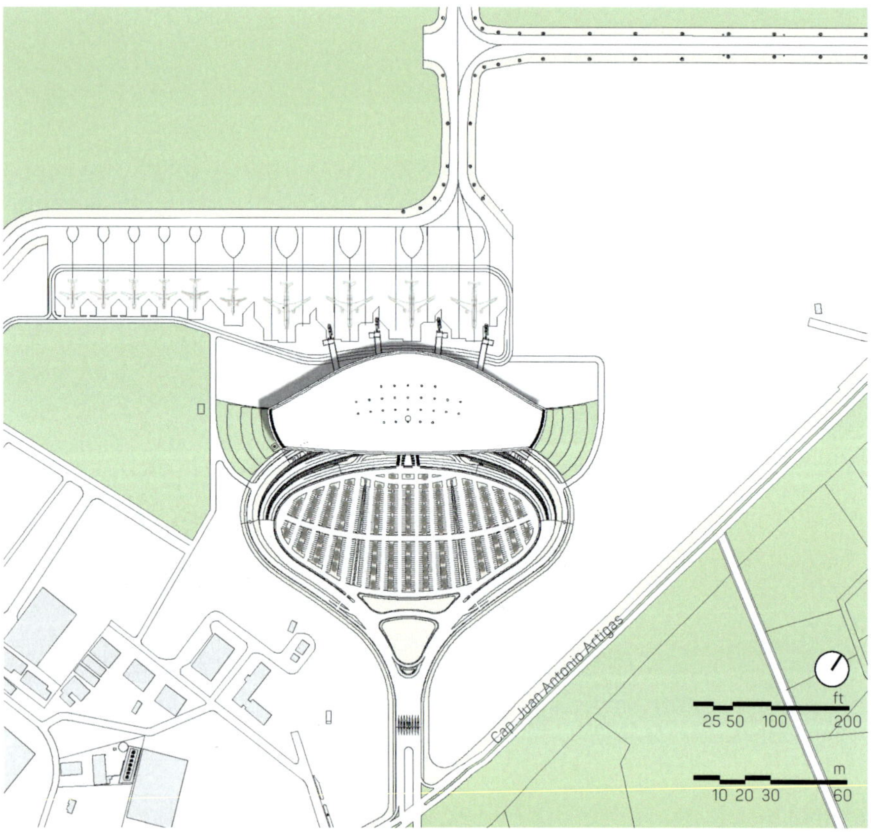

Site plan

Building Section.

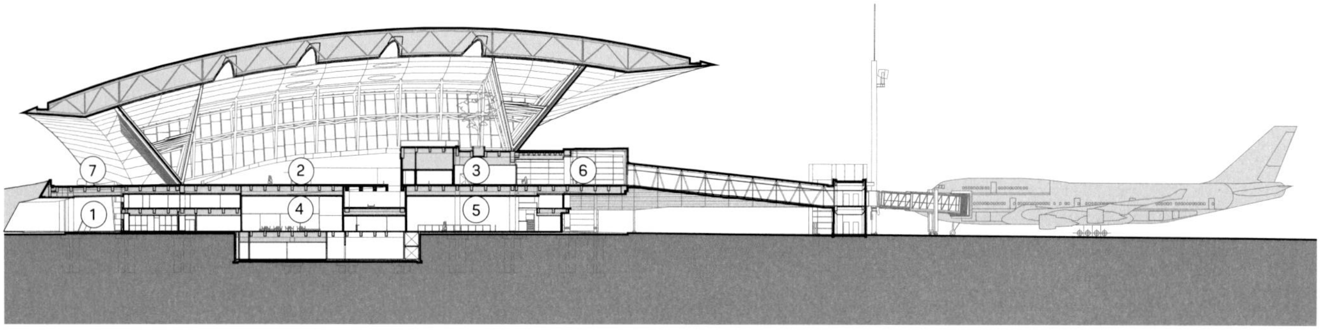

1 Passenger pick-up
2 Departure hall
3 Security control
4 Arrival hall
5 Baggage claim
6 Waiting area
7 Passenger drop-off

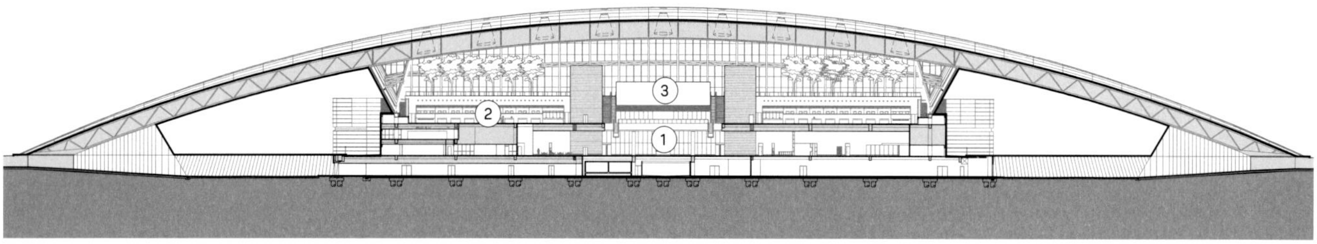

1 Arrival hall
2 Check-in/departure hall
3 Waiting area/bar

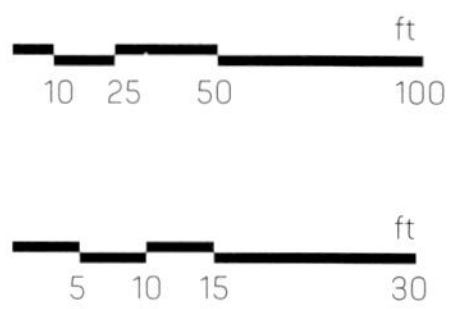

Roof structure diagrams showing shape, placement, and distribution of structure.

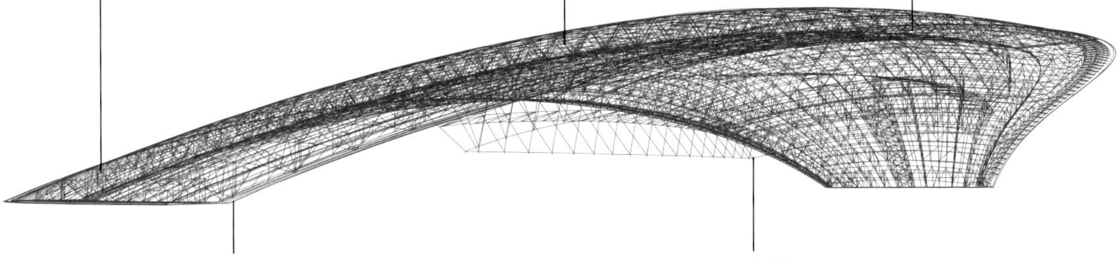

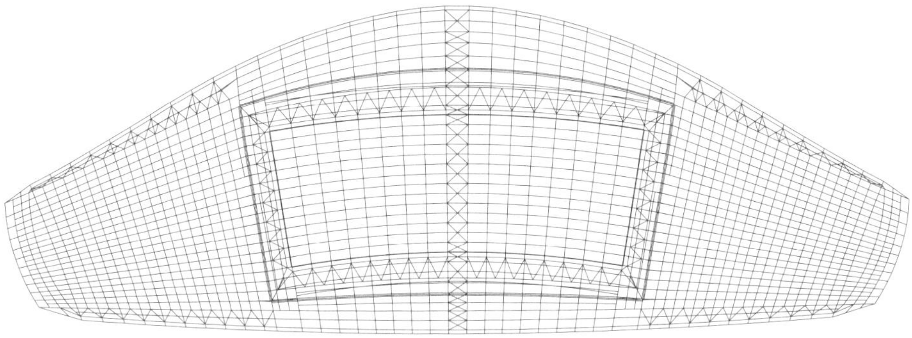

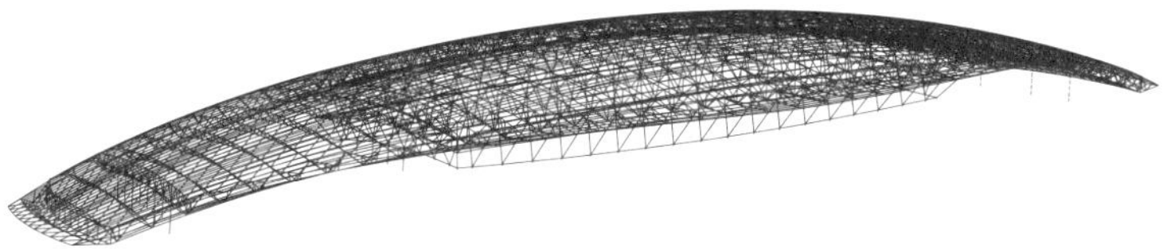

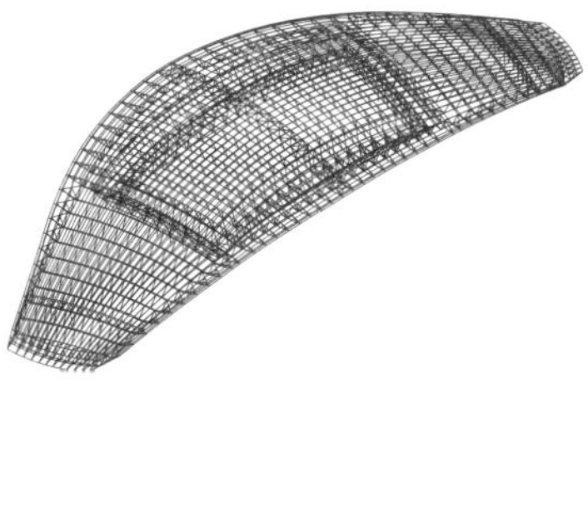

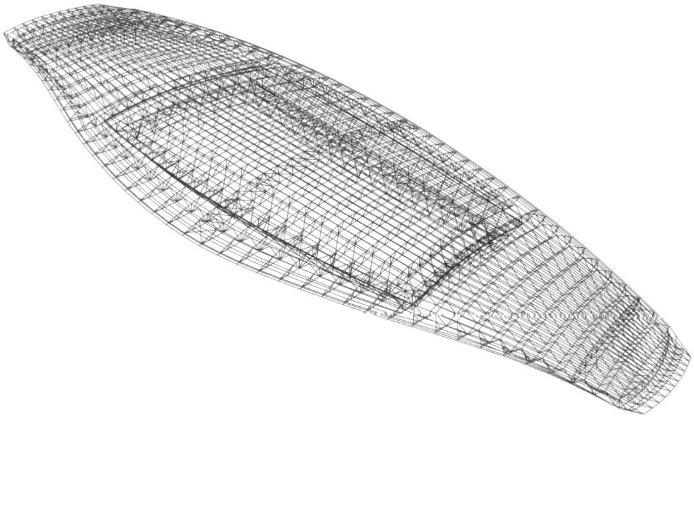

BING CONCERT HALL

842-seat concert hall

Palo Alto, USA

2009

Architectural ambition

The Bing Concert Hall in Stanford, California, "exemplifies the seamless integration of architecture, acoustics and technology to transform the practice, study, and experience of the performing arts,"[1] as proclaimed by the architects, Ennead Partners. As a concert venue designed in an oval, vineyard-style hall, it has terraced seating surrounding a sunken performance stage. Large, convex interior sails made of FRP, designed in partnership with acoustician Dr. Yasuhisa Toyota of Nagata Acoustics and fabricated by Kreysler & Associates, provide the optimal acoustic shape and properties for the 842-seat concert hall.

Design and engineering

Lead designer Richard Olcott, a partner at Ennead Architects, states that some 50 iterations of the concert hall were designed and provided to Nagata Acoustics (in the form of a Rhino model) for acoustic modeling with digital tools. The modeling software allowed the acousticians to then provide specific feedback on the design of the concert hall space—a sophisticated method that has meant that "the process of designing spaces where sound is important is largely data-driven."[2]

The issue was that the desired oval room of a vineyard-style hall tends to concentrate sounds, creating unwelcome acoustic effects. This necessitated the addition of large convex surfaces to evenly reflect and distribute sound throughout the space, generating the pleasing reverberation that is a trait of well-designed acoustic spaces.

opposite
Interior view of the concert hall showing the FRP interior acoustic "sails".

The designers came up with giant, convex, acoustic sails to be mounted around the upper walls of the interior. Furthermore, it was determined that the sails would benefit from having a surface texture that would add to the richness of the sound—yet the texture couldn't be a repeating pattern, which would create echoes at certain frequencies.

Ten in total, the large convex surfaces (the sails) were made from molded FRP. The acoustic shapes range from 7.92 m (26 ft) in the smallest dimension to 15.24 m (50 ft) in the largest, with a custom non-repeating texture designed by the architects CNC-milled into the surfaces of the sails. A central acoustic cloud suspended from the ceiling was 38.71 m (127 ft) long and 19.20 m (63 ft) wide, integrating lighting, sprinklers, and speaker boxes.

The desired mass of 117.18 kg/m^2 (24 lb/ft^2) for acoustic purposes was achieved using a 3/8 in thick FRP shell backfilled with concrete after it was determined that a fully concrete sail would be overly thick and massive.

These FRP and concrete shapes were then mounted into a steel tube frame for rigidity and installed by Kreysler & Associates.

Conclusion

The Bing Concert Hall in Stanford, California, is an example of the ability of FRP materials and technology to realize the complex integration of design intent, specific material property engineering, and acoustic performance modeling.

1 Ennead website.
2 Bernstein.

Panel during fabrication showing the surface patterning.

top and right
Panels being fitted with support structures for mounting and installation.

Cloud panel mold being cut on a CNC router.

Farm Fresh
To You

THE FERRY BUILDING

Office space, retail marketplace

San Francisco, USA

2005

Architectural ambition

This project was the renovation and restoration of a historic Beaux Arts building in the Embarcadero District at the northern edge of San Francisco. Having survived numerous earthquakes since its original completion in 1898 (architect A. Page Brown), it was now being redeveloped after the 1989 Loma Prieta earthquake significantly altered the surrounding Embarcadero area.

The redevelopment was intended to revitalize the area with a marketplace, offices, and retail space in an historic building. Architects SMWM (since incorporated into Perkins + Will), with Baldauf Catton von Eckartsberg retail designers and Page & Turnbull preservation specialists, designed a renovation that "held to strict preservation standards while applying innovative techniques and using new materials to stabilize the structure and update the building systems," as the EDRA Great Places Award announcement states.

Design and engineering

The SMWM design was distinguished by its "quiet balance of old and new," as well as its fully restored sky-lit nave with historic brick arches. But further investigation determined that little original brickwork capable of being salvaged remained, and seismic concerns meant that new masonry construction would have been problematic. What was needed was something that could mimic the appearance of the original brickwork but be lightweight and strong enough for the enhanced structural demands.

opposite
Interior view of nave with FRP interior elements.

Restoration specialists Page & Turnbull turned to Kreysler & Associates to create FRP replicas of the original brickwork. The team at Kreysler & Associates built plugs (positive shapes) for the brickwork using wood, foam, and plaster. They then applied their proprietary blend of fire-retardant unsaturated polyester resin, aggregate, and fiberglass onto these molds. The resulting fiberglass panels were then sandblasted and finished by artist Jacquelyn Giuffre to mimic the appearance of weathered stone.

Conclusion

In a project where the interior architecture needed to be both structurally sound and esthetically specific, FRP composite materials proved to be a perfect fit.

opposite top
Exterior view of Ferry Building in San Francisco.

opposite bottom
Interior second floor view with FRP interior elements.

FRP molds in progress.

BLOOM HOUSE AND LANTERN

Residence

Southern California, USA

2008

Architectural ambition

The Bloom House is located on a beach in Southern California. The interiors of the house, which respond to a client's desire for space that was both open and continuous while intimate and cozy, was designed by "curving, folding, puckering, and looping surfaces" to make discrete spaces. The first floor is also defined by a luminous fiberglass lantern that stretches along the length of the space, providing illumination and connecting the discrete spaces along the ground floor.

Design and engineering

The lantern is composed of twenty-two fiberglass panels joined at the flanges. The lantern extends from outside of the building, through to the interior, terminating near the office and powder room.

The lantern was fabricated of glass fiber reinforced polymers (gFRP) by Kreysler & Associates.

Conclusion

The fiberglass lantern by Greg Lynn is an example of an indoor FRP element that serves multiple functional and spatial purposes, being simultaneously an architectural-scale esthetic feature and a translucent FRP light source.

opposite
Interior view with FRP lantern.

Fabrication and installation images of the translucent FRP lantern element for the Bloom House, showing mold preparation, laminate lay-up, and final part assembly.

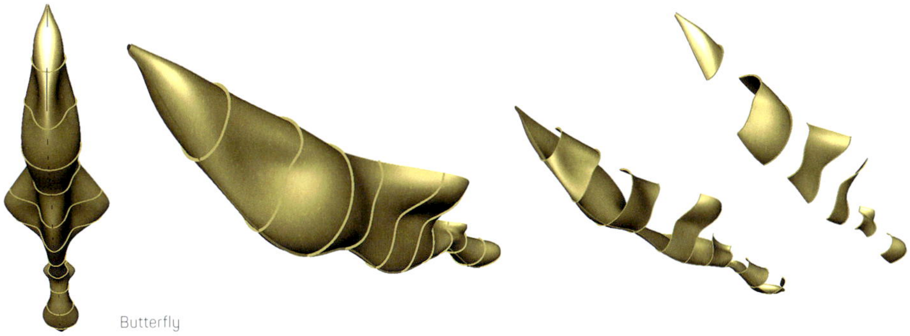

Design renderings of the lantern element.

Finished part being held up to the light to check quality and consistency of translucency.

CASE STUDIES
STRUCTURES

BLUE DREAM

Single-family residence

Long Island, New York, USA

2016

Architectural ambition

The Blue Dream is the first single-family residence completed from the ground up by architects Diller Scofidio + Renfro (DS+R) (their seminal Slow House was never completed). This residence continues the studio's exploration and interrogation of fundamental architectural ideas and elements. The ambition for this building, sited in the sandy dune beaches of Long Island, New York, was to articulate a vocabulary of space-making that took its inspiration from the local landscape.

Diller Scofidio + Renfro, working with ideas of domesticity, gradation, and landscape, and using advanced composite technologies, has realized a conceptually audacious building located in this historic testing ground for adventurous modernist houses.

Design and engineering

The structural system, developed in partnership with structural engineers LERA and composites engineers Optima Projects Ltd., has a monocoque gFRP roof structure atop a hybrid steel and concrete substructure. gFRP cladding extends seamlessly from the roof down to shape the soffits, exterior walls, ground, and hardscape.

The primary structural component for the building is the monocoque gFRP structural roof. The roof was composed of numerous individual gFRP sandwich panels, which were seamed together on site to bond them into one

opposite
Design rendering.

structural monocoque, allowing the tensile and compressive stresses to be carried across the entire length and width of the roof without any internal structure.

Each panel was composed of a varying number of layers of vinyl ester impregnated glass fiber placed over milled blocks of polyethylene terephthalate (PET) foam. The glass fiber and vinyl ester resin formula were chosen for their structural capacity and their ability to meet specific flammability performance criteria set out in the building codes. The foam was chosen for its shear resistance and offered a sustainability bonus of being completely composed of recycled plastic water bottles.

The structure had to meet stringent requirements for wind loading on this coastal site, while accommodating the spatial and architectural goals of open, column-free spaces with large cantilevers. Finite element analysis (FEA) models were developed using multiple load combination cases to understand deflections and movements under stresses from wind, live loads, dead loads, and thermal expansion.

The gFRP panels vary in shape, depth, fiber weave, foam specification, and a combination thereof, allowing the form to respond to local structural needs as well as architectural effect and programmatic requirements. Details accommodating skylights, chimneys, exhaust air vents, drainage, drip lines, and interfaces with other materials, such as the glazing and structural steelwork, were able to be designed and integrated into the shape of the gFRP panels. In contrast to traditional framed structures, the basic concept of the structural gFRP roof shape means the structure and the architecture are constantly in dialog at the surface level. The finished skin serves as the structure, and vice versa.

Fabrication and construction

The development of the finished shape was done by continually coordinating the engineering and fabrication parameters. This task called for the use of CATIA, a parametric software platform robust enough to handle the continually developing design criteria and able to interface with the fabrication tools that were to be used—all initially developed for applications in the aerospace industry. Control over the esthetic expression had heightened meaning, given the architectural and structural roles the roof played.

Erection and installation of the structural components required advanced geospatial locating systems as well as teams familiar with boat-building materials and methods.

Conclusion

The structural gFRP roof, exterior cladding, and interior shapes created a spatial, formal, and structural expression that would not have been possible in any other material. This capability advanced the ambitions of the architect by layering in a new technical, structural, and material intelligence.

Construction photo: view standing on top of the roof structure after the panels were seamed together on site.

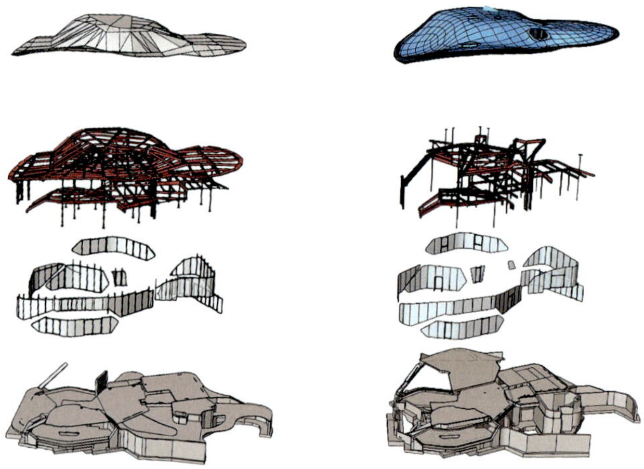

top
Screenshot of the building information modeling system used to coordinate design shape and building systems, as well as construction and fabrication parameters.

left
Diagrammatic comparison of two differently engineered structural systems that were developed for this building; the left one composed of steel beams, metal decking, and concrete, and the right using the FRP structure on a reduced steel frame. The difference in weight between the two systems was around 220 tons of structural material.

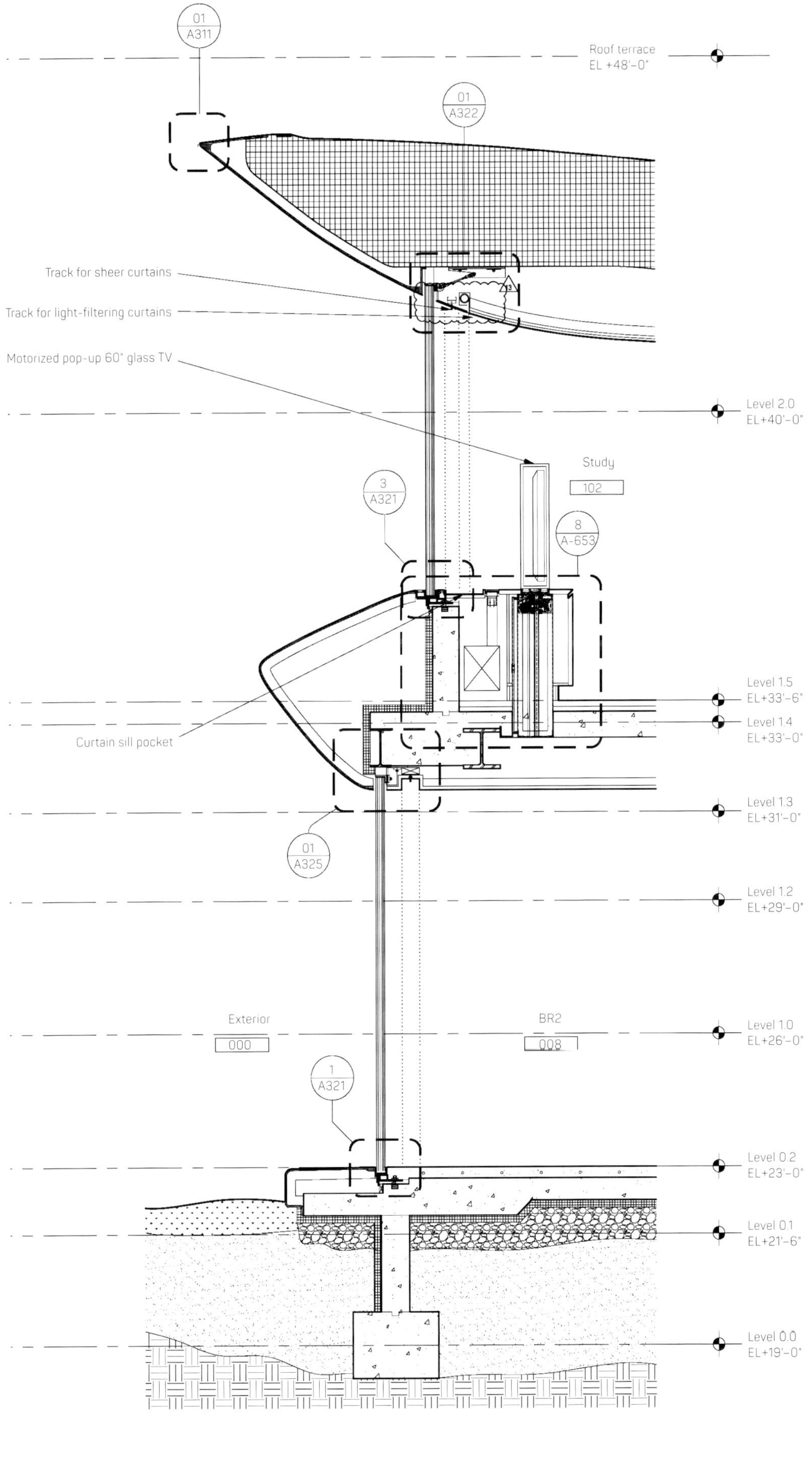

Detail drawing showing the relationship between the structural FRP sandwich roof panels, FRP cladding at soffit and exterior walls, glazing interface, and structural steel and concrete frame.

FEA analysis diagrams showing deflections under dead load.

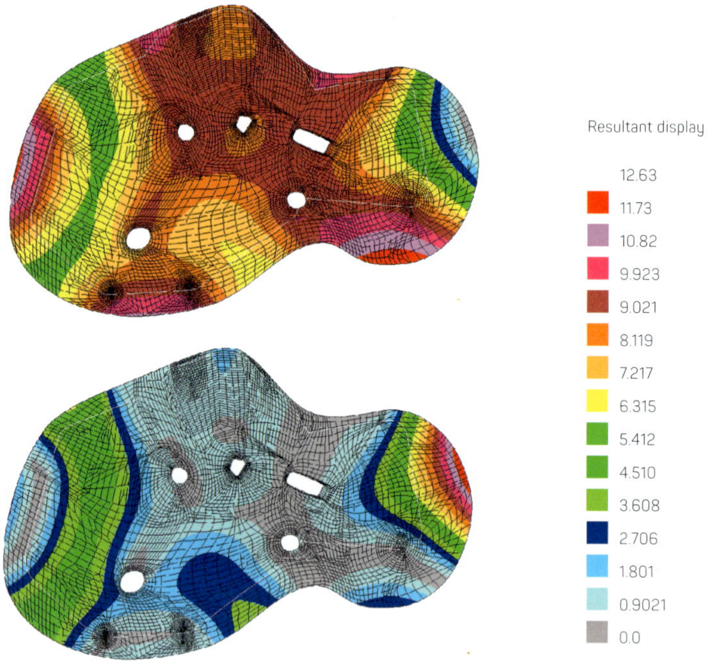

opposite top
Construction photo showing completed structural elements in place.

opposite bottom
Structural FRP panels being hoisted into place, with mounting points, center of gravity, and erection order calculated for precise field placement.

Photograph of foam blocks being CNC milled in a facility typically dedicated to aerospace and nautical tooling.

Component structural panels being hand laid and wetted-out with multiple layers of FRP.

APPLE

Retail stores and theater

Various locations worldwide

2014–2019

Architectural ambition

The technology company Apple has been popularizing its design vision for many years through the industrial design of its extremely popular consumer products, particularly its phones and computers. With the recently completed headquarters in Cupertino, California, and recent Apple retail stores throughout the world, Apple, working with the architects Foster + Partners, has translated that design vision into architecture.

The minimalist design ethos of Apple, with its emphasis on primary shapes, refined industrial materials, and a quest for greater and greater levels of transparency and thinness, finds its most fitting architectural material in carbon fiber (cFRP).

The buildings completed by Apple using carbon fiber so far include the Apple Store in Zorlu, Istanbul (2014), the Apple Store in Kunming, China (2016), the Michigan Avenue Apple Store in Chicago (2017), the Apple Store in Dubai (2017), the Steve Jobs Theater and the Visitor Center in Cupertino, California (2017), and the Apple Store in Xinyi, Taipei, Taiwan (2019). All of them, save for the Dubai location, utilize carbon fiber as a structural roof element; the Dubai store utilizes double-height, vertically spanning, operable "solar wing" window frames made of carbon fiber.

opposite
Interior view of the Steve Jobs Theater. The 155 ft diameter roof is entirely supported by the glass with no columns or walls.

Apple Stores

Beginning around 2014, Apple began installing a series of Apple Stores throughout the world using carbon fiber as a primary structural element.

The first of these retail centers was built in Zorlu, Turkey, designed and built in conjunction with the architects Foster + Partners and Premier Composite Technologies (a collaborating composite manufacturing company based in Dubai). This store, continuing the architectural language of earlier Apple Stores, has a large, glass, rectangular volume projecting from the ground surface, with the retail spaces all located underneath. In contrast to the famous all-glass example on Fifth Avenue in Manhattan (recently re-engineered to be composed of 21 glass panels encompassing a cubic void with all sides measuring 32.8 ft (10 m)), the Zorlu location uses only 4 panels of glass, each measuring 32.8 ft × 9.8 ft (10 m × 3 m), topped by a one-piece, thin, carbon-fiber roof some 1076 ft^2 (100 m^2) in area. The carbon-fiber roof rests on the glass, with no columns or walls or any mechanical fasteners, and all five panels are structurally bonded together with silicone.[1]

In 2016, in Kunming, Yunnan province, China, Apple installed the next example in the evolution of their retail architectural thinking. Here, Apple began the move away from the architectural motif of a cubic glass lantern above a subterranean store. Here, a large carbon-fiber disk measuring 52.5 ft (16 m) in diameter sits on structural glass; it is a cylindrical glass lantern topped with a giant, thin-edged carbon-fiber disk that now signifies the entrance to the store. Hong Kong-based IDA architects served as the architectural partner for this store, also with Premier Composite Technologies and structural engineers Eckersley O'Callaghan.

Two new Apple Stores opened in 2017, one located in Dubai and the other in Chicago, both utilizing carbon fiber as a structural element, though in different ways. Foster + Partners were the architects for both, in collaboration with Premier Composite Technologies and Eckersley O'Callaghan.

The Dubai Apple store is situated in the indoor Dubai Mall, with a large, double-height balcony overlooking a marina. It has 18 motorized, 36 ft (11 m) tall, operable "solar wings" made of gold-painted carbon fiber. In use, they shield and protect the glazing and interior spaces from solar heat gains during challenging times of day/year. Each of the operable panels was made from around 340 carbon fiber rods, the patterning and design of which were inspired by Arabic mashrabiyas. The pattern of cFRP rods is denser at the top than at the bottom, providing solar shading while allowing light to come in and views outwards.

In Chicago Apple built an ambitious flagship retail center at the heart of one of America's great architectural cities. Oriented at the center of a wide set of stairs that lead from an urban plaza along busy Michigan Avenue down to the Chicago River, the store aims to be "a source of creativity, education and entertainment."[2] A thin, carbon-fiber roof in the shape of a rounded rectangle floats above, measuring 108 ft × 95 ft (33 m × 29 m), supported by 4 slender columns at the center. The thin roof and minimal columns allow unobstructed views from the street down to the river, where 9.84 ft × 32.8 ft (3 m × 10 m) panels of glass enclose the space (including curved panes at the corners).

Apple Park

Apple's corporate headquarters, called Apple Park, is a 6.6 ha (175 acre) campus in Cupertino, California. Alongside the donut-shaped main building are two smaller buildings, both of which utilize structural carbon fiber. These two buildings are the Visitor Center, used to greet and orient visitors to the campus, and the Steve Jobs Theater, housing a 1000-seat theater used for publicity and other large events on the campus.

The Steve Jobs Theater offers one of the most pure and striking examples of the Apple design vision on a building scale. The plan is a perfect circle; the interior space of the building a perfect cylinder in volume. An impossibly thin roof cantilevers beyond the curved glass walls, and no columns or walls exist at all on the ground floor. The carbon fiber roof, the largest structure of its kind in the world, spans a full 155 ft (47.2 m) across its diameter (135 ft (41.1 m) between structural glass walls) and is light enough to be entirely supported by the curved glass forming the exterior envelope.[3] Building systems such as electrical and mechanical equipment are routed from the basement up to the roof imperceptibly through the silicone joints between the panels of glass.

The building program, a 1000-seat theater, is buried completely underground, and the only indication of programmatic function from outside is a glass elevator (which does not touch the 22 ft (6.7 m) high ceiling) and the tops of stone handrails that indicate an arcing staircase descending underground.

"The idea is very simple: a delicate hovering roof providing shelter in the middle of a beautiful Californian landscape. Making it feel effortless was among the hardest technical and engineering challenges we ever had to solve."[4] So said Senior Executive Partner Stefan Behling of architects Foster + Partners.

To accomplish this very simple idea but difficult technical challenge, the architects and engineers used a completely carbon fiber-reinforced epoxy polymer (cFRP) composite structural roof. This allowed the largest, thinnest possible structural roof, with a weight low enough to allow it to rest completely on the glazing with no columns or walls for support.

The roof is composed of 44 radial wedge-shaped cFRP panel sections, each approximately 70 ft (21.3 m) long and 11 ft (3.35 m) wide.[5] They were fabricated in Dubai at Premier Composite Technologies, shipped to Cupertino, then re-assembled at the job site.

Each wedge-shaped cFRP panel consists of an inverted U-shape, with a top surface sandwich laminate construction and two webs of monolithic laminate cFRP. These panels were bolted together at the webs and to a central cFRP hub approximately 15 ft (4.6 m) in diameter. The hub and each radial panel are roughly 5 ft (1.5 m) in depth at the thickest point, toward the center of the structure. They then taper out in depth to the thinnest profile at the outermost edge of the structure. A circumferential monolithic cFRP beam serves as the mounting point for the structural connection between the roof and the supporting glass panels.

The roof is fully self-supporting, carrying the self-imposed dead loads, the finish ceiling loads, maintenance live loads, and the lateral loads from the glazing and California seismic requirements. Acoustic concerns for the roof meant the structure was tested to meet ISO 140-18 acoustic standards.

All mechanical, electrical, and plumbing systems, including sprinklers, were routed from underground through the silicone joints between glazing panels up into the ceiling, requiring extensive design coordination. The effect was to eliminate those building services systems from view, allowing the glazing to create the effect of complete transparency between the ground plane and the roof.

Once all the panels had been shipped and bolted together on site at a staging location adjacent to the final position, the roof was then hoisted in one piece into its final position atop the structural glass panels. The assembled roof weighs a total of 80.7 tons (73 tonnes), is 155 ft (47.2 m) in diameter, and is the largest self-supporting fully carbon fiber roof in the world, in addition to being the world's largest all-glass-supported structure.

While 80 tons may seem like a lot for a unitary structure encompassing close to 19,000 ft^2 (1765 m^2), no other material would have come close to the minimal weight and dimensions that would have allowed this structural and architectural expression to be realized.

The Apple Visitor Center, also located within the campus of Apple's corporate headquarters at Cupertino, is a specially designed gateway point for visitors, housing a store, café, roof terrace, and small event space.

The carbon-fiber roof cantilevers out dramatically from the stone-clad cores within the building, tapering to a thin edge with no visible thickness from the ground, similar in profile to the roof of the Steve Jobs Theater. The roof requires no other columns or walls; the mullion-free glazing contributes to the effect of a floating roof.

See Detail Magazine, issue 3/2018 for more information.

Only through the use of carbon fiber were Apple and Foster + Partners able to find the most complete and pure realization of their design ambitions, illustrating a type of architecture achievable with the structural possibilities of FRP.

1 Premier Composite Technologies website, accessed 8/5/2019 via http://www.pct.ae/projects.php#architectural.

2 Foster + Partners website. Accessed 8/5/2019.

3 Kelly, Samantha Murphy. "The Spaceship Rises: A First Look at Apple's New Campus." *Mashable*, 7 Mar. 2016, mashable.com/2016/03/07/apple-campus-2-photos-spaceship/.

4 Foster + Partners. (2017). The Steve Jobs Theater at Apple Park [press release]. Retrieved from https://www.fosterandpartners.com/news/archive/2017/09/the-steve-jobs-theater-at-apple-park/.

5 Foster + Partners.

top
Diagram showing the respective column-free spans achieved by various Apple stores using glass and carbon fiber.

bottom
Photo from the exterior of the Steve Jobs Theater. Notice the lack of any columns or interior walls supporting the carbon fiber roof structure (the roof is light enough to be supported entirely by the glass envelope).

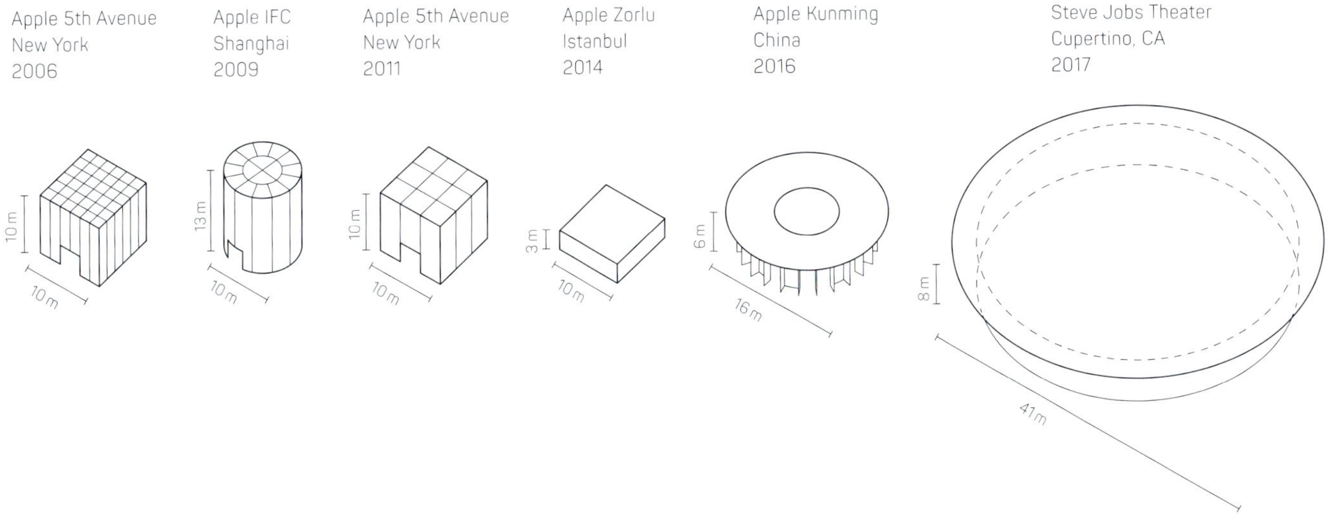

top
Exterior view, showing operable carbon-fiber "solar wings" in open position.

left
Interior view of Apple Dubai, showing the operable carbon-fiber "solar wings".

bottom
Exterior view of the Apple Store on Michigan Avenue in Chicago, USA.

Apple store in Xinyi, Taipei,
Taiwan.

Exterior view of the Apple
Park Visitor Center
with carbon-fiber roof.

Photo of the Apple Store
in Kunming, China.

See photo of the Apple Store
in Zorlu, Turkey on page 20.

NOVARTIS ENTRANCE PAVILION

Entry pavilion and reception

Basel, Switzerland

2018

Architectural ambition

The entrance pavilion serves as the first point of contact for visitors to the Novartis Campus in Basel, Switzerland, which strikes an immediate impression of clarity, openness, transparency, and innovation. A curved, monolithic roof reminiscent of an airplane wing cantilevers over glass with no visible beams or columns to support it. Serving as form, structure, enclosure, and thermal insulation all at the same time the gFRP roof achieves an architectural effect impossible with any other material.

Design, engineering, fabrication and construction

From the architect: The gFRP roof integrates all roof functions in a single, monolithic body: load-bearing structure, shape and surface finish, shading through overhang, thermal insulation, waterproofing, airtightness, and noise insulation. The roof's shape is an analogy to a cut-off wing tip with dimensions of 21.6 m × 18.5 m. Three edges are thinly rounded, whereas the western edge shows the "cut" side. The radii of the upper and lower faces vary continuously from east to west.

The roof is made of 460 gFRP-wrapped PUR foam cores of various densities. Their vertical faces create internal webs which, in combination with the face sheets, form the load-bearing structure. The foam cores define the roof's shape, which was modeled using CATIA®. CNC-controlled machines cut the foam into shapes, including all necessary recesses. gFRP laminates were

opposite
Exterior view.

added in several steps in hand lamination, thereby creating ever larger pieces: from individual blocks to block strips and finally to four large roof elements.

Approximately 100 small-scale tests were done to assist in the dimensioning and detailing of the laminates, including tensile tests on laminate strips and shear tests on overlapping joints. Four large-scale tests were performed on 23.6 ft × 2.95 ft × 0.98 ft (7.2 m × 0.9 m × 0.3 m) beams to verify various aspects of dimensioning, including large-scale tensile strength of the face sheets, buckling resistance of the face sheets and webs, tensile strength in the thickness direction at face sheet deviations, creep behavior and shear lag in the face sheets.

All vertical and horizontal loads are transferred through the all-glass façade into the foundation. The U-shaped façade elements each consist of an insulating glass unit, which is stiffened by glass fins on each vertical edge. They are connected at the top by a steel band, thereby creating a stiff wall against in-plane loads. The roof is vertically supported near each glass fin. Horizontal loads are introduced into the connecting steel bands at one point on each façade. Tension rods between the glass fins secure the roof against uplift. They are anchored in steel inserts in the gFRP roof.

The four roof elements were produced on a scaffold with adjustable support elevations. Block strips were arranged upside-down on the scaffolding and epoxy bonded on their vertical faces. Tolerances in the block strips were smoothed out and a continuous face sheet was added by hand lamination. A topcoat guarantees waterproofing and resistance to UV light. On the underside, the block strips were joined by gFRP plates, which was necessary for turning the element over. After that, the second face was made in the same way.

The four roof elements were transported overnight on trucks in stacks of two. The easternmost element was placed on the fixed part of a scaffolding and the remaining three elements were added on a movable part of the scaffolding. The elements were joined by epoxy strips on the webs and gFRP laminate strips on recesses in the face sheets. Local unevenness was smoothed out and the topcoat was completed along the joints. The glass façade was put in place after completion of the roof. The façade elements were bolted to steel consoles at the bottom and to the steel band at the top, which was integrated into the roof. After completion of the façade, the scaffolding was lowered and removed.

The focus of quality control was on geometric tolerances and on the correct application of the gFRP laminates. The geometry of all foam blocks was checked before lamination. In order to check the laminate structure, 1.57 in (40 mm) diameter samples were cut out of the face sheets. The laminate thickness was measured and the architecture of the glass fibers was checked after burning off the polyester matrix.

Conclusion

In conclusion, the composite material construction of the roof allowed an architectural expression impossible with any other material.

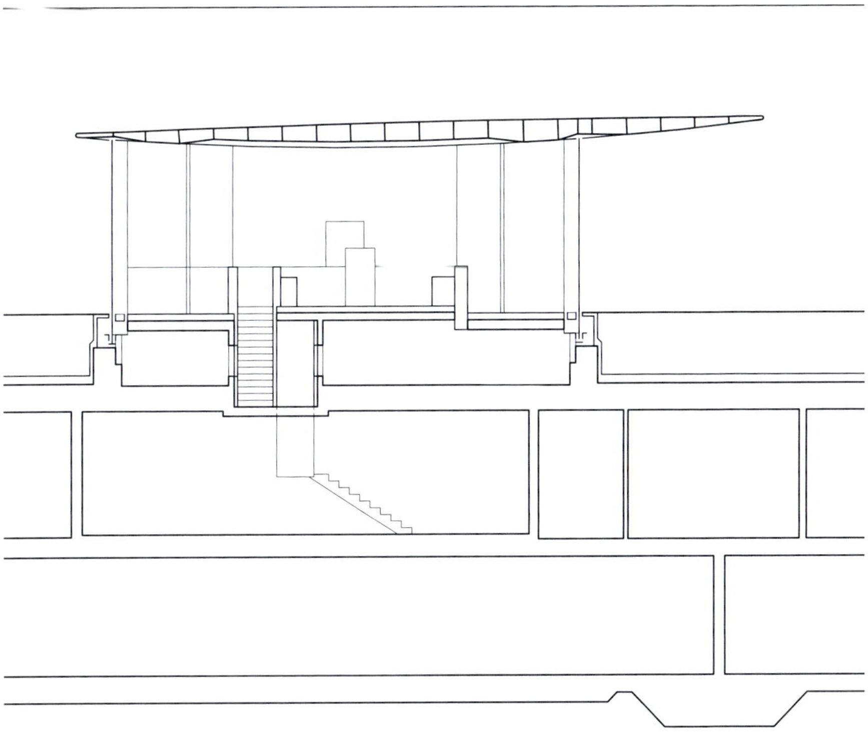

top
Exterior view.

left
Cross section of reception building.

top
Interior view.

bottom
Construction photos.

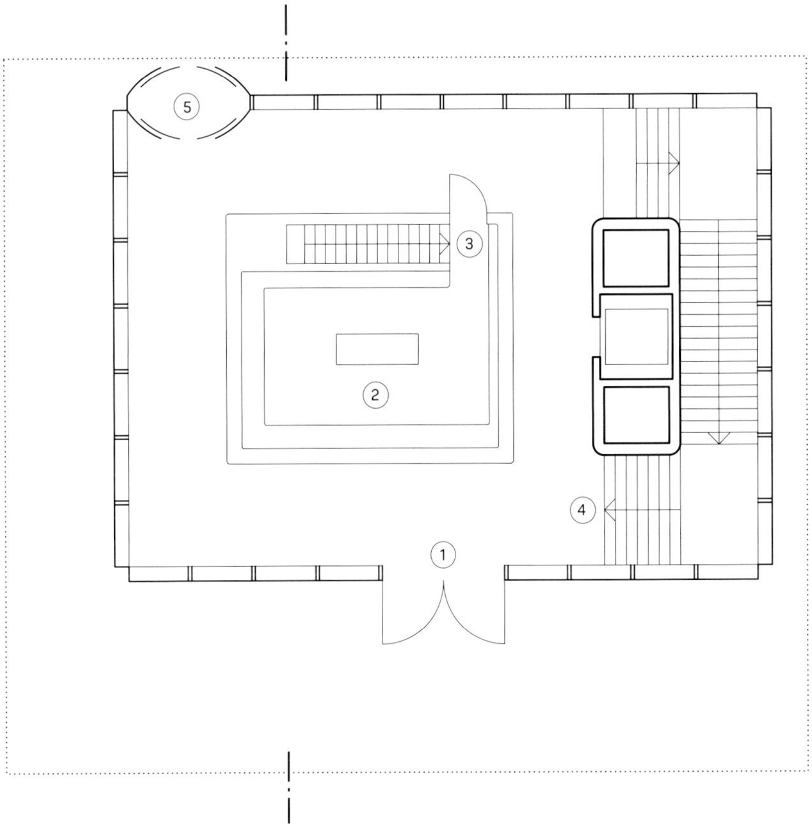

top
Floor plan of reception building.

bottom
Site plan showing entrance pavilion building in relation to the rest of the Novartis Campus.

1 Main entrance
2 Reception
3 Employee entrance
4 Access to underground parking garage
5 Access to campus
6 Entrance building
7 Novartis Campus

Vertical section of east façade.

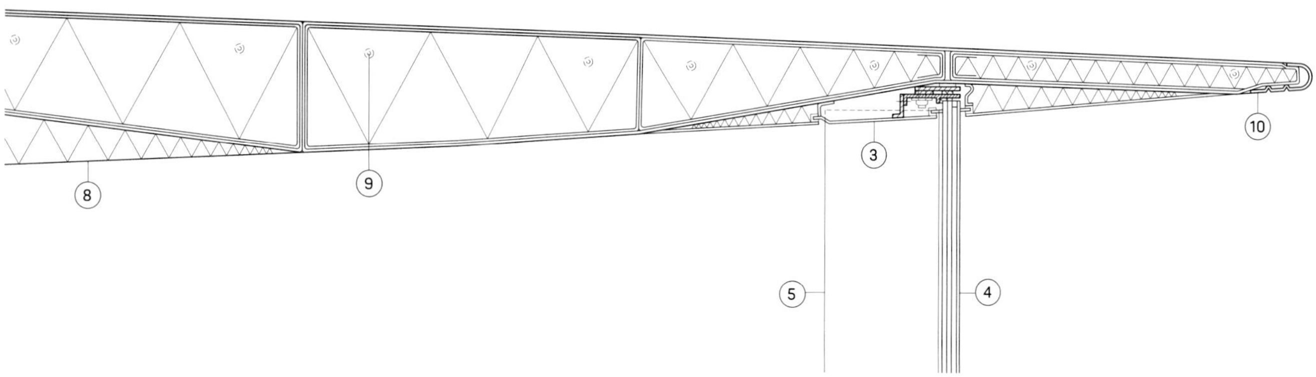

Detail of roof section.

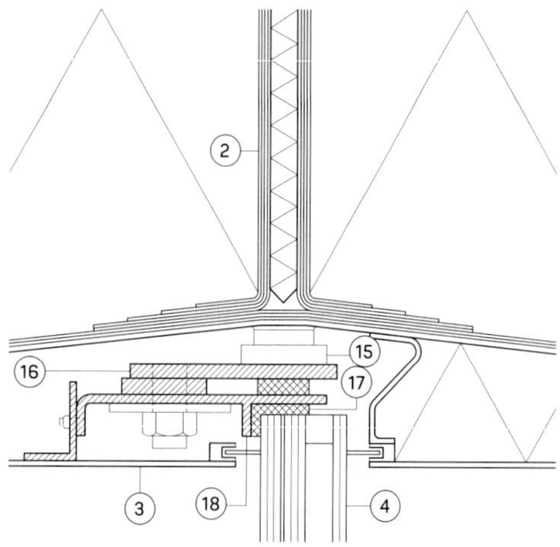

Glazing detail.

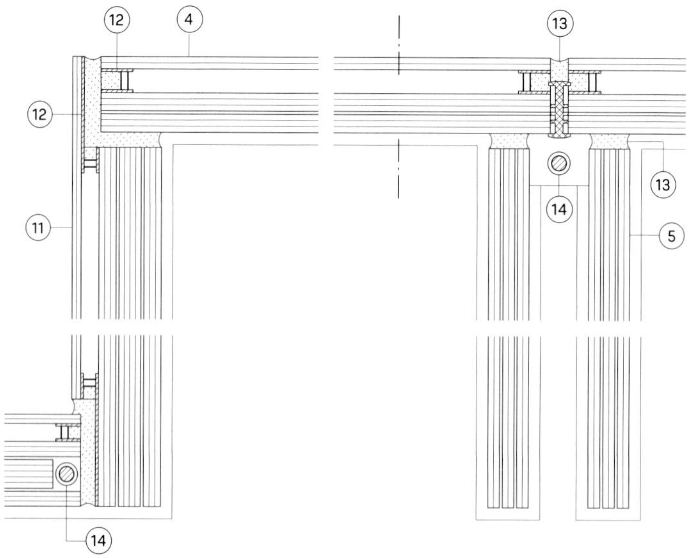

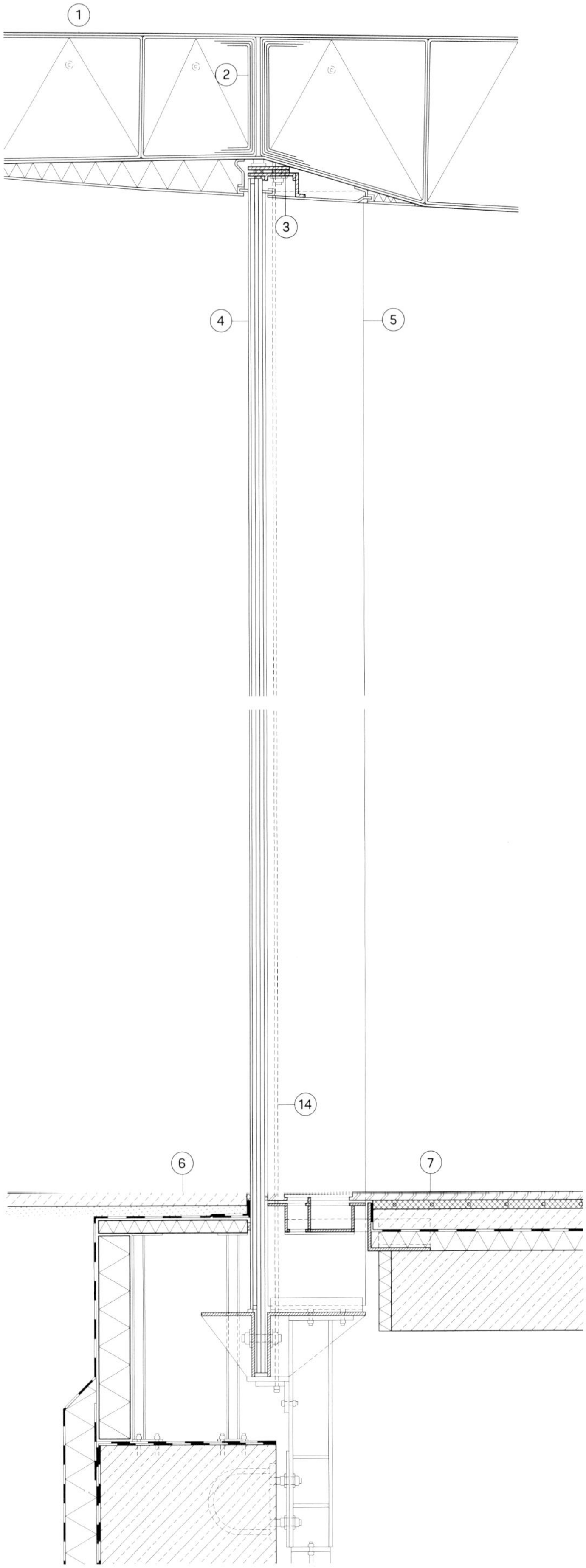

1 70–600 mm PUR block, laminate covering 6–10 mm gFRP; polyester topcoat, UV-resistant, self-extinguishing
2 15 mm rigid foam board between 2 × 12 mm to 2 × 18 mm multi-wall gFRP sheet
3 gFRP cover, removable
4 structural double glazing; 8 mm toughened glass + 16 mm cavity + laminated safety glass of 2 × 12 mm heat-strengthened glass with 1.52 mm PVB foil
5 glass fin: laminated safety glass of 3 × 8 mm heat-strengthened glass with 2 × 1.52 mm PVB foil; frame above: 50/35 mm stainless-steel channel below: 60 mm stainless-steel channel
6 65 mm asphalt
7 25 mm marble, 7 + 18 mm underfloor heating, 70 mm concrete floor base, 0.2 mm PE foil, 60 mm thermal insulation, 250 mm reinforced concrete deck
8 acoustic ceiling: 3 mm fabric netting, mineral-wool acoustic mat
9 control bolts for CNS fabrication
10 moulded gFRP weather drip
11 corner column: double glazing, 6 mm toughened glass + 12 mm cavity + laminated safety glass of heat-strengthened glass 12 + 15 + 12 mm
12 enamelled edge strip
13 silicone adhesive
14 steel tension rod 12 mm diameter encased in acrylic-glass sheath
15 sliding bearings (at intervals) 45 / 170 / 10 mm stainless-steel section
16 120 / 8 mm steel flat
17 synthetic resin injection as tolerance compensation
18 5 mm stainless-steel section

KOMATSU SEIREN

Offices, in-house exhibition halls

Nomi, Japan

2015

Architectural ambition

Komatsu Seiren, a fabric and textile manufacturing company, selected architects Kengo Kuma to seismically retrofit their offices and in-house exhibition halls with carbon fiber produced by the company. Located in Nomi, Ishikawa Prefecture, Japan, the concrete office building houses the company offices and showrooms, including the Fab Labo, a museum about the company's fabric innovations.

Design, engineering, fabrication and construction

To structurally brace the building against earthquakes, the architects searched for a novel way of using carbon fiber, a material produced by the client. Earthquakes, it is worth noting, are a common occurrence in Japan, and seismic building technology has been a focal point of the country's building research. The proprietary carbon fiber composite produced by Komatsu Seiren is called CABKOMA Strand Rod and is composed of synthetic and organic fibers finished with a thermoplastic resin.

Kengo Kuma and Associates came upon a novel way of building using the carbon fiber strand rods: internal carbon fiber-braced frames inside the building connected to a curtain of exterior carbon-fiber strand rods terminating in the ground outside the building. According to Kengo Kuma, the strand rods draw upon the rope-braiding techniques for which the local region is renowned. Draping the carbon fiber strand rods on the exterior

opposite
Exterior view showing carbon fiber strand rods spanning from the roof to the ground.

creates the main visual impact, while also providing the structural elements to resist lateral forces. This completely novel building method takes advantage of carbon fiber's inherent tensile strength, while also emphasizing the unique visual and esthetic possibilities of a structure based on fibrous strands.

On the rooftop, the dedication to material exploration continues, with a green roof made of porous ceramic panels composed of industrial by-products.

Conclusion

Kengo Kuma has built a practice around the careful consideration and exploration of materials, and this building is a testament to the many novel ways that carbon fiber's properties can be used to striking structural and esthetic effect.

Lateral bracing diagram.

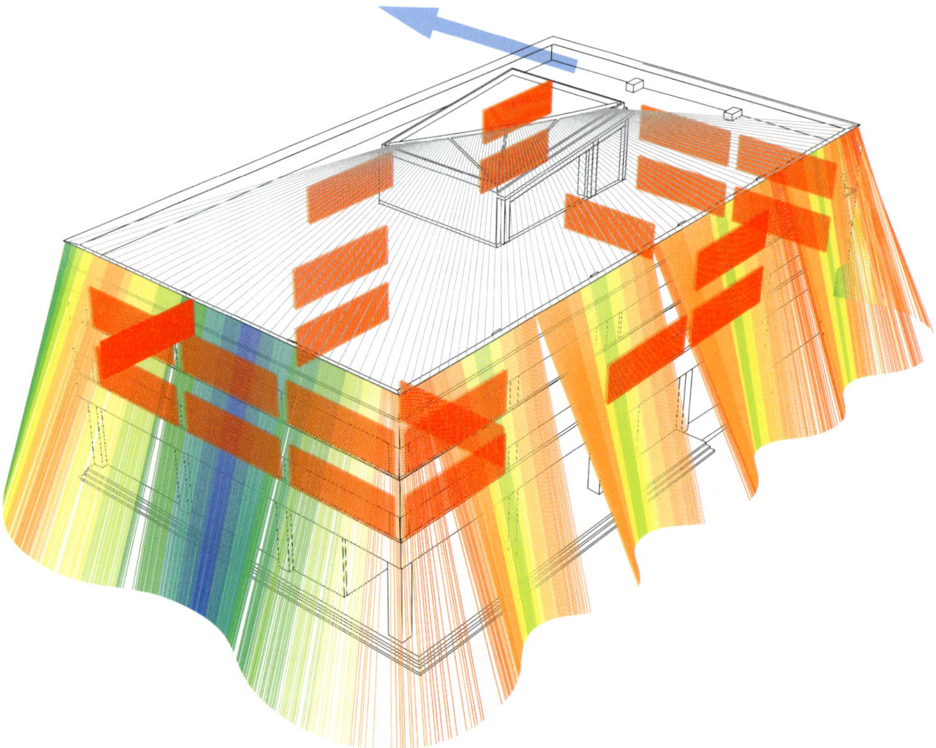

Aerial exterior view.

Site section showing lateral bracing system.

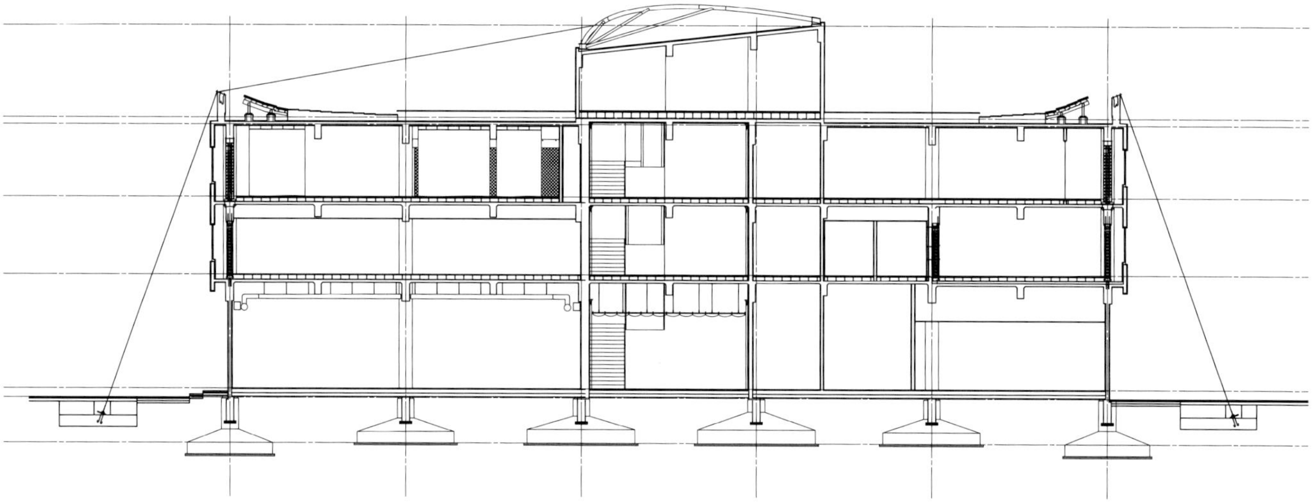

Site plan showing pattern of carbon fiber rod attachments at ground level.

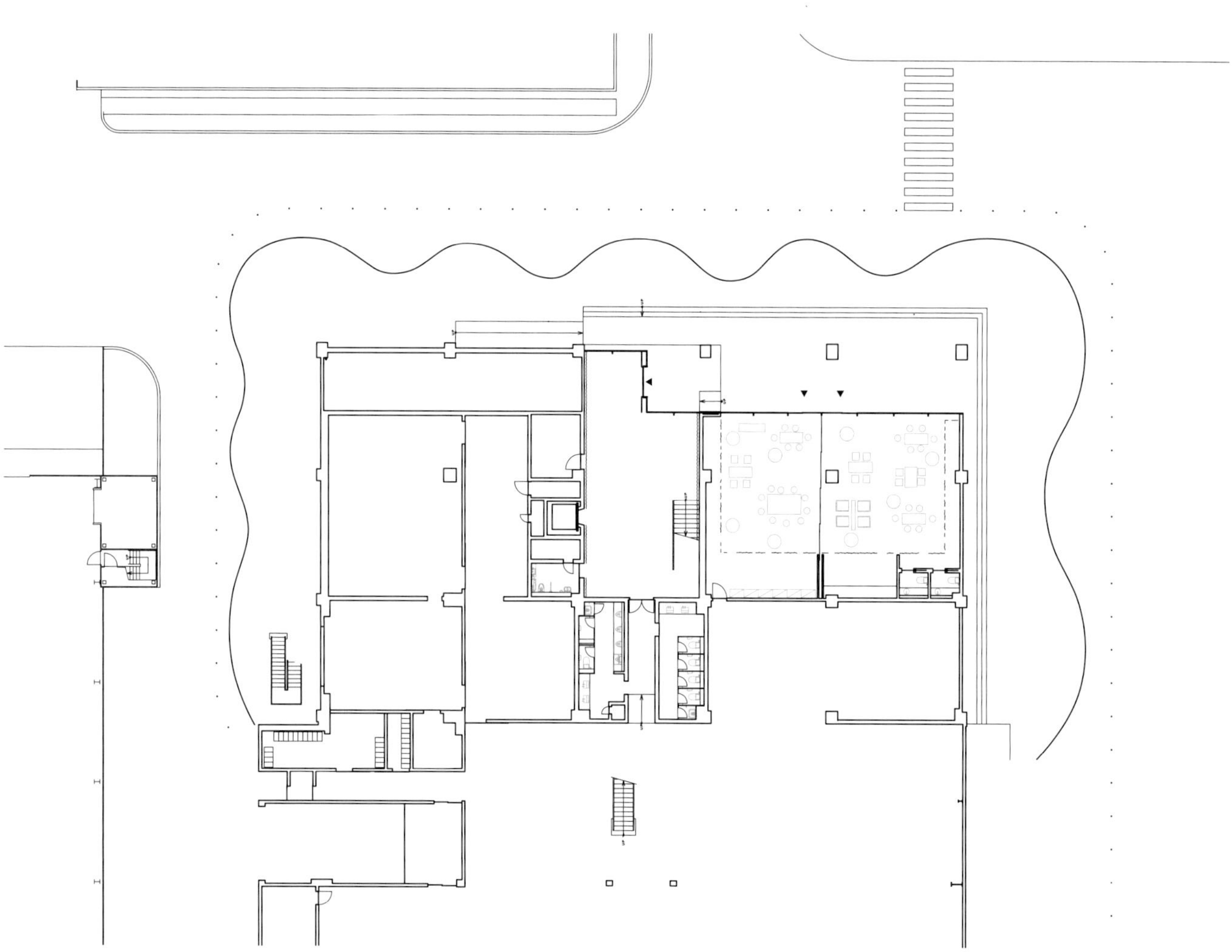

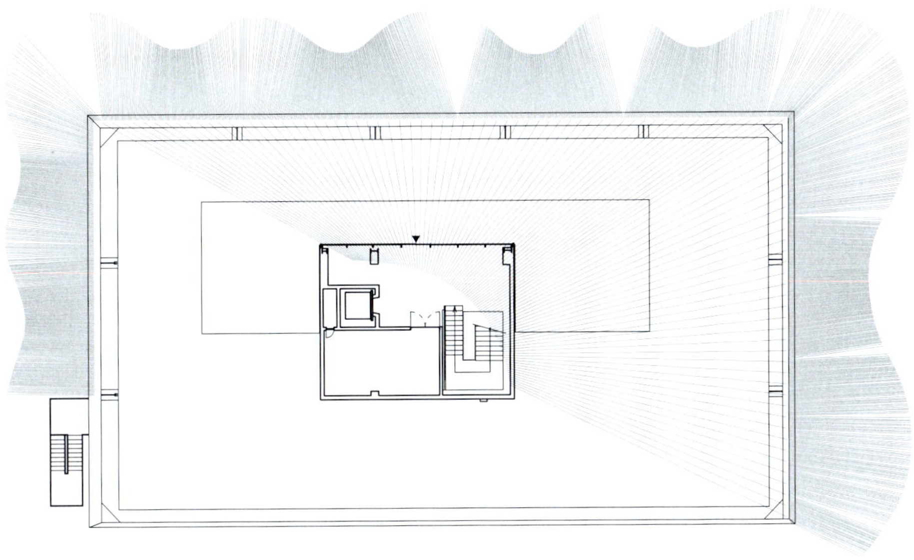

Roof plan showing carbon fiber rod placement and patterning between roof and ground.

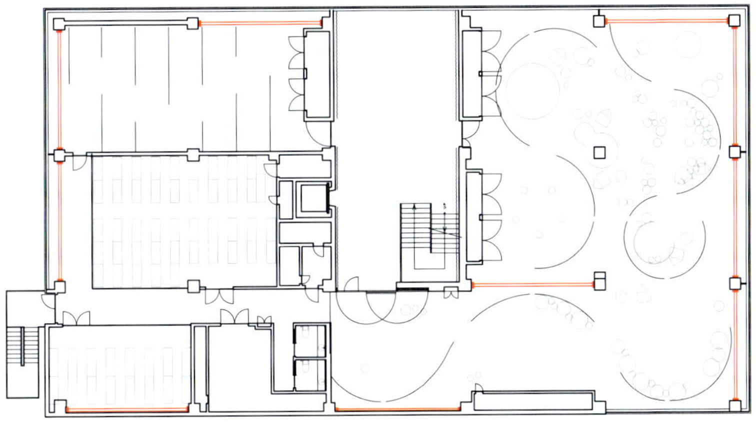

Third floor plan showing lateral bracing elements in red.

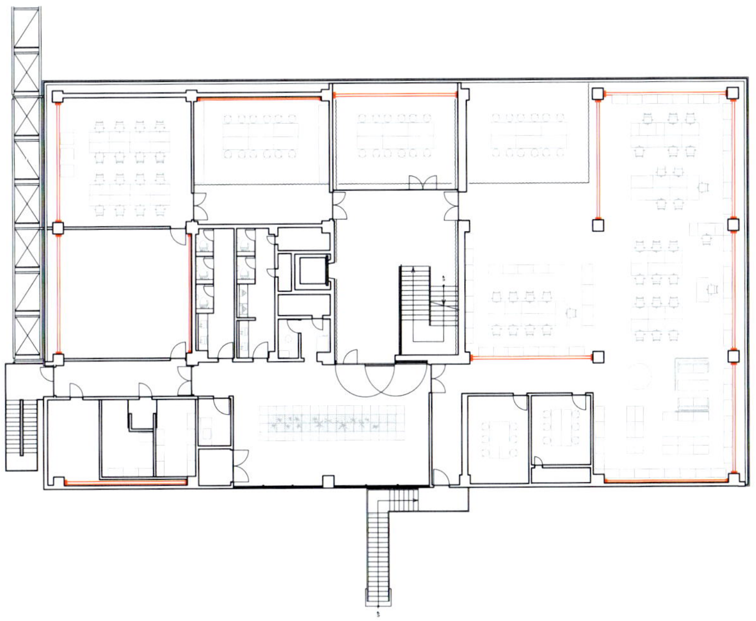

Second floor plan showing lateral bracing elements in red.

Elevation and section detail of interior lateral bracing elements.

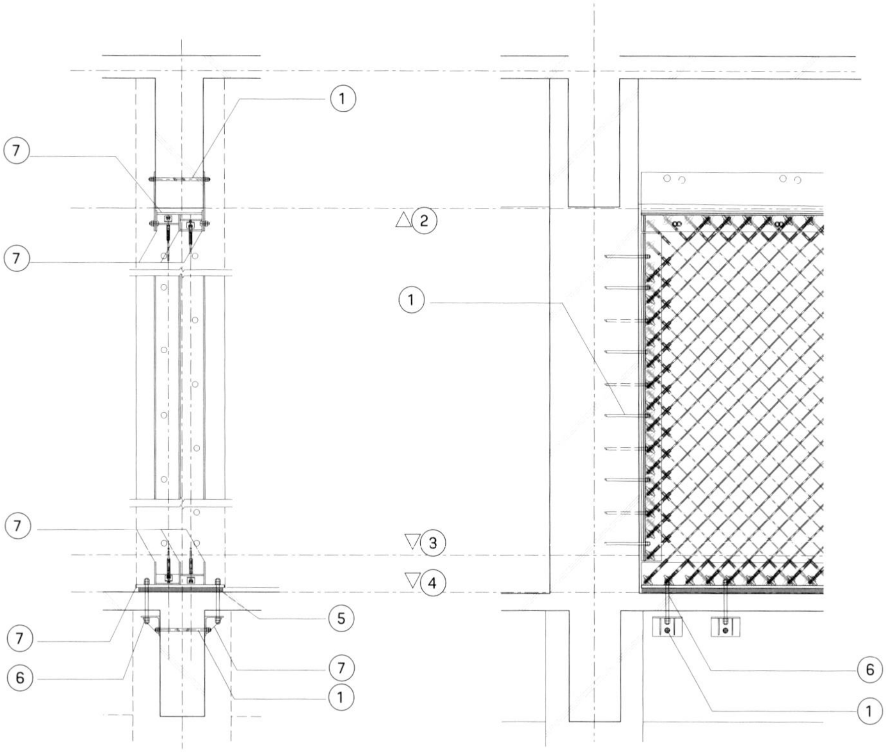

1 Post-installed anchor
2 Bottom of beam
3 Top of floor
4 Top of structural slab
5 Non-shrink grout
6 Slab penetration bolt
7 Steel plate

Section detail of exterior carbon fiber structure at roof and foundation.

1 Galvanized washer
2 Threaded bolt
3 Adhesive filled carbon fiber rod receiving sleeve
4 Carbon fiber rod
5 Steel plate
6 Anchor bolt
7 Steel strut
8 Sheath tube
9 Turnbuckle
10 Foundation lift prevention
11 Floor level -1100
12 Floor level -500

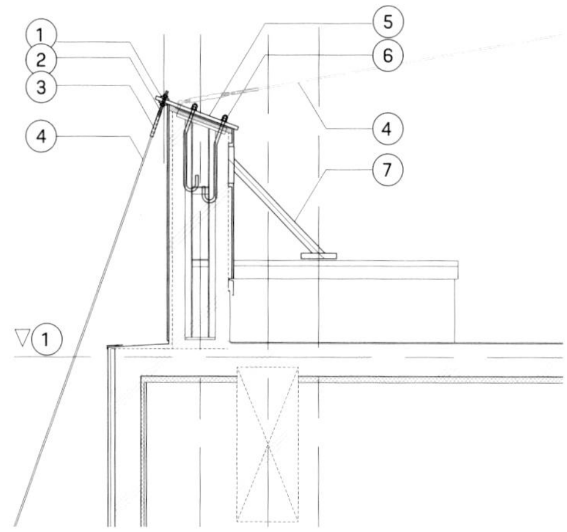

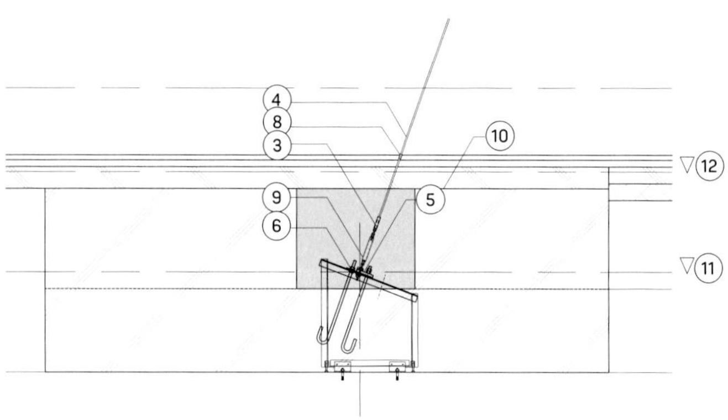

opposite top
Exterior view of carbon fiber cables at rooftop mounting points.

opposite middle left
Exterior view of carbon fiber cables.

opposite middle right
Exterior view of carbon fiber cables at ground mounting points.

opposite bottom left
Exterior view of carbon fiber cables during installation.

opposite bottom right
Construction photo: carbon fiber shear wall.

CASE STUDIES
SPECIAL CASES

HALLEY VI ANTARCTIC RESEARCH STATION

Laboratories, offices, living, and social areas

Brunt Ice Shelf, Antarctica

2013

Architectural ambition

Proving the suitability and capabilities of composite materials at the most extreme ends of the environment, the Halley VI Antarctic Research Station demonstrates several notable composite properties.

Halley VI is a science research station operated by the British Antarctic Survey, located on the Brunt Ice Shelf in Antarctica. It contains scientific laboratory spaces, offices, sleeping quarters, group social spaces, and living accommodation. The station is subject to extreme environmental conditions: temperatures down to -55 °C, solar gain temperatures on surfaces up to 30 °C, and wind speeds above 124 mph (200 kph). Air infiltration had to be minimized to protect the interior air quality. It also had to take into consideration construction and erection in those conditions, with a weight limit imposed by the need to transport the entire assembly, and have it sit safely on the ice shelf, and be moved in its entirety once fully assembled in the event of an emergency.

In addition to its peculiar transport and erection requirements, as a fully self-supporting and physically isolated building, it also had to meet very tight flammability requirements due to its remoteness.

Design and engineering

opposite
Exterior view of Halley VI Research Station in Antarctica.

The Halley VI Antarctic Research Station was designed as a series of composite FRP sandwich panels clad over a steel frame, elevated on hydraulic legs. The composite sandwich panels were composed of FRP skins on either side of a thick polyisocyanurate (PIR) fire-retardant foam core. The FRP skins were corrugated or ribbed and overlapped at the edges to prevent delamination. The total thickness of each panel was approximately 8 in (200 mm).

Each panel was manufactured using a vacuum infusion process in open molds. Fire-retardant polyester resin was used for the laminate skins and then finished with a special intumescent paint for further flame spread resistance on the interior and with an automotive polyurethane acrylic paint with extreme UV-fade resistance on the exterior.

Fabrication and construction

Finally, the entire surface had to be painted. To avoid any variations in the painting, the entire façade had to be spray painted in one pass for each coating. A UV-resistant paint used in the marine and aerospace industries was chosen and applied by boat painters. The finish has proven to show little fading and to be remarkably easy to clean.

Conclusion

The Halley VI Antarctic Research Station demonstrates an extreme range of properties that can be achieved with the use of FRP materials. The architects had this to say about FRP materials: "It is a hi-tech product drawing upon manual processes, and it is important to recognize this dichotomy when selecting FRP as a construction solution."

top
Cutaway view of the central/ social module.

bottom
Section through the central/ social module.

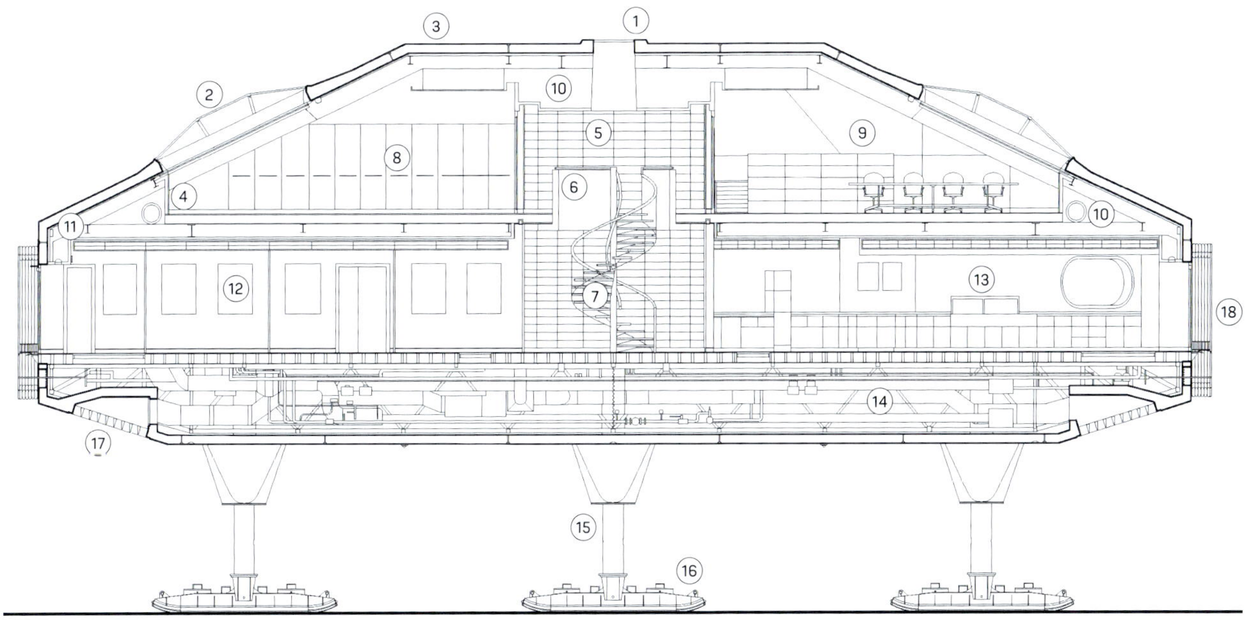

1 Triple glazed rooflight centered over spiral stair
2 Double glazed curved oval cockpit rooflight allows full views of auroral displays in winter
3 Painted GRP cladding incorporating PIR closed cell foam insulation with overall U-value of 0.113 W / m²k
4 Painted glass fiber faced Fermacell wall linings with integral movement joints
5 Lebanese cedar veneered curved wall panels to stair hub
6 Solid balustrade to upper landing of spiral stair
7 Satin stainless steel, cherry and glass spiral stair
8 Gym
9 TV lounge and meeting room
10 Service distribution to upper level
11 Intumescent coated steel superstructure
12 Bar lounge with historical photos mounted on wall
13 Servery
14 Service distribution to lower level with space frame superstructure
15 Hydraulic operated CHS leg wrapped in high performance insulation and mandrel wrapped with GRP skin
16 Steel skis
17 Pultruded GRP grille to air intake and extract
18 Insulated double skin flexible silicone rubber connectors between modules

Cladding detail.

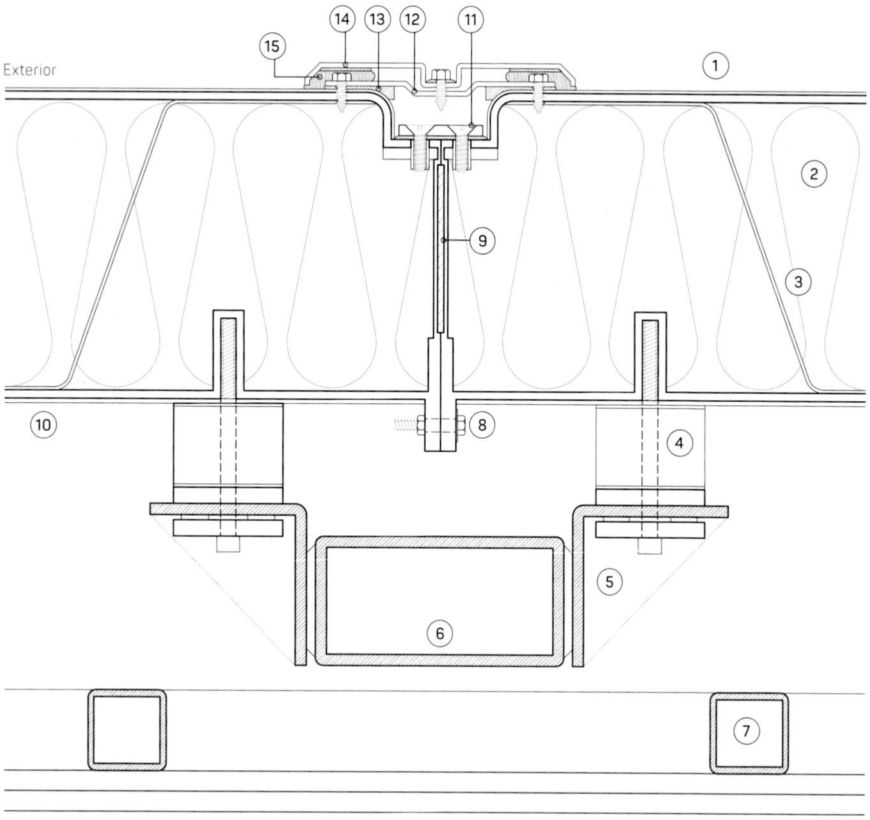

1 Fiber-reinforced polymer (FRP) outer skin to panels finished with gel coat and oversprayed with polyurethane acrylic automotive paint to ensure UV stability. Filled polyesther resin used to achieve 30 minutes fire resistance
2 190mm polyisocyanurate (PIR) closed-cell foam insulation to give U-value of 0.113 WsqmK
3 Resin-infused cross fibers prevent delamination under wind load
4 Flexible elastic silicone cladding mounting screwed into FRP "hard points" cast into panels
5 Steel cladding brackets welded to primary steel superstructure
6 Steel superstructure finished in intumescent coating to achieve 1-hour fire resistance. Steel grade selected for performance at extreme low temperature
7 Steel structure of prefabricated room pods (bedrooms, bathrooms, offices, etc). Pods lined in Fermacell board selected for rigidity and acoustic performance
8 Panels bolted together through FRP flanges using stainless steel fixings
9 Continuous compressible neoprene insulation maintains thermal performance at joints. Insulation finished with PTFE to reduce friction during installation.
10 Fiber-reinforced polymer inner skin to panels finished with intumescent paint to achieve C-s3d2 (Class 0) surface spread of flame characteristics
11 Panels jointed with FRP jointing strip fixed with countersunk M10 stainless steel cap screws through compressed foam neoprene gasket
12 Extruded aluminum internal cover mounting strip
13 Aluminum mounting strip fixed with coach screws. Foamed EPDM compressed gasket seal between mounting strip and panel.
14 Extruded aluminum external cover strip finished with polyurethane acrylic automotive paint to match panel finish, fixed to internal aluminum mounting strip with self-drilling stainless steel fasteners
15 Junction cover gasket formed in foamed EPDM

opposite top
Exterior view of modules.

opposite bottom
Construction photo, as cladding is applied to one of the standard modules.

Merit

CHANEL MOBILE ART PAVILION

Pavilion

Hong Kong, New York, Tokyo, Paris

2008–2010

opposite
Aerial view in front of the Institut du Monde Arabe.

Architectural ambition

In 2007, the French fashion label Chanel commissioned 20 artists to create works of art inspired by Chanel handbags; the resulting works were then exhibited in a specially designed mobile art pavilion designed by Zaha Hadid Architects. The pavilion needed to be temperature and humidity controlled for the display of art and capable of handling large crowds, but also able to be assembled, disassembled, and shipped to various locations for re-installation.

As the architects' press release states, "The Mobile Art Pavilion is inspired by one of Chanel's signature creations, the quilted bag. [It] is the very latest evolution of Hadid's architectural language that generates a sculptural sensuality with a coherent formal logic. This new architecture flourishes via the new digital modeling tools that augment the design process with techniques of continuous fluidity."

Design, engineering, fabrication and construction

The design is based on a parametrically distorted torus, about 7534 ft^2 (700 m^2) in floor area, with a central courtyard and an ethylene tetrafluoroethylene (ETFE) pillow roof. The panelization scheme represents a logic of subdivisions within a sphere, combined with the size requirements of shipping. "The partitioning seams become a strong formal feature of the exterior façade cladding, while these seams also create a spatial rhythm of perspective views within the interior exhibition spaces."

The double-curvature façade panels were made of a core-insulated fiberglass with high-gloss lacquer on the outside. The panels were fabricated in the UK by Stage One Creative Services, and then attached to a steel skeleton. Each panel was created with strict transportation constraints in mind; no panel is larger than 7.6 ft × 39.4 ft (2.3 m × 12 m), i. e. transport container dimensions. The composite FRP material's strength, durability, ability to fabricated to conform to the design, and light weight meant a perfect fit for the architectural and performance goals of the pavilion.

Conclusion

The Mobile Art Pavilion, utilizing FRP exterior panels to facilitate both the architectural design language and the performance requirements of a traveling pavilion, represents some of the architectural possibilities made reality by the technology of composites. Zaha Hadid is quoted as saying, "The complexity and technological advances in digital imaging software and construction techniques have made the architecture of the Mobile Art Pavilion possible. It is an architectural language of fluidity and nature, driven by new digital design and manufacturing processes which have enabled us to create the pavilion's totally organic forms—instead of the serial order of repetition that marks the architecture of the industrial 20th century."

Rendering.

Section.

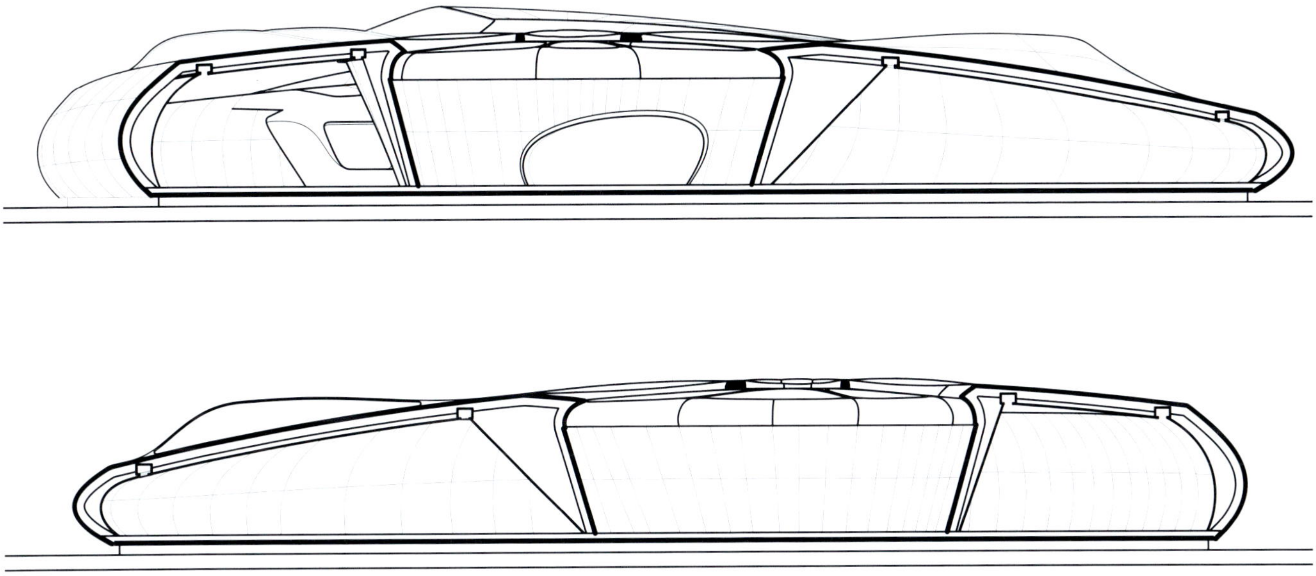

Design diagrams.

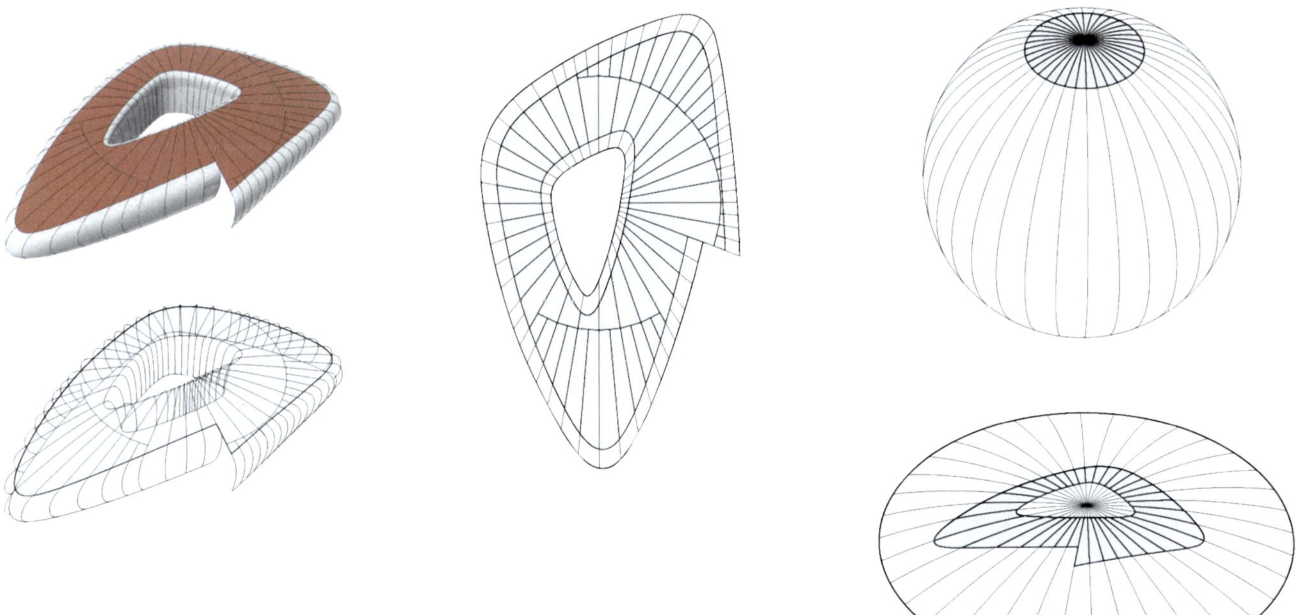

Ground floor plan.

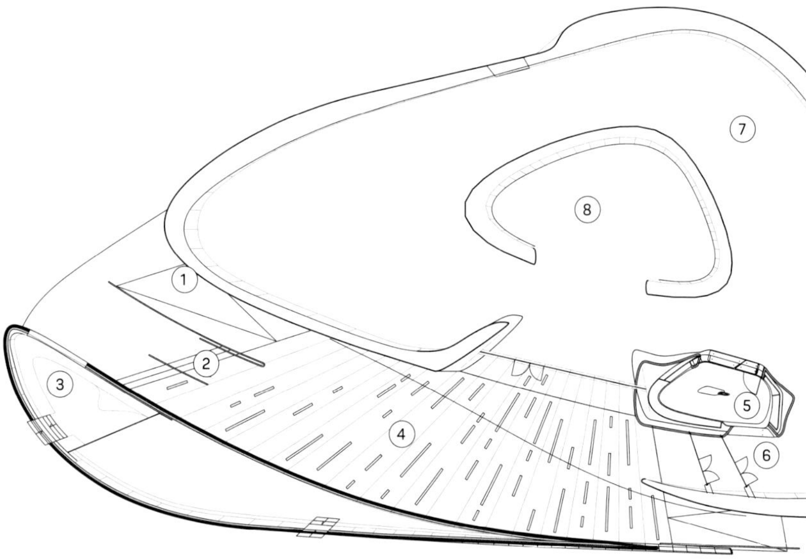

1 Ramp
2 Stairs
3 Ticket house
4 Terrace
5 Cloak room
6 Entrance
7 Exhibition space
8 Courtyard

Roof plan.

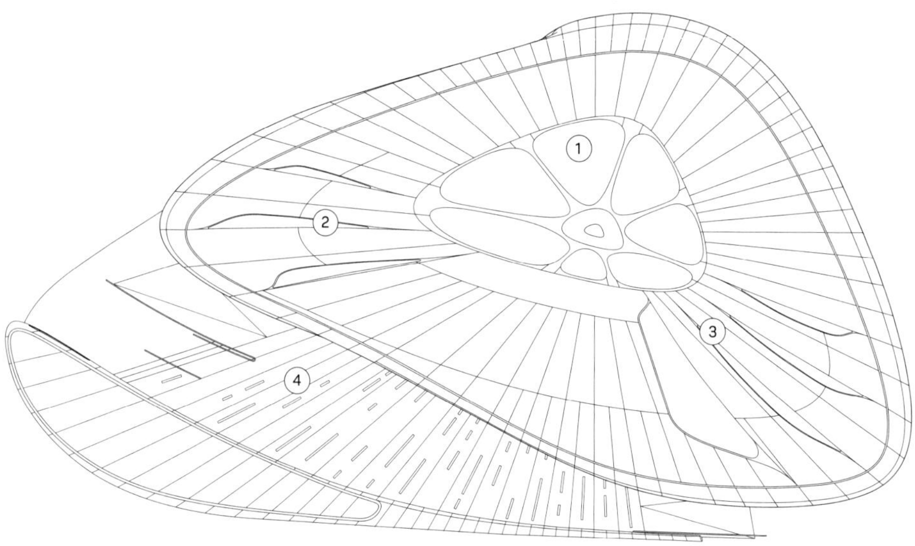

1, 2, 3 Transparent glass cushions
4 Light panels

Axonometric view of the structural steel framework.

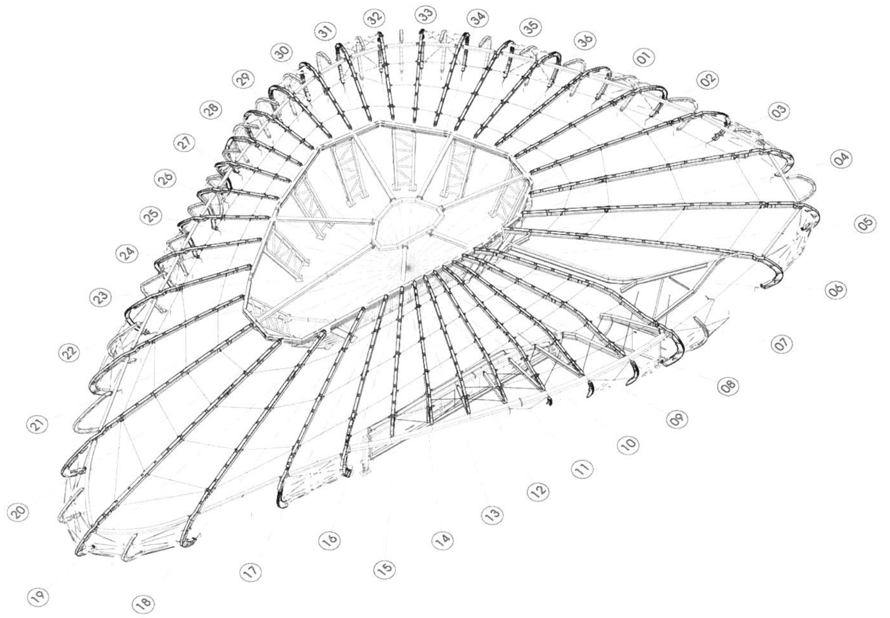

Elevation view of a structural steel framework member.

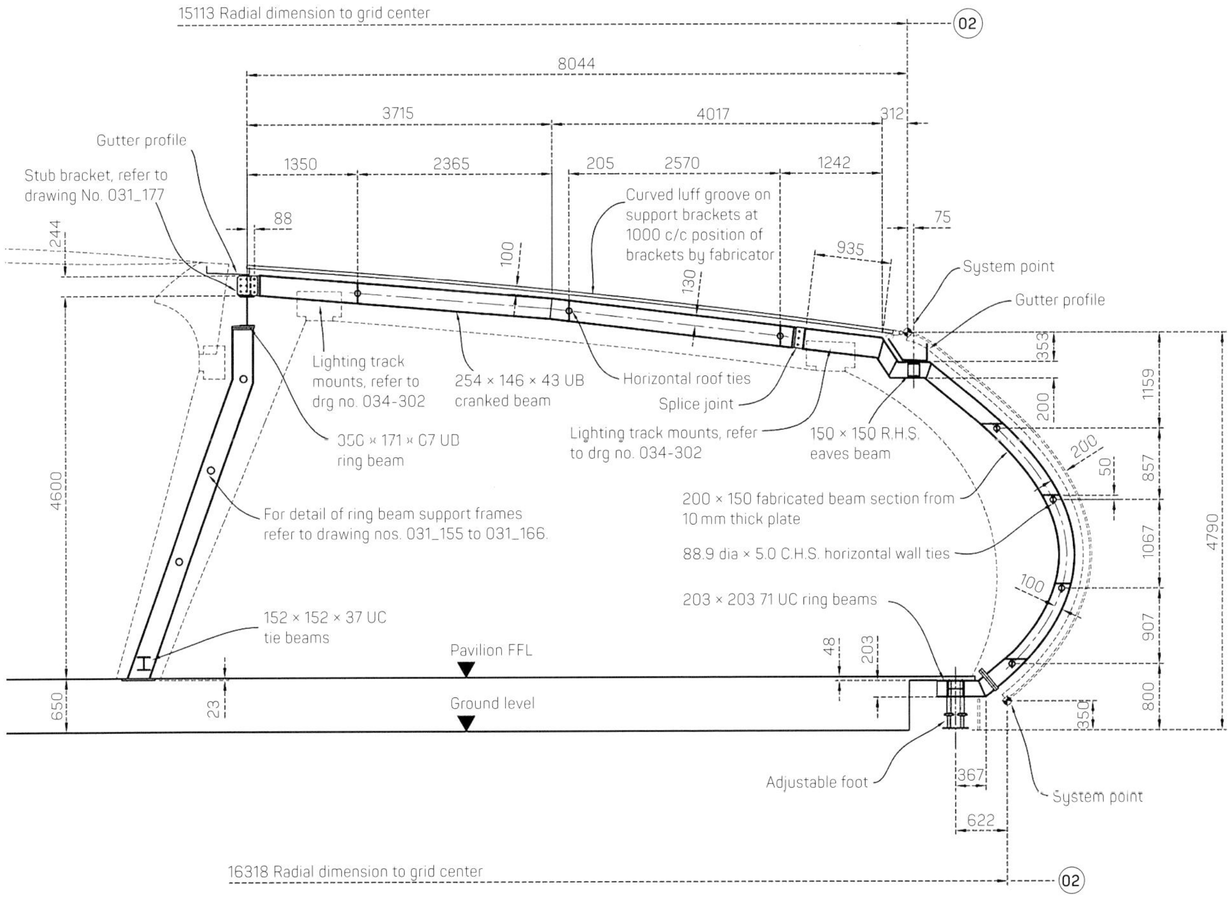

Cladding detail.

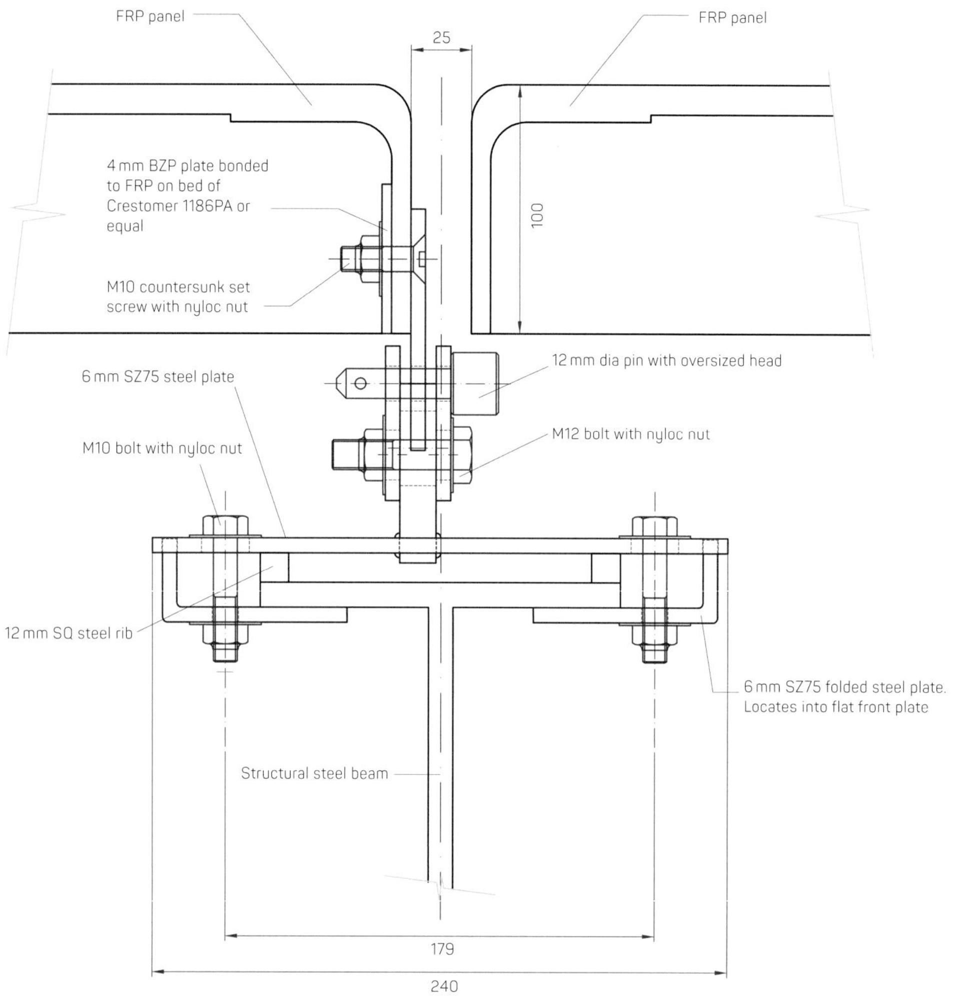

Detail of FRP panel mounting hardware.

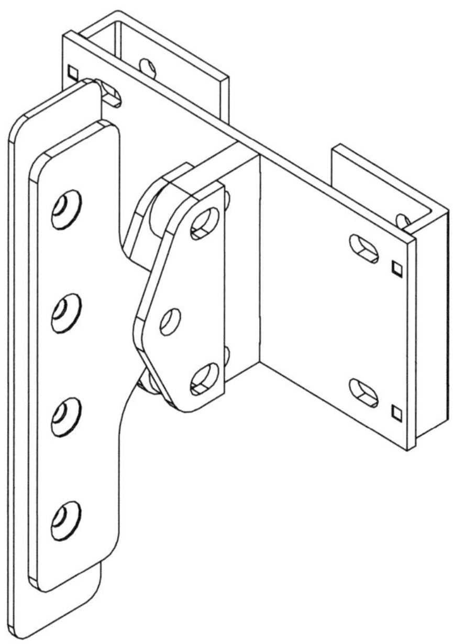

View of the pavilion set up in front of the Institut du Monde Arabe in Paris.

Interior view of the pavilion, showing artwork, furniture, and models pertaining to the pavilions design.

FLOTSAM AND JETSAM

Pavilion

Miami, USA and Nairobi, Kenya

2016

Architectural ambition

Designed for the Design Miami exhibition, the initial brief specified a few broad parameters: the installation must be assembled within five days, span generous distances to host a variety of programmatic events, showcase an innovative construction method, and support easy transport and reassembly.

"At once glamorously amorphous and rigorously defined, the dual pavilions of *Flotsam and Jetsam* evoke the geometries of current-borne sea life from diatoms to jellyfish."[1] The innovative construction materials and methods explore the formal, structural, and procedural possibilities of robotic additive manufacturing with carbon fiber and bio-composite materials.

Design, engineering, fabrication and construction

SHoP Architects, in partnership with Dassault Systèmes, Thornton Tomasetti, Branch Technology, and the Oak Ridge National Laboratory (ORNL) used parametric modeling to explore gridshell structures (as advanced by Russian engineer Vladimir Shukhov) with additive manufacturing technology and robotic fabrication. Critical capabilities of additive manufacturing technology include customizable material distribution, geometric freedom, and parts consolidation, minimizing waste and simplifying the fabrication and construction process.

The optimization of print time and material volume in conjunction with structural loading was a primary constraint, necessitating intensive coordination among the engineers, the architects, and the developers of the proprietary material technology.

opposite
View inside the pavilion.

Branch Technology manufactured the primary structural elements using a carbon fiber-reinforced ABS polymer and a proprietary method called Cellular Fabrication™, an additive manufacturing process. This process relies on adapted industrial robotics to bring 3D printing into broader use as a full-scale, practical means of construction.

A second material printing technology was provided by ORNL using a biodegradable bamboo-polylactic acid (PLA) substrate. This new material, invented in-house by ORNL, offered a green and renewable alternative to petroleum-based thermoplastics and adds to the new and exciting research being done in bio-composites.

The pavilions, while considered to be outdoor semi-permanent structures, still required a fire-rating for installation. This was resolved by using a clear-coat spray application on the final printed product to ensure the necessary rating requirements.

The architects state: "The combination of a free-form additive manufacturing process employed for the carbon fiber composite coupled with a laminar printing process for the bamboo polymer yielded construction tolerances that, until the final assembly week, remained unknown as the two printed mediums were arriving on site from two different fabricators. It is a testament to the collaborative design process and SHoP's direct-to-fabrication methodology that the construction and assembly came together better and faster than expected."

Conclusion

Though initially designed to be part of Design Miami's temporary installation program, the pavilions have served in residence as a public amenity for two years in the Design District's Jungle Plaza, been re-installed twice within the civic realm (hosting weekend events such as farmer's markets), withstood several Florida storms, and been shipped to Nairobi, Kenya, where they were installed again as part of the United Nations Environment Assembly there. *Flotsam and Jetsam* remains in use at the University of Nairobi. As the architects state, "Through this journey, there exists the inevitable wear from external forces, yet this project's continued application and redeployment serves as a case study testament to the inherent strength and sustainability of composite materials."

1 Email interview with SHoP Architects, March, 2019.

bottom
Part and component diagram.

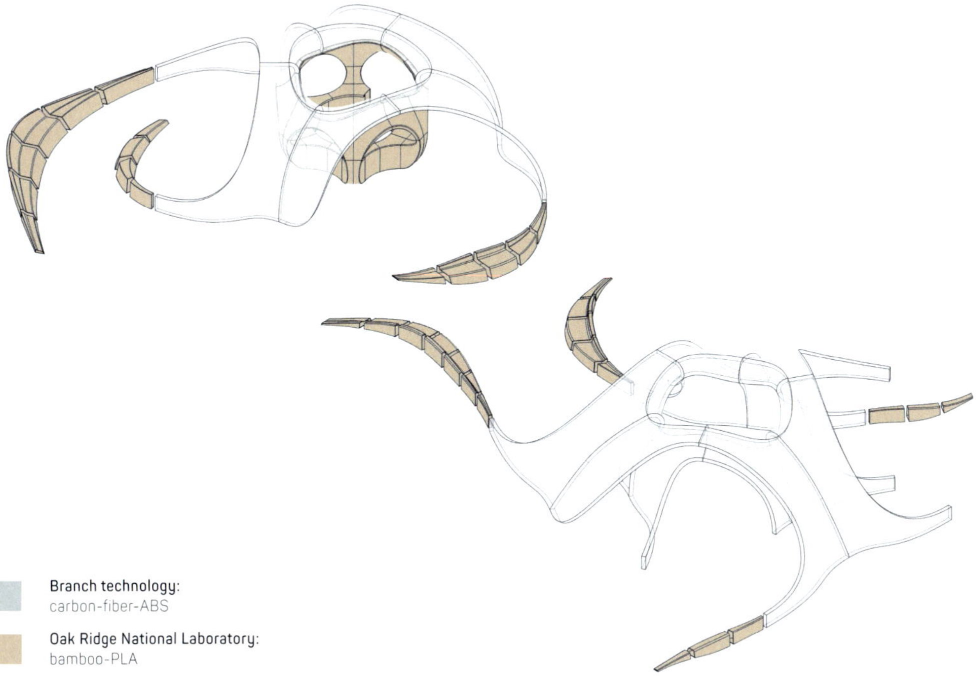

Branch technology:
carbon-fiber-ABS

Oak Ridge National Laboratory:
bamboo-PLA

Rudy

Build Envelope:
47.7' (L)
5.6' (W)
7.6' (H)

Parts:
E / D / M / N / W / W2 / q / q2 /
A / H / C / O / O2 / J / T / T2 / R

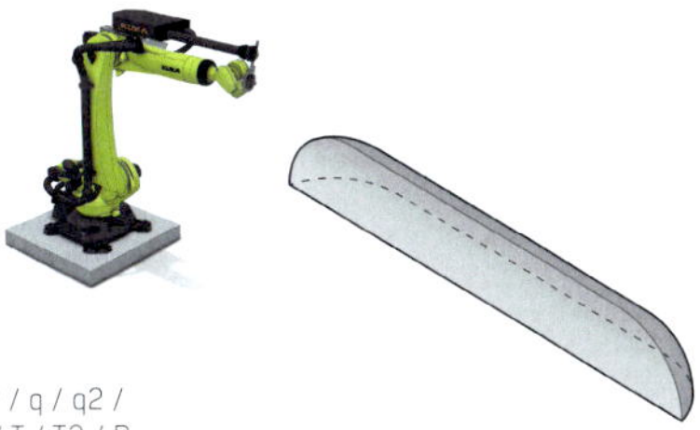

Walker & Tex

Build Envelope:
16.6' (L)
5.1' (W)
7.2' (H)

Parts:
G / F / B / L / K / I
S / P / P2 / U / V / V2

Aerial view of the pavilions.

Detail view of 3D-printed carbon fiber.

The pavilions as installed in Nairobi.

3D-printing of the pavilion.

KUKA
KUKA

ICD / ITKE RESEARCH PAVILIONS

Research Pavilion

Stuttgart, Germany

2012–2019

At the University of Stuttgart in Germany, the Institute for Computational Design (ICD) and the Institute of Building Structures and Structural Design (ITKE) have collaborated over the past several years on a series of annual pavilions that are some of the best explorations of emerging material and process technologies as they relate to the craft of building.

The joint ICD/ITKE Research Pavilions from 2012–2019 all vary slightly but are united in their interdisciplinary approach (involving the departments of biology, textile design, aerospace, and geoscience, in addition to the architecture, computational design, and engineering departments), exploration of computational and robotic methods, fibrous composite material usage, and biologically inspired forms/tectonic resolution.

Each one merits study for the specific design, technical, and process resolutions achieved.

opposite
A student of the ICD/ITKE at the University of Stuttgart controlling the robotic fabrication process for the carbon-fiber pavilion.

Exterior view of the finished pavilion.

Detail view of the cured carbon fiber structure.

2012

Architectural ambition

The initial ICD/ITKE Pavilion, completed in 2012, looked to biologic models for inspiration in the design and fabrication of structures using computational and robotic tools. Or, as their press materials state, the pavilion "investigates the possible interrelation between biomimetic design strategies and novel processes of robotic production. The research focused on the material and morphological principles of arthropods' exoskeletons as a source of exploration for a new composite construction paradigm in architecture."

Central to the project was the idea of transposing "the fibrous morphology" of biologic models "to fiber-reinforced composite materials, the anisotropy of which was integrated from the start into the computer-based design and simulation processes." This meant studying natural materials, many of which are fibrous in nature, and understanding what parallels may be found between those materials, their form, and contemporary composite material processes.

Integration of the design, analysis, and fabrication methods was fundamental to the project. This contrasts with the more linear, sequential mode of conventional building design. "Form finding, material and structural design were directly integrated in the design process, whereby the complex interaction of form, material, structure and fabrication technology could be used as an integral aspect of the biomimetic design methodology."[1] The finished pavilion has a shell thickness of 0.157 in (4 mm) capable of spanning 26.2 ft (8 m), achieving a remarkable structural and material efficiency.

Design, engineering, fabrication and construction

Research began by studying a wide range of different invertebrates before settling upon the lobster (*Homarus americanus*) as the biologic model for design. In particular, the lobster's exoskeleton, which is made of chitin, was the source of inspiration. The exoskeletal shell of the lobster is a locally materially differentiated structure, meaning that the microscopic material of the shell is distributed, oriented, and geometrically arranged for structural efficiency.

The principles of local material variation and placement were then applied to the design of the pavilion. Using filament winding as a basis, the designers then searched for a method that would free them from the constraints of a positive mold, typical for composite filament winding processes but impractical for architectural applications. They settled upon a method using a temporary, lightweight steel armature with defined anchor points, between which a robot could stretch continuous strands of resinous fibers. Through a layering of different fibrous materials, with intermediate curing times, the pavilion could achieve a "heterogeneity, hierarchy, and functional integration" of materials, traits that were identified as integral to biologic structures.

Computationally, the direct linking of architectural form, finite element analysis, and material testing information allowed the efficient simulation of numerous variations. Fiber material, layer arrangement, and geometric form were optimized to create a highly efficient structure with minimal use of material.

The pavilion was fabricated on site with a purpose-built, weather proof, 6-axis robotic arm that stretched toward a rotating platform. The robotic arm had a specially built tool that saturated the fibers in resin immediately before placement upon the temporary armature. This setup allowed a structure approximately 26.2 ft (8 m) in diameter and 11.5 ft (3.5 m) in height, a build volume that was specific to the method generated by the designers.

The final structure weighs 705 lb (320 kg), spans 26.2 ft (8 m) in diameter, and "reveals the system's structural logic through the spatial arrangement of the carbon and glass fibers."[2] "The concurrent integration of the biomimetic principles of the lobster's cuticle and the logics of the newly developed robotic carbon and glass fiber filament winding within the computational design process, enable a high level of structural performance and novel tectonic opportunities for architecture."[3]

1 Press materials from University of Stuttgart.
2 Press materials from University of Stuttgart.
3 Press materials from University of Stuttgart.

Site plan drawing.

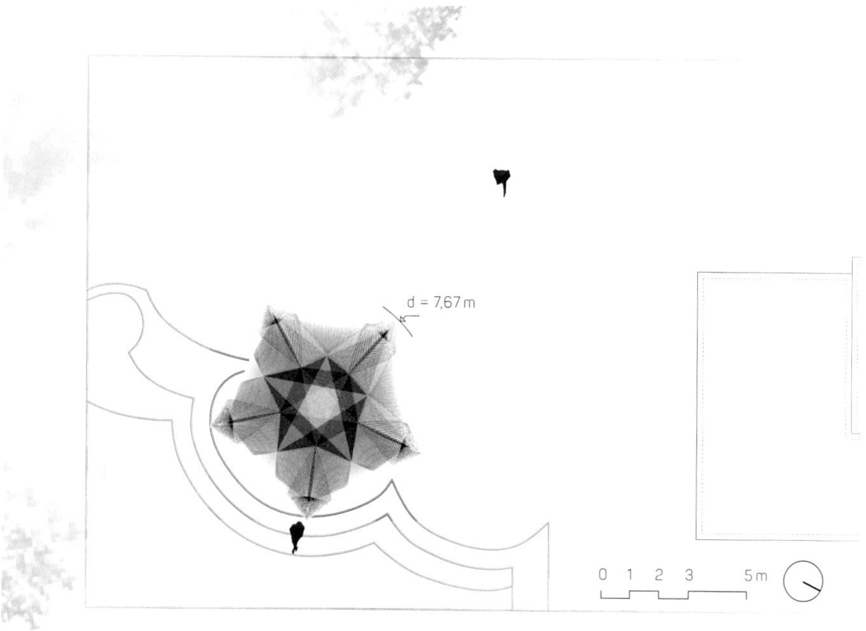

top
Site elevation.

bottom
Finite element analysis (FEA) for the material and fiber orientation of the pavilion structure.

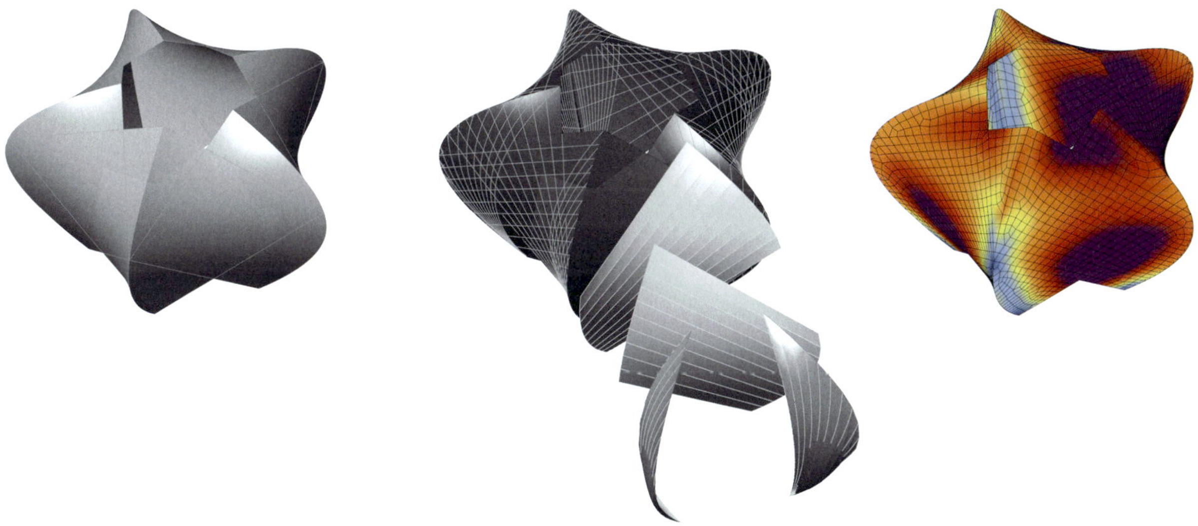

Parameter values
Top height: 3.8798 m
Top radius: 1.865 m
Middle height: 2.4926 m
Middle radius: 4.431 m
Bottom height: 0.0 m
Bottom radius: 2.497 m

Material and fiber orientation
Layer 1: gFRP
Layer 2: gFRP
Layer 3: cFRP
Layer 4: cFRP

Feedback
Max. deformation: 1.14187 m
von Mises stress: 4.9121e + 5 N/mm²
Material utilization: 3.84488

top
Winding logic of the fibers.

bottom
Form-finding and engineering analysis of the fiber wrapping routine.

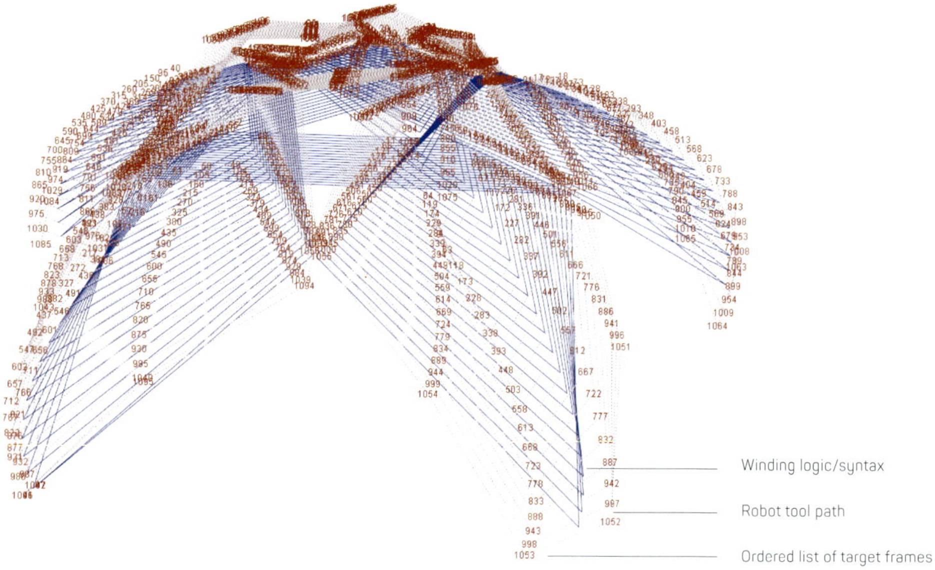

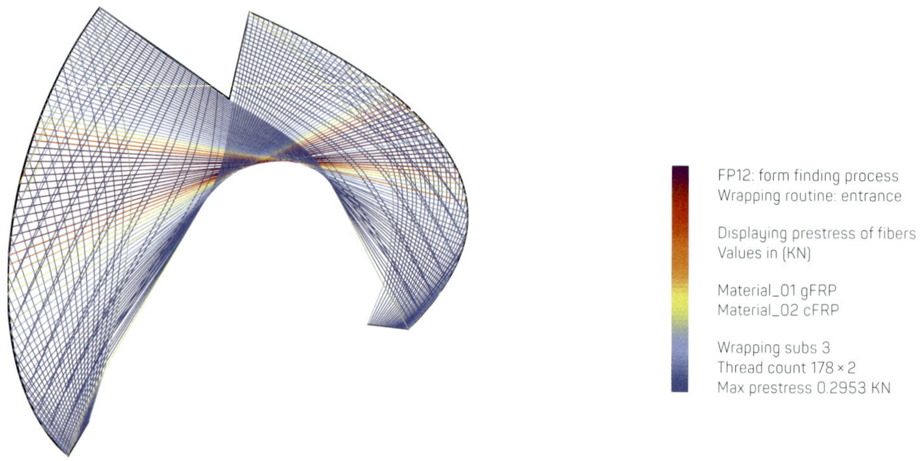

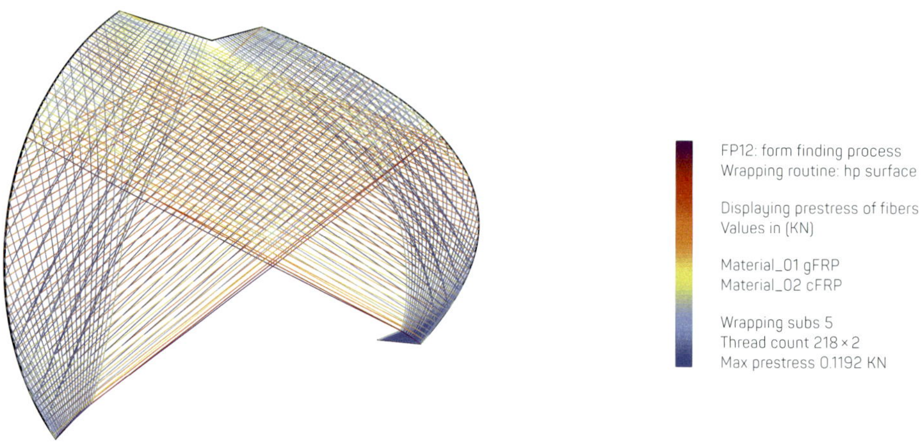

top
Part diagram for the fabrication setup.

bottom
Process photo of the fabrication setup.

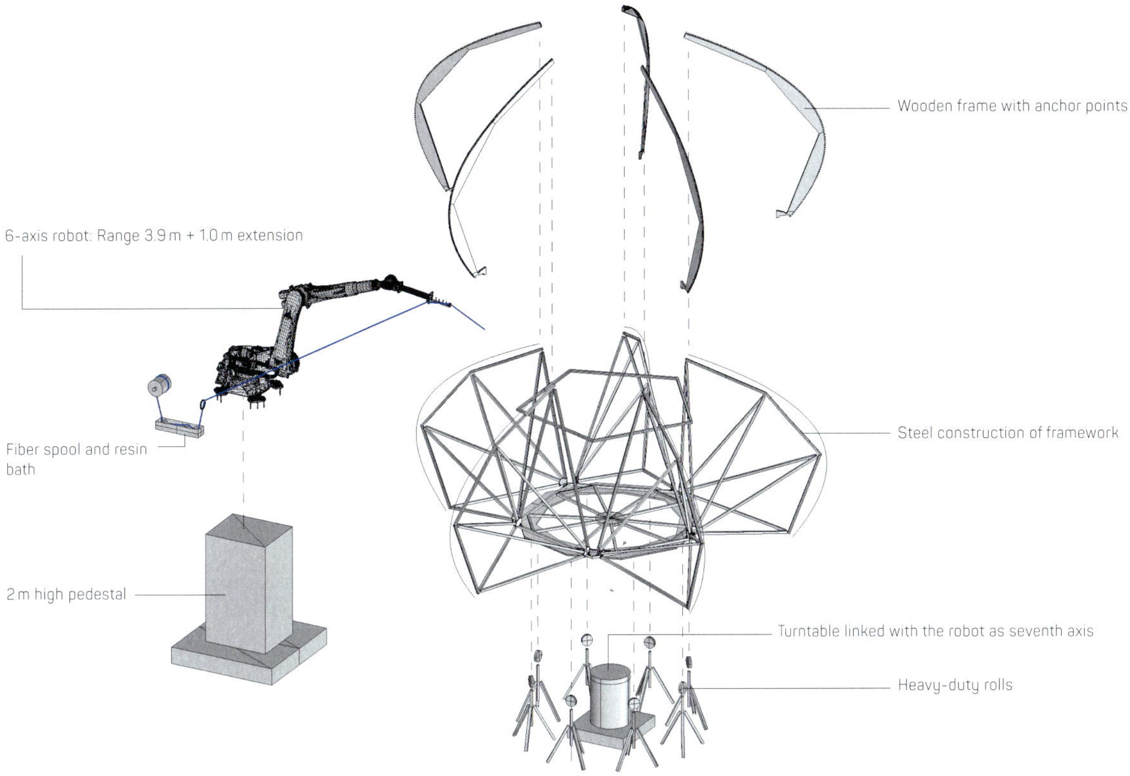

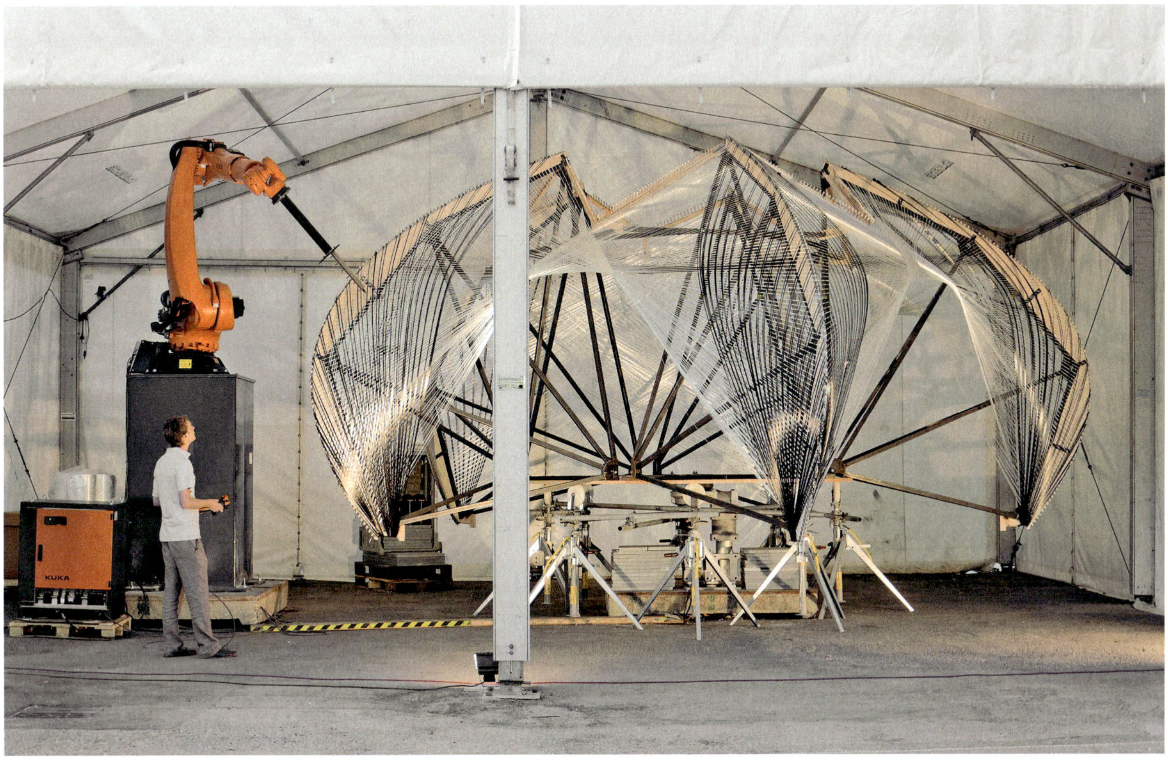

Exterior view of the finished pavilion.

Assembly process of 36 lightweight fiber composite components on site.

2013–2014

Architectural ambition

The second iteration of the joint-effort pavilion by the ICD and ITKE at the University of Stuttgart carried over many of the same principles of the first pavilion of 2012, using a multi-disciplinary approach to explore the craft of building. "The project is part of a successful series of research pavilions which showcase the potential of novel design, simulation and fabrication processes in architecture. The project was planned and constructed within one and a half years by students and researchers within a multi-disciplinary team of biologists, paleontologists, architects and engineers."[1] A study of biological models inspired computational design, structural analysis, and robotic fabrication of fiber-based materials. Besides the departments of structural engineering, architecture, and computational design, this year's pavilion also involved the Institute of Evolution and Ecology and the department of paleobiology. Freedom from typical composite processes depending on molds and geometric freedom were, again, part of the primary fabrication goals.

Design, engineering, fabrication and construction

The biological inspiration came from a detailed study of beetle shells. Using radiation and scanning electron microscope (SEM) scans of natural samples, 3D models of the shells were extracted and analyzed. The geometry, layering, and locally differentiated nature of the fibrous chitin in the composition of the beetle shells generated the structural principles upon which the form of the pavilion was computationally designed.

A robotic filament winding process was developed to create modular, double-layered composite structural parts, which were then assembled to create the pavilion's enclosure.

With glass and carbon fibers as the selected materials, the strands of each material were wound between two custom steel frames, each held by one of two collaborating 6-axis robots. The sequence and pattern of material wound generated a double-curvature surface formed by the tensioning of the carbon and glass fibers across the steel frame. In total, 36 individual structural elements were fabricated from one robotic fabrication setup. The largest element was an 8.5 ft (2.6 m) diameter steel, glass, and carbon fiber part with a weight of 53 lb (24.1 kg).

These 36 structural elements were then assembled to create a pavilion covering an area of 538 ft^2 (50 m^2), with a volume of 4308 ft^3 (122 m^3), and weighing only 1307 lb (593 kg).

1 Press materials from University of Stuttgart.

Biological sources of design inspiration.

- a Comparison of internal elytron architecture in flying and flightless beetles.
- b Elytra cross sections based on microcomputed tomography scans by Dr. Thomas van de Kamp at the ANKA Synchrotron Radiation Facility of Karlsruhe Institute of Technology (KIT).
- c SEM scans of a Colorado potato beetle (*leptinotarsa decemlineata*) elytron scanned by Prof. Oliver Betz at University of Tübingen.
- d Correlation of fiber layout and structural morphology in trabeculae.

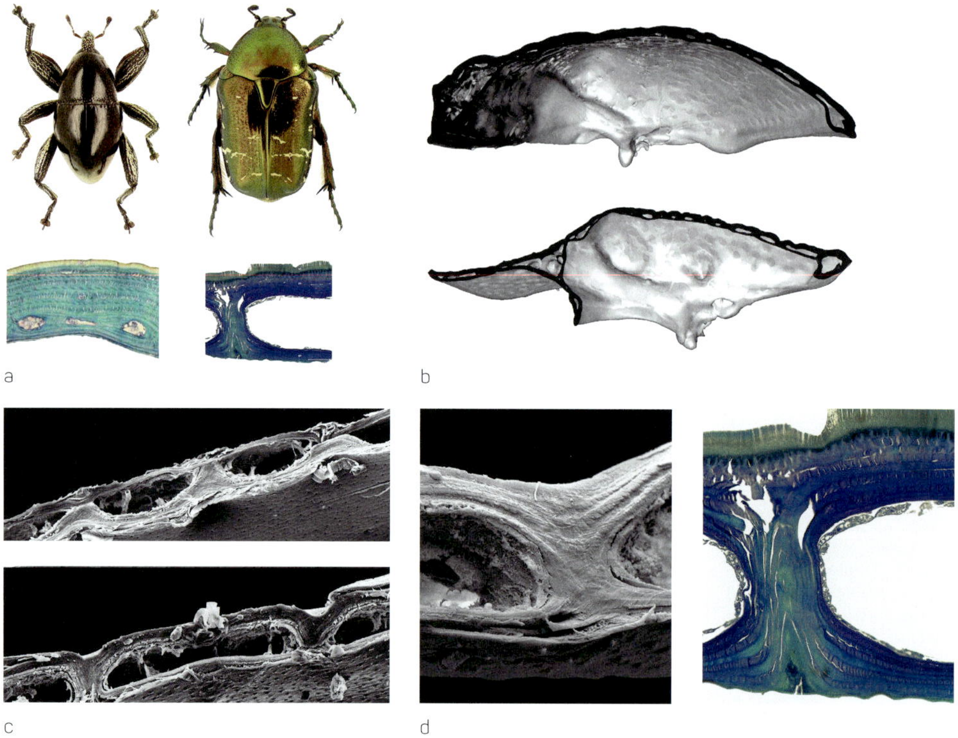

Integration of multiple process parameters into a component-based construction system.

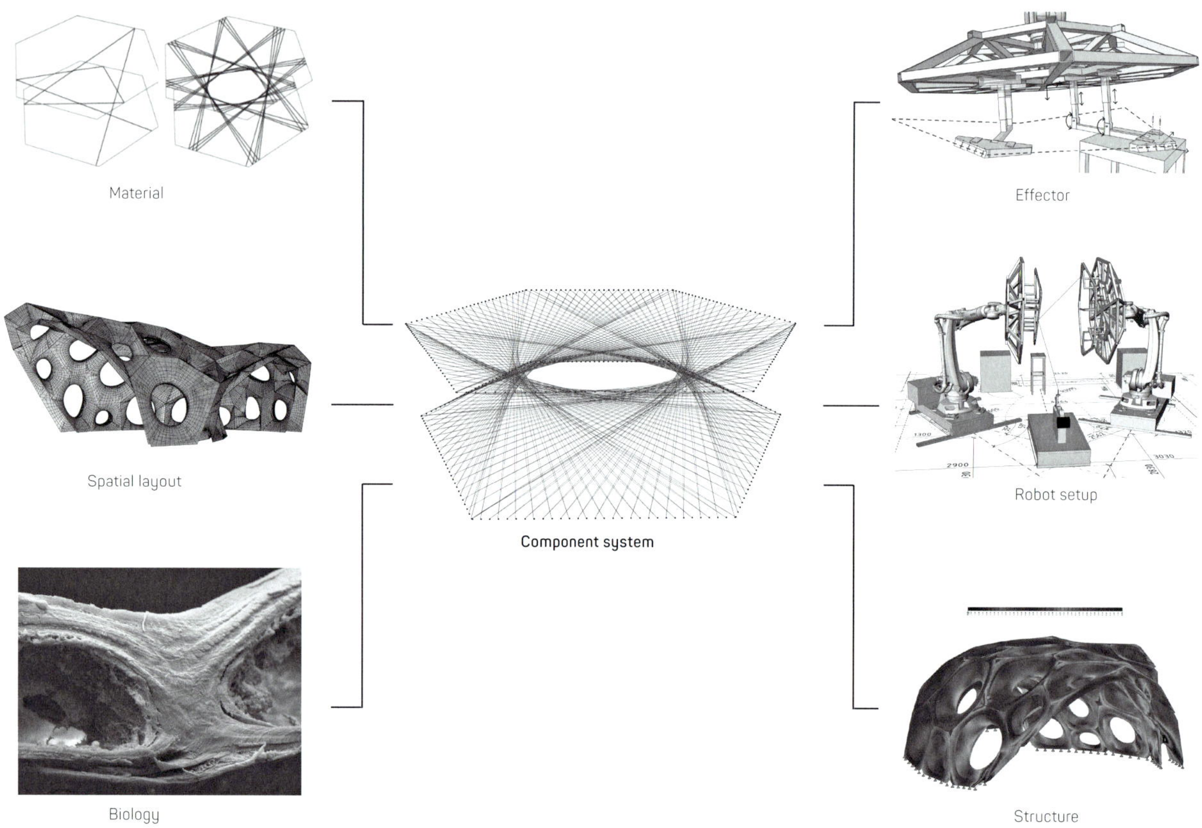

Diagram of integrative design and fabrication strategy.

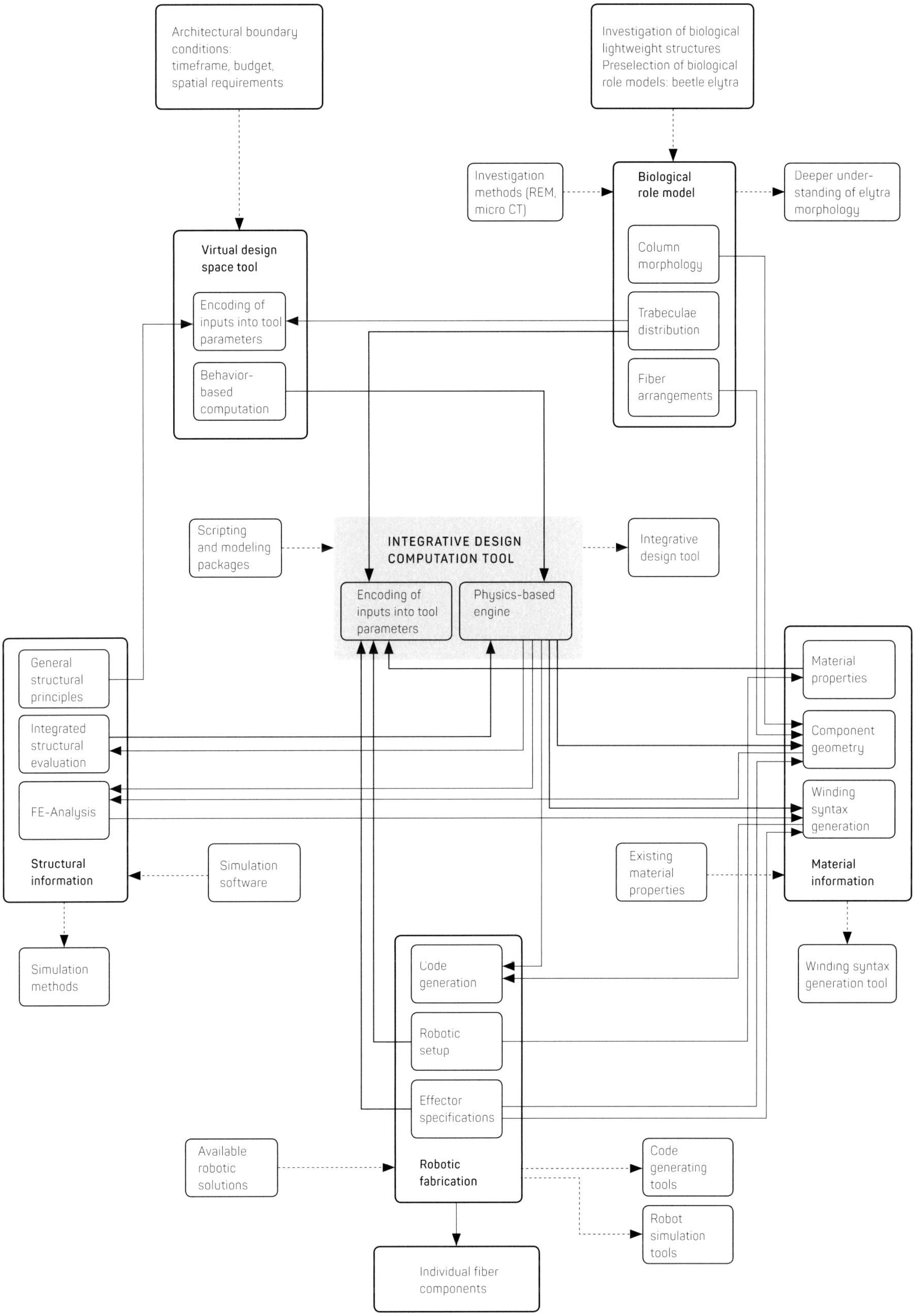

top
Finite element analysis of global force flows and their transfer into structural carbon fiber reinforcements.

bottom
Fiber layout for one component.

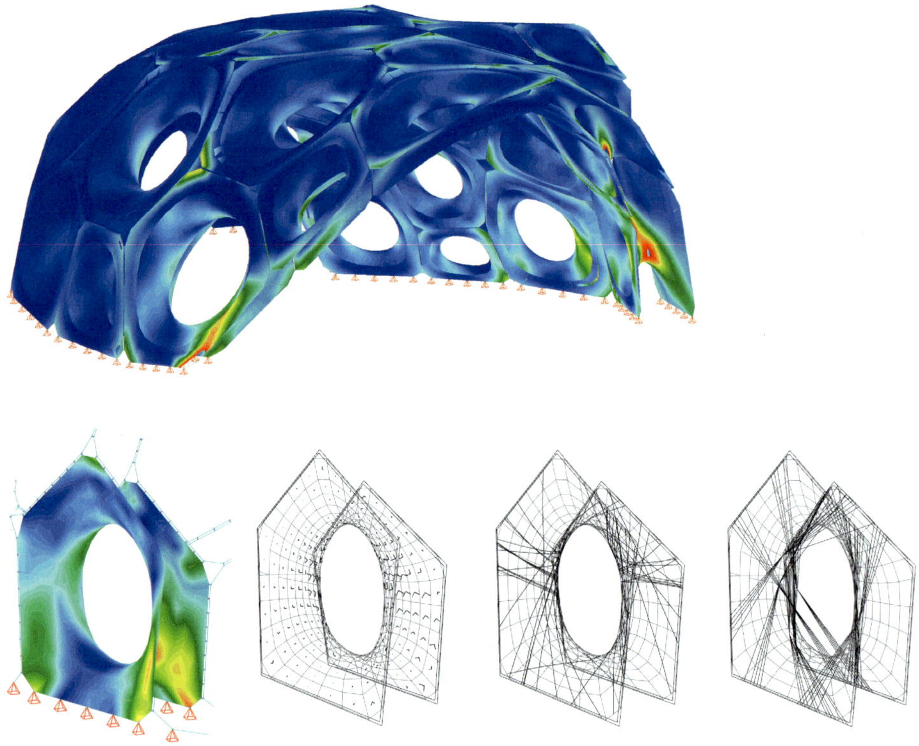

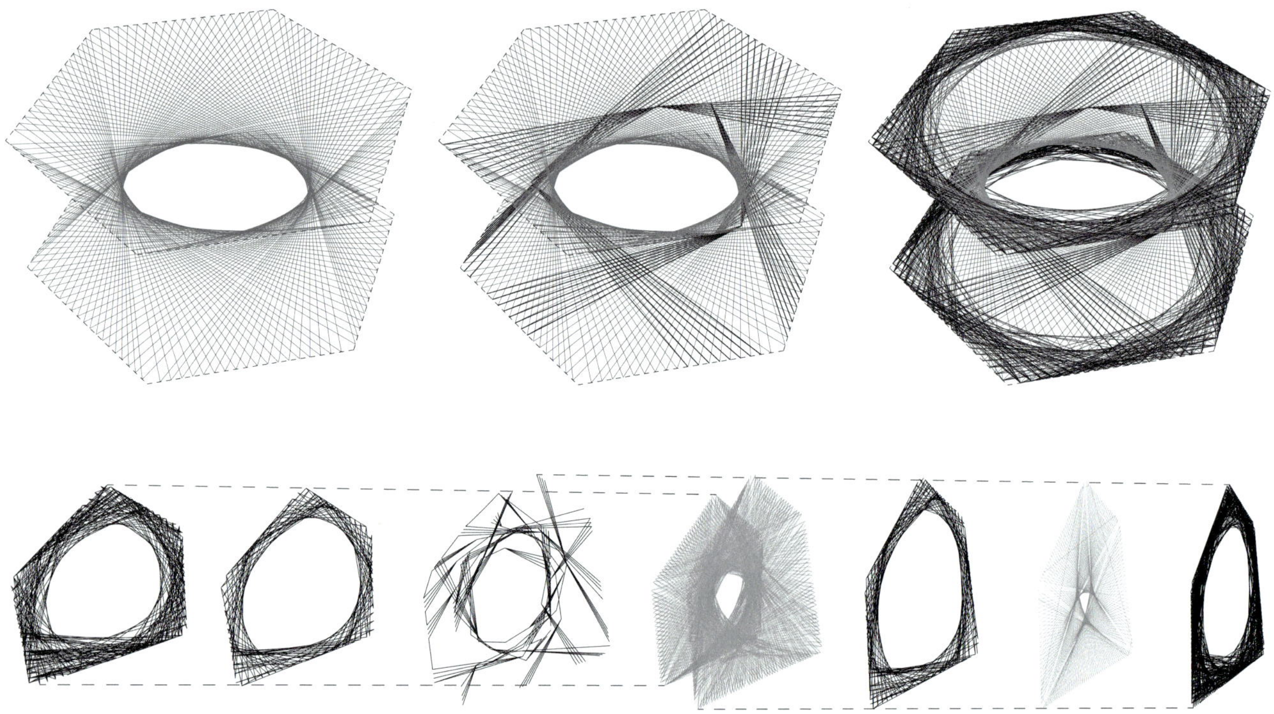

Robotically assisted effector adjustment.

Coreless filament winding.

Dual robot fabrication setup.

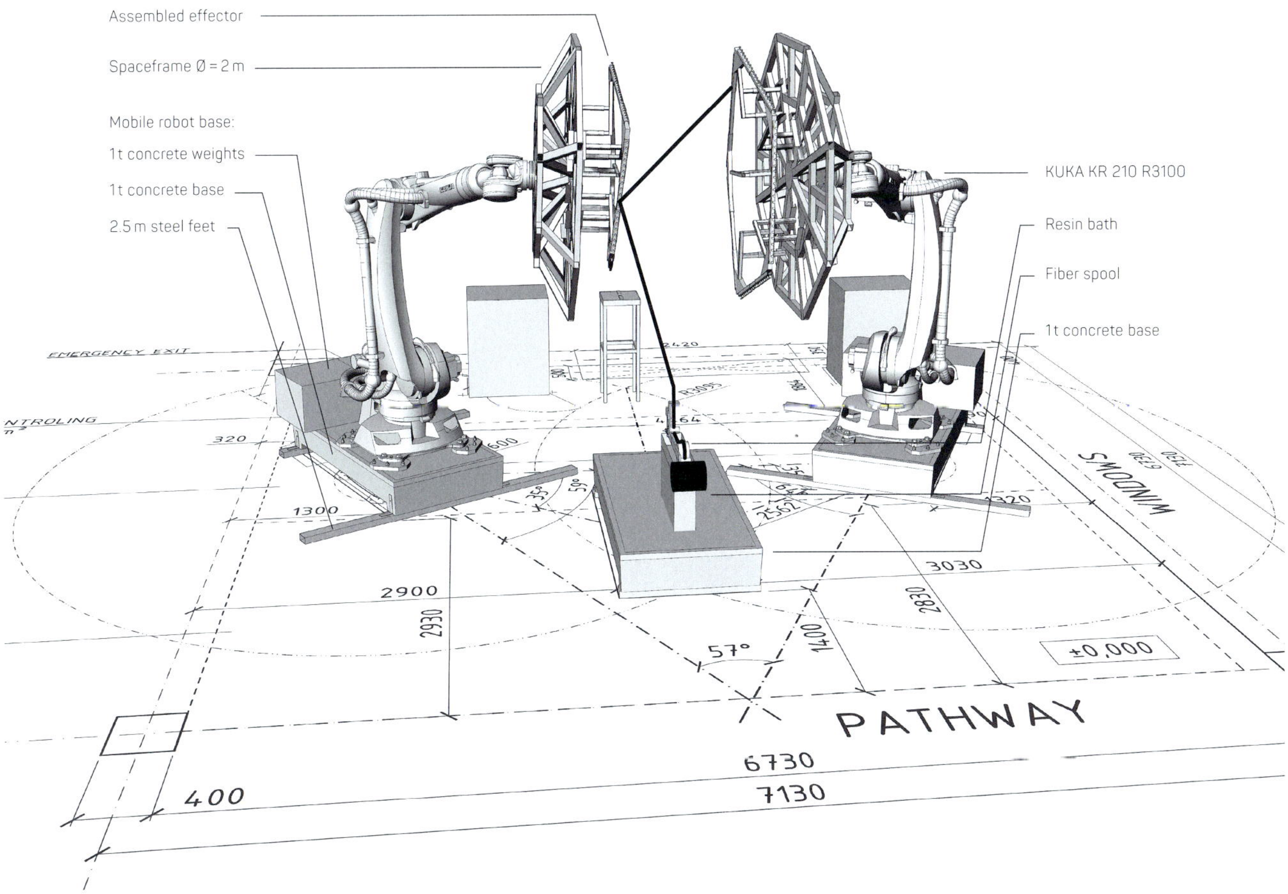

Exterior view of finished pavilion installed at the University of Stuttgart.

Pneumatic formwork with robotic fiber reinforcement.

2014–2015

Architectural ambition

The ambitions of the jointly developed pavilion for the year 2014–2015 carry over from previous years; in this iteration, the underwater nest of the water spider provided the source of inspiration. Again, material and structural efficiency were the primary goals; computational design tools and robotic fabrication were the means. The typical composite material process reliance on molds was addressed in this design by using a pneumatic supporting formwork, which was gradually reinforced with robotically placed carbon fibers. As stated in their documents, "The ICD/ITKE Research Pavilion 2014–15 serves as a demonstrator for advanced computational design, simulation and manufacturing techniques and shows the innovative potential of interdisciplinary research and teaching. The prototypical building articulates the anisotropic character of the fiber composite material as an architectural quality and reflects the underlying processes in a novel texture and structure. The result is not only a particularly material-effective construction, but also an innovative and expressive architectural demonstrator."

Design, engineering, fabrication and construction

For this pavilion, the process of creating an inhabitable underwater air bubble by the diving bell water spider (*Agyroneda aquatica*) was the inspiration. By studying the principles and process of the water spider, the ICD, ITKE, and collaborating departments of biology, paleontology, and aircraft design were able to generate an analogous process using a pneumatic air structure, robotically placed carbon fiber, and computational design simulation and analysis.

In this process, an industrial 6-axis robot was placed inside an air-supported ethylene tetrafluoroethylene (ETFE) membrane. This membrane is gradually reinforced by the robotic placement of carbon fibers, selectively applied where required for structural reinforcement. During this process, the fiber placement and geometry of the shell were generated using a form-finding computational method integrating fabrication constraints and structural analysis.

One of the challenges faced by the design team was understanding the changing stiffness of the pneumatic formwork and the resultant fluctuations in deformation during fiber placement. This was addressed by integrating an embedded sensor system into the robot arm, allowing constant feedback between actual conditions and digital environments.

In total, 28 miles (45 km) of carbon fiber was laid at an average speed of 2 ft/min (0.6 m/min) on 3.1 miles (5 km) of total robot tool path. "This additive process not only allows stress-oriented placement of the fiber composite material, but it also minimizes the construction waste associated with typically subtractive construction processes."[1]

The 2014–2015 pavilion had a footprint of 431 ft² (40 m²), an internal volume of 4591 ft³ (130 m³), with a span of 24.6 ft (7.5 m) and height of 13.5 ft (4.1 m). Total construction weight was just 573 lb (260 kg).

1 Press materials from University of Stuttgart.

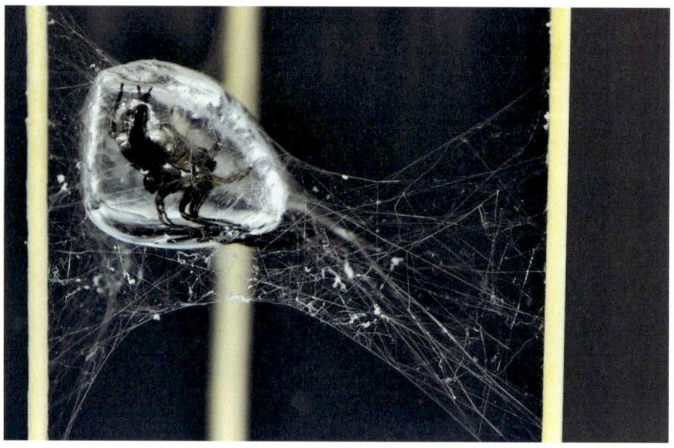

Diving bell water spider (*Agyroneda aquatica*) reinforcing an air bubble from the inside.

bottom
Diagram of integrated design criteria.

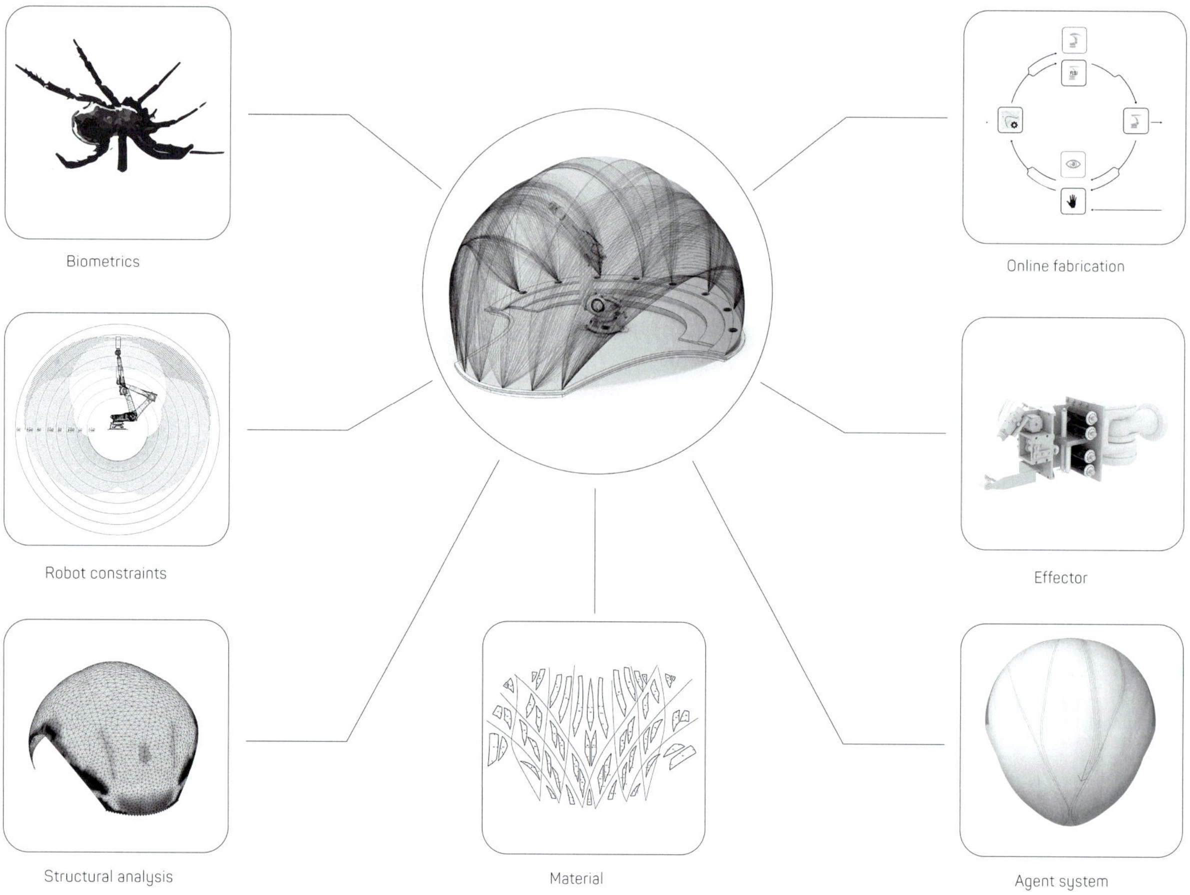

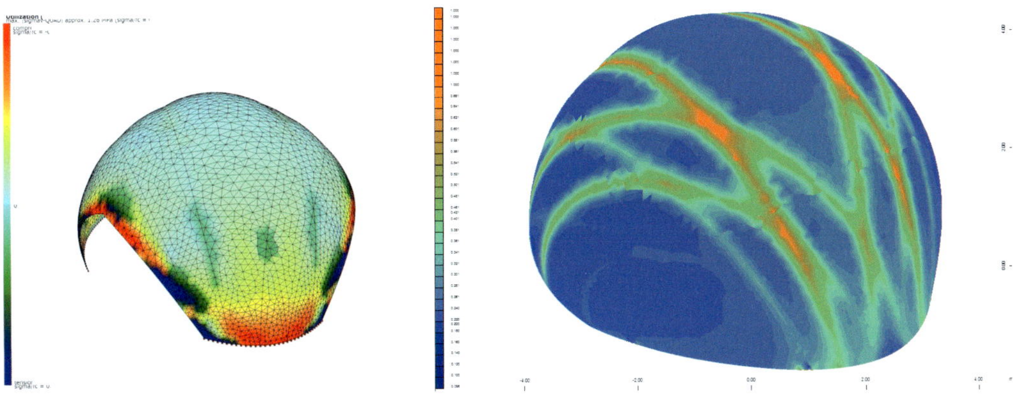

Finite element analysis of pretensioned pneumatic membrane and composite shell, bottom right.

below
Comparison of various fiber reinforcement strategies.

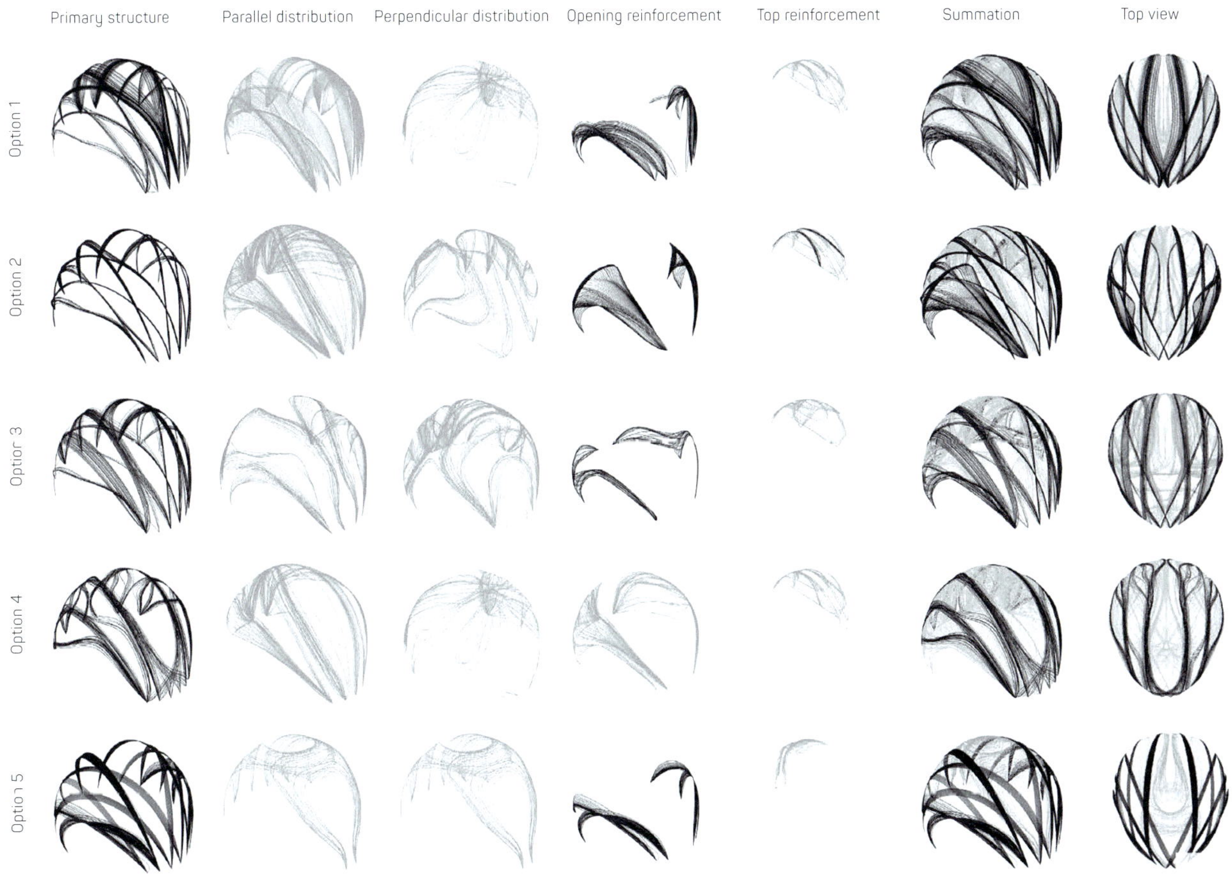

Conceptual fabrication strategy diagram.

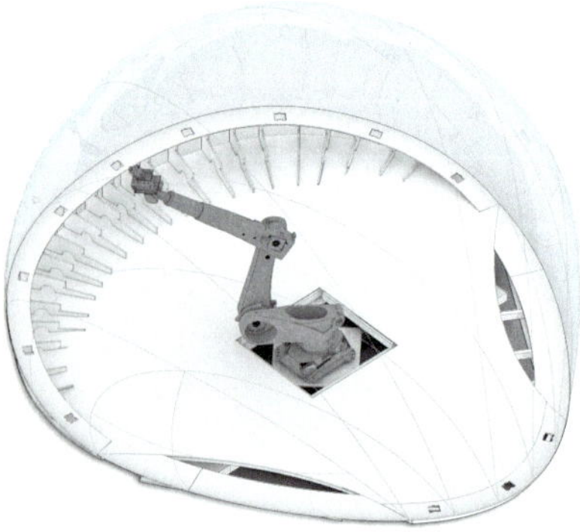

Inflated pneumatic membrane

Robotically reinforce membrane with carbon fiber from inside

Stable composite shell.

right
On-site sensor interface for adaptive fiber placement process.

far right
On-site robotic fiber placement of reinforcement fibers with parallel distribution.

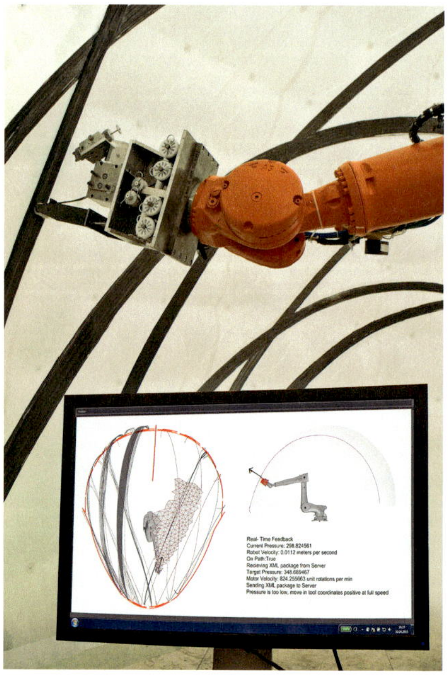

Cyber-physical fiber placement process.

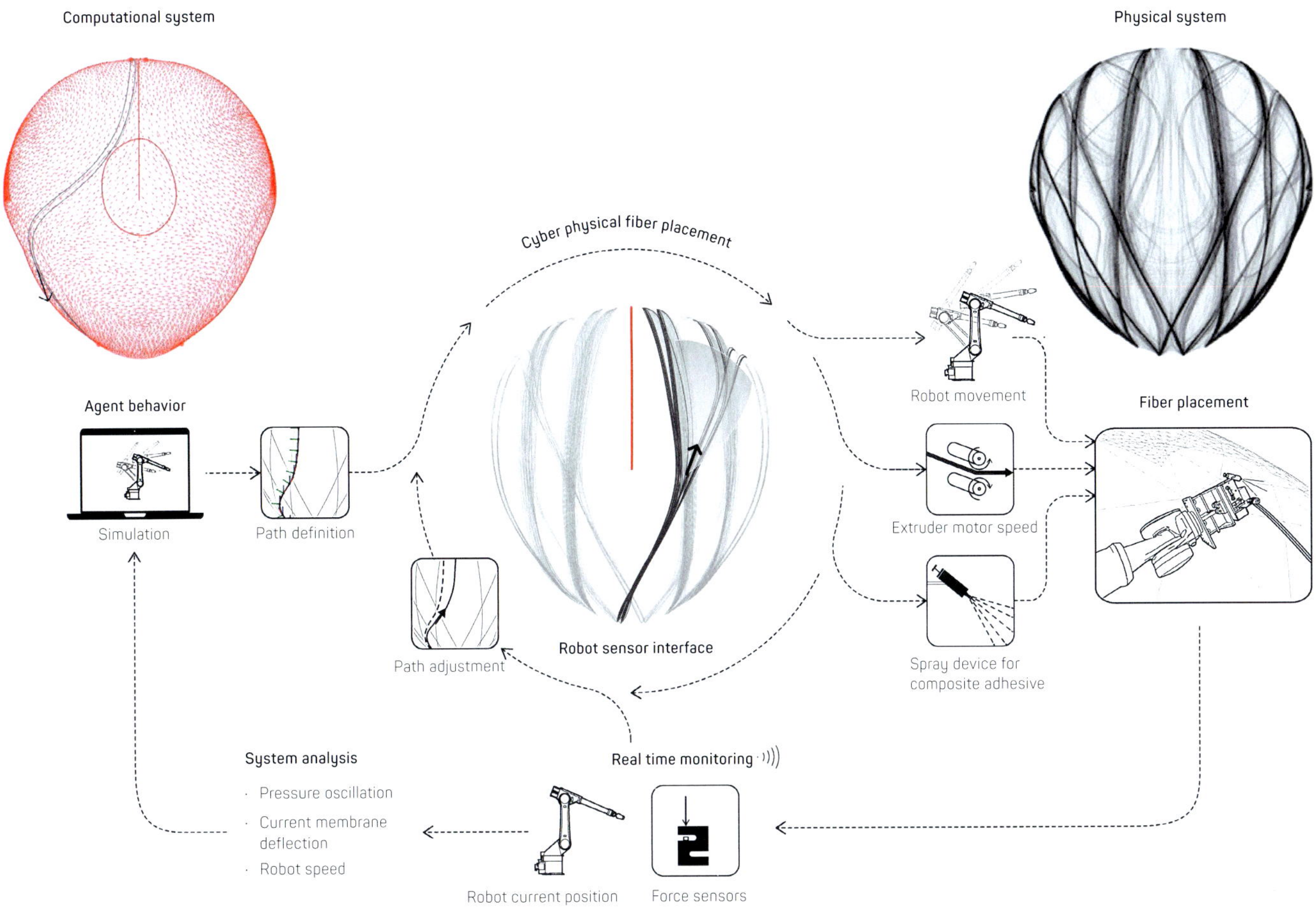

Exterior view of completed pavilion.

2016–2017

Architectural ambition

The interdisciplinary team of researchers at the University of Stuttgart, including the ICD and ITKE in collaboration with biologists, paleontologists, and aircraft designers, continued their successful series of pavilions exploring construction technology, biological inspiration, and computational tools. The pavilion of 2016–2017 specifically explores the long-span possibilities of fiber-based construction materials and robotic tools, including unmanned aerial vehicles (UAVs, or drones).

Here, as in all the previous pavilions, the problem of composite material fabrication free from the constraints of molds was primary. But this pavilion attempted to break from the limitations of the robotic tools, specifically, the build volume and reach of the 6-axis robotic arms. "Previous research at the ICD and ITKE has explored fiber composite construction without the need for surface molds or costly formwork. These novel manufacturing processes have been utilized to create highly differentiated multi-layered structures, functionally integrated building systems and large element assemblies. They have freed the relatively formable material from the limitations of traditional fiber composite fabrication processes. However, the scale of these early investigations has been limited by the working space of the industrial robotic arms that were utilized. The goal of the ICD/ITKE Research Pavilion 2016–17 is to envision a scalable fabrication process and to test alternative scenarios for architectural application by developing a manufacturing process for long span continuous fiber structures."[1]

Design, engineering, fabrication and construction

The silk "hammocks" that the leaf miner moths (*Lyonetia clerkella* and *Leucoptera erythrinella*) spin between bent leaves were identified as a biological model for adaptation. From the long-span fibrous construction of those silk structures, the designers abstracted structural principles to be transferred into fabrication concepts. These included a "bending-active substructure and coreless wound fiber reinforcement to create an integrated composite winding frame, fiber orientation and hierarchy over a long span structure and multi-stage volumetric fiber laying processes for the generation of complex three dimensional geometries."[2]

To realize the long-span fabrication setup, the designers sought to create a collaborative multi-machine process, where multiple different robotic systems could interface and communicate seamlessly. The reach of multi-axis robots would be extended and supplemented by drones (UAV). In this case, "combining the untethered freedom and adaptability of the UAV with the robots, opened up the possibilities for laying fibers on, around or through a structure, creating the potential for material arrangements and structural performance not feasible with the robot or UAV alone."[3]

The designers then set about creating a control, communication, and sensor system that allowed all the different machines to interact throughout the fiber-winding and -laying process. "The series of adaptive behaviors and integrated sensors lay the foundation for developing novel multi-machine, cyber-physical fabrication processes for large scale fiber composite production."[4]

In total, the pavilion of 2016–2017 used 114 miles (184 km) of resin-impregnated glass and carbon fiber, creating a single, long span cantilevering 39.4 ft (12 m). The area covered was roughly 431 ft^2 (40 m^2) and the structure weighed about 2200 lb (1000 kg). As the designers conclude, "This research showcases the potential of computational design and construction through the incorporation of structural capacities, material behavior, fabrication logics, biological principles and architectural design constraints into integrative computational design and construction. The prototypical pavilion is a proof-of-concept for a scalable fabrication processes of long-span, fiber-composite structural elements, suitable for architectural applications."

1 Press materials from University of Stuttgart.
2 Press materials from University of Stuttgart.
3 Press materials from University of Stuttgart.
4 Press materials from University of Stuttgart.

Diagram of integrated design space.

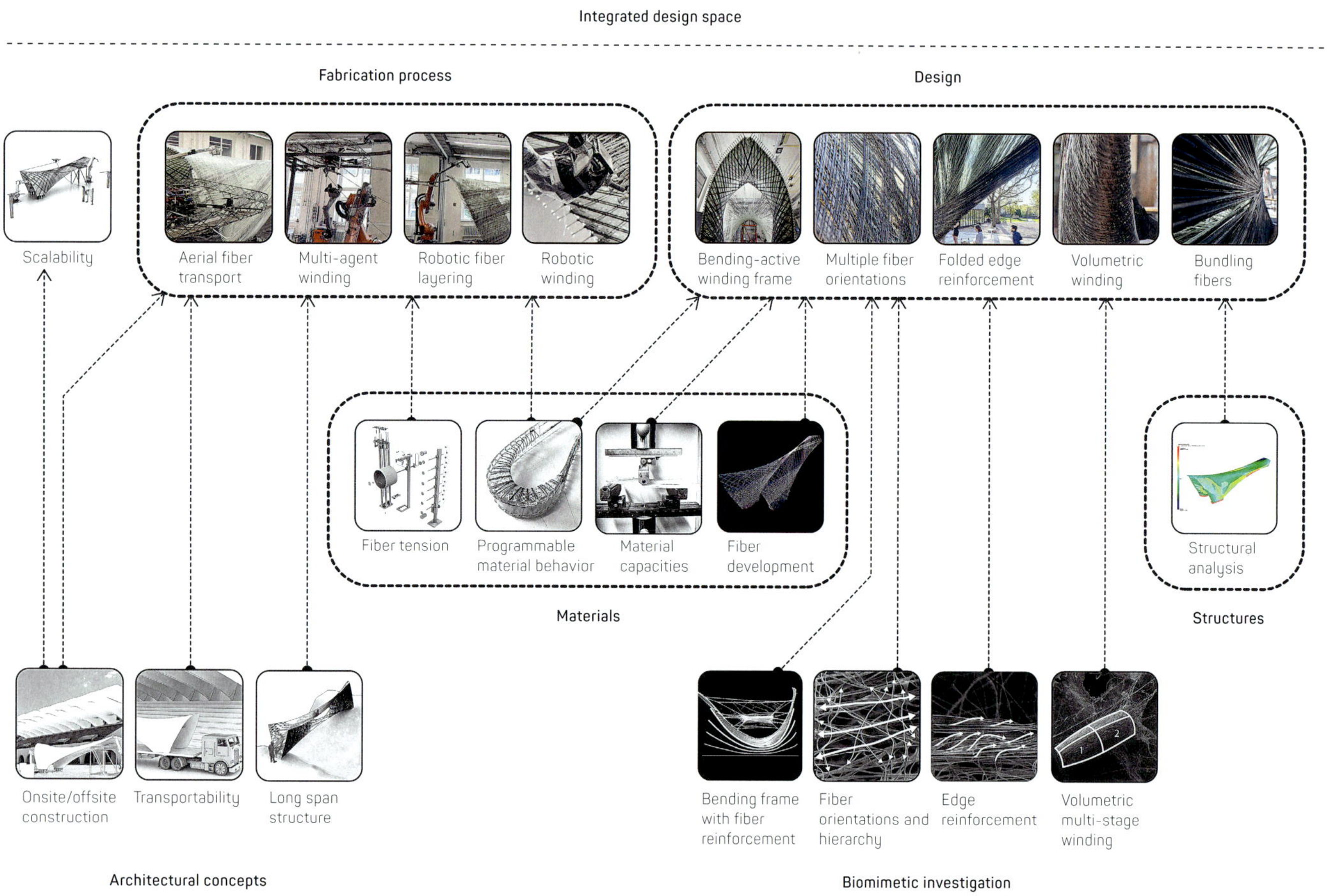

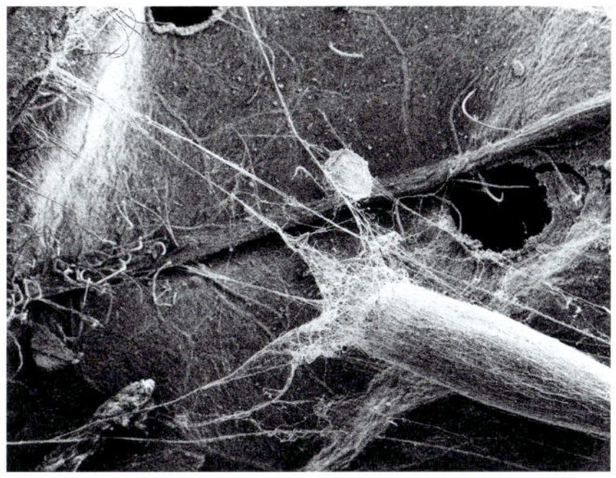

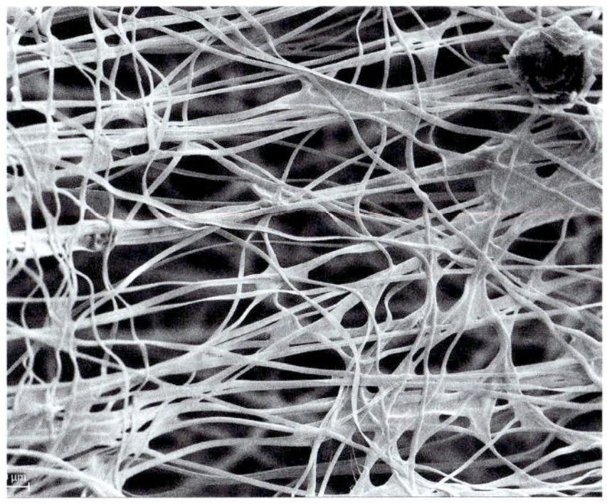

clockwise

Lyonetia prunifoliella, apple leaf miner cocoon.

Microscopic image of an apple leaf miner cocoon, illustrating volumetric structure.

Microscopic image of an apple leaf miner cocoon, illustrating fiber hierarchy and directionality.

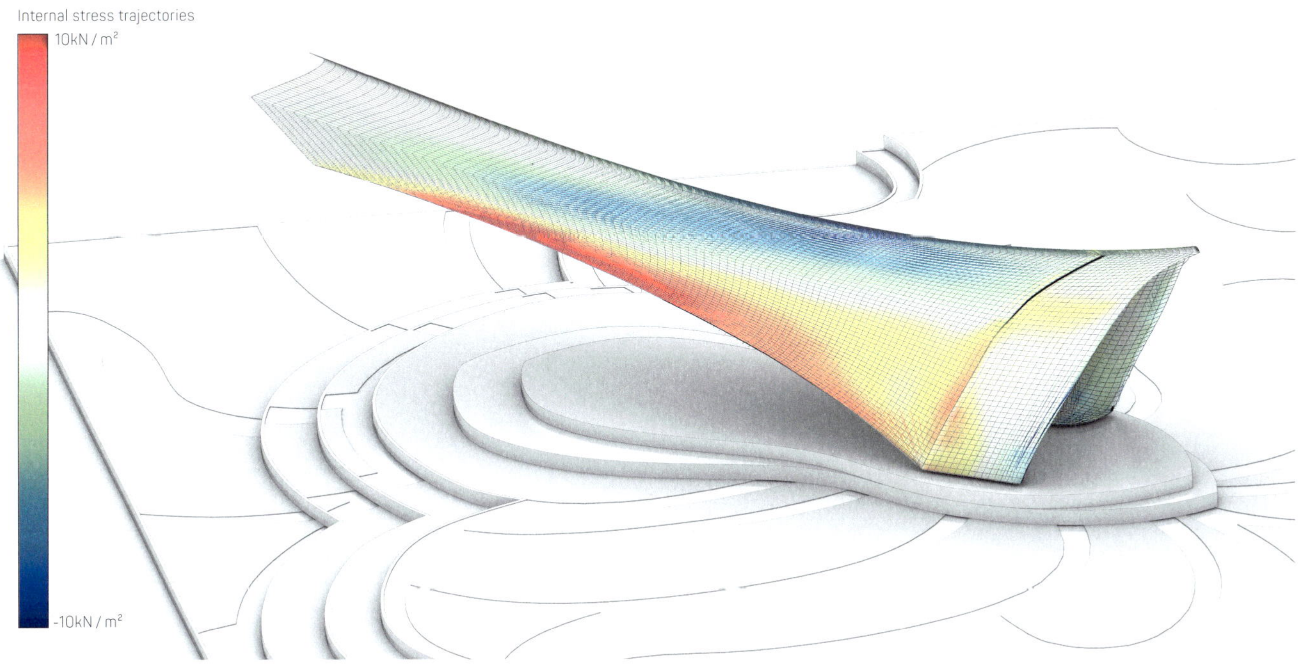

Diagram of structural simulation showing internal stress trajectories.

For diagram of structural development process, see page 116.

top
Exploded diagram of custom autonomous drone.

bottom
Diagram of tension control mechanism.

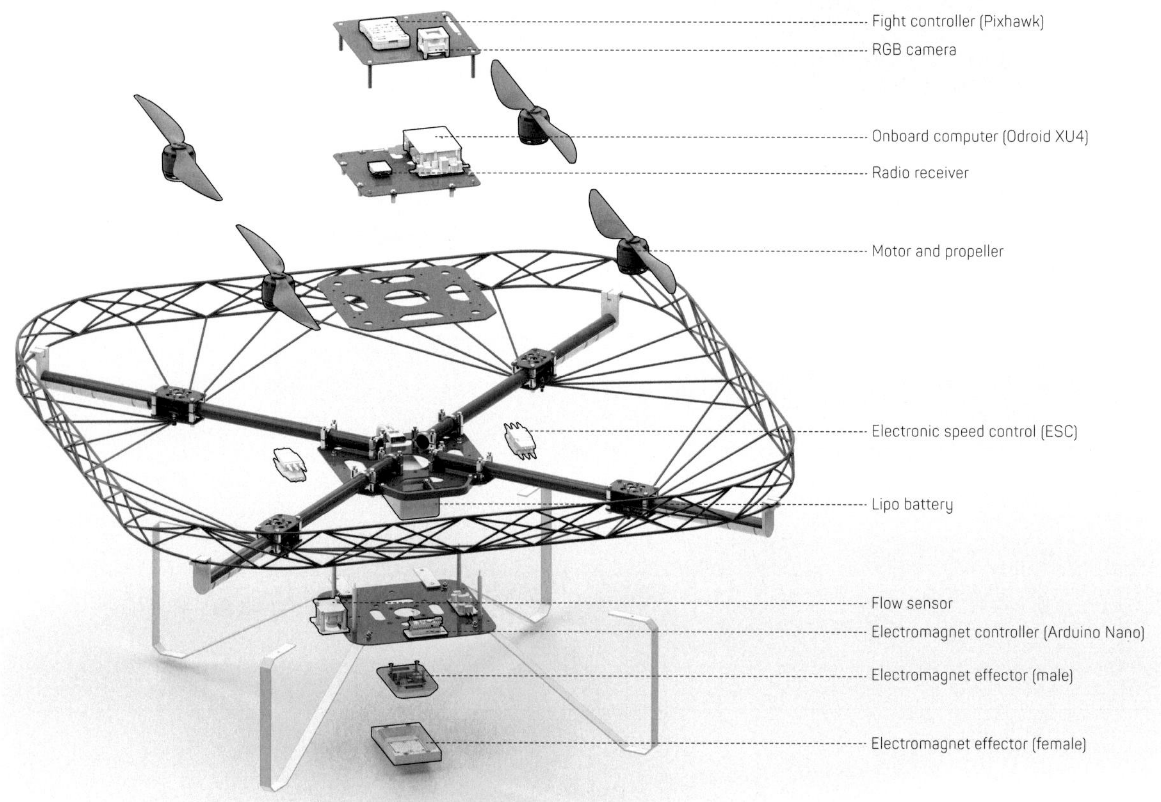

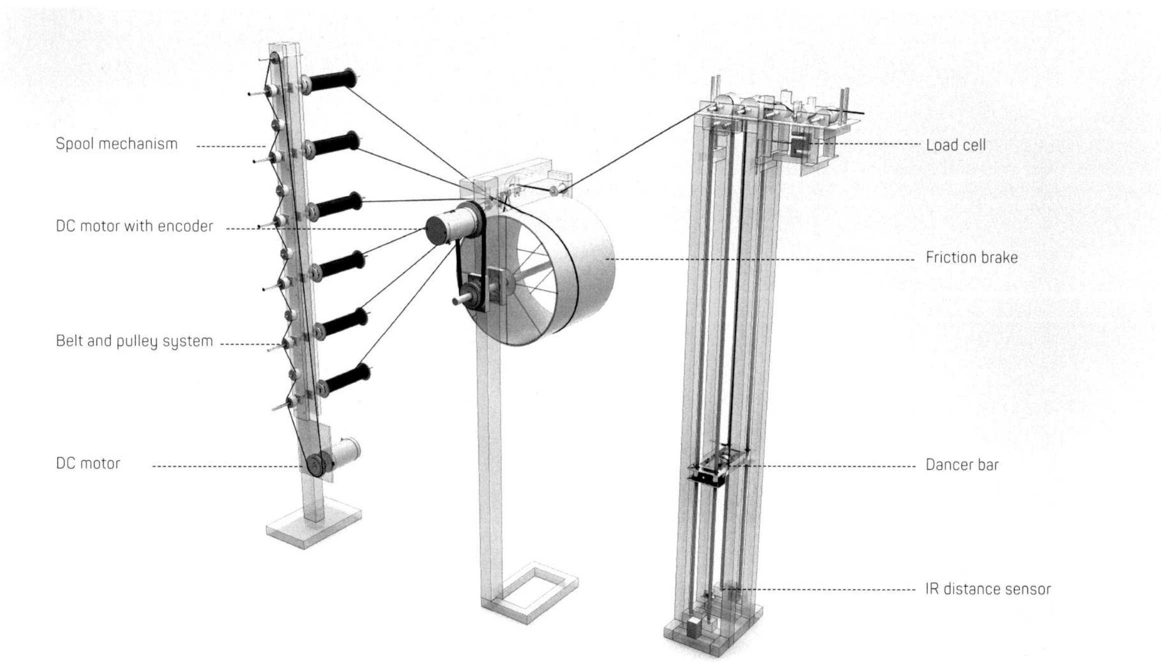

Diagram of multi-machine communication for long-span fiber winding process.

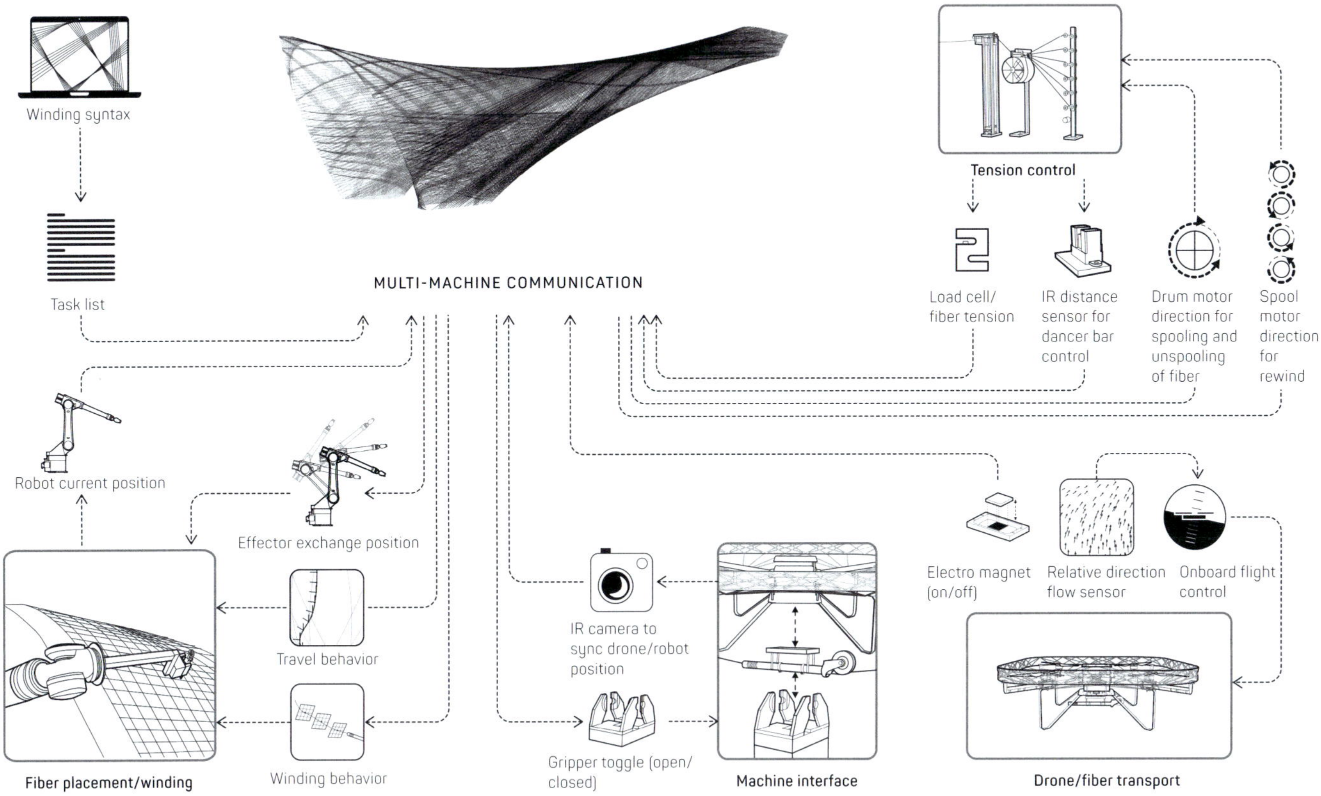

Autonomous flight of custom drone carrying a fiber between robots.

Completed pavilion.

BUGA FIBER PAVILION

Architectural ambition

In contrast to previous pavilions jointly developed by the ICD and ITKE, the pavilion of 2019 was installed in the grounds of the Bundesgartenschau (BUGA), a biennial horticultural show in Germany. However, the main thematic strands of research animating the researchers and designers at the University of Stuttgart continued: interdisciplinary collaboration, biomimetic design, computational technologies, and fiber composite materials.

This research began with the insight that most load-bearing structures in nature are fiber composites, such as cellulose, chitin, collagen, or wood. "The BUGA Fiber Pavilion aims to transfer this biological principle of load-adapted and thus highly differentiated fiber-composite systems into architecture. Manmade composites, such as the glass- or carbon-fiber-reinforced plastics that were used for this building, are ideally suited for such an approach, because they share their fundamental characteristics with natural composites. It shows how an interdisciplinary exploration of biological principles together with the latest computational technologies can lead to a truly novel and genuinely digital fiber composite building system."[1]

Design, engineering, fabrication and construction

Building on some of the technology and insight from previous ICD/ITKE pavilions, this pavilion uses robotic, coreless, filament winding, eliminating the traditional reliance of composite manufacturing on molds and adapting some of the principles of additive manufacturing. A robot places glass and carbon fiber strands between two rotation scaffolds. The shape of the final structural part is defined by the interaction of the strands placed between the scaffolds, and the material is completely glass or carbon fiber. This allows for completely custom shapes within one fabrication setup with no waste or molds, resulting in "highly load-adapted components with a highly distinct architectural appearance." Sixty load-bearing structural composite elements were fabricated in this fashion, each taking about four to six hours to fabricate from 3281 ft (1000 m) of glass fiber and 5249 ft (1600 m) of carbon fiber on average. Furthermore, testing proved that each structural component could carry a compressive force of more than 56,202 lbf (250 kN) (roughly equivalent to 15 cars).

The final pavilion covers 4306 ft^2 (400 m^2), spanning 75 ft (23 m) from edge to edge. The final pavilion is further enclosed in a transparent ETFE membrane, with the entire structure weighing only 1.6 lb/ft^2 (7.6 kg/m^2). As the designers conclude, "The pavilion shows how a truly integrative approach to computational design and robotic fabrication enables the development of novel, truly digital fiber composite building systems that are fully compliant with the stringent German building regulations, exceptionally light, structurally efficient and architecturally expressive."

1 Press materials from University of Stuttgart.

top
Site plan.

bottom
Section.

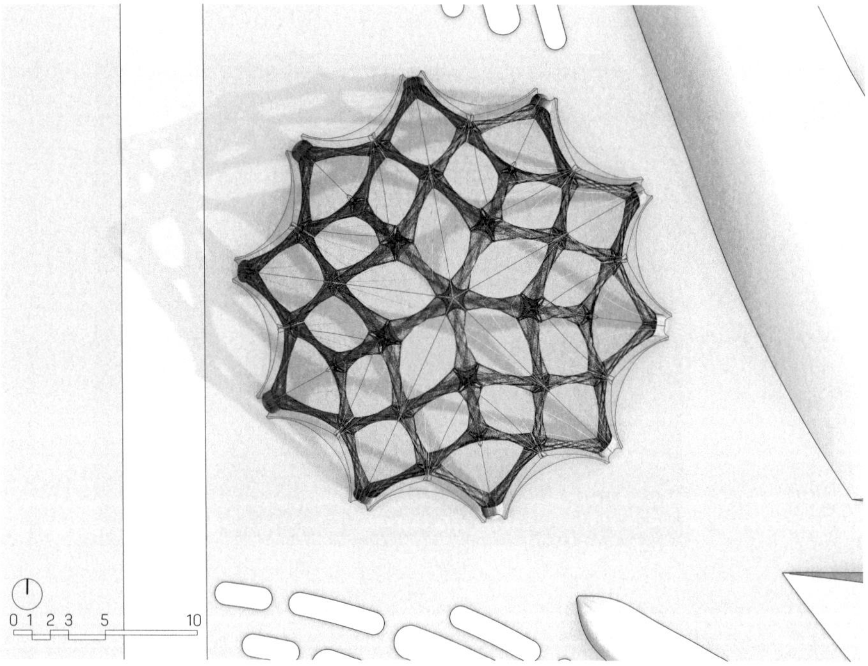

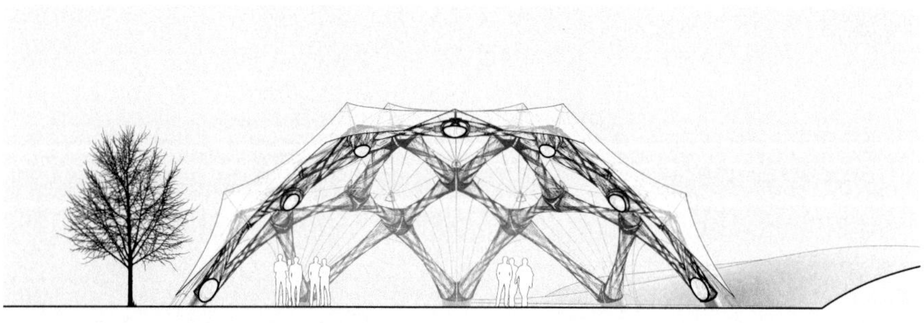

BIBLIOGRAPHY

Ascione, L., J. F. Caron, P. Godonou, K. Van IJselmuijden, J. Knippers, T. Mottram, M. Oppe, M. Gantriis Sorensen, J. Taby, and L. Tromp. "Prospect for new guidance in the design of FRP." *JRC Report EUR* 27666 (2016). Published in Italy, Luxembourg: Publications Office of the European Union, 2016.

Bai, Jiping, ed. *Advanced fibre-reinforced polymer (FRP) composites for structural applications*. Elsevier, 2013.

Bank, Lawrence C. *Composites for construction: structural design with FRP materials*. John Wiley & Sons, 2006.

Barbero, Ever J. *Introduction to composite materials design*. CRC press, 2017.

Bell, Michael, and Craig Buckley. *Permanent Change: Plastics in Architecture and Engineering*. New York: Princeton Architectural Press, 2014.

Berardi, Umberto, and Nicholas Dembsey. "Thermal and Fire Characteristics of FRP Composites for Architectural Applications." *Polymers 7, no. 11* (2015): 2276–289.

Berardi, Umberto. "Building energy consumption in US, EU, and BRIC countries." *Procedia engineering 118* (2015): 128–136.

Berardi, Umberto. "Sustainability assessment in the construction sector: rating systems and rated buildings." *Sustainable Development 20, no. 6* (2012): 411–424.

Berge, Bjørn, Chris Butters, and Filip Henley. *The Ecology of Building Materials. Second ed.* London: Routledge, 2009.

Blonder, Arielle, and Yasha Jacob Grobman. "Design and fabrication with fibre-reinforced polymers in architecture: a case for complex geometry." *Architectural Science Review* 59, no. 4 (2016): 257–268.

Cabeza, Luisa F., Lídia Rincón, Maria Vilariño, Gabriel Perez, and Albert Castell. "Life Cycle Assessment (LCA) and Life Cycle Energy Analysis (LCEA) of Buildings and the Building Sector: A Review." *Renewable and Sustainable Energy Reviews 29* (2014): 394–416.

Campbell, Flake C. *Structural composite materials*. ASM international, 2010.

Chalmers, D. W. "Experience in design and production of FRP marine structures." *Marine Structures 4, no. 2* (1991): 93–115.

Ching, Francis D. K., and Mark Mulville. *European Building Construction Illustrated*. Hoboken, New Jersey: John Wiley & Sons, 2014.

Ching, Francis D. K., and Steven R. Winkel. *Building Codes Illustrated: A Guide to Understanding the 2015 International Building Code. 5th ed.* Hoboken, New Jersey: Wiley, 2016.

Daniel, Ryszard A., "Environmental Considerations to Structural Material Selection for a Bridge." *European Bridge Engineering Conference*, Rotterdam, March 2003.

Das, Sujit. "Life cycle assessment of carbon fiber-reinforced polymer composites." *The International Journal of Life Cycle Assessment 16, no. 3* (2011): 268–282.

Dao, and Asaro. "A Study on Failure Prediction and Design Criteria for Fiber Composites under Fire Degradation." *Composites Part A 30, no. 2* (1999): 123–31.

De Paola, Silvia, Cristiano Fragassa, Giangiacomo Minak, and Ana Pavlovic. "Green Composites: a review of state of art." *CARBON 1, no. 4000* (2013): 230–240.

DuBois, John Harry. *Plastics History USA*. Cahners Books, 1972.

Ehlen, Mark A. "Life-cycle Costs of Fiber-reinforced-polymer Bridge Decks." *Journal of Materials in Civil Engineering 11, no. 3* (1999): 224–30.

Ehlen, Mark A. "Life-cycle costs of new construction materials." *Journal of Infrastructure systems 3, no. 4* (1997): 129–133.

Goldin, Aaron, Adam Jongeward, Lauren Scammell, and Cris Wise. "Architectural Façades for the Heydar Aliyev Cultural Center: A Life Cycle Assessment." Stanford University term paper, published online by www.kreysler.com. http://www.kreysler.com/wp-content/uploads/2013/08/CEE-226-Baku-Facade.pdf (accessed 2018).

Hale, Justin. "Boeing 787 From the Ground Up." *Aero Qtr_04, 06 (2006)*. Internal company publication.

Herakovich, Carl T. "Mechanics of composites: a historical review." *Mechanics Research Communications* 41 (2012): 1–20.

Hinton, M. J., A. S. Kaddour, and P. D. Soden. *Failure Criteria in Fibre Reinforced Polymer Composites The World-Wide Failure Exercise. 1st ed.* Amsterdam; San Diego, CA; Oxford: Elsevier, 2004.

Hodkinson, Mark. "Back to the Futuro." *Guardian* [London, England], August 22, 2018.

Hollaway, Leonard C., and Jin-Guang Teng, eds. *Strengthening and rehabilitation of civil infrastructures using fibre-reinforced polymer (FRP) composites*. Elsevier, 2008.

Hollaway, L. C. *Advanced polymer composites and polymers in the civil infrastructure*. Elsevier, 2001.

Hollaway, L. C. "Sustainable energy production: key material requirements." In *Advanced Fibre-Reinforced Polymer (FRP) Composites for Structural Applications*, pp. 705–736. 2013.

Hollaway, L. C. "A review of the present and future utilisation of FRP composites in the civil infrastructure with reference to their important in-service properties." *Construction and building materials* 24, no. 12 (2010): 2419–2445.

Hollaway, L. C. "The evolution of and the way forward for advanced polymer composites in the civil infrastructure." *Construction and Building Materials* 17, no. 6–7 (2003): 365–378.

Howarth, Jack, Sada SR Mareddy, and Paul T. Mativenga. "Energy intensity and environmental analysis of mechanical recycling of carbon fibre composite." *Journal of Cleaner Production 81* (2014): 46–50.

Hull, Derek, and Trevor W. Clyne. *An introduction to composite materials*. Cambridge University Press, 1996.

Ilg, Patrick, Christoph Hoehne, and Edeltraud Guenther. "High-performance materials in infrastructure: a review of applied life cycle costing and its drivers–the case of fiber-reinforced composites." *Journal of Cleaner Production 112* (2016): 926–945.

The International Building Code 2015, 2018. Accessed from [https://codes.iccsafe.org].

Jain, Ravi, and Luke Lee, eds. *Fiber reinforced polymer (FRP) composites for infrastructure applications: Focusing on innovation, technology implementation and sustainability*. Springer Science & Business Media, 2012.

Jang, Bor Z., and ASM International. *Advanced Polymer Composites*. Materials Park, OH: ASM International, 1994.

Jones, Robert M. *Mechanics of composite materials*. CRC press, 2014.

Kazmierski, Chuck. "Growth Opportunities in Global Composites Industry, 2012–2017." *Lucintel*, Irving, TX (2012): 21–23.

Kasapoglou, Christos. *Design and Analysis of Composite Structures*. Hoboken, N.J.: Chichester: John Wiley, 2010.

Kendall, David. "Building the future with FRP composites." *Reinforced Plastics* 2007; 51(5).

Khatib, Jamal M., ed. *Sustainability of construction materials*. Woodhead Publishing, 2016.

Kreysler, Bill, et al. *Guidelines and Recommended Practices for Fiber-Reinforced-Polymer (FRP) Architectural Products*. Industry group publication: ACMA, 2016.

Kreysler, William. "Qualifying FRP Composites for High-Rise Building Façades." *Fabricate 2017* (2017): 130–137.

Kulshreshtha, Anand K., and Cornelia Vasile, eds. *Handbook of polymer blends and composites*. Vol. 1. Rapra Publishing, 2002.

Lacombe, Alain, Thierry Pichon, and Marc Lacoste. "3D carbon-carbon composites are revolutionizing upper stage liquid rocket engine performance by allowing introduction of large nozzle extension." *50th AIAA / ASME / ASCE / AHS / ASC Structures, Structural Dynamics, and Materials Conference 17th AIAA / ASME / AHS Adaptive Structures Conference 11th AIAA* No, p. 2678. 2009.

Lee, Luke S., and Ravi Jain. "The role of FRP composites in a sustainable world." *Clean Technologies and Environmental Policy 11, no. 3* (2009): 247–249.

Lehne, Johanna, and Felix Preston. "Making Concrete Change, Innovation in Low-carbon Cement and Concrete." *Chatham House Report, Energy Environment and Resources Department*: London, UK (2018): 1–66.

Loschke, S. K. (Ed.). *Materiality and Architecture*. London: Routledge (2016).

Mafeld, Andrew. *The Future of Building: The growing use of composites in construction and architecture*. JEC (2017).

Mallick, Pankar K. *Fiber-reinforced composites: materials, manufacturing, and design*. CRC press, 2007.

Mara, Valbona, Reza Haghani, and Peter Harryson. "Bridge decks of fibre reinforced polymer (FRP): A sustainable solution." *Construction and Building Materials 50* (2014): 190–199.

Marsh, George. "50 Years of Reinforced Plastic Boats." *Reinforced Plastics* 50, no. 9 (2006): 16–19.

McMullen, P. "Fibre/resin Composites for Aircraft Primary Structures: A Short History, 1936–1984." *Composites* 15, no. 3 (1984): 222–30.

Meiarashi, S., I. Nishizaki, and T. Kishima. "Life-cycle cost of all-composite suspension bridge." *Journal of Composites for Construction* 6, no. 4 (2002): 206–214.

Menges, Achim, and Jan Knippers. "Fibrous tectonics." *Architectural Design 85, no. 5* (2015): 40–47.

Milewski, John V., and Dominick V. Rosato. "History of reinforced plastics." *Journal of Macromolecular Science—Chemistry* 15, no. 7 (1981): 1303–1343.

Palardy, Genevieve. "Resin Volumetric Changes and Surface Finish Characterization of Composite Automotive Panels." 2007, ProQuest Dissertations and Theses.

Pepis, Betty. "House of molded plastic is leaving dream stage." *New York Times*, Jun 11, 1956.

Quarmby, Arthur. *The Plastics Architect*. London: Pall Mall Press, 1974.

Rackard, N. "Buckminster Fuller's 50-Foot 'Fly's Eye' Dome to be Restored." [online] *ArchDaily*. Available at: https://www.archdaily.com/343036/buckminster-fullers-50-foot-flys-eye-dome-to-be-restored [Accessed 12 Dec. 2018].

Reinhart, Theodore J., Cyril A Dostal, and ASM Handbook Committee. *Composites. Engineered Materials Handbook; v. 1*. Metals Park, Ohio: ASM International, 1987.

Rosenberg, Debra. "Plastics." *Newsweek* 130, no. 22 (1997): 44–45.

Rowe, Jason. *Advanced Materials in Automotive Engineering*. Woodhead Publishing. Philadelphia, Pa.: Woodhead Pub., 2012.

Saint, Andrew. *Architect and engineer: a study in sibling rivalry*. Yale Univ Press, 2007.

Savage, G. "Formula 1 composites engineering." *Engineering Failure Analysis* 17, no. 1 (2010): 92–115.

Scala, E. Pete. "A brief history of composites in the US—the dream and the success." *JOM* 48, no. 2 (1996): 45–48.

Schröpfer, Thomas. *Material design: informing architecture by materiality*. Walter de Gruyter, 2012.

Seymour, Raymond Benedict, and Rudolph D. Deanin, eds. *History of polymeric composites*. VSP, 1987.

Smil, Vaclav. *Making the Modern World: Materials and Dematerialization*. Chichester, West Sussex, United Kingdom: John Wiley & Sons, 2014.

Song, Young S., Jae R. Youn, and Timothy G. Gutowski. "Life cycle energy analysis of fiber-reinforced composites." *Composites Part A: Applied Science and Manufacturing 40, no. 8* (2009): 1257–1265.

Starr, Trevor. *Carbon and High Performance Fibres Directory and Databook*. Springer Science & Business Media, 1995.

Starr, Trevor F. *Composites: A Profile of the Worldwide Reinforced Plastics Industry, Markets and Suppliers: Market Prospects to 2005*. Elsevier, 1999.

Strong, A. Brent. *Fundamentals of composites manufacturing: materials, methods and applications*. Society of Manufacturing Engineers, 2008.

Sudha, P., K. Nasreen, and P. Angelin Vinodhini. "Natural fiber composites and applications." *Green Polymers and Environmental Pollution Control*, edited by Moayad Khalaf, p. 335–358. Boca Raton: CRC Press, 2016.

Tsai, Stephen W. "Three decades of composites activities at US Air Force Materials Laboratory." *Composites science and technology* 65, no. 15–16 (2005): 2295–2299.

Uddin, Nasim, ed. *Developments in fiber-reinforced polymer (FRP) composites for civil engineering*. Cambridge: Woodhead Publishing, 2013. ISBN: 9780857092342

Walker, Anthony. "Plastics: The Building Blocks of the Twentieth Century." *Construction History* 10 (1994): 67–88.

Watts, Andrew. *Modern Construction Handbook*. Basel/Berlin/Boston: Walter de Gruyter, 2016. Accessed November 15, 2018. ProQuest Ebook Central.

Wilcke, Gerd. "Plastics producers seek a here and now for the house of the future." *New York Times*. Jan 11, 1970.

Winfield, Armand G. "Fifty years of plastics." *Plastics Engineering*, May 1992, 32.

Witten, Elmar, B. Jahn, and D. Karl. "Composites Market Report 2012: Market developments, trends, challenges and opportunities." *AVK-Industrievereinigung Verstärkte Kunststoffe (Federation of Reinforced Plastics)*, Germany, 2012.

Zhishen, Wu, Wang Xin, and Wu Gang. "Advancement of structural safety and sustainability with basalt fiber reinforced polymers." *CICE2012*, Rome 13 (2012): 15–29.

"ALL-PLASTIC HOME FOR FUTURE." 1956. *New York Times* (1923-Current File), May 13, 354.

Hastak, M., D. W. Halpin, and T. Hong. "Constructability, Maintainability, and Operability of Fiber Reinforced Polymer (FRP) Bridge Deck Panels." Publication FHWA/IN/JTRP-2004/15. Joint Transportation Research Program, Indiana Department of Transportation and Purdue University, West Lafayette, Indiana, 2004. doi: 10.5703/1288284313163.

Pavlović, Marko, and Milan Veljković. "08.08: Prefabricated demountable concrete and FRP decks in composite structures." *ce/papers* 1, no. 2–3 (2017): 1889–1898.

Sahirman, Sidharta, and Robert C. Creese. Fiber Reinforced Polymer (FRP) Bridge Deck Life-cycle Cost Analysis, 2009, ProQuest Dissertations and Theses. Cover: Photo © Abdelmalek Bensetti

IMAGE CREDITS

Cover: Photo © Abdelmalek Bensetti

Back cover: © James Morris, courtesy Hugh Broughton Architects

p. 6: Photo © Jasmine Park

pp. 12–13: Photo © Digital Building Technologies Group / ETH Zurich

p. 14: Photo © ICD/ITKE

p. 16 top: Chart adapted from CES EduPack 2019, ANSYS Granta © 2020 Granta Design

p. 16 bottom: Illustration © the author, using data compiled from Ansys / Granta Design

p. 17 bottom left: Charles-Dominique-Joseph Eisen (1720–1778), Frontispiece from Essai sur l'architecture, second edition, 1755. Engraving.

p. 17 bottom right: Photo © ICD/ITKE

p. 18: Photo © BMW

p. 19 top left: Photo © CNB Yacht Builders

p. 19 top right: Photo copyright holder unknown

p. 19 bottom: Photo © Boeing

p. 20 top: Photo © Antony Dubber

p. 20 bottom: Photo © Gary Allen

p. 21 bottom: Photo by Richard G Hawley licensed under CC BY-ND 2.0

p. 23: Image © Neri Oxman

p. 26 clockwise from top left: Image by Berkshire Community College Bioscience Image Library licensed under CC0; photo by Piergiorgio Rossi in the public domain; photo by wikimedia user Torr68 licensed under CC BY-SA 3.0; photo copyright holder unknown

p. 30: Movie still from *The Graduate*. Directed by Mike Nichols. Screenplay by Calder Willingham and Buck Henry. Hollywood, CA: Lawrence Turman Productions, 1967.

p. 31 top: Photo in the public domain

p. 31 middle: Image by William Warby licensed under CC by 2.0

p. 32 top: Photo by U.S. Air Force / Staff Sgt. Bennie J. Davis III, in the public domain

p. 32 middle: Photo by Staff Sgt. Aaron Allmon II, in the public domain

p. 32 bottom: Illustration adapted from diagrams by Boeing

p. 33 top left: Photo by John Chapman, licensed by CC BY-SA 3.0

p. 33 top right: Photo by Flickr user W9NED, licensed by CC BY-NC-ND 2.0

p. 34 bottom: Photo in the public domain

p. 35 top left and right: Photo © Volvo

p.p. 35 bottom: Photo in the public domain

p. 36 bottom: Photo by Rob Croes / Anefo, in the public domain

p. 37 top: Illustration adapted from Van Den Einde, Lelli, Lei Zhao, and Frieder Seible. "Use of FRP composites in civil structural applications." Construction and building materials 17, no. 6–7 (2003): 389–403.

p. 37 middle: Illustration adapted from Hollaway, L. C. "A review of the present and future utilisation of FRP composites in the civil infrastructure with reference to their important in-service properties." Construction and building materials 24, no. 12 (2010).

p. 38 middle and bottom: Images by Greg Janky and Sean Horita, via CC BY-NC-ND 4.0

p. 39: Photo by Advanced Infrastructure Technologies / University of Maine

p. 40 top: Photo by Orange County Archives, licensed by CC BY-2.0

p. 40 bottom left: Photo by Jean-Pierre Dalbéra, licensed by CC by 2.0

p. 40 bottom right: Photo by Astrid Westvang, licensed by CC BY-NC-ND 2.0

p. 41 middle: Photo by Flickr user Kristjan, licensed by creative CC BY-NC-ND 2.0

p. 41 bottom: Photo by Flickr user Phillip Pesar, licensed by CC BY 2.0

p. 42 all: Photo © Fondazione Renzo Piano (Via P. P. Rubens 30A, 16158 Genova, Italy)

p. 44: Photo © U.S. Department of Energy, Oak Ridge National Laboratory

pp. 46–47: Charts adapted from CES EduPack 2019, ANSYS Granta © 2020 Granta Design

p. 50 clockwise from top left: Photo by wikimedia user Cjp24, licensed by CC BY-SA 3.0; photo © Danish Technological Institute; photo by Brett Jordan, licensed by CC BY 2.0; photo by wikimedia user bodyarmor, licensed by CC BY-SA 3.0

p. 52: Photo © the Smithsonian Institution National Air and Space Museum

p. 55: Chart adapted from Larry Cox, Structurlite Composites Consultants

p. 58: Photo © Siemens AG, Munich / Berlin

p. 59: Photo © SHoP Architects

p. 60: Composite Panel Building Systems

p. 62: illustration © ICD/ITKE

p. 63 left and right: Photo © Andrei Jipa, courtesy of the BRG at ETH Zurich

p. 64 top and middle: Photo © Digital Building Technologies Group / ETH Zurich

p. 64 bottom: Illustration © Digital Building Technologies Group / ETH Zurich

p. 66: © Andreas Gursky / Courtesy Sprüth Magers / 2019, ProLitteris, Zurich

p. 69: Illustration © each respective company

p. 74 top and bottom: Charts adapted from CES EduPack 2019, ANSYS Granta © 2020 Granta Design

p. 75: Diagram adapted from diagram © EPRS | European Parliament Research Service – Publications Management and Editorial Unit

p. 77: Photo by Petar Milošević, licensed by CC BY-SA 4.0

p. 78 left: Photo by wikimedia user Auyon, licensed by CC BY-SA 3.0

p. 78 right: Photo by Christian Gahle, nova-Institut GmbH, licensed by CC BY-SA 3.0

p. 79 all images: Photo © ELG Carbon Fiber

p. 82 top and bottom: Illustration © Armacell

p. 84: Photo © Henrik Kam

p. 87 top left: Photo by Mark J. Handel, licensed by CC BY 2.0

p. 87 top right: Photo by wikimedia user Cjboffoli, in the public domain

p. 87 middle: Photo © Sam Burrell, courtesy of Hugh Broughton Architects

p. 87 bottom: Photo © Hugh Broughton Architects

p. 89 top: Chart adapted from CES EduPack 2019, ANSYS Granta © 2020 Granta Design

p. 90 bottom: Illustration © the author, based on Section 703 of the IBC 2018

p. 94 top: Excerpted from the 2003 International Building Code; © 2017; Washington, D.C.: International Code Council. Reproduced with permission. All rights reserved. www.ICCSAFE.org

p. 94 bottom: Illustration adapted from Ching

pp. 97–101: Flowchart © ACMA, originally printed in „Guidelines and Recommended Practices for FRP Architectural Products"

p. 103 top: Illustration copyright © the European Union, 2018

p. 103 bottom: Chart adapted from CES EduPack 2019, ANSYS Granta © 2020 Granta Design

p. 105: Photo by Rob Oo, licensed by CC BY 2.0.

p. 106: Chart adapted from CES EduPack 2019, ANSYS Granta © 2020 Granta Design

p. 107: Photo © Jannes Linders

p. 108: Photo © Young & Ayata

p. 110: Photo © Andreas Gursky / Courtesy Sprüth Magers / 2019, ProLitteris, Zurich

p. 113: Image in the public domain

p. 114: Drawing © Peter Eisenman

p. 115: Photo © Mateenbar

pp. 116–117: Illustration © ICD / ITKE

p. 118: Movie still from The Fountainhead. Directed by King Vidor. Henry Blanke Productions / Warner Bros. Studio, 1949.

p. 119 top: Drawing © Young & Ayata

p. 119 bottom: Photo and Illustration © Joris Laarman

p. 120: Drawings and illustrations © Van Wijnen

p. 121: Photo © Michael Hansmeyer

p. 123: Photo © Young & Ayata

pp. 124–125: Photo © Jeff Goldberg / Esto – Courtesy of Ennead Architects

p. 126: Photo © Henrik Kam

p. 128: Photo © Henrik Kam

pp. 132–135: Drawings and photos © Snøhetta

p. 136 top: Photo © Henrik Kam

pp. 136–137: Photos © Snøhetta

pp. 138–139: Photo © Henrik Kam

p. 140: Photo © Abdelmalek Bensetti

pp. 143–144: Drawings © Zaha Hadid Architects

p. 145 top, middle, and bottom: Photo © Luke Hayes

pp. 146–147: Photo © Abdelmalek Bensetti

p. 148: Photo © Jasmine Park, courtesy of Morphosis Architects

pp. 151–157: Drawings, diagrams and phots © Morphosis Architects

pp. 158–159: Photo © Jasmine Park, courtesy of Morphosis Architects

p. 160: Photo © Jannes Linders

pp. 164–168 top: Drawings and photos © Benthem Crouwel Architects

p. 168 bottom: Diagram © Teijin Limited

p. 169 top, middle, and bottom: Drawing © Benthem Crouwel Architects

pp. 170–171: Photo © Jannes Linders

p. 172: Photo © Joaquín Michavila Mas

pp. 174–175: Drawings © Herzog & de Meuron

p. 176: Photo © Joaquín Michavila Mas

p. 179: Photo © Menno Emmink, courtesy of Broekbakema Architects NL

pp. 180–183: Drawings © Broekbakema Architects NL

pp. 184185 top left and top right: Photos © Holland Composites

p. 185 bottom: Photo © Menno Emmink, courtesy of Broekbakema Architects NL

pp. 186–187: Photo © Timon Jacob, courtesy of Broekbakema Architects NL

p. 188: Photo © Richard Powers

p. 190: Photo © Daniela MacAdden, courtesy of Rafael Vinoly Architects

p. 192: Drawing © Rafael Vinoly Architects

p. 193 top and bottom: Photo © Daniela MacAdden, courtesy of Rafael Vinoly Architects

pp. 194–195: Drawings © Rafael Vinoly Architects

pp. 198–199: Photos © Kreysler & Associates

p. 200: Photo © Port of San Francisco, licensed by CC BY 2.0

p. 202 bottom left and right: Photo © Kreysler & Associates

p. 203 top: Photo by wikimedia user JaGa, licensed by CC BY-SA 4.0

p. 203 bottom: Photo by Frank Schulenburg, licensed by CC BY-SA 4.0

p. 204: Photo © Richard Powers

pp. 206–207: Photos and rendering © Greg Lynn Form

p. 208: Photo © Andrew W. Kearns

p. 210: Rendering © Diller Scofidio + Renfro

p. 214–216 top: Diagrams and drawing © Diller Scofidio + Renfro

p. 218: Photo © Andrew W. Kearns

p. 223 bottom: Photo © Stan Dye

p. 224 top right: Photo by Flickr user lhongchou, licensed by CC BY-NC-ND 2.0

p. 224 top left: Photo © Piotr Kowalski

p. 224 bottom: Photo © Erik Wolf

p. 225 top: Photo by Flickr user 淺草靈 licensed by CC BY-NC-ND 2.0

p. 225 middle: Photo by Gregory Varnum, licensed by CC BY-SA 4.0

p. 225 bottom: Photo by Junyi Lou, licensed by CC BY-SA 4.0

pp. 226, 229 top: Photos © Marco Serra

p. 229 bottom: Drawing © DETAIL, originally published 5 – 2008

p. 230: Photos © Marco Serra

p. 231–233: Drawings © DETAIL, originally published 5 – 2008

p. 234: Photo © Takumi Ota, courtesy of Kengo Kuma Architects

p. 236: Diagram © Kengo Kuma Architects

p. 237: Photo © Takumi Ota, courtesy of Kengo Kuma Architectspp. 238–240: Drawings © Kengo Kuma Architects

p. 241 top, middle left, middle right: Photo © Takumi Ota, courtesy of Kengo Kuma Architects

p. 241 bottom left and bottom right: Photo © Kengo Kuma Architects

p. 242: Photos © Francois Lacour, courtesy of Institut du Monde Arabe

p. 244: Photo © Dan Earl

pp. 247–248: Drawings © Hugh Broughton Architects

p. 249 top: Photo © James Morris, courtesy of Hugh Broughton Architects

p. 249 bottom: Photo © Andy Cheatle, courtesy of Hugh Broughton Architects

p. 250: Photo © Francois Lacour, courtesy of Institut du Monde Arabe

p. 252: Rendering © Zaha Hadid Architects

p. 253–256: Drawings © Zaha Hadid Architects

p. 257: Photos © Francois Lacour, courtesy of Institut du Monde Arabe

p. 258: Photo © Robin Hill, courtesy of SHoP Architects

pp. 261–263: Diagram and photos © SHoP Architects

pp. 264–297 all photos, diagrams, drawings, and images, except page 274 top and page 284 bottom: © ICD / ITKE University of Stuttgart

p. 274 top: a) © Dr. Thomas van de Kamp, Prof. Dr. Hartmut Greven. b) © ICD/ITKE University of Stuttgart.
c) © Prof. Oliver Betz, Anne Buhl, University of Tübingen.
d) © Dr. Thomas van de Kamp, Prof. Dr. Hartmut Greven | Prof. Oliver Betz, Anne Buhl, University of Tübingen

p. 284 bottom: Photo © Laurian Ghinitoiu

p. 298: Photo © ICD/ITKE University of Stuttgart

Copyright of the images by the featured photographers, architects and companies. Not credited images by the author.

Concept / Texts
Quang Truong

Copy editing
Raymond Peat

Project management
Freya Mohr, Alexander Felix

Production
Amelie Solbrig

Layout, cover design and typesetting
Dörte Nielandt

Paper
Magno Volume, 135 g/m²

Printing
optimal media GmbH, Röbel / Müritz

Library of Congress Control Number
2020940780

Bibliographic information published by the German National Library
The German National Library lists this publication in the Deutsche Nationalbibliografie; detailed bibliographic data are available on the Internet at http://dnb.dnb.de.

ISBN 978-3-0356-1940-9
e-ISBN (PDF) 978-3-0356-1952-2

P.O. Box 44, 4009 Basel, Switzerland
Part of Walter de Gruyter GmbH, Berlin / Boston

9 8 7 6 5 4 3 2 1
www.birkhauser.com